Oracles, Heroes or Vill

M000287172

IMF Managing Director Christine Lagarde declared central bankers and finance ministers to be the heroes of recent economic crises for taking corrective action while national politicians squabbled. What enabled them to do so? In the wake of Brexit, chaotic trade policies in the United States, and resurgent nationalism around the world, national politicians are quarrelling again, meanwhile the markets are roiling. Can we again depend on economic technocrats to save the day for these national politicians and the rest of us? What happens if they fail or, perhaps worse, go too far? In this timely book, Shambaugh answers these question using recent economic crises in Argentina, the United States and Europe as case studies for analysing the intersections of power, politics and markets. By specifying the interactions between political uncertainty, market intervention, and investor risk, Shambaugh predicts how economic technocrats manage market behaviour by shifting expectations regarding what national politicians will do and whether their policies will be effective.

GEORGE E. SHAMBAUGH, IV, is Associate Professor of International Affairs and Government in the Edmund A. Walsh School of Foreign Service, Georgetown University. His authored books include *States, Firms, and Power: Successful Sanctions in United States Foreign Policy* (1999), and, as co-author *The Art of Policymaking: Tools, Techniques, and Processes in the Modern Executive Branch* (2nd edition, 2016).

Oracles, Heroes or Villains

*Economic Policymakers, National Politicians
and the Power to Shape Markets*

George E. Shambaugh, IV

Georgetown University

CAMBRIDGE
UNIVERSITY PRESS

CAMBRIDGE
UNIVERSITY PRESS

University Printing House, Cambridge CB2 8BS, United Kingdom

One Liberty Plaza, 20th Floor, New York, NY 10006, USA

477 Williamstown Road, Port Melbourne, VIC 3207, Australia

314–321, 3rd Floor, Plot 3, Splendor Forum, Jasola District Centre, New Delhi – 110025, India

79 Anson Road, #06–04/06, Singapore 079906

Cambridge University Press is part of the University of Cambridge.

It furthers the University's mission by disseminating knowledge in the pursuit of education, learning, and research at the highest international levels of excellence.

www.cambridge.org
Information on this title: www.cambridge.org/9781108493987
DOI: 10.1017/9781108624978

First published 2019

Printed in the United Kingdom by TJ International Ltd. Padstow Cornwall

A catalogue record for this publication is available from the British Library.

Library of Congress Cataloging-in-Publication Data
Names: Shambaugh, George E., 1963– author.
Title: Oracles, heroes or villains : economic policymakers, national politicians and the power to shape markets / George Shambaugh.
Description: Cambridge, UK ; New York, NY : Cambridge University Press, 2019. | Includes bibliographical references and index. | Summary: "Economic Policymakers, National Politicians and the Power to Shape Markets"– Provided by publisher.
Identifiers: LCCN 2019010786 | ISBN 9781108493987 (hardback) | ISBN 9781108713795 (paperback)
Subjects: LCSH: Monetary policy–Europe. | Monetary policy–United States. | Europe–Economic policy | United States–Economic policy. | Markets–Europe. | Markets–United States.
Classification: LCC HG925 .S49 2019 | DDC 339.5/3094–dc23
LC record available at https://lccn.loc.gov/2019010786

ISBN 978-1-108-49398-7 Hardback
ISBN 978-1-108-71379-5 Paperback

I dedicate this book to Jacqui, Emily and Natalie.

Contents

Figures

Preface

Adults in the Room

In September of 2018, reports that senior appointees in the White House were attempting to shape the content of national policy provoked "volcanic" reactions by President Trump including accusations of "treason" and an internal hunt for disloyal personnel in the West Wing.[1] The accounts detailed by Bob Woodward in *Fear: Trump in the White House*[2] and by an unknown senior member of the president's staff in an editorial provocatively titled, "I Am Part of the Resistance Inside the Trump Administration," describe a chaotic policy environment in which a president demands complete deference from his staff yet is surrounded by many "senior officials in his own administration [who] are working diligently from within to frustrate parts of his agenda and his worst inclinations."[3] The anonymous editorial writer describes efforts by senior members of President Trump's staff to make sure that Russian President Vladimir Putin is held accountable for poisoning a former Russian spy in Great Britain and for offenses committed against the United States despite President Trump's reluctance to do so.[4] Woodward, in turn, recounts an instance when, following a phone call in which President Trump raised the possibility of assassinating Syrian President Bashar al-Assad, US Secretary of Defense James Mattis told a senior aide, "We're not going to do any of that. We're going to be much more measured."[5]

---

[1] H. Jackson, K. Welker & P. Alexander (2018). "On the hunt for a betrayer, a 'volcanic' Trump lashes out." *NBC News*, September 6. www.nbcnews.com/politics/donald-trump/hunt-betrayer-volcanic-trump-lashes-out-n906941.

[2] B. Woodward (2018). *Fear: Trump in the White House*. New York: Simon & Schuster.

[3] "I am part of the resistance inside the Trump administration" (2018). *New York Times*, September 5. www.nytimes.com/2018/09/05/opinion/trump-white-house-anonymous-resistance.html.

[4] Ibid.

[5] P. Rucker & R. Costa (2018). "Bob Woodward's new book reveals a 'nervous breakdown' of Trump's presidency." *The Washington Post*. September 4. www.washingtonpost.com/politics/

Some of the actions described appear truly extraordinary – such as removing a piece of legislation from the President's desk so that it remained unsigned – yet interventions by "adults in the room" who take advantage of their positions to constrain the policies of overly exuberant politicians are not specific to the Trump administration or to the United States.[6] He is neither the first nor will he be the last leader of a democratic country who demands deference from his advisors, appoints loyalists and fires critics, interprets his authority broadly and attempts to bypass or disrupt institutional constraints on his actions. Nor is his administration the only one in which appointees and senior civil servants actively seek to constrain as well as bolster the executive's agenda, even when doing so involves taking actions that extend beyond the traditional bounds of their authority.[7]

The key issue raised by these revelations is not that senior appointees are trying to shape the policy-making process or that they occasionally take extraordinary actions to do so. These behaviors are relatively common.[8] Rather, the essential unanswered questions are about their impact: When and under what circumstances can unelected senior policymakers affect the contents and consequences of national policy decisions?

Economic Crises as Laboratories

Contemporary commentators offer immediate responses to these questions, but their assessments are often limited by a focus on current policies whose consequences cannot yet be fully known.[9] To better

bob-woodwards-new-book-reveals-a-nervous-breakdown-of-trumps-presidency/2018/09/04/ b27a389e-ac60-11e8-a8d7-0f63ab8b1370_story.html?utm_term=.c94e2b6578e5.

[6] Examples include the Madisonian division of authority among the executive, legislative and judicial branches of the US government.

[7] G. Shambaugh & P. Weinstein (2016). *The Art of Policymaking: Tools, Techniques, and Processes in the Modern Executive Branch*. Washington, DC: CQ Press.

[8] Unapproved leaks like those to Bob Woodward and *The New York Times*, defined as information that is provided to people outside of the formal decision-making apparatus without the knowledge or consent of the executive, are relatively common across US administrations when members of the policy-making community feel that their view or concern is not being presented to or considered by the President. Shambaugh & Weinstein, *Art of Policymaking*, p. 270.

[9] Examples include: P. Musgrave (2017). "President Trump should stop tweeting. Now." *Washington Post*, June 8. www.washingtonpost.com/posteverything/wp/2017/06/08/ president-trump-should-stop-tweeting-now/?utm_term=.937145a1c67f; K. Vanden Heuvel (2018). "Forget the Trump circus. Focus on his ruinous policies." *Washington Post*, September 11. www.washingtonpost.com/opinions/forget-the-trump-circus-focus-instead-on-his-ruinous-policies/2018/09/11/d8dcfed2-b51a-11e8-94eb-3bd52dfe917 b_story.html?utm_term=.0132a2ee869d; J. Scarborough (2018). "Woodward's 'Fear' is

understand these dynamics, I examine the role of senior unelected policy experts in the formulation and implementation of economic policy in Argentina, the United States and Europe over the past thirty years. Their collective experiences provide a laboratory for analyzing how changing power dynamics among national politicians and senior technocrats affect the contents and consequences of economic policy in different contexts.

The US Federal Reserve Chairs Alan Greenspan, Ben Bernanke and Janet Yellen, European Central Bank Presidents Jean-Claude Trichet and Mario Draghi, and Argentine Ministers of the Economy Domingo Cavallo and Roberto Lavagna are widely acknowledged as having played key roles in shaping economic policy and taming market behavior before, during and after the economic crises that hit Argentina in the 1990s, the United States in 2007, and Europe in 2010. Some of these technocrats interpreted their mandates narrowly and remained deferential to political leaders, while others took a broader view and were willing to do "whatever it takes" to manage market expectations and achieve broader policy goals. Some succeeded in securing the authority, deference and political support necessary to shape national economic policy. Others had their authority curtailed and their policies ignored. Still others were left without sufficient political backing to generate or sustain supporting legislation. Consequently, as is playing out in the Trump administration today, some technocrats succeeded in reducing policy uncertainty and changing market behavior with mere words, while others manipulated extraordinary incentives and threats to little avail.

Managing Director of the International Monetary Fund Christine Lagarde proclaimed central bankers to be the heroes of the recent crises because they took corrective action while political leaders squabbled.[10] I argue that under the right conditions, central bankers, treasury secretaries and finance ministers (a group that I will refer to as "economic technocrats" or "economic policymakers") can manage market expectations and behavior by reducing uncertainty about how national governments are likely to respond to changing circumstances and whether their chosen policies will be effective.

The adage that "markets abhor uncertainty" is suggestive, but not very informative. I increase its utility by specifying the relationships among

depressing – and heartening." *Washington Post*, September 5. www.washingtonpost.com/opinions/woodwards-fear-is-damning-depressing–and-heartening/2018/09/05/0a7ee502-b149-11e8-aed9-001309990777_story.html?utm_term=.9473a8accbfc.

[10] C. Lagarde (2012). "Promises to keep: the policy actions needed to secure global recovery," interview with K. Ryssdal. *American Public Media, Marketplace*, September 24. www.marketplace.org/topics/world/european-debt-crisis/imfs-christine-lagarde-urges-action-fiscal-cliff-euro-crisis.

investor risk, political uncertainty and different types of government intervention in the economy using what I call the Risk Intervention Curve (RIC). Economic policymakers can reduce political uncertainty by altering the economic policy options available to national politicians. They can also increase expectations that desired outcomes will be achieved by validating the chosen policies (i.e., reducing policy risk), altering general market conditions (i.e., reducing market risk), and assisting financial institutions and countries in distress or compelling them to alter their behavior (i.e., reducing specific actor risk).

The ability of economic technocrats to reduce these uncertainties and risks varies with their ability to assert authority over economic policy, to generate deference from national politicians to their policies and to standing institutional obligations, and to secure supporting legislation as needed. The constitutive power dynamics among economic technocrats and national politicians are reflected in (1) the degree to which the locus of authority over economic policy is accepted or contested, (2) the degree to which national politicians defer to or demand deference from economic policymakers and conform to or shirk their responsibilities to extant agreements, and (3) the degree to which political leaders have the will and capacity to implement supporting legislation. Variations in authority, deference and implementation capacity generate six distinct patterns of political and market behavior that have reoccurred repeatedly in Argentina, the United States and Europe over the past thirty years.

Oracles, Heroes or Villains?

In the 1990s and early 2000s, Federal Reserve Chairman Alan Greenspan was lauded as an oracle who understood the complex dynamics of modern financial markets. Federal Reserve Chairman Paul Volcker is renowned as the hero who slayed inflation and brought the United States out of the economic doldrums of the 1970s; in parallel, Argentine Finance Minister Domingo Cavallo is the hero who slayed inflation and transformed Argentina from a basket case into a poster child of economic development in the 1990s. European Central Bank President Mario Draghi is the hero who restored investors' confidence in Europe in 2012 by asserting he would do "everything it takes" to preserve the euro. Federal Reserve Chairman Ben Bernanke was anointed by *Time* magazine as the "Person of the Year" in 2009 for using his mastery to minimize its severity.

At the same time, many would-be oracles and heroes have failed. Some central bankers, finance ministers and treasury secretaries secured the power to shape policy, yet made poor decisions. In April and July of 2011, for example, Jean-Claude Trichet infamously misread market expectations and raised interest rates despite high levels of policy uncertainty generated by Moody's decision to downgrade Portugal's debt to junk status and the stalled negotiations regarding a bailout for Greece.[11] Trichet's authority to raise rates was not questioned, but raising interest rates unsettled markets by compounding growing uncertainties across Europe about the ECB's willingness to recognize and respond to economic downturns in member countries. This likely, stalled growth and worsened the debt crisis.[12] Other technocrats had compelling policy ideas yet failed to acquire the right balance of authority, deference and political support needed to shape, validate or sustain desired economic policies. Consequently, they were unable to reduce political or policy uncertainty and failed to reduce investors' perceptions of risk. Misguided and failed interventions have generated asset bubbles and exuberant spending; they have also stalled economic growth, triggered bank runs and sparked capital flight.

Furthermore, even when central bankers and other economic policy-makers achieve their objectives, the benefits of their actions are often not evenly distributed across society. Monetary policy is a blunt instrument. It can reinvigorate economic systems, but it is a poor substitute for legislative policy when it comes to allocating benefits. Aggregate indicators of economic recovery and the successful recapitalization of the financial sector are little solace to those who remain unemployed or feel like they have been left behind. Consequently, even some technocrats who were once lauded as oracles and heroes – including both Alan Greenspan[13] and Domingo Cavallo – have fallen from grace. Some were summarily dismissed by disgruntled politicians. Others had their authorities reduced or were simply ignored or not given the supporting legislation needed for their policies to succeed. Still others have become reviled as villains who are blamed for the crises and the inequities of the post-crisis recoveries. In addition, seemingly impervious institutions – like the Argentine currency board, the euro, the European Union, and the Federal Reserve – have been chastised. Rather than being all-powerful, their impacts on political behavior and market expectations have been

---

[11] J. Kollewe (2011). "ECB raises interest rates despite debt crisis." *The Guardian*, July 7. www.theguardian.com/business/2011/jul/07/ebc-raise-interest-rates-debt-crisis; "ECB raises interest rates to 1.5%" (2011). *The Financial Times*, July 7. www.ft.com/content/a4f92816-a87f-11e0-8a97-00144feabdc0.

[12] J. Surowiecki (2011). "Europe's big mistake." *The New Yorker*, September 5. www.newyorker.com/magazine/2011/09/05/europes-big-mistake.

[13] S. Mallaby (2010). *The Man Who Knew: The Life and Times of Alan Greenspan*. New York: Bloomsbury Publishing.

revealed to be highly contingent on shifts in the degrees of authority, deference and political support they command.

Today, in the face of continued economic policy uncertainty generated by bickering among national politicians and the rise of nationalist leaders who are threatening to tear down long-standing economic agreements and institutions, a growing number of us – political leaders, investors and citizens alike – have put our trust in economic technocrats – central bankers, finance ministers, treasury secretaries and other regulators – to reduce uncertainty and manage the economy. We hope they will reinvigorate growth, create jobs and protect us from inflation and other dangers. Many of us join Managing Director Lagarde in hoping that they will keep us happy, healthy and wealthy when our intricately interconnected markets go awry.

Twenty years after the financial crisis hit Argentina and ten years after the crises hit the United States and Europe, the global financial system has been rebuilt and economic growth is returning for many. Yet, despite this apparent success, national politicians continue to squabble, and our hopes often turn to angst because the abilities of these technocrats to exercise power in an age of political upheaval and economic interdependence, though great, do not match our expectations.[14] This sentiment is reflected in Neil Irwin's aptly named article, "The Policymakers Saved the Financial System. And America Never Forgave Them."[15] This paradox persists in much of the world because neither people on the street nor the politicians nor the technocrats themselves fully understand the nature of this power or the consequences of its use. The experiences of Argentina, the United States and Europe can help resolve this paradox by providing a laboratory for enriching our understanding of the nature and consequences of exercising power in politically turbulent and highly interdependent times.

[14] Just two years after her declaration of central bankers as heroes, Ms. Lagarde described the global economy as covered by clouds of the "new mediocre," with economic challenges (e.g., low levels of growth, investment and inflation in many countries and resurgent inflation in others), financial challenges (e.g., high interest-rate spreads, volatility and the resurgence of under-regulated shadow banking), social challenges (e.g., persistently high unemployment and growing income inequality in many countries), institutional challenges (e.g., widespread distrust and rejection of long-standing norms and institutions at the core of the liberal democratic order) and political challenges (e.g., rising polarization, stalemating political opposition and extremism on the left and right around the world) fueled by public backlashes against austerity and the lack of recovery for many. C. Lagarde (2014). "World financial growth still falling short," speech delivered at Georgetown University on October 2. www.georgetown.edu/news/christine-lagarde-imf-director-speaks-2014.html.

[15] N. Irwin (2018). "The policymakers saved the financial system. And America never forgave them." *New York Times.* September 12. www.nytimes.com/2018/09/12/upshot/financial-crisis-recession-recovery.html.

Acknowledgments

This book benefited from contributions by many people. My wife, Jacqui, and daughters, Emily and Natalie, provided inspiration, encouragement and humor throughout the process. I am also grateful for the substantive input and editorial assistance that they and others provided along the way. Colleagues that deserve special recognition include Kelsey Larsen, Christopher Shorr, Madison Schramm, Carol Sargent, Cara Dienst, Arie Kacowicz and members of the Political Economy Working Group at Georgetown University. I also appreciate and benefited greatly from many conversations with Roberto Lavagne and many other senior economic policymakers who shied away from attribution but willingly shared their experiences and insights. Finally, this project would not have begun without a grant from the Smith Richardson Foundation that enabled me to step away from the university for a semester to begin field research in Argentina.

Abbreviations

ABSPP	Asset-Backed Securities Purchase Programme
AIG	American International Group
AMLF	Asset-Backed Commercial Paper Money Market Mutual Fund Liquidity Facility
APP	Asset Purchase Program
BCRA	Central Bank of the Argentina Republic
Brexit	British Exit from the European Union
CBPP	Covered Bond Purchase Programme
CEO	Chief Executive Officer
CFTC	Commodities Futures Trading Commission
CGT	*Confederación General del Trabajo*
CIFS	Credit Institutions Financial Support Scheme
CJEU	Court of Justice of the European Union
CONADEP	*Comisión Nacional sobre la Desaparición de Personas*
CPFF	Commercial Paper Funding Facility
CSPP	Corporate-Sector Purchase Programme
DF	Deposit Facility
EC	European Commission
ECB	European Central Bank
EFSF	European Financial Stability Facility
ELA	Emergency Liquidity Assistance
EONIA	Euro Overnight Index Average
ESF	Exchange Stabilization Fund
ESM	European Stability Mechanism
EU	European Union
FCC	Federal Constitutional Court of Germany
FDIC	Federal Deposit Insurance Company
FED	Federal Reserve Bank of the United States
FOMC	Federal Open Market Committee
FPV	Progressive Front Alliance
FrePaSo	Front for a Country in Solidarity
GDP	Gross Domestic Product

G-Fund	Government Securities Investment Fund
GIPSI	Greece, Ireland, Portugal, Spain and Italy
Grexit	Greek Exit from the European Union
GSP	Generalized System of Preferences
ICSID	International Centre for the Settlement of Investment Disputes
IMF	International Monetary Fund
INDEC	*Instituto Nacional de Estadística y Censos*
LEBAC	Letters of the Central Bank of Argentina
LIBOR	London Interbank Offer Rate
LTCM	Long-Term Capital Management
LTRO	Longer-Term Refinancing Operations
M3	Money Supply
MMIFF	Money Market Investor Funding Facility
MRO	Main Refinancing Operations
NCUA	National Credit Union Administration
NEC	National Economic Council
OAS	Organization of American States
OCC	Office of the Comptroller of the Currency
OMT	Outright Monetary Transactions
OTC	Over-the-Counter Derivatives
OTS	Office of Thrift Supervision
PJ	Justicialist Party
PSI	Private-Sector Involvement
PSPP	Public-Sector Purchase Programme
QE	Quantitative Easing
REPO	Repurchase Contract
RIC	Risk Intervention Curve
RUFO	Rights upon Future Offers
SEC	Securities and Exchange Commission
SGP	Stability and Growth Pact
SMP	Securities Markets Programme
TARP	Troubled Asset Relief Program
TED	Treasury–EuroDollar Rate
TLTRO	Targeted Longer-Term Refinancing Operation
TROIKA	European Commission, European Central Bank and International Monetary Fund
UCR	*Unión Cívica Radical*
UN	United Nations
UNCITRAL	United Nations Commission on International Trade Law
VLTRO	Very-Long-Term Refinancing Operation
YPF S.A.	*Yacimientos Petrolíferos Fiscales*

1   Reaching for the Bazooka

1.1   Misfiring the Economic Bazooka

Speaking before the Senate Banking Committee on July 15, 2008, US Treasury Secretary Henry Paulson petitioned Congress for the authority to use taxpayer funds to prevent America's mortgage giants Fannie Mae and Freddie Mac from collapsing.[1] The hearing addressed widespread homeowner mortgage defaults that had sent stock prices plummeting and investors fleeing.[2] Paulson argued that if investors came to understand that the government would not allow Fannie and Freddie to go under, stock prices would stabilize and a larger crisis could be averted. In a statement that would be repeated in news stories for years to come, Paulson speculated, "If you have a bazooka in your pocket and people know it, you probably won't have to use it."[3] In this instance, the "bazooka theory" failed: Paulson not only had to fire his bazooka shortly after acquiring it, but its blast proved grossly inadequate to calm market uncertainty and forestall what became the worst financial crisis to hit the United States since the Great Depression.[4] In spite of Paulson's newly acquired money and authority, investors dumped Fannie and Freddie shares, both organizations fell into government conservatorship, political

---

[1] Fannie Mae and Freddie Mac are privately held corporations created by the US Congress known as government-sponsored enterprises. Their purpose is to encourage credit in agriculture, home finance and education by reducing the risk of capital losses to investors. www.freddiemac.com.

[2] US Senate Committee on Banking, Housing and Urban Affairs Hearings (2008). "Recent Developments in U.S. Financial Markets and Regulatory Responses to Them," July 15. www.banking.senate.gov/hearings/recent-developments-in-us-financial-markets-and-regu latory-responses-to-them.

[3] C. Isidore (2008). "Paulson in hot seat over Fannie, Freddie," *CNN Money*, July 15. https://money.cnn.com/2008/07/15/news/economy/Freddie_Fannie_Senate.

[4] C. Barr (2008). "Fortune special report: Paulson readies the 'bazooka.'" *CNNMoney*, September 6. https://money.cnn.com/2008/09/06/news/economy/fannie_freddie_paulson .fortune/index.htm.

criticisms of bailouts grew louder and the whirlpool of uncertainty swirled ever faster.[5]

Given the very high-profile failure of Paulson's bazooka theory, one might have reasonably imagined that this crisis management strategy would have been discarded permanently. Quite to the contrary, central bankers in Argentina, Japan, the United Kingdom and continental Europe have all tried to shape market expectations by wielding their own economic bazookas.[6] Just four years after Paulson's metaphorical weapon failed to stop the oncoming economic crisis in the United States, European Central Bank (ECB) Chairman Mario Draghi cocked his own economic bazooka to fight a crisis in Europe. At the time, banking and sovereign debt crises had made it prohibitively expensive for several countries to raise revenue on international markets, and fears that contagion could threaten the integrity of the Eurozone and its common currency, the euro, were rising. The growing levels of perceived risk can be seen in the dramatic increases in interest rates that investors demanded from Greece, Ireland, Portugal, Spain and Italy (i.e., GIPSI countries) in order to buy their bonds. The differences in their rates relative to "safe" countries like Germany also reflect the relative cost of raising money (see Figure 1.1). To calm market expectations, reduce this risk premium for GIPSI countries and forestall further contagion, Draghi declared boldly, "The ECB is ready to do whatever it takes to preserve the euro. And believe me, it will be enough."[7]

Draghi's bazooka consisted of the newly created Outright Monetary Transactions (OMT).[8] Under the OMT, the ECB can purchase limitless amounts of government-issued bonds from countries who are pursuing European Union (EU) economic adjustment programs and agree to pursue specified domestic economic policies.

Several factors suggest that Draghi's bazooka was less likely to succeed in calming market fears than Paulson's had been. Paulson had congressional approval and had put his money on the table; in short, he

---

[5] "Fire the bazooka: it's time to nationalize America's mortgage giants – and then to dismantle them" (2008). *The Economist,* August 28. www.economist.com/node/12009702; "America's mortgage giants: suffering a seizure" (2008). *The Economist,* September 8. www.economist.com/node/12078933.

[6] The capacity of central bankers to generate large amounts of official liquidity quickly makes this tool attractive.

[7] M. Draghi (2012). "Verbatim of the remarks made by Mario Draghi at the Global Investment Conference in London." *European Central Bank,* July 26. www.ecb.europa.eu/press/key/date/2012/html/sp120726.en.html.

[8] "Press release: technical features of outright monetary transactions" (2012). *European Central Bank,* September 6. www.ecb.europa.eu/press/pr/date/2012/html/pr120906_1.en.html.

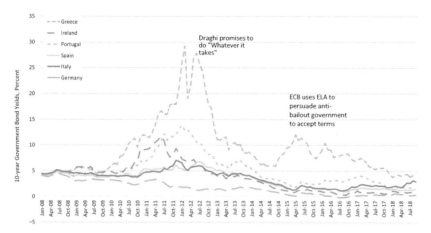

Figure 1.1 Intervention and investor risk in Europe.
Source: Organization for Economic Co-operation and Development, Long-Term Government Bond Yields: 10-year: Main (Including Benchmark) for Germany, Italy, Spain, Portugal, Ireland and Greece, retrieved from FRED, Federal Reserve Bank of St. Louis; https://fred.stlouisfed.org/, December 17, 2018.

had both the authority and the capacity to act. Draghi, on the other hand, faced political opposition and his authority to act was being challenged by Europe's principal financier, Germany. Draghi also kept his bazooka in his pocket. Indeed, to date, no one has taken any money from the OMT. Yet, Draghi's contested and untested promise worked while Paulson's bazooka failed. As shown in Figure 1.1, Draghi's announcement was followed by a significant drop in interest rates in Greece and across Europe. By 2014, countries that had been "bailed out" were once again able to raise money on international financial markets at affordable rates. With their return to global financial markets, the second phase of the European economic crisis came to a successful – if fleeting – end.

Uncertainty returned to Europe in 2015 when a newly elected, anti-austerity government in Greece challenged the repayment terms for its debt and raised the prospect of exiting from the EU. The ECB responded with a two-part strategy designed to bolster market activity in the Euro-zone and reduce specific-actor risk. First, it instituted a broad-based monetary stimulus program that included the use of negative interest rates in its deposit facility, expanded targeted longer-term refinancing operations designed to promote bank lending, and an asset purchase program that was similar to the quantitative easing (QE) programs adopted by Japan, the United States and the United Kingdom.[9] It also committed to communicating its intentions about these and other initiatives through a forward guidance program. Second, the ECB reduced specific-actor risk by compelling wayward states countries to change their behavior. For example, the ECB governing council manipulated collateral requirements and the amount of funding available to Greek banks through the emergency liquidity assistance (ELA) program to persuade Greece's anti-austerity government to accept the terms of a third bailout.[10] The ECB used a similar strategy to compel Ireland, Spain, Italy and Cyprus to alter their economic policies. The US Treasury and Federal Reserve similarly sought to restore market confidence by targeting particular companies they deemed to be "too big to fail." These actions generated significant backlashes from the private sector (many of whom interpreted bailouts as indicators of failure rather than as safety nets) private citizens (many of whom considered bailouts to be illegitimate), and national politicians. Consequently, many governments and firms only accepted the bailouts under duress.

This activism by the Federal Reserve, ECB and other economic policymakers and the varying levels of their effectiveness are difficult to explain using prominent theories of political economy which, before the crises, idealized central banks as apolitical, autonomous entities whose principal task was to fight inflation. From this traditional perspective, the primary political role of an independent central bank is to increase the credibility of a country's inflation-fighting commitments by limiting the ability of national politicians to forsake their inflation-fighting promises when political or economic circumstances change (e.g., to solve a time-inconsistency problem).[11] With a few exceptions, debates about the politics of central banking focused on the degree of central bank autonomy from political influence, the effects of transparency in central bank decision-making, or the ability of

---

[9] "Monetary policy decisions" (2018). *European Central Bank*. www.ecb.europa.eu/mopo/decisions/html/index.en.html; B. Fawley & C. Neely (2013). "Four Stories of Quantitative Easing." *Federal Reserve Bank of St. Louis Review* 95(1), 51–88; "Japan's quantitative easing: a bigger bazooka" (2014). *The Economist*, October 31. www.economist.com/blogs/banyan/2014/10/japans-quantitative-easing.

[10] J. Kanter & N. Kitsantons (2015). "E.C.B. agrees to extend lifeline to Athens." *New York Times*, June 19. www.nytimes.com/2015/06/20/business/international/ecb-greece-debt-meeting.html; "Greece's creditors allow a bit more money to flow" (2015). *The Economist*, July 16. www.economist.com/blogs/freeexchange/2015/07/ecb-and-greek-banks.

[11] For a review of central bank independence literature before the 2008 financial crisis, see: M. Arnone, B. J. Laurens, J.-F. Segalotto & M. Sommer (2007). "Central Bank Autonomy: Lessons from Global Trends." IMF Working Paper, WP/07/88.

independent central banks and fixed-exchange-rate regimes to serve as complements or substitutes in the fight against inflation.[12] The varying successes and failures of national governments in shaping market behavior are also puzzling for theories of international political economy which emphasize the disciplining effects of markets on economic policy and argue that dependence on foreign capital should lead to a convergence of economic policies that reflect the preferences of investors.[13]

In the aftermath of the recent crisis, political economy debates have swung from idealizing central bankers as apolitical technocrats to recasting them as strategic political actors. An increasing number of memoires and personal accounts provide vivid details of the roles that specific individuals have played in shaping economic policy.[14] Other research emphasizes the capacity of central bankers to alter the rules of the game

---

[12] C. Crowe & E. Meade (2008). "Central Bank Independence and Transparency: Evolution and Effectiveness." IMF Working Paper, 08/119; P. Keefer & D. Stasavage (2003). "The Limits of Delegation: Veto Players, Central Bank Independence, and the Credibility of Monetary Policy." *American Political Science Review* 97(3), 407–423.

[13] W. R. Clark & M. Hallerberg (2000). "Mobile Capital, Domestic Institutions, and Electorally Inducted Monetary and Fiscal Policy." *American Political Science Review* 94 (2), 323–346; W. R. Clark, U. N. Reichert, S. L. Lomas & K. L. Parker (1998). "International and Domestic Constraints on Political Business Cycles in OECD Economies." *International Organization* 52(1), 87–120; W. R. Clark (2002). "Partisan and Electoral Motivations and the Choice of Monetary Institutions under Fully Mobile Capital." *International Organization* 52(1), 725–749; D. Andrews (1994). "Capital Mobility and State Autonomy: Toward a Structural Theory of International Monetary Relations." *International Studies Quarterly* 38(2), 193–218; B. Cohen (2000). *The Geography of Money.* Ithaca: Cornel University Press; J. Frieden & R. Rogowski (1996). "The Impact of the International Political Economy on National Policies: An Analytical Overview." In *International Organization and Domestic Politics*, eds. R. Keohane & H. Milner. New York: Cambridge University Press, pp. 25–47; S. Maxfield (1998). "Effects of International Portfolio Flows on Government Policy Choice." In *Capital Flows and Financial Crises*, ed. M. Kahler. Ithaca: Cornell University Press, pp. 69–92; B. Stallings (1992). "International Influence on Economic Policy: Debt, Stabilization, and Structural Reform." In *The Politics of Economic Adjustment: International Constraints, Distributive Conflicts and the State*, eds. S. Haggard & R. Kaufman. Princeton: Princeton University Press, pp. 41–88; G. Shambaugh (2004). "The Power of Money: Private Capital and Policy Preferences in Newly Emerging Market Economies." *American Journal of Political Science* 48(2), 281–295; G. Shambaugh & E. Shen (2018). "A Clear Advantage: The Benefits of Transparency to Crisis Recovery." *European Journal of Political Economy* 55, 391–416.

[14] L. Ahamed (2009). *Lords of Finance: The Bankers Who Broke the World.* New York: Penguin Group; C. Bastasin (2015). *Saving Europe: Anatomy of a Dream.* Washington, DC: Brookings Institution; B. Bernanke (2015). *The Courage to Act: A Memoir of a Crisis and Its Aftermath.* New York: W. W. Norton; N. Irwin (2014). *The Alchemists: Three Central Bankers and a World on Fire.* New York: Penguin Group; T. Geithner (2014). *Stress Test: Reflections on Financial Crises.* New York: Crown Publishers; A. Greenspan (2007). *The Age of Turbulence: Adventures in a New World.* New York: Penguin Group; H. Paulson (2010). *On the Brink: Inside the Race to Stop the Collapse of the Global Financial System.* New York: Hachette Book Group.

in domestic and international finance.[15] Scholars like Bruce Hall emphasize the extraordinary power that central bankers derive from their status functions. These include the authority to create and destroy money and to delineate the roles and functions that individual actors play in the global economy.[16] Some blame these unelected technocrats for pursuing policies that enabled the crises to take place. Others criticize them for the inequities generated by their crisis-response and post-crisis policies.[17]

The recent financial crises have inspired a wide range of productive research on the roles that central bankers and other senior economic policymakers play in shaping economic policy, yet even today central bankers chafe at the suggestion that they may not be apolitical. Perhaps as a result, we often fail to appreciate their responsiveness to changing political as well as economic circumstances. As reflected in the chapters to follow, many politicians and citizens alike express surprise when "politically independent" central bankers promote particular policy agendas and help national leaders circumvent their critics. Many are also angered when these unelected technocrats compel national governments to accept conditional assistance, impose austerity or shift the burden of bad investment decisions to taxpayers.

At the same time, many place undue confidence in the ability of these technocrats and the economic institutions they manage to shield them from risk. They mistakenly conflate the delegation of economic policy-making authority and declarations of fidelity to experts and institutions with actual changes in political and market behaviors. Many continue to assume these technocrats and the institutions they manage are all-powerful and discount the frequency with which their authorities are contested or rescinded. Many also continue to underestimate the extent to which the power that these economic policymakers and institutions exert over market behavior is contingent on the degree to which national politicians are willing to defer to their recommendations and are willing and able to implement supporting legislation. Consequently, many of us are often uncertain about their motives, yet are perplexed by their failures and concerned about the inequities of their successes.

[15] B. Hall (2010). *Central Banking as Global Governance: Constructing Financial Credibility.* Cambridge: Cambridge University Press.
[16] Ibid.
[17] A. Bowman et al. (2013). "Central Bank-Led Capitalism?" *Seattle University Library Review* 36, 455; L. Jacobs & D. King (2016). *Fed Power: How Finance Wins.* Oxford: Oxford University Press; J. Kirchner (2002). *Monetary Orders: Ambiguous Economics, Ubiquitous Politics.* Ithaca: Cornell University Press.

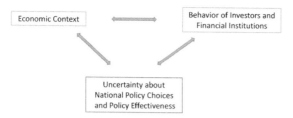

Figure 1.2 The dynamics of intervention.

Lessons from Argentina, the United States and Europe suggest that we need not be perplexed. Variations in the degree to which authority over economic policy is accepted or contested, policy deference is granted or demanded, and the capacity to implement and sustain supporting legislation is high or low generate distinct patterns of political behavior and market outcomes that persist over time in different contexts across Argentina, the United States and Europe. Understanding these patterns enables us to understand the roles these actors play and the impacts they are likely to have on policy and markets in the future.

1.2 The Argument in Brief

The rise of private-sector liquidity as a dominant component in global liquidity markets has created a web of financial interdependence that links the fates of investors, financial institutions and national governments to one another.[18] As demonstrated by the recent crises, the behaviors of each of these actors can generate uncertainties that motivate shifts in capital flows, alter the availability and cost of credit, and motivate changes in financial asset and property prices with significant consequences for all. I argue that this connectivity creates opportunities for the exercise of second-order power because it means that the behaviors of investors, financial institutions and governments are mediated by their expectations about what the others will do and what the consequences of their actions will be (see Figure 1.2).[19]

---

[18] As defined in Chapter 2, private-sector liquidity is generated by investors engaged in processes that include cross-border banking, interbank and interfirm lending, portfolio flows and investment funds, trading in primary and secondary bond and security markets and the exchange of over-the-counter derivatives and other financial instruments. See: J. P. Landau, ed. (2011). "Global Liquidity – Concept, Measurement and Policy Implications." *Committee on the Global Financial System (CGFS) Papers, No. 45: Bank of France, Bank for International Settlements.*

[19] R. Keohane & J. Nye (1977). *Power and Interdependence.* New York: Longman.

Under the right conditions, economic policymakers can alter the behaviors of investors and financial institutions by reducing political and policy uncertainties. They can reduce uncertainty about how national governments are likely to act (i.e., political uncertainty) by increasing or decreasing policy-making flexibility and by supplementing or limiting policy options. They can reduce uncertainty about policy outcomes (i.e., policy uncertainty) by validating specific policies or policy agendas, altering market conditions and mitigating specific-actor risks. I define this as the exercise of second-order power because the ability of economic policymakers to change market behavior is a second-order effect of their power to reduce political and policy uncertainty.

The relationships among political uncertainty, policy uncertainty and risk under different economic conditions can be represented in stylized form by the Risk Intervention Curve (RIC). The level of political and policy uncertainty in a particular country is a function of the pulling and hauling among national politicians and economic policymakers over economic policy. It varies based on the degree to which authority over economic policy is contested, the degree to which national politicians defer to economic policymakers and extant policy agreements, and the degree to which these politicians have the will and capacity to implement supporting legislation as needed. The ability of central bankers and other economic policymakers to alter these uncertainties and shift their countries' positions along the RIC (e.g., thereby to lower investor risk, attract or retain capital, increase the availability and lower the cost of credit, and manage inflation) varies with their ability to secure the authority, deference and implementation capacity needed to shape economic policy. As discussed in detail in Chapter 2, variations in authority, deference and implementation capacity generate six patterns of political behavior and market outcomes. These patterns reappear consistently over the past thirty years of economic policymaking in Argentina, the United States and Europe.

The interaction among markets, national governments and market actors is dynamic. Changes in market conditions can alter the ability of economic policymakers to secure the authority, deference and implementation capacity needed to shape economic policy. At the same time, economic policymakers often attempt to loosen or tighten general market conditions to incentivize investors and financial institutions to alter their behaviors. They also often attempt to change market uncertainties by assisting firms and countries in distress or by compelling them to change undesirable behaviors.

I analyze these interactions through a three-step process of: (1) specifying the relationships among political uncertainty, policy uncertainty and investor risk under different economic conditions; (2) specifying strategies for reducing risk by managing political and policy uncertainties; and (3) specifying conditions under which economic policymakers are likely to succeed in implementing these policies and shaping market behavior.

1.2.1　Political Uncertainty, Policy Uncertainty and Risk

I begin by developing a model of investor risk based on political uncertainty under different economic conditions that I call the Risk Intervention Curve (RIC). The RIC builds on insights from recent research by Andrew MacIntyre who posits that the policy preferences of investors reflect a trade-off between policy constraint and policy flexibility.[20] *Ceteris paribus*, policy constraint – resulting from checks and balances in the policy-making process, institutional commitments and other factors that limit the discretion of national politicians to shape economic policy – improves policy predictability and the credibility of policy commitments. Yet, if these constraints are too severe, they can limit the ability of national governments to adapt and respond to changing economic conditions. Alternatively, giving national politicians a freer hand to manage economic policy by reducing the number of veto players and institutional constraints in the policy-making process increases policy adaptability. Yet, if policy flexibility is too high, it could reduce the predictability of future policy decisions and decrease the reliability of policy commitments. Consequently, the relationship between policy flexibility and risk is expected to be concave upward. High levels of risk are associated with both high levels of policy constraint and high levels of policy flexibility; lower levels of risk are associated with a midrange between the two extremes (see Figure 1.3). With the caveat that the risk tolerance of investors can vary widely, the comfort level of a stylized investor can be included to suggest a comfort zone of policy flexibility for a generic investor.

The RIC adds dynamism to existing models that link policy flexibility and investor risk by recognizing that this relationship is context specific. The RIC presumes, for example, that risk and policy constraint will be negatively correlated in inflationary environments in which investors place a premium on the credibility of politicians' commitments to fiscal discipline. In such circumstances, the trade-off between flexibility and risk will become skewed, with a relatively higher level of risk associated with policy flexibility and a relatively lower level of risk associated with

---

[20] See Chapter 2 for a discussion of MacIntyre's veto player model of investor preferences. A. MacIntyre (2001). "Institutions and Investors: The Politics of the Economic Crisis in South East Asia." *International Organization* 55(1), 81–122.

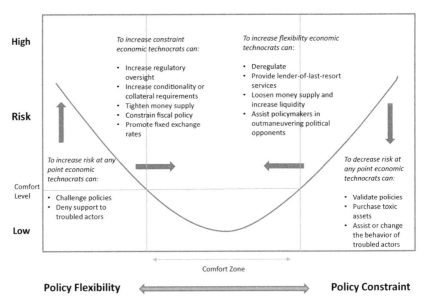

Figure 1.3 The risk intervention curve.

policy constraint. In contrast, risk and policy constraint are expected to be positively correlated in circumstances where private capital is scarce or prohibitively expensive and investors are uncertain about whether the government will step in as a lender of last resort. Consequently, in periods of capital scarcity or other phenomena in which government intervention is desired, the RIC will be skewed in the opposite direction, with a relatively lower level of risk associated with policy flexibility and a relatively higher level of risk associated with policy constraint.

1.2.2   Strategies for Reducing Risk by Managing Political and Policy Uncertainties

The RIC also adds agency to existing models that link policy flexibility and investor risk by treating economic policymakers and national politicians as strategic actors who often attempt to anticipate, respond to and shape investor expectations. I specify two dominant strategies that economic policymakers can use to reduce investor risk. The first involves reducing political uncertainty by increasing or decreasing the likelihood of government intervention, expanding or limiting available policy options, or enabling or constraining the policy discretion of national politicians over economic policy. Economic policymakers can increase the level of constraint in a variety of ways including asserting their statutory authorities, increasing oversight, adding conditionality or raising collateral requirements for loans, promoting the adoption of fixed exchange rates and creating other institutional constraints. Alternatively, they can increase policy flexibility by promoting deregulation, providing lender-of-last-resort functions, increasing access to public sources of liquidity and helping national politicians outmaneuver political opponents. When successful, these efforts can reduce risk and policy uncertainty by shifting their country's position along the RIC.

A second strategy involves decreasing policy uncertainty by altering expectations regarding particular policy outcomes. Economic policymakers can do this by validating particular policy decisions. National politicians often appoint or retain specific personnel to signal policy consistency. In addition to reducing uncertainty about what the government is going to do, such appointments can also reduce policy uncertainty by suggesting that a known expert will be involved in the policymaking process. In contrast, placing a sycophant in a significant advisory position increases policy uncertainty because such individuals are unlikely to be seen as expert and neutral assessors of government policy.

Economic policymakers can also change the likelihood of particular outcomes by altering general market conditions or changing the behavior of particular market actors. Central bankers, for example, often manipulate interest rates, purchase bonds or engage in other measures to adjust the supply and cost of capital in order to persuade banks to lend, consumers to borrow, and investors to buy bonds. They may also intervene to bail out companies whose failure could pose system-wide risk and compel countries whose policies are potentially destabilizing to change their behavior.

1.2.3   The Power to Act and to Change Behavior

I argue that the power to influence investor risk begins at home with the pulling and hauling among national politicians and economic policymakers over the authority to shape economic policy, the content of economic policy and the means of implementation. The ability of particular central bankers and other economic policymakers to prevail in this arena – and thus to move their country's position along the RIC and to alter investors' perceptions of risk at any particular point along the RIC – is a function of constitutive power dynamics as defined by their willingness and capacity to: (1) exploit their institutional positions and expand their authority and/or limit the authority of others over economic policy as needed; (2) build and maintain deference from national politicians and essential private-sector stakeholders; and (3) secure sufficient political

The Power to Act			Prediction		
Authority to Act	Deference to Technocrats	Implementation Capacity of National Politicians	Impact of Technocrats		Behavior
Reflected in the degree to which the scope, domain, magnitude and tools of authority over economic policy are accepted	Reflected in the appointment of potential critics with reputations for success or expertise and degree of unity or division of policymakers	Reflected in national politicians' popularity, their ability to promote their legislative agendas and electoral outcomes	Reflected in the ability to manage political uncertainty by altering policy flexibility	Reflected in the ability to manage policy uncertainty by altering the likelihood of policy outcomes	Reflected in political and market behavior
1 High, Uncontested	High, Deference Granted	High or Not Necessary	Can constrain or expand policy flexibility	Can validate policy, targeted and broad strategies may be effective	Maximum bargaining power
2 High, Uncontested	High, Deference Granted	Low	Can constrain or expand policy flexibility if legislative support is unnecessary	Can validate policy, targeted strategies may be disruptive, broad strategies may be effective	Weak politicians appoint technocrats to bolster implementation capacity, but may abandon them
3 Low, Contested	High, Deference Granted	High or Not Necessary	Can constrain or expand policy flexibility if additional authority is not needed	Can validate policy, targeted and broad strategies may be effective	Technocrats will attempt to expand authority
4 Low, Contested	High, Deference Granted	Low	Can constrain or expand policy flexibility if additional authority and legislative support are not necessary	Can validate policy, targeted strategies may be disruptive, broad strategies may be effective	Technocrats can help leaders outmaneuver political opponents, but long-term uncertainty remains
5 High or Low	Low, Deference Demanded	High or Not Necessary	Confrontational technocrats likely to be replaced with sycophants	Cannot validate policy, targeted and broad strategies by politicians possible	No economic validation, political exuberance likely
6 High or Low	Low, Deference Demanded	Low	Technocrats are impotent	Cannot validate policy, broad strategies by politicians may be effective	Minimum bargaining power, maximum uncertainty

Figure 1.4 Shaping policy and behavior.

capacity to implement and sustain complementary policies. Variations in the degree to which authority over economic policy is accepted or contested, the degree of deference given to those in positions of authority and extant agreements, and the degree to which supporters have the capacity to implement supporting legislation as needed generate six distinct patterns of behavior. Each of the six patterns corresponds to an enumerated category in the rows of Figure 1.4. As shown in subsequent chapters, these patterns of behavior and outcomes have persisted across Argentina, the United States and Europe over the past thirty years. Each case also provides complementary insights into the exercise of power in highly interdependent and often politically turbulent environments.

1.3   Insights from the Cases

Contrary to the expectations based on traditional conceptions of economic technocrats as apolitical, central bankers, treasury secretaries and finance ministers in Argentina, the United States and Europe have been highly responsive to politics and economics. They have interacted extensively with national politicians and have influenced the contents and consequences of economic policy. They have generally been nimbler than national political leaders and played important roles in shaping their countries' responses to economic and political crises. They have also shaped the trajectory of national economic policies and augmented their countries' abilities to respond to and manage investor behavior.

1.3.1   Argentina's Tango

Argentina's efforts to manage competing forces of democratization and financial globalization since the late 1980s foreshadow many of the challenges, choices and consequences that currently haunt Europe and the United States. Argentina's experimentation with fixed exchange rates demonstrates their extraordinary potential for taming inflation and stabilizing investors' expectations, while also highlighting their fragility and dependence on continued deference and legislative support from national politicians. In a prelude to Draghi's efforts to save the euro in 2012, Minister of the Economy Domingo Cavallo succeeded in saving Argentina's fixed exchange rate system, the Convertibility Plan, from potential ruin in 1994 and 1995. His efforts, like Draghi's, restored investor confidence and triggered an economic recovery.

The Argentine experience demonstrates how changing political and economic circumstances affect the degree to which national political leaders are willing to defer to economic policymakers are willing and able to bring the recommended policies to fruition. When circumstances are poor, national politicians are often willing to defer to economic technocrats, delegate authority over monetary policy to central bankers and commit to institutional constraints. Argentine presidents often accepted institutional constraints on monetary policy (such as the Austral Plan of 1985 and the Convertibility Plan of 1991) and appointed strong ministers of the economy (such as Juan Vital Sourrouille, Domingo Cavallo and Roberto Lavagna) to enhance policy credibility when economic conditions were poor. Unfortunately, while important, such displays of deference were often not sufficient to shape policy or market behavior when national politicians lacked the capacity to implement or sustain supporting legislation. Minister of Finance Juan Vital Sourrouille, for example, was left unsupported politically and his Austral Plan failed.

In contrast, when times are good, the legislative capacity of national politicians tends to increase, but their willingness to defer to others or to accept constraints on their authority tends to diminish. When conditions improved, Argentine presidents tended to dismiss economic technocrats who challenged them and appoint more sympathetic ministers of the economy or central bank presidents. In addition, their compliance with legal and institutional constraints on their behavior diminished and progress toward economic reform stalled. For example, reforms stalled when foreign capital inflows surged in 1996, 1998 and 2003–2004. The same dynamic occurred in Greece when capital inflows surged after it joined the euro in 2001, as well as in the United States in 2011–2012 when capital flew in as investors sought to escape worsening conditions in Europe.

The Argentine case also demonstrates that national governments will go to great lengths to placate foreign investors (including raiding pension funds – a strategy copied by the state of California). At the same time, it highlights the ability of national governments to extract enormous concessions from both foreign companies and bondholders. Argentina also provides several vivid examples of the consequences of political corruption and of not providing accurate statistics about national finances.

1.3.2   The US Division of Powers

As in Argentina, individual technocrats influenced how the United States responded to economic pressures at home and financial flows from abroad. Federal Reserve chairman and Treasury secretaries actively promoted financial liberalization and self-regulation in the 1990s and early 2000s. They were first responders to the economic crisis in 2007 and played very active roles in coordinating the US crisis response. In the postcrisis period beginning in 2010, their roles transformed from serving as lenders-of-last resort to reducing political uncertainty generated by ongoing political battles with the Republican Congress and President Obama over economic policy.

The US experiences demonstrate the malleability of political institutions, the enabling as well as constraining effects of these institutions, and the importance of the reputation, creativity and identity of the individual leaders within them. Over the past thirty years, leaders of the Federal Reserve and Treasury repeatedly demonstrated high levels of ingenuity. They exploited unused aspects of their statutory authority and requested additional authority when needed. While they repeatedly took actions that had dire political consequences, they also often bolstered and enabled national politicians. The Federal Reserve provided additional liquidity at home and abroad when none was available from the Treasury; it also intervened when the executive branch was unwilling or unable to do so. The Secretary of the Treasury, in turn, assisted the Federal Reserve by helping it to secure the cooperation of firms in the financial sector with government efforts to recapitalize the system.

Furthermore, while members of Congress often tried to limit the activities of the President, the Treasury and the Federal Reserve, they ultimately granted them the capacity to act by enabling bailouts, financial reforms, economic stimuli, and debt management to take place.

1.3.3   Europe's Odyssey

Like Argentina, Europe's journey toward the ideal of ever-denser integration involved declarations of fidelity to a fixed exchange rate regime and other agreements designed to limit fiscal expenditures. As they discovered, such constraints are neither always effective nor always desirable. The ECB attempted to ameliorate market risks during the crisis using broad-based initiatives to manage liquidity in euros and dollars across Europe. It did so using traditional monetary policy tools, by creating dollar swap lines, developing new lending facilities to provide access to credit, and engaging in "extraordinary" tactics such as buying government bonds, employing negative interest rates and engaging in QE programs.

The ECB also intervened in narrow and targeted ways by assisting banks and countries in distress and compelling wayward governments to accept conditionality-laden bailouts. It did so in part by making access to lending facilities and other programs conditional on policy changes that conformed to its guidelines and those of the European Commission and the International Monetary Fund.

Despite holding a narrower mandate than the Federal Reserve, the ECB has continued to expand the scope and domain of its activities. Many people in Europe have responded to the perceived inequities resulting from the ECB's actions with the same angst shown by their Argentine and American cousins. On the one hand, their angst is generating a resurgence of nationalism and anti-European sentiments. On the other hand, the EU has granted the ECB new powers to oversee the banking sector across Europe. Consequently, concern and reliance on the ECB continue to go hand in hand.

1.4   Conclusion: Economic Policymakers Go Political

The basic premise of this book can be summed up as follows: economic policymakers – including central bankers, treasury secretaries and finance ministers – are strategic political actors. Over the past thirty years, they have attempted to shape economic policy and manage investor behavior by manipulating the institutions, rules and tools that delineate what political stakeholders can do in the economic policy arena and what private-sector actors can do in domestic and global markets. They have also issued promises and threats, manipulated conditional incentives and penalties, provided and withheld information, and been more and less transparent about their intentions.

Some of these efforts have been broadly targeted and intended to shape market behavior by altering general economic conditions and expectations (examples include adjusting interest rates to stimulate or slow down economic activity and setting reserve standards for commercial banks to increase their resilience and decrease the likelihood of bank runs). Other efforts have been targeted narrowly and intended to shape market expectations by changing the conditions or behaviors of specific actors whose circumstances or actions pose systemic risks (examples include offering lender-of-last-resort services to firms that are deemed "too big to fail," requiring banks to conduct "stress tests" to evaluate their ability to withstand future crises and compelling national governments like Greece to pursue financial reforms).

The success and failure of these efforts vary as a function of a dynamic process of pulling and hauling among national politicians and economic technocrats over economic policy. The ability of economic technocrats to reduce political uncertainty by augmenting or limiting policy flexibility and reduce policy uncertainty by altering the likelihood that economic policy will be effective is a function of constitutive power. Their constitutive power varies with their ability to secure the authority, deference and political support needed to shape national economic policy. Variations in the degree to which their authority is contested, the degree to which deference is granted or denied, and the degree to which national politicians have the capacity to implement supporting legislation consistently generate distinct behaviors and policy outcomes.

These arguments are developed in Chapter 2. Their propositions are evaluated using the experiences of Argentina, the United States and Europe in Chapters 3, 4 and 5. The implications of the findings for economic policy and the study of power in highly interdependent and politically turbulent environments are explored in Chapter 6.

2   Preferences, Power and Predictions

2.1   The Challenge of Managing Private Capital

With the creation of the Brady Plan – a program developed by US Treasury Secretary Nicholas Brady in 1989 to convert national debt into bonds following the Latin American debt crisis – emerging market countries joined their wealthier cousins as important participants in global bond and equity markets. The subsequent profitability and popularity of emerging market bonds combined with the securitization of other debts (most notably the packaging of mortgages into tradable securities), the creation of a wide range of increasingly sophisticated finance instruments and the normalization of free capital mobility led to a dramatic surge in the growth of private-sector liquidity and sparked the development of the extraordinarily highly interconnected global financial marketplace that we live in today. The resulting globalization of finance has transformed the international financial system from one dominated by official, public sources of capital to one in which private-sector components of liquidity now permeate virtually all facets of the financial system.[1]

The penetrating web of financial interdependence increasingly links the fates of investors, financial institutions and national governments to one another. These connections can be highly profitable and can provide readily accessible sources of private-sector liquidity. At the same time, the behavior of each of these actors can generate uncertainties that motivate shifts in capital flows, alter the availability and cost of credit, and generate changes in financial asset and property prices with significant domestic and global consequences. Private-sector liquidity can

---

[1] Private sector liquidity is generated through processes that include cross-border banking, interbank and interfirm lending (often in very short-term time frames), portfolio flows and investment funds, trading in primary and secondary bond and security markets and the exchange of over-the-counter derivatives and other financial instruments. J. P. Landau, ed. (2011). "Global Liquidity – Concept, Measurement and Policy Implications." *Committee on the Global Financial System (CGFS) Papers, No. 45. Bank of France, Bank for International Settlements.*

potentially expand endlessly, but will do so only as long as private-sector entities are willing to fund one another. The high degree of connectivity and the ease with which capital can shift from one location to another mean that economic policy choices in relatively small countries or the failure of even relatively small companies can quickly ripple through the global economy. When uncertainties rise and private capital becomes scarce or expensive, markets often look to national governments, central banks and international financial institutions for help.

International Monetary Fund (IMF) Managing Director Lagarde highlights the challenge of financial interdependence and its consequences as follows:

The [2008] crisis also gave us cause to rethink the extent to which the world is interconnected. A bankruptcy in the United States in 2008 brought the world economy to its knees. Then Eurozone troubles shook the global economy again. Another worry today is the risk of a slowdown in emerging markets pulling back growth everywhere.[2]

Indeed, varying levels of uncertainty about how national governments would respond to changing economic and political conditions (i.e., political uncertainty) and what the consequences of their actions would be (i.e., policy uncertainty) within this dense web of interdependence triggered and shaped the market reactions to the Argentine inflation crisis of 1989–1990, the Mexican Tequila Crisis of 1994–1995, the East Asian financial crisis of 1997, the Russian financial crisis of 1998, the Argentine economic crisis of 2001–2002, the US financial crisis of 2008, the Eurozone crisis of 2010, the British referendum in 2016 and the Argentine and Turkish economic crises of 2018. Even in noncrisis periods, uncertainty about what governments are likely to do and what effects their actions are likely to have can compound market uncertainty with deleterious effects on economic growth, competitiveness and societal well-being.

I argue that high levels of interdependence among investors, financial institutions and national governments create opportunities for the exercise of second-order power. One of the principal consequences of extensive financial connectivity is that the behavior of investors, financial institutions and governments is mediated by their expectations about what the others will do and what the consequences of their actions will be. Under the right conditions, central bankers and other economic policymakers can exploit this interdependence to influence the behavior

---

[2] C. Lagarde (2013). "The Global Calculus of Unconventional Monetary Policies." Speech at Jackson Hole. www.imf.org/en/News/Articles/2015/09/28/04/53/sp082313.

of investors and financial institutions and, by doing so, influence capital flows, credit dynamics and price levels in their countries.

They can exercise second-order power by reducing uncertainty about how national governments are likely to act in particular economic and political circumstances, and by reducing uncertainty about the consequences of government outcomes. They can do so by validating policy choices, managing general economic conditions (e.g., reducing market risks) and assisting financial institutions and countries in distress or compelling them to alter undesirable behaviors (e.g., reducing specific-actor risks). I define this as the exercise of second-order power because the impact on market behavior is a second-order effect of the ability of economic policymakers to reduce political and policy uncertainty.

Implementing second-order power strategies successfully is a two-step process. The first step is to specify the level of risk that investors are likely to attribute to particular policies under prevailing economic conditions. This can be done using the Risk Intervention Curve (RIC). The second step is for national governments to take actions that reduce uncertainty about what types of policies they will adopt and what consequences those policies will have. Political and policy uncertainty vary with the extent to which authority over economic policy is contested, deference to particular policies is high or low, and supporting legislation can be implemented as needed. To the extent that economic policymakers assert their authority, command deference or enforce policy compliance, and secure the implementation of supporting legislation as needed to shape economic policy, they can reduce political and policy uncertainty. All else being equal, this can reduce perceptions of risk and help to promote desirable market behaviors.

Thus, within the broad field of international economic governance, I focus narrowly on a subset of actors and institutions involved in shaping the content and consequences of national economic policy choices. I focus in particular on economic policy-making in Argentina, the United States and Europe since the early 1990s when these countries began adapting to the rise of financial globalization. Since then, these countries have experienced dramatic shifts in capital flows, the availability and cost of credit, consumer prices, property prices and asset prices. Each experienced periods of economic growth, recession, crisis and recovery. Economic policymakers in each country also faced changing political environments. Some politicians asserted their authority over economic policy while others delegated that authority; some politicians demanded deference while others were willing to defer to economic technocrats. Some politicians began with strong electoral positions then weakened; others were weaker to begin with but gained strength over time. In short, the independent variables that affect the ability of economic policymakers to alter political and policy uncertainty (e.g., the degree to which authority over economic policy is asserted, delegated or contested; the degree to which deference to particular policymakers, policies, or institutions is granted; and the capacity of political leaders to implement supporting legislation as needed) vary over time and across these cases. The dependent variables of interest (e.g., investor risk as reflected in the availability and cost of capital and the rate of inflation or deflation) also vary over time and across these cases. Though there are obvious differences within and among Argentina, the United States and Europe over time, common variations in the variables of interest suggest that there are important lessons to be learned from comparing each of them.

In this chapter, I develop the argument introduced in Chapter 1. I define and operationalize the variables of interest and develop specific hypotheses about how constitutive power dynamics among economic policymakers and national politicians are likely to alter policy-making behavior and market outcomes.

I begin by specifying the relationships among political uncertainty, policy uncertainty and investor risk under different economic conditions. These relationships can be represented in stylized form in the RIC. Next, I specify the conditions under which these strategies are likely to be effective. I argue that the ability of particular central bankers and other economic policymakers to prevail – and thus move their country's position along the RIC or alter investors' perceptions of risk at any particular point along the RIC – is a function of their willingness and capacity to: (1) exploit their institutional positions and expand their authority and/or limit the authority of others over economic policy as needed; (2) build and maintain deference from national politicians and essential private sector stakeholders; and (3) secure sufficient political capacity to implement complementary policies. Variations in the degree to which the exercise of authority over economic policy is accepted or contested, deference to those in positions of authority is given or demanded, and national politicians have the will and capacity to implement supporting legislation as needed generate six distinct hypotheses about government behavior.

2.2   Investor Preferences and the RIC

I begin by developing a model of investor preferences for particular types of market interventions known as the RIC. The RIC builds on insights from recent research by Andrew MacIntyre who posits that the policy preferences of average investors reflect a trade-off between policy predictability and the ability to notational governments adapt to changing circumstances.[3] This approach posits that, *ceteris paribus*, constraints on economic policy-making – resulting from checks and balances in the policy-making process, institutional commitments and other factors that limit the discretion of national politicians to shape economic policy – improve policy predictability and the credibility of policy commitments. Yet, if these constraints are too severe, they could limit the ability of national governments to adapt and respond to changing economic conditions.

Alternatively, giving national politicians a freer hand to manage economic policy by reducing the number of veto players and institutional constraints in the policy-making process increases policy adaptability, yet it could also decrease the reliability of policy commitments and reduce the predictability of future policy decisions. Consequently, the relationship between policy flexibility and risk is expected to be concave upward. High levels of risk are associated with both high levels of policy constraint and high levels of policy flexibility; lower levels of risk are associated in the midrange between the two extremes.

In his study of investor behavior in Southeast Asia following the 1997 crisis, MacIntyre argues that economic policies in countries like Thailand whose leaders face a relatively high level of institutional constraint will be relatively rigid and inflexible in the face of changing economic circumstances.[4] In contrast, economic policies in countries like Indonesia and Malaysia whose leaders face relatively few institutional constraints will be highly responsive but also more unpredictable. Investors are expected to be wary of the extremes associated with both economic policy rigidity and policy flexibility and prefer a middle zone between two. As predicted, investors returned more quickly to the Philippines following the 1997 crisis because they expected its economic policies to be more flexible than those in Thailand and more predictable than those in Indonesia and Malaysia.

2.2.1   Institutional Constraints and Investor Preferences

The basic model of the relationship between perceptions of risk and the policy flexibility–policy rigidity spectrum using the veto-player model is

---

[3] A. MacIntyre (2001). "Institutions and Investors: The Politics of the Economic Crisis in South East Asia." *International Organization* 55(1), 81–122.

[4] Ibid.

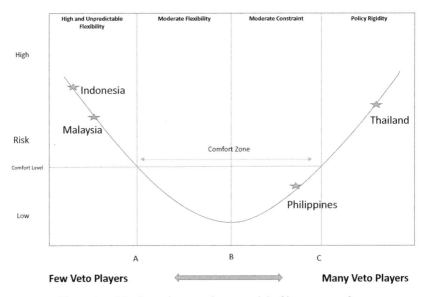

Figure 2.1 MacIntyre's veto-player model of investor preferences.

reflected in a symmetric inverted curve presented in Figure 2.1. MacIntyre estimates investor risk in terms of the differential rate at which investors returned to different countries in Southeast Asia following the 1997 Asian financial crisis. He estimates policy flexibility in terms of the number of institutionalized veto players in a country's policy-making process. A veto player is defined as an individual or set of individuals whose consent is required before policies can change.[5] The relative degree of policy flexibility of Indonesia, Malaysia, the Philippines and Thailand is approximated by the relative number of veto players and institutional constraints that exist within each country's policy-making processes.

While the risk tolerance of individual investors may vary significantly, an idealized comfort zone of policy flexibility can be approximated for any comfort level of risk. For an investor with the comfort level for risk designated in Figure 2.1, countries with levels of policy flexibility between A and C will be more attractive than those that fall outside that range. Countries located to the left of point A on the horizontal axis have fewer veto players and institutionalized checks in their policy-making

---

[5] G. Tsebelis (2002). *Veto Players: How Institutions Work*. Princeton: Princeton University Press.

processes. Consequently, they are expected to be more adaptive, but also potentially more erratic and unpredictable. These leaders can be expected to implement new policies quickly, but the freedom to make economic policy decisions without securing the approval or validation of others in the policy-making process makes policy outcomes less certain. It also suggests that the executive could readily shape economic policy for political or personal purposes. This decreases the credibility of policy commitments and increases the possibilities for potential problems of corruption, cronyism and collusion.

In contrast, countries located to the right of point C on the horizontal axis are more highly constrained. The policy-making process may be constrained by a variety of institutional mechanisms including the delegation of monetary policy to an independent central bank, the adoption of a fixed-exchange-rate regime or treaty commitments. These constraints can be commitment enforcing and credibility enhancing, but they may also limit the ability of policymakers to adapt to changing circumstances in a timely manner.

2.3   Adding Dynamism to Create the RIC

MacIntyre's veto-player curve provides a useful and straightforward way to assess the relative attractiveness to investors of comparable countries under comparable circumstances. It is difficult, however, to apply his model over time or across countries when economic and political conditions vary. To expand its applicability, I redefine investor risk, operationalize the policy-flexibility spectrum in terms of political uncertainty rather than the number of veto players, and add the consideration of uncertainty regarding policy outcomes. The resulting RIC infuses MacIntyre's veto-player model with dynamism by treating the level of policy flexibility as a variable that can be manipulated strategically. It also enables the manipulation of market risks, specific-actor risks and other factors that affect policy impacts. These considerations suggest that level of risk associated with a given policy choice – and thus the shape of the curve – is context specific. For example, market risks and thus the shape of the RIC can differ in inflationary versus deflationary environments. Changes in specific-actor risks, in turn, can affect the level of risk associated with a particular level of policy flexibility at any point along the curve. For example, the potential failure of a systemically important bank could make an otherwise acceptable level of policy constraint riskier than normal by raising concerns about the ability of policymakers to provide a bailout in a timely manner.

2.3.1   Defining Risk and Uncertainty

I argue that investors' perceptions of risk vary as a function of uncertainty regarding what a government is likely to do and what the consequences of its actions are likely to be. The RIC depicts this relationship. Risk is associated with the likelihood of loss. Uncertainty is associated with the inability to determine the likelihood and/or magnitude of an event. I focus in particular on four aspects of risk that are shaped by four parallel aspects of uncertainty. They include political risk and political uncertainty, policy risk and policy uncertainty, market risk and market uncertainty, and specific-actor risk and specific-actor uncertainty.

- *Political risk* is generally defined as "the risk that an investment's returns could suffer as a result of political change or instability in a country."[6] *Political uncertainty* involves expectations that a government will respond to changing political or economic circumstances in a particular way.
- *Policy risk* is generally defined as the extent to which an investment's returns could suffer because the policy is considered inappropriate or suboptimal or is otherwise expected to be ineffective. *Policy uncertainty* involves expectations about whether a chosen policy will achieve its objectives. Policy uncertainty can be reduced if the policy at hand is validated by credible experts, market risks are reduced or specific-actor risks are reduced.
- *Market risk* (also widely referred to as *systemic risk*) is generally defined as the possibility that an investor will experience losses due to overall performance in economic and financial markets.[7] High levels of market risk may be associated with concerns about macroeconomic performance, inflation or deflation, exchange rate appreciation or depreciation, asset bubbles, recessions and unemployment. *Market uncertainty* can be reduced by factors that alter general market conditions in desirable ways or otherwise increase confidence about future economic or financial performance.
- *Specific-actor or product risk* relates to the potential losses from situations uniquely attributable to a particular product or actor.[8] It might pertain to a particular country, bank or company; a specific stock, bond or investment vehicle; a specific regulation or policy; or small

---

[6] "Political risk." *Investopedia*. www.investopedia.com/terms/p/politicalrisk.asp?layout=orig.

[7] "Market risk." *Investopedia*. www.investopedia.com/terms/m/marketrisk.asp?layout=infini&v=5B&orig=1&adtest=5.

[8] "Specific risk." *Investopedia*. www.investopedia.com/terms/s/specificrisk.asp?layout=infini&v=5B&orig=1&adtest=5B.

numbers of any of these. If the behavior or condition of one or a small number of specific market actors or products has potentially negative repercussions for a large number of other actors, then they could pose market or systemic risks. *Specific-actor uncertainty* can be reduced in a variety of ways, including removing problematic products (e.g., "toxic assets") from the marketplace, acting as a lender of last resort for troubled firms and compelling wayward countries to adopt recommended policy changes.

2.3.2 Strategies for Managing Uncertainty and Reducing Risk

The RIC adds agency to the veto-player model of investor risk by relaxing the assumption that degree of policy flexibility is fixed by the number of veto players and formal checks and balances that exist within a country's policy-making process. While useful as a first approximation of relative policy flexibility, this approach cannot account for the wide variation in policy-making flexibility within Argentina, the United States and Europe over periods of time when their formal policy-making structures – including the number of veto players and institutional commitments – remained unchanged. I argue that the impact of individuals and institutions on policy-making is contingent on the degree to which their authorities are accepted or contested, national politicians defer to or demand deference from them, and national politicians have the capacity to implement supporting legislation as needed. As Bruce Hall notes, even core statutory authorities – like the de jure independence of central banks and the stability of fixed-exchange-rate regimes – are highly contingent.[9] Recognizing this contingency, I posit that policy flexibility and the efficacy of policy decisions are shaped by ongoing strategic interactions among national politicians, economic policymakers, and the institutions through which they operate.

As introduced in Chapter 1, economic policymakers and national politicians often attempt to anticipate, respond to and shape investor expectations. Economic policymakers can increase policy flexibility and expand the number of policy options available to national policymakers and private sector actors in a variety of ways. Examples include lowering interest rates or reserve requirements, promoting deregulation, providing lender-of-last-resort services to banks in distress and increasing access to public liquidity. Alternately, they can reduce policy flexibility and limit the discretion of national politicians by asserting their statutory authority

[9] B. Hall (2010). *Central Banking as Global Governance: Constructing Financial Credibility.* Cambridge: Cambridge University Press.

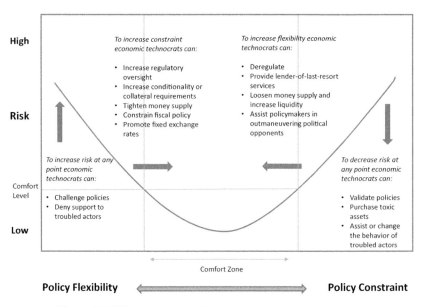

High

To increase constraint economic technocrats can:

- Increase regulatory oversight
- Increase conditionality or collateral requirements
- Tighten money supply
- Constrain fiscal policy
- Promote fixed exchange rates

To increase flexibility economic technocrats can:

- Deregulate
- Provide lender-of-last-resort services
- Loosen money supply and increase liquidity
- Assist policymakers in outmaneuvering political opponents

Risk

To increase risk at any point economic technocrats can:

- Challenge policies
- Deny support to troubled actors

To decrease risk at any point economic technocrats can:

- Validate policies
- Purchase toxic assets
- Assist or change the behavior of troubled actors

Comfort Level

Low

Comfort Zone

Policy Flexibility   **Policy Constraint**

Figure 2.2 The risk intervention curve.

and oversight of economic policy, adding conditionality to lending, raising interest rates or collateral requirements and promoting and reinforcing commitments to fixed exchange rates and other institutional constraints. When successful, these efforts can reduce risk and policy uncertainty by shifting their country's position along the RIC (see Figure 2.2).

Economic policymakers can also increase policy flexibility by helping national politicians overcome political opposition and by intervening in ways that compensate for political inertia. Throughout much of his administration, for example, President Barack Obama faced extraordinary opposition from the US Congress. Political polarization became so severe that major legislation generally passed only by way of party-line votes. In the summer of 2011, Standard & Poor's downgraded the credit rating of the United States because the President and Congress were unable to reach an agreement on managing the budget. In October of 2013, Congress even forced the US Government to shut down rather than reach a compromise on the Affordable Care Act. Throughout this period, however, the Secretaries of the Treasury and Chairs of the Federal Reserve added flexibility to an otherwise highly rigid US policy environment. Treasury Secretaries Geithner and Lew exploited their access to intragovernmental funds to keep the United States from going into default while the President and members of Congress fought the budgets. Federal Chairman Bernanke intervened repeatedly to stimulate the economy. As is highlighted in Chapter 4, many of the Federal Reserve's interventions – including Operation Twist and various quantitative easing programs – coincided with political stalemates and peaks in political infighting. These interventions helped to compensate for political uncertainty and the risk of policy rigidity.

Economic policymakers can also increase the likelihood that particular policy choices will be successful by reducing market risk and specific-actor risks. Targeted threats have been used to compel changes in behavior. In October of 2015, for example, the European Central Bank (ECB) threatened to deny Irish banks access to emergency liquidity assistance (ELA) in order to compel Ireland to accept a conditional bailout program. Incentives have also been used. In March of 2016, the ECB tried to encourage lending by launching a series of targeted longer-term refinancing operations (TLTRO-II) at interest rates that decreased based on the number of loans that the banks issued.

2.3.3 Considering Context

The RIC considers the relationship between risk and policy flexibility to be context specific. Furthermore, it presumes that the level of risk associated with a particular level of policy flexibility will vary depending on expectations that the chosen policy will achieve its objectives. In inflationary environments or in the run-up to elections when fears of fiscal exuberance are high, for example, the level of risk associated with policy flexibility will tend to increase and the level of risk associated with policy constraint will tend to decrease. In these circumstances, strategies designed to constrain economic policy options and limit the ability of national politicians to engage in potentially inflationary behavior are likely to be associated with lower levels of risk. These circumstances reflect the conventional wisdom that investors will be attracted to countries that delegate monetary authority to a politically autonomous central bank, adopt a fixed-exchange-rate regime or commit to agreements designed to limit the economic policy discretion of national politicians. A RIC in inflationary environments and run-ups to elections is presented in Figure 2.3. While risk acceptance levels vary, the comfort zone for a stylized investor is included for reference purposes.

In contrast, in circumstances in which investors would like the government to step in as a lender of last resort or as a first responder to a crisis, the level of risk associated with policy constraint is expected to be higher than normal and the level of risk associated with policy flexibility is

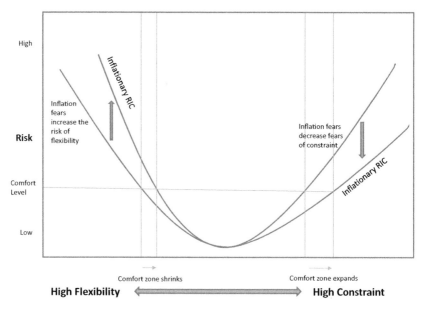

Figure 2.3 The risk intervention curve in inflationary environments.

expected to be lower. This is likely in periods of capital scarcity, when the risk of contagion is high and when growth has stagnated or the economy is deflationary. In the aftermath of the collapse of the US economy in September of 2008, for example, investors responded positively to coordinated stimulus activities (see Figure 2.4).

2.4   The Power to Manage Risk and Uncertainty

The power to influence investor risk begins at home with the pulling and hauling among national politicians and economic policymakers over the authority to shape economic policy, the content of the policy and the means of implementation. The ability of particular central bankers and other economic policymakers to prevail in this arena – and thus move their country's position along the RIC or alter investors' perceptions of risk at any particular point along the RIC – is a function of their constitutive power dynamics as defined by their willingness and capacity to: (1) exploit their institutional positions and expand their authority and/or limit the authority of others over economic policy as needed; (2) build and maintain deference from

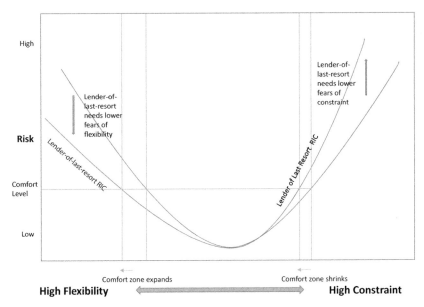

Figure 2.4 The risk intervention curve in lender-of-last-resort environments.

national politicians and essential private-sector stakeholders; and (3) secure sufficient political capacity to implement and sustain complementary policies and engage in behavior.

2.4.1 Authority

From the perspective of the New Haven School of International Law, a rule or institution is considered authoritative if actors in the relevant policy-making process perceive it to be so and, thus, it is *opinio juris*. As articulated by Anthony Arend, the level of authority varies based on the frequency, spread and significance of manifestations of the authority and the frequency, spread and significance of contrary manifestations of the authority.[10] Manifestations of authority include statutory documents and legislative policy actions that amend such documents, actions by the judiciary that interpret and evaluate the implementation of these documents, and actions taken by the executive or others who themselves have the authority to delegate

---

[10] A. Arend (1999). *Legal Rules and International Society.* New York: Oxford University Press, pp. 87–98.

responsibility and appoint, manage or oversee the individuals or institutions in question. Manifestations of authority also include less formal actions by members of the executive, legislative or judicial branches of government that express support for or conform to a particular set of guidelines or practices specified by those in authority. Contrary manifestations of authority are challenges contesting any of the above.

For the purposes of this book, authority will be considered highly contested if explicit legislative, political or legal actions are taken to challenge an assertion of authority or the promulgation of a regulation, or if such actions are taken to limit the future assertion of authority or regulatory action. Authority will be considered less contested if legislative, political or legal actions are muted or not taken when a particular actor or institution asserts or expands the scope, domain, magnitude or use of tools associated with its authority. Legitimacy and contestation are inversely related: those who contest the exercise of authority by others generally consider it to be illegitimate because it falls outside of expected parameters of scope or domain, or the magnitude or the tools used are inappropriate.

The level of authority is also a function of the clarity of lines of responsibility and accountability within a country's policy-making process. Authority will be considered contested if multiple parties attempt to assert authority over a specific issue. The acceptance or contestation of authority within the policymaking process can be delineated in terms of scope, domain, magnitude and use of particular tools. Points of contention generally include:

- *Scope*: For what set of issues is the individual or institution responsible or accountable? When multiple issues are involved, how are their prioritized?
- *Domain*: What entities fall under the jurisdiction of the individual or institution? If multiple entities are involved, which take precedence?
- *Magnitude*: How much change can be required or requested by those in positions of authority?
- *Tools*: Over what resources does the individual or institution have discretion?

One or more of these components may be respected while others are contested. In the cases presented below, for example, the authority of the Federal Reserve and ECB to conduct monetary policy using traditional tools was broadly accepted. Nonetheless, critics of the Federal Reserve contested its extension of bailouts to private companies and nonbank financial institutions. Critics of the ECB, in turn, contested its purchase of government bonds and the extent of economic policy reforms demanded by the Troika as part of its bailout packages.

2.4.2   Deference

I define deference as "the respectful submission or yielding of judgment, opinion, will, etc., of another" person or institution.[11] Having the "ear" of the president or prime minister and having the confidence and trust of private-sector stakeholders often matters more than the one's administrative position when seeking to shape policy. This is particularly true when multiple technocrats are attempting to shape policy or multiple agencies have authority over different aspects of economic policy-making.

The level of deference given or demanded by national politicians and economic policymakers often varies across different administrations. Some presidents and prime ministers delegate most of the responsibility for monetary policy to their economic teams and defer to their policy recommendations. Argentine President Carlos Menem deferred to Minister of the Economy Domingo Cavallo with regard to the creation and maintenance of the Convertibility Plan that pegged the peso to the dollar throughout the 1990s. Similarly, US President George W. Bush deferred to his senior economic advisors Chairman of the Council of Economic Advisors Edward Lazear and Treasury Secretary Henry Paulson regarding how to respond to the emerging financial crisis in the summer of 2008.

Others, like Argentine President Néstor Kirchner and US Presidents Bill Clinton and Barack Obama, took more active roles in economic policy-making, often collaborating closely with broader economic teams. President Obama also tried to reduce policy uncertainty by appointing Timothy Geithner as Treasury Secretary and Larry Summers as Chairman of the Council of Economic Advisors, and by reappointing Ben Bernanke as Chairman of the Federal Reserve.

Still others, like Argentine President Cristina Fernández de Kirchner and US Presidents Richard Nixon and Donald Trump, demanded a high degree of deference from their economic team. President Fernández de Kirchner famously fired the President of the Argentine Central Bank Martin Redrado when he refused to allow her to use pension funds to pay foreign investors. In commenting about working for President Nixon, Chairman of the Federal Reserve Arthur Burns mused, "I knew that I would be accepted in the future only if I suppressed my will and yielded completely – even though it was wrong at law and morally – to his authority."[12]

---

[11] "Deference" (n.d.). *Dictionary.com.* http://dictionary.reference.com/browse/deference.

[12] Cited in N. Irwin (2014). *The Alchemists: Three Central Bankers and a World on Fire.* New York: Penguin Group, p. 11.

Neil Irwin summarizes nicely the distinction between the having the legal authority to shape economic policy independently from political pressure and the level of deference granted by political leaders to economic technocrats in positions of authority:

> The Bank of England gained legal independence in 1997; the central banks of France, Italy and many other Western European nations that aren't Germany weren't truly independent as late as the 1990s, when there began a push to create the ECB. The Federal Reserve gained independence in the 1951 Treasury–Fed accord, but sure didn't act like it in the 1970s, when the Nixon administration used all manner of tools to encourage easy money policies out of the central bank (and resulting high inflation). It was Fed Chief Paul Volcker's willful leadership, serving in the Carter and Reagan administrations, that brought independence to the Fed in practice, if not in law.[13]

Presidents and prime ministers often appoint particular economic policymakers to signal their deference to a particular set of policy ideas. For example, President Clinton renewed Alan Greenspan's appointment on January 4, 2000 to signal policy continuity despite animosity between many in the administration and Greenspan over his decision to raise interest rates several months ahead of the 1994 midterm elections. The message was well received, with the Dow Jones index increasing 124 points. President George W. Bush's appointment of Henry Paulson, the former Chairman of Goldman Sachs, as Treasury Secretary was similarly well received by Wall Street. European markets also responded positively in November of 2011 when Mario Monti, a well respected economist and former European Commissioner, replaced Silvio Berlusconi as Prime Minister of Italy.

The degree of deference given to or demanded by political leaders and senior economic technocrats can also vary within a single administration in response to changing economic and political circumstances. For example, when economic conditions were poor Argentine presidents often accepted institutional constraints on monetary policy (like the Austral Plan of 1985 and the Convertibility Plan of 1991) and appointed strong ministers of the economy (like Juan Vital Sourrouille, Domingo Cavallo and Roberto Lavagna) to enhance policy credibility. Their deference to these institutions and individuals was, however, almost always temporary. When economic conditions improved, Argentine presidents

---

[13] N. Irwin (2013). "The Bank of Japan is coordinating policy with the Japanese government. That is a big deal." *Washington Post*, January 22. www.washingtonpost.com/blogs/wonkblog/wp/2013/01/22/the-bank-of-japan-is-coordinating-policy-with-the-japanese-government-that-is-a-big-deal; cited in "Central bank independence in Japan – not what you would expect" (2013). *Reszat Online*, January 1. http://reszatonline.wordpress.com/2013/01/27/central-bank-independence-in-japan-not-what-you-would-expect.

tended to replace assertive technocrats with more sympathetic individuals, their compliance with legal constraints on their behavior diminished and progress toward economic reform stalled.

National governments often react to capital inflows and permissive economic conditions as if they are rewards for good behavior, even when they are the result of other exogenous factors. Capital inflows surged into Argentina following the Asian and Russian financial crises of 1997 and 1998, and again when soybean prices surged in 2003–2006; they surged into Greece when it adopted the euro in 2001, and into the United States when the economic crisis hit Europe in 2010. In each case, as capital flooded in the level of deference granted to economic technocrats by national politicians declined. Protesting finance ministers and central bankers were ignored or dismissed as national politicians took advantage of the permissive conditions.

For the purposes of this book, deference will be evaluated in terms of (1) whether national politicians appoint, retain or dismiss economic policymakers who are known for their expertise or policy successes and have shown a willingness to pursue prudent economic policies regardless of the political consequences, (2) the degree to which a policy consensus exists among senior policymakers, (3) the frequency, spread and significance of acts of compliance and noncompliance with existing protocols and agreements, and (4) the extent to which the policies are considered successful.

2.4.3   Implementation Capacity

Implementation capacity involves the will and ability of national governments to implement and sustain supporting economic policies. It is also reflected in the ability of national politicians to support their economic team in the face of social and political backlashes.

For the purposes of this book, implementation capacity is expected to be high when public approval of national political leaders is high, when they or their parties have experienced electoral successes and when they have been able to implement other components of their policy agendas. Implementation capacity will be considered low when public approval of national political leaders is low, when they or their parties have experienced electoral defeats or when they are unable to implement other aspects of their policy agendas.

2.5   Predictions

Variations in the degree to which authority over economic policy is accepted or contested, deference to those in positions of authority is

The Power to Act			Prediction		
Authority to Act	**Deference to Technocrats**	**Implementation Capacity of National Politicians**	**Impact of Technocrats**		**Behavior**
Reflected in the degree to which the scope, domain, magnitude, and tools of authority over economic policy are accepted.	*Reflected in the appointment of potential critics with reputations for success or expertise and degree of unity or division of policymakers*	*Reflected in national politicians' popularity, their ability to promote their legislative agendas and electoral outcomes*	*Reflected in the ability to manage political uncertainty by altering policy flexibility*	*Reflected in the ability to manage policy uncertainty by altering the likelihood of policy outcomes*	*Reflected in political and market behavior*
1 High, Uncontested	High, Deference Granted	High or Not Necessary	Can constrain or expand policy flexibility	Can validate policy, targeted and broad strategies may be effective	Maximum bargaining power
2 High, Uncontested	High, Deference Granted	Low	Can constrain or expand policy flexibility if legislative support is unnecessary	Can validate policy, targeted strategies may be disruptive, broad strategies may be effective	Weak politicians appoint implementation capacity, but may abandon them
3 Low, Contested	High, Deference Granted	High or Not Necessary	Can constrain or expand policy flexibility if additional authority is not needed	Can validate policy, targeted and broad strategies may be effective	Technocrats will attempt to expand authority
4 Low, Contested	High, Deference Granted	Low	Can constrain or expand policy flexibility if additional authority and legislative support are not necessary	Can validate policy, targeted strategies may be disruptive, broad strategies may be effective	Technocrats can help leaders outmaneuver political opponents, but long-term uncertainty remains
5 High or Low	Low, Deference Demanded	High or Not Necessary	Confrontational technocrats likely to be replaced with sycophants	Cannot validate policy, targeted and broad strategies by politicians possible	No economic validation, political exuberance likely
6 High or Low	Low, Deference Demanded	Low	Technocrats are impotent	Cannot validate policy, broad strategies by politicians may be effective	Minimum bargaining power, maximum uncertainty

Figure 2.5 Shaping policy and behavior.

given or demanded, and supporters have the capacity to implement legislation as needed generate six distinct patterns of behavior and predictable outcomes. These are reflected in the enumerated categories in the rows of Figure 2.5.

2.5.1   United We Stand

Category 1 in Figure 2.5 represents an ideal in which the authority of economic policymakers is uncontested and the rules and institutions they lead are expected to be controlling, deference is granted to economic technocrats and the policies prescribed by international agreements, and implementation capacity is high. Uncontested authority implies that economic policymakers should not receive any legislative or legal challenges for actions taken within the purview of their mandates. The high level of deference indicates that their policy recommendations and those prescribed by international agreement will be accepted. The high implementation capacity suggests that supporting legislation will be enacted and sustained. Consequently, the country's economic policies will be considered economically credible and politically viable. Thus, political uncertainty and policy uncertainty will be low.

Since the deference and implementation capacity are high, the policies proposed by economic policymakers are likely to be reinforced by supporting legislation as needed. A restrictive monetary policy is likely to be matched with a restrictive fiscal policy, a decision to fix the exchange rate will likely be matched with fiscal discipline, and requests by technocrats for additional funding to address economic concerns will likely be supported politically. This means that the economic technocrats and national decision-makers can act in unison to stay the course or shift national policy in response to market fluctuations as needed. This coordination enhances the bargaining capacity of the government vis-à-vis other market actors. Consequently, the ability of the government to reduce market uncertainty and specific-actor uncertainty will be high.

The confluence of uncontested authority, high levels of deference and sufficient legislative capacity can be benign. It characterizes many regular, uncontroversial economic policy activities such as normal open-market operations and the periodic review of banks and other financial institutions. In such circumstances, maintaining transparency and providing forward guidance are generally sufficient to manage expectations about future monetary policy decisions, and the consequences of any particular intervention are likely to be understood and highly predictable. In essence, this situation is seemingly ideal for central bankers whose ambition, as described by Former Governor of the Bank of England Mervyn King, is to be boring.[14]

For economic policymakers with broader ambitions or challenges, however, the confluence of authority, deference and legislative capacity offers extraordinary opportunities to shape economic policy and alter market behavior. Investors who observe clear lines of policy-making authority and evidence of deference and legislative capacity can make credible assumptions that economic policymakers are contributing to the policy-making process, that a general policy consensus exists and that chosen policies are likely to be implemented and sustained. Consequently, consistent with traditional arguments about central bank autonomy, economic policymakers have the capacity to limit the policy-making discretion of national politicians if warranted to fight inflation or other ills. On the other hand, they also have the capacity to promote particular

---

[14] M. King (2000). "Balancing the Economic See-Saw." Speech to the Plymouth Chamber of Commerce and Industry's 187th Banquet, April 14. www.bis.org/review/ r000417d.pdf.

policies and policy agendas, and assist national politicians in overcoming potential veto players and other obstacles to change.

It is important to recognize that the confluence of authority, deference and implementation capacity does not dictate what type of policy will be pursued. In 1991, collaboration between Argentina's President Carlos Menem and his Minister of the Economy Domingo Cavallo led to the implementation of a fixed-exchange-rate regime and policy shift toward economic liberalization that heralded a golden decade of economic growth. Similarly, American President Bill Clinton's willingness to collaborate with National Economic Council (NEC) Director Robert Rubin and Fed Chairman Alan Greenspan led to the 1993 Economic Plan which prioritized monetary over fiscal policy and generated a surge in investor confidence and economic growth. In contrast, the close relationship between Argentina President Néstor Kirchner and his Minister of the Economy Roberto Lavagna enabled them to pursue a series of populist policies and helped Argentina challenge international investors. The confluence of authority, deference and implementation capacity between 2003 and 2005 helped Argentina settle its debts with the IMF, fix the price that foreign companies could charge their consumers for utilities and then renegotiate its external debt at the extraordinarily discounted rate of twenty-three cents on the dollar.

2.5.2   Appoint Oracles and Heroes to Build Strength, but Be Ready to Abandon Old Friends

Category 2 in Figure 2.5 represents the situation in which the authority of economic policymakers is uncontested and the rules and institutions they lead are expected to be controlling, deference is granted to economic technocrats and the policies prescribed by international agreements, but implementation capacity is low. As in category 1, this combination implies that economic policymakers can expect to operate within their mandates without legal or political challenges and their policy recommendations are likely to be accepted. Unlike category 1, however, they are unlikely to be able to secure legislative support for their policy initiatives.

In these circumstances, weak politicians often appoint well-known central bankers, finance ministers and treasury secretaries to enhance the credibility of their economic policies. Reappointing economic policymakers from previous administrations is a useful means of demonstrating that deference is high and that policy consistency is likely. In addition, if previously successful economic policymakers are successful again, they may become heroes and bolster the political status and implementation capacity of their president or prime minister.

If, however, the president or prime minister remains weak, he or she may be unable or unwilling to sustain the economic policies that the economic team recommends. Over the past twenty-five years, many politicians delegated authority to central bankers and finance ministers but then lacked the will or political capacity to follow through with supporting legislation. After its initial success in lowering inflation in 1985, for example, the Austral Plan faltered when Argentine President Alfonsín succumbed to societal pressures to raise military and public-sector wages. In doing so, he violated the policies recommended by his Minister of Economy Sourrouille. The resulting political and policy uncertainties led to a run on the currency, suspension of financing by the IMF, hyperinflation and the early demise of the Alfonsín regime. Similarly in the United States, the legislative defeat of Secretary Paulson and Chairman Bernanke's first Troubled Asset Relief Program (TARP) proposal on September 29, 2008 by congressmen in the President's political party led to a panic that turned the burgeoning economic crisis into a calamity.

The lack of implementation capacity also suggests that the ability of central bankers to compel wayward governments to accept conditional bailouts may be insufficient to restore market confidence. For example, while Mario Draghi was able to compel the government of Greece, Ireland, Spain, Italy and Cyprus to accept conditional bailouts, several of the politicians who accepted those terms were quickly thrown out of office and replaced with more populist-leaning leaders. Consequently, even though these countries eventually recovered, the initial impacts of the ECB's interventions were destabilizing politically and economically.

2.5.3   *May I Please Have More Authority?*

Categories 3 and 4 in Figure 2.5 represent situations in which the authority of economic policymakers is insufficient to achieve their object-ives or is likely to be contested, deference of high, and implementation capacity varies. The high level of deference suggests that economic policymakers may have the ear of the president or prime minister. Con-sequently, they may succeed in asking for supplemental authority, though those in category 4 may have difficulty and may face a legislative backlash for their efforts.

The combination of low or contested authority and mixed implemen-tation capacity means that economic policymakers who attempt to take actions outside the bounds of their traditional mandates will likely face a legal challenge and political backlash. As discussed in Chapter 4, the US Congress repeatedly challenged the Treasury Department's use of "extraordinary means" to assist Presidents Clinton and Obama during their debt limit fights by extending the period of time before the government would default on its public debt payments. It also criticized the Federal Reserve for "bailing out" financial firms and other companies that were outside of its normal jurisdiction.

On the other hand, if deference is high, then markets may interpret an assertion of authority by economic technocrats positively despite legal or political contestation. Investors responded well to interventions by the Treasury and Federal Reserve during the 2008–2010 crisis in the United States despite Congressional criticisms that these agencies had exceeded their mandates. Similarly, investors across Europe responded well to ECB President Draghi defense of the Outright Monetary Transactions (OMT) despite legal challenges from Germany. Indeed, Draghi's perseverance despite the legal challenge gave the OMT a high level of credibility and helps to explain its extraordinary success.

2.5.4   You are with Us or against Us!

Categories 5 and 6 in Figure 2.5 represent situations in which deference to economic policymakers is low. Regardless of de jure authority neither economic policymakers nor existing economic agreements or institutions will have much influence over the activities of political leaders or private-sector stakeholders. Presidents and prime ministers are likely to ignore undesired recommendations. They are also likely to replace policy critics with like-minded supporters or sycophants. Argentine Presidents Menem, Néstor Kirchner and Cristina Fernández de Kirchner replaced Ministers of Finance Domingo Cavallo and Roberto Lavagna and Central Bank President Martín Redrado, respectively. US President Bush similarly replaced Treasury Secretary Paul O'Neill. In each case, their replacements were more like-minded and compliant than their predecessors. If the president or prime minister does not defer to the counsel of his or her economic team and has a high level of implementation capacity, then political exuberance, corruption and cronyism are likely. Political uncertainty will be low because implementation capacity is high, but policy uncertainty will be high.

If the president or prime minister is not deferential and is weak, then political uncertainty and policy uncertainty will be high. Economic technocrats will be impotent, countries will be prone to contagion and crises will be likely.

2.6   Conclusion

The power to shape markets begins at home with the pulling and hauling among national politicians and economic policymakers over economic policy. Shifts in authority, deference and implementation capacity generate distinct patterns of political behavior. Given the right combinations of these variables, economic policymakers can expand or restrict national economic policy choices. By doing so, they can reduce uncertainty about what national governments are likely to do in response to changing circumstances. Political uncertainty matters to investors and financial firms because of the penetrating web of interdependence that links their fates with those of national governments.

The relationship between risk and uncertainty can been represented in the RIC. The RIC is dynamic and changes shape based on prevailing market conditions and uncertainties about the effectiveness of government policies and the behaviors of specific actors or products who could potentially destabilize the economy. The RIC also responds to agency. To the extent that economic policymakers can reduce market uncertainties, reduce specific-actor risk, or validate national policy decisions they can reduce policy uncertainty and risk at any point along the RIC.

Consequently, the ability to manage political uncertainty and policy uncertainty provides economic policymakers with a source of second-order power to shape the behavior of investors and financial institutions by reducing risk and, in so doing, manage the cost and availability of capital, inflation and other prices.

In the chapters that follow, I demonstrate these dynamics by comparing the experiences of economic policymakers in Argentina, the United States and Europe as they navigate their countries through often tumultuous economic and political changes.

3   The Argentine Tango

3.1   The Argentine Tango

Like the bittersweet drama of tango dancers performing on Calle Florida for shoppers leaving Buenos Aires' posh *Galerias Pacífico* shopping center, Argentina's political and economic leaders stepped out of Latin America's sorrowful "lost decade" of the 1980s with a series of dramatic policy changes that led the country through grand successes, devastating failures and postcrisis resurgences. Like the dancers shifting to changes in musical tempo, Argentine presidents and ministers of the economy responded to fluctuations in global markets and domestic politics with dips and twirls, driving forward and occasionally reversing direction with great fanfare. Their moves generated both praise and scorn, winning Argentina the diverse imprimaturs – at different moments in time – of "poster child" of the Washington Consensus, "defaulting pariah" of international bondholders, "vanguard" of Latin American populism and the "victim of vulture investors" that threatened to undermine debt restructuring agreements around the globe.

Argentina's dynamic and often flamboyant efforts to engage the global economy over the past thirty years provide vivid demonstrations of how power dynamics among national politicians and economic technocrats affect the way that national governments and investors respond to market fluctuations. Argentine governments often inherited large debts, inflation and other economic problems from their predecessors. They experienced periods of extreme market pressure resulting from high debt obligations and reliance on sometimes scarce financing from abroad, the ever-present danger of rampant inflation and the scourge of capital flight. They also experienced more permissive economic conditions, including surging capital inflows and a high demand for Argentine exports. Like Greece, Argentina confronted both the benefits and the costs of a fixed-exchange-rate system, condition-laced financial assistance from international financial institutions and successful debt renegotiations tinged with the ire of recalcitrant lenders. As highlighted in Chapter 1, investor actions throughout were mediated by their expectations regarding the policies that the Argentine government was likely to pursue and whether those policies were likely to be effective.

The varying success of Argentina's ministers of the economy in managing investor expectations by reducing uncertainty regarding likely economic policy choices and policy outcomes in differing economic and political circumstances provides important insights for Greece, the rest of Europe and the United States. Like many political leaders in Europe, Argentine Presidents often attempted to increase their inflation-fighting credibility by declaring fidelity to economic institutions and agreements and promising to defer to their ministers on matters of economic policy. One of the central lessons from their experiences is that the effectiveness and durability of these institutions and agreements – including the Austral Plan and the Convertibility Plan – are contingent on continued attention and maintenance. Economy ministers in Argentina were able to bolster these regimes when they succeeded in securing deference and political support from the president. In the absence of deference and supporting legislation, these regimes failed to be controlling. In other words, the existence of authoritative institutions was insufficient to constrain presidential actions. When deference or implementation capacity declined, these regimes lost their ability to reduce political uncertainty.

Argentine influence over investors' expectations was greatest when influential presidents reinforced and were reinforced by highly respected economy ministers, as happened with Presidents Carlos Menem and Economy Minister Domingo Cavallo from 1991 to 1996, and with President Néstor Kirchner and Economy Minister Roberto Lavagna from 2003 to 2005. When economy ministers were unable to secure supporting legislation or when they lost credibility or were replaced with sycophants to the president, their ability to manage investors' expectations declined.

Economic conditions affected both internal power dynamics and external bargaining outcomes. On one hand, favorable economic conditions and access to alternative sources of financing bolstered the government's ability to bargain with international investors. On the other hand, the willingness of national politicians to accept institutional constraints, share authority and defer to their ministers or central bankers declined when economic conditions improved. Consequently, more often than not, favorable economic conditions generated cycles of political uncertainty and inflation.

The ability of international actors to bargain with Argentina also varied with the degree to which they were able to assert their authority, generate deference and/or exploit electoral capacity to their advantage. Like the several European politicians who used their domestic authorities and institutions to challenge the European Central Bank – by, for example, calling for a referendum to challenge austerity measures or asserting the jurisdiction of national courts and legislatures over international agreements – bond-holder holdouts asserted their contractual authority and the jurisdiction of a US court to keep Argentina from completing a debt reduction agreement.

This chapter explains Argentina's economic policy roller coaster across four distinct periods. Period I, from 1983 to 1996, was a time of great inflation battles. Period II, from 1997 to 2002, was a time of political exuberance, financial inflows and economic crisis. Period III, from 2003 to 2015, was a time of postcrisis populist recovery. Period IV, from 2016 to the present, has been a time of rocky reentry into international markets. Constitutive power dynamics among national presidents and economic technocrats shifted dramatically during each of these periods. Each section concludes with an assessment of behavior and market influence relative to predictions based on shifts in authority, deference and implementation capacity among them.

3.2   Period I: The Great Inflation Battles, 1983–1996

Between 1983 and 1996, Argentina struggled against and eventually won its war against hyperinflation. Its repeated failures and ultimate success during this thirteen-year period demonstrate that while delegating authority to economic technocrats and creating new institutions can mitigate political uncertainty and alter investor behavior, their success is highly contingent. These efforts succeeded when the minister of the economy was able to maintain deference from the president and private-sector stakeholders and when he or the president was willing and able to mobilize sufficient political support to sustain supporting legislation.

President Alfonsín entered office in 1983 with the goals of building popular support for democratic rule and promoting economic opportunity following the turmoil of Argentina's military dictatorship. The combination of high external debt left over from the military regime and demands from the public sector and the military for higher wages created fertile ground for government spending and ever more inflation. As is reflected in Figure 3.1, inflation was a problem throughout this period, reaching over 500 percent in 1984 and then surging to over 3000 percent in 1989. Although hyperinflation subsided in 1991, fears of rekindling inflation did not subside until after Argentina succeeded in maintaining price stability despite shockwaves created by the Mexican peso crisis from

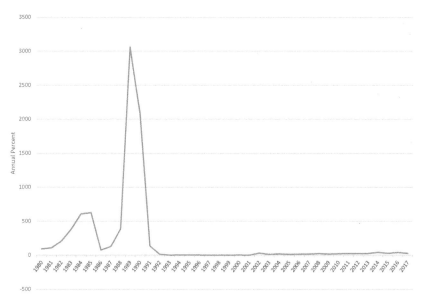

Figure 3.1 Inflation in Argentina (GDP deflator).
Source: World Bank (1980–2017). "World Development Indicators." http://
databank.worldbank.org/.

1994 to 1995. This success helped President Menem win reelection on May 14, 1995, and gave birth to Argentina's reputation as the poster child of economic development in Latin America.

Given this context, the risk intervention curve (RIC) from 1983 to 1995 reflects relatively high level of risk associated with high levels of policy flexibility (see Figure 3.2). Consequently, international lenders and investors are expected to respond positively to interventions that increase policy stability and negatively to those that increase in policy flexibility. While risk tolerance is expected to vary, a general risk comfort level and comfort zone are specified to provide a frame of reference.

3.2.1   *The First Wayward Steps toward Liberalism*

The 1980s was Latin America's "lost decade" of crushing external debt, uncertainty at home and weakness abroad.[1] It was in this context that Argentina took its first wayward steps out of a tumultuous period of

---

[1] L. Manzetti (1994). "Institutional Decay and Distributional Coalitions in Developing Countries: The Argentine Riddle Reconsidered." *Studies in Comparative International Development* 29(2), 82–114.

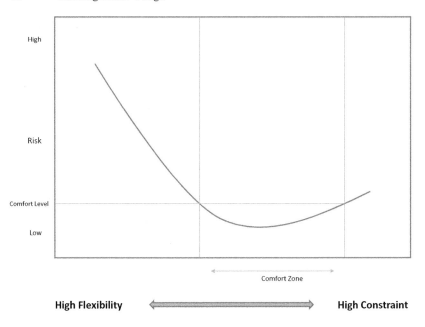

Figure 3.2 Inflation fears in Argentina, 1983–1996.

military rule and toward political and economic liberalism. Raúl Alfonsín Foulkes began his presidency in a relatively strong political position. He and Victor Hipólito Martínez of the *Unión Cívica Radical* (UCR) won the 1983 Presidential and Vice Presidential election with 51.7 percent of the vote and 317 votes of the Electoral College.[2] President Alfonsín assumed office on December 10, 1983, following the early departure of President Reynaldo Bignone. Bignone was the last of the military leaders from the National Reorganization Process Party. He and the military juntas had been discredited by internal factions, military defeats in the Falkland Islands, brutal domestic suppression and violence against potential domestic critics throughout the period known as the Dirty War (*Guerra Sucia*) from 1976 to 1983.

   President Alfonsín entered office with a high level of popular support based on his reputation for assisting people whose friends and families had disappeared during the Dirty War and his role in creating the Permanent Assembly for Human Rights in 1975. Immediately after assuming office, he created the National Commission on the

---

[2] Edmund A. Walsh School of Foreign Service, Center for Latin American Studies. *Political Database of the Americas.* http://pdba.georgetown.edu/Elecdata/Arg/arg.html.

Disappearance of Persons (*Comisión Nacional sobre la Desaparición de Personas*; CONADEP),[3] rescinded a self-amnesty law that the military dictatorship had enacted, sponsored the "Trial of the Juntas" in the Supreme Court of Justice and supported the prosecution of members of the military leadership. He also took steps to rebuild Argentina's foreign relations by normalizing relations with the United Kingdom following the failed conflict over the Falkland Islands and signing a Treaty of Peace and Friendship with Chile.

Unfortunately, President Alfonsín was unable to translate his political popularity into support for his economic policies. He faced a hostile economic environment characterized by high external debt, high interest rates and an economy close to collapse.[4] Borrowing by the military government had swelled Argentina's external debt from US$8 billion in 1976 to over US$43 billion in 1983.[5] President Alfonsín and his first Economy Minister, Bernardo Grinspun, attributed much of the debt to dubious policies promoted by the military regime's last Economy Minister, Martínez de Hoz.[6] The International Monetary Fund (IMF), however, rejected their efforts to nullify the debt or alternately set the terms of its repayment. The United States threatened Argentina with sanctions if it failed to meet its debt obligations to its commercial banks. Grinspun tried to respond by creating a countervailing Latin American debt cartel but was unsuccessful.[7] In the summer of 1984, Argentina capitulated. It agreed to pay US$350 million in overdue liabilities to commercial banks. The IMF reciprocated by agreeing to roll over US$13 billion in existing loans.[8] However, when Argentina failed to meet its repayment deadline in February 1985, the IMF refused to release a scheduled payment. Minister Grinspun resigned.

President Alfonsín appointed Juan Vital Sourrouille as the new Minister of the Economy. Rather than trying to avoid debt repayments, Minister Sourrouille focused on fighting what he called "the inertial effects of

---

[3] CONADEP ultimately published a detailed report entitled *Never Again* (*Nunca Más*), which documented the abuses of over 9,000 people by the military regime.

[4] Though undeclared, Argentina had gone into default prior to Mexico in 1982 during the Malvinas War.

[5] M. Braun (2006). *The Political Economy of Debt in Argentina, or Why History Repeats Itself.* Washington, DC: World Bank.

[6] One poignant example was a decision by the Central Bank in late 1982 to reward banks and companies that were loyal to the military regime by nationalizing their debt (so called *plata dulce* or "sweet money"). M. Rogers (2011). "2001–2011: The Making of a Crisis." *The Argentina Independent*, December 27.

[7] See K. Veigel (2009). *Dictatorship, Democracy and Globalization: Argentina and the Cost of Paralysis, 1973–2001.* University Park: Pennsylvania University Press, pp. 130–147, for an excellent review of this period.

[8] Ibid., p. 144.

inflation" through the Austral Plan.[9] With the backing of President Alfonsín, Sourrouille created a new currency, the austral, at a rate of 1,000:1 with the peso, and pledged that the Central Bank would not print money to finance government operations. He also implemented price controls, wage freezes on public workers and reforms designed to increase government revenue and decrease government expenditures.[10]

The Austral Plan succeeded initially. Tax revenue increased, fiscal expenditures decreased and inflation fell from its peak in July of 1985 of 1129 percent to an annual rate of 300 percent in January 1986 and a low of 50.1 percent in July.[11] This economic success (combined with President Alfonsín's willingness to try military leaders in court) helped spur an electoral victory for the UCR in parliamentary elections. In November 1985, the UCR and its allies won 43 percent of the votes, securing 130 out of 254 seats, compared with the Peronists and their allies, who won 34.5 percent of the vote and secured 103 seats in the Chamber of Deputies.[12]

This moment in time was the peak in President Alfonsín's political capacity. It was also a high point in deference and legislative capacity. Alfonsín worked in coordination with a minister of the economy to create a new currency, pass supporting legislation and accept new institutional constraints on economic policy-making. Based on the argument presented in Chapter 2, the combination of high implementation capacity, deference and authority to create new constraints on the President's discretion over economic policy should shift Argentina to the right along the flexibility–constraint spectrum. Given inflation fears and the relatively low risk associated with high levels of policy constraint, shifting to the right along the RIC should decrease uncertainty about the sustainability and effectiveness of economic policy. This should lower investors' perceptions of risk and increase Argentina's bargaining leverage abroad. As predicted, inflation fell and the government was able to secure additional funding from the IMF, the World Bank and international creditors in exchange for promises to meet fiscal targets.

Unfortunately, President's Alfonsín's political strength was short-lived. Even though the rate of inflation fell substantially, it was still 50 percent in mid-1986. This had disparate effects on wages. Public sector wages were

---

[9] Ibid., pp. 130–147.
[10] R. Fernández (1991). "What Have Populists Learned from Hyperinflation?" In *The Macroeconomics of Populism in Latin America*, eds. R. Dornbusch & S. Edwards. Chicago: University of Chicago Press, p. 123.
[11] "Argentina's inflation rate" (n.d.). *TradingEconomics.com*. www.tradingeconomics.com/argentina/inflation-cpi.
[12] Edmund A. Walsh School of Foreign Service, Center for Latin American Studies. *Political Database of the Americas*. http://pdba.georgetown.edu/Elecdata/Arg/arg.html.

fixed by policy, but private-sector wages were not – and they were rising.[13] Inflation continued to increase, reaching an annual rate of 110 percent in July of 1987 and 322 percent in July of 1988, where it stayed until June of 1989, Then it exploded, reaching an annual rate of 12,085 percent in February of 1990.[14] As inflation grew, President Alfonsín faced pressure from military personnel and other public employees for salary increases. Military personnel also demanded that their former officers not be prosecuted. In the face of general strikes, the potential for military unrest and growing opposition within his own party, President Alfonsín relented. On April 4, 1986, his administration adopted a "Flexibilization" plan to increase wages in the military and public sectors and established a crawling peg exchange rate regime. As predicted, the decline in Alfonsín's political capacity and his willingness to break with Sourrouille's policy guidelines undercut the effectiveness of the Austral Plan. Consequently, Argentina began shifting to the left on the flexibility–rigidity spectrum of the RIC and the level of risk increased.

Confidence in the credibility of Argentina's efforts to fight inflation were further undermined by divisions within the economic team. As discussed in Chapter 2, disagreements among economic policymakers can raise uncertainty about political viability and policy efficacy and thus increase perceptions of risk. Bernardo Grinspun, now the Planning Secretary, and the President of the Central Bank Juan Concepción opposed the Austral Plan and criticized Economy Minister Sourrouille for pursuing a tight monetary policy.[15] In response, Sourrouille threatened to resign unless President Alfonsín removed Juan Concepción from his position. Alfonsín agreed and replaced Concepción with José Luis Machinea as President of the Central Bank on August 22, 1986.[16] Machinea was a conservative economist who agreed with Sourrouille's approach of constraining the economy to fight inflation. He promoted raising interest rates and maintaining a tight monetary policy. With these personnel problems resolved, political uncertainty declined temporarily and Sourrouille successfully reached an agreement with the IMF in February of 1987 for assistance in exchange for a commitment to reduce inflation and meet a balance of payment target. In April of that year, he also reached an agreement with commercial banks to reschedule nearly US$2 billion in external debt.

---

[13] M. Kiguel (1989). *Inflation in Argentina: stop and go since the Austral Plan*. Washington, DC: World Bank, p. 17.

[14] "Argentina's inflation rate" (n.d.). *TradingEconomics.com*. www.tradingeconomics.com/argentina/inflation-cpi.

[15] Veigel. *Dictatorship, Democracy and Globalization*, p. 142.   [16] Ibid., p. 146.

Sourrouille's success did not reduce the social pressure on President Alfonsín. In the face of growing challenges from labor and public-sector groups, he appointed a former union leader, Carlos Alderete, as Minister of Labor in April of 1987. Alderete promoted increasing wages and prices in the public sector. Despite a concession by Sourrouille regarding wages, union opposition to the administration continued to grow. The leader of the workers' union *Confederación General del Trabajo* (CGT), Saúl Ubaldini, promoted a series of general strikes and many smaller strikes throughout the country. The government responded by making more concessions. With each capitulation, Argentina shifted to the left on the flexibility–rigidity spectrum of the RIC and the level of risk increased. By June of 1987, Argentina began failing to meet its inflation targets.[17] With is inflation-fighting credibility diminishing, speculators withdrew their investments and the austral declined from 2.55 to the dollar in June to 4.05 to the dollar in September of 1987.

The government's growing weakness was confirmed by a devastating political defeat in legislative elections. On September 6, 1987, the UCR won only 38 percent of the vote. It lost 13 seats in the Argentine Congress, for a total of 117 seats in the Chamber of Deputies. It also lost five of the seven provincial governorships it had held prior to the election, including the defeat of Governor Alejandro Armedáriz of the Province of Buenos Aires. In contrast, the rival Peronist party won 43 percent of the vote for a total of 108 seats in the Chamber of Deputies, increasing the number of Justicialist governors from twelve to seventeen.[18]

As his political position weakened, the president softened his approach to the military. On December 24, 1986, President Alfonsín promoted passage of the Final Point law (*Ley de El Punto Final*, Ley 23492), which ended the investigation and prosecution of those accused of violence during the Dirty War. He also suspended trials of military officers through the Law of Due Obedience (*Ley de Obediencia Debida*, Ley 23521, June 4, 1987). These laws, as well as seemingly light punishments given to a radical military group known as the *Carapintadas* following insurrections in 1987 and 1988, suggest the president's capacity to implement economic policies that challenged the military was minimal at best.[19]

---

[17] Ibid., p. 149.

[18] Edmund A. Walsh School of Foreign Service, Center for Latin American Studies. *Political Database of the Americas.* http://pdba.georgetown.edu/Elecdata/Arg/arg.html.

[19] See "Military Uprisings," www.yendor.com/vanished/uprisings.html. Both laws were repealed in 2003 and both were deemed unconstitutional by the Supreme Court of Justice on June 14, 2005.

Minister of the Economy Sourrouille and Minister of Public Works and Services Rodolfo Terragno tried again to promote economic reforms to slow inflation (these included raising taxes on imports, income and checking accounts, and liberalizing the exchange market), but they failed to secure sufficient political support to bring their policies to fruition.[20] As an alternative, Sourrouille attempted to limit inflation by issuing a debt moratorium on commercial bank loans. This policy failed. In June, the IMF declared Argentina noncompliant and suspended further disbursements. Minister Sourrouille, Central Bank President José Luis Machinea and Treasury Secretary Mario Brodersohn attempted to placate the IMF by implementing the Spring Plan (*Plan Primavera*), which included wage and price controls, tight fiscal and monetary policies and the adoption of a fixed exchange rate.[21] The Spring Plan slowed inflation briefly, but never gained domestic or international support. Within a month, the CGT and others were engaged in violent strikes.

Roque Fernández summarized the lack of popular and international confidence in the system as a return to a common refrain:[22]

The traditional approach to stabilization in Argentina was to announce a program of fiscal discipline plus price controls; the traditional result was increasing inflation after a short period of stabilization. The Austral Plan confirmed this tradition, since, after a few months, inflation accelerated again, this time reaching a two-digit monthly rate by the beginning of 1988. ...

[When the Spring Plan was implemented, the] strong credibility available at the beginning of the Austral Plan was gone, and the side effects of orthodox measures in the absence of credibility was taking a significant political toll. The lack of credibility and the fear of repudiation of the government debt increased interest rates to levels never seen before in Argentina. Government borrowing in the domestic financial system, at the beginning of 1988, took place at annual effective rates of more than 30 percent for operations adjusted to the U.S. dollar; that is, at four times the LIBOR rate.

In the face of increasing capital flight and declining reserves, the World Bank refused to disburse US$350 million at the end of February 1989, and a commercial bank steering committee said they would not engage in additional negotiations unless an agreement was reached with the IMF. Lacking reserves, the Central Bank suspended its efforts to defend the austral. On February 7, on what became known as "Black Tuesday," the austral lost 40 percent of its value relative to the US dollar. The government initiated a wide variety of economic policy responses in quick

---

[20] Fernández. "What Have Populists Learned from Hyperinflation?" p. 126.

[21] H. Schamis (2002). *Re-forming the State: The Politics of Privatization in Latin America and Europe.* Ann Arbor: University of Michigan Press, p. 132.

[22] Fernández. "What Have Populists Learned from Hyperinflation?" pp. 123, 132.

succession, but the economy collapsed. Sourrouille resigned on February 30, 1989.

President Alfonsín appointed Juan Pugliese and Jesús Rodríguez in quick succession as ministers of the economy, but he lacked the political capacity to support any of the policies either recommended. As the US Embassy noted: "Alfonsín administration has a figurehead economic team in place which is merely able to apply Band-Aids to economic ills when radical surgery is needed."[23] In March of 1989, the monthly inflation rate was 17 percent, in April it was 33.4 percent and in May it reached 78.5 percent.[24] Argentina approached the United States for aid, but the US Embassy said that it was not willing to provide any until the country restored the stability needed for growth.[25] On May 14, 1989, Carlos Menem won the presidential election. In the face of ongoing protests, President Alfonsín agreed to step down on July 8 rather than wait for inauguration day on December 10.

In sum, in the absence of sustained deference and political support from the president, neither economic technocrats nor the institutions they created were able to constrain economic policy decisions sufficiently to placate the IMF, World Bank and other loan holders. The Austral Plan failed because there was insufficient political will and capacity to stop adjusting public-sector wages and the money supply to inflation.[26] Even though Sourrouille and other economic ministers used their authority to promote institutional reforms and generate other inflation-fighting policies, their efforts did not receive the level of political support from the president or Congress necessary to bring them to fruition. Instead, national political leaders counteracted Sourrouille's actions by raising wages in response to societal pressure. As Klaus Veigel notes, one of Sourrouille's closest advisors complained, "An important reason for the failure of the Austral Plan was that the economic team lacked support within the UCR. It was a small group of seven people. The majority of the UCR hated us."[27] Without the deference and support of national leaders, the economic team lacked the means to sustain their policies. As a consequence, Argentina moved to the left on the RIC, risk increased, banks refused to cooperate without IMF involvement, the IMF and World Bank refused to disperse negotiated loans and private-sector investors fled.

---

[23] Veigel. *Dictatorship, Democracy and Globalization*, p. 157.
[24] Fernández. "What Have Populists Learned from Hyperinflation?" p. 133.
[25] Veigel. *Dictatorship, Democracy and Globalization*, p. 156.
[26] Kiguel. *Inflation in Argentina*, p. 31.
[27] Veigel. *Dictatorship, Democracy and Globalization*, p. 142.

3.2.2   *Uncertainty Continues in a New Political Regime: 1989–1990*

President Menem initially received substantial support from Congress, the business community and other former critics of the Peronist party. During his first two years, President Menem demonstrated a remarkable ability to shape national policy as he chose. Based on the model presented in Chapters 1 and 2, the lack of policy constraints suggests that investors would likely remain wary because his policies would be considered unpredictable and their effects uncertain.

President Menem entered office five months ahead of schedule. Thus, though he began in July, his Peronist party would not have the majority in Congress until they entered office in December. To compensate for this misalignment, President Menem extracted a pledge from the UCR party in Congress to withdraw a sufficient number of votes so that his Peronist party could pass legislation. With this authority in hand, Menem passed two emergency laws that centralized control of the economy: the State Reform Law and the Economic Emergency Law.

The State Reform Law effectively gave the president the ability to create policy without the consent of the legislature through the use of Decrees of Necessity and Urgency (DNUs). President Menem exploited this power extensively, ultimately issuing 545 DNUs. This is an extraordinarily high number when compared to the 25 such decrees by Argentine leaders from 1853 to 1983.[28] A decade later, President Néstor Kirchner continued this trend by issuing 249 DNUs during his first four-year term, while his wife and successor President Cristina Fernández de Kirchner issued 29 DNUs between 2007 and 2011.[29] President Menem also made extensive use of presidential vetoes, issuing 37 full vetoes and 41 partial vetoes between 1989 and 1993.[30]

The Economic Emergency Law, in turn, gave the president the ability to control the budget, eliminate subsidies, modify taxes, alter bond payments and reorganize social security. It also gave the president the power to give preference to local investors in the privatization process. This enabled President Menem to develop close relationships with many large local businesses such as Pérez Companc, Techint-Rocca, Bunge & Born, Bridas-Bulgheroni, SOCMA-Macri, Soldati, Loma Negra and Astra-Grüneisen, who were given opportunities to benefit from the privatizations.[31]

---

[28] Interview with Ricardo López Murphy, Cordoba 637, Buenos Aires. July 2012.
[29] "Lapicera veloz: CFK firma un DNU cada mes y medio" (2014). *La Tecla*, December 8. www.latecla.info/3/nota_1.php?noticia_id=45923.
[30] Schamis. *Re-forming the State*, p. 139.
[31] Manzetti. "Institutional Decay and Distributional Coalitions."

President Menem also expanded his control over the Supreme Court by increasing the number of justices from five to nine (Ley 23744) in April of 1990. Two judges resigned, so Menem was able to appoint six of the nine.[32] Thus, by May 1990, Menem controlled the court and both houses of Congress. He also tried to bolster his support within the military by pardoning 39 military officers charged with human rights abuses and 164 of the *Carapintadas* accused of aiding military rebellions in October of 1989.[33] Those pardoned included former military presidents Jorge Videla and Roberto Viola, as well as Admiral Emilio Eduardo Massera. General Videla had been convicted for the murder of 66 people and the torture of 93 others; Admiral Massera had been found guilty of three murders, the torture of 12 people and the detention of 79.[34] President Menem also pardoned former Economy Minister José Alfredo Martínez de Hoz who had been accused of kidnapping and extortion.[35] Ironically, despite President Menem's many pardons of people who worked for the military dictatorship, the *Carapintadas* attempted a coup on December 3, 1990. Though the coup was unsuccessful, Menem capitulated to military pressure by pardoning many of those convicted for actions taking during the Dirty War a few days later. Seventeen years later, in 2007, these pardons were deemed unconstitutional and those released were sent back to prison.[36]

In terms of economic policy, President Menem reversed course from his populist campaign rhetoric and shifted toward what became known as the "Washington Consensus."[37] Menem created an alliance with the Union of the Democratic Centre (UCeDe), which was known for its free-market, anti-Peronist agenda. Counter to the traditional Peronist agenda, he privatized a wide range of businesses including media and

[32] Schamis. *Re-forming the State*, p. 138.

[33] Associated Press (1989). "200 military officers are pardoned in Argentina." *New York Times*, October 8. www.nytimes.com/1989/10/08/world/200-military-officers-are-pardoned-in-argentina.html; "Pardon of Argentine officers angers critics of military" (1989). *New York Times*, October 8. www.nytimes.com/1989/10/09/world/pardon-of-argentine-officers-angers-critics-of-the-military.html; "Argentina cancels junta pardons" (2007). *BBC News*, April 27. http://news.bbc.co.uk/2/hi/americas/6594127.stm.

[34] "Argentina cancels junta pardons" (2007). *BBC News*, April 27. http://news.bbc.co.uk/2/hi/americas/6594127.stm.

[35] G. Marx (1990). "Argentina's president pardons leaders of 'Dirty War' on leftists." *Chicago Tribune*, December 30. http://articles.chicagotribune.com/1990-12-30/news/9004170832_1_pardoned-two-former-military-presidents-dirty-war.

[36] "Menem: Pardon our dirty war" (1991). *Los Angeles Times*, January 6. http://articles.latimes.com/1991-01-06/opinion/op-10843_1_dirty-war.

[37] J. Williamson (2002). "What Washington means by policy reform." *Peterson Institute for International Economics*, November 1. https://piie.com/commentary/speeches-papers/what-washington-means-policy-reform.

television companies, oil exploration and extraction businesses, the Argentine telephone company and the national airlines.[38]

Reflecting his tight connection with the business community, President Menem appointed a succession of businessmen – Néstor Rapanelli and Antonio Erman González – to serve as economy minister. Both men were senior executives of the large Argentine multinational firm Bunge & Born. The close connections to the business community in Argentina did not improve investor confidence in the predictability or anticipated effectiveness of economic policy reform. Within a few months of taking office, President Menem's new coalitions had begun to break down. Minister Rapanelli was unable to secure the cooperation of the business community, which raised prices and refused to accept the government's tax reform proposals. Nor was he able to constrain provincial spending. Pushback from Peronist labor unions and divisions within the Peronist party intensified over a wide range of issues including cabinet selections, economic and foreign policy, the treatment of the military and the alliance with business.[39] The resulting political uncertainty compounded market uncertainty. Investors who held government debt responded by rushing to convert their austral-denominated debts into dollars.[40] Facing a run on the austral and resurgent inflation, Néstor Rapanelli resigned in December of 1989.

President Menem replaced Minister Rapanelli with Antonio Erman González. Economy Minister González implemented a stabilization plan and attempted to overcome shortfalls in liquidity by issuing short-term Bonex bonds. Divisions among ministers within the Menem administration, however, undercut support for the Bonex Plan. González and the Minister of Public Works and Services, José Roberto Dromi, accused one another of being responsible for irregularities in the privatization process of Aerolíneas Argentinas. In January of 1991, the situation deteriorated further with a bribery and corruption scandal involving a US company, Swift Armour S.A., which was involved in the privatization process. As a result, Minister Dromi and the president of the Central Bank resigned, and Minister González became Minister of Defense. President Menem responded by appointing Domingo Cavallo as the new Minister of the Economy and giving him the added responsibilities of the Ministry of Public Works and Services. The political situation remained unstable in

---

[38] Schamis. *Re-forming the State*, p. 133.

[39] For a timeline of events, see: J. Corrales (1997a). "Do Economic Crises Contribute to Economic Reform? Argentina and Venezuela in the 1990s." *Political Science Quarterly*, 112(4), 643–644.

[40] Fernández. "What Have Populists Learned from Hyperinflation?" p. 138.

February, with Cavallo receiving a poor reception during his first visit to the Argentine Congress, inflation continuing and rural unions going on strike.

In sum, President Menem consolidated political power immediately. In an effort to placate business, he appointed two businessmen to the position of Minister of the Economy. Neither was successful. Their abilities to shape economic policy and quell inflation fears were undermined by divisions within the cabinet and charges of incompetence and corruption. Consequently, while President Menem was able to implement a variety of economic policies, his initiatives lacked validation and policy uncertainty remained high. Thus, Argentina remained at the far left side of the RIC in Figure 3.2 with high levels of policy flexibility and risk.

3.2.3   The Glory Days of Neoliberalism and Victory over Inflation, 1991–1996

Political and economic uncertainties were high in January and February of 1991. Relations between President Menem and the ruling Peronist party were openly hostile, and the President's own cabinet was divided. His economic team had been discredited by scandal and policy failure. Facing hyperinflation and a dysfunctional cabinet, Menem shifted course and strategy in ways that ultimately transformed the Argentine government, restoring confidence in Argentina's political and economic leadership and pushing Argentina down the RIC into the glory days of neoliberalism.

Politically, President Menem rebuilt his political coalition with the Justicialist Party (PJ) members in Congress by reorganizing his cabinet and instituting a practice of negotiating directly with party leaders and legislators rather than going through union and business coalitions. He also agreed to safeguard issues of Peronist concern. He coopted and divided his opponents by splitting the CGT in two and offering union leaders a share of privatization revenues, social security benefits and other perks if they mobilized political support for the privatizations.[41] To expand gubernatorial support, he devolved responsibility for public services like health, education and social assistance programs to the provinces, thus both increasing governors' authority while making them increasingly dependent on federal tax revenue through co-participation agreements.[42] As summed up by Javier Corrales, "For the first time,

---

[41] Schamis. *Re-forming the State*, p. 135.

[42] The devolution of authority was not, unfortunately, matched with increased oversight over provincial expenditures. Provincial spending rose dramatically throughout the 1990s, eventually constituting almost half of consolidated public spending. Braun. *The Political Economy of Debt*, pp. 18–22.

an Argentine executive was able to convey unambiguously that the populist sectors of the country now stood with the reform process."[43]

Economy Minister Domingo Cavallo complemented the President's efforts by seeking congressional approval for his plan to tie the peso to the US dollar at a rate of 1:1, which was known as the Convertibility Plan, and promising to secure congressional approval for future privatizations. Cavallo's willingness to make these commitments even though President Menem had already acquired the authority to run the privatization process by decree gave added weight to the President's efforts to demonstrate that he valued congressional input and was willing to relinquish some of his recently consolidated authority. To reinforce the message, Cavallo established the *Secretaría de Relaciones Institucionales* within the Ministry of the Economy to institutionalize congressional involvement in economic affairs. He also agreed to negotiate directly with Peronist leaders with regard to the privatization of pensions and the distribution of public funds.[44]

Some attribute Cavallo's engagement to his experience serving as a member of Congress at a time when Congress was largely ignored by the President; others attribute it to the importance he gave to the rule of law.[45] Regardless of the motivation, the strategy increased procedural legitimacy and, by so doing, increased congressional support for his economic policy reforms.[46] As Javier Corrales argues:

Once the Argentine executive began to court the party, this reform [the Convertibility Plan] became possible. Since the approval of the law, the ruling party has been the most adamant defender of the regime, despite the fact that the regime became the most controversial element of the reforms until at least 1994. Between 1991 and early 1996, the party defended even the harshest aspects of the reform, such as the government's tough stand against pensioners and labor strikes.[47]

President Menem had been expected to pursue Peronist orthodox policies, but when he reversed course, he did so without hesitation.[48] Efforts by both President Menem and Economy Minister Cavallo to rebuild political support for these policy changes were critical. Their

[43] Corrales. "Do Economic Crisis Contribute to Economic Reform?"   [44] Ibid.
[45] J. Corrales (1997b). "Why Argentines Followed Cavallo: A Technopol between Democracy and Economic Reform." In *Technopols: The Role of Ideas and Leaders in Freeing Politics and Markets in Latin America in the 1990s*, ed. J. I. Domínguez. University Park: Penn State Press, pp. 49–93.
[46] G. Shambaugh & P. Weinstein (2016). *The Art of Policymaking: Tools, Techniques and Processes in the Modern Executive Branch*. Washington, DC: CQ Press.
[47] Corrales. "Do Economic Crisis Contribute to Economic Reform?"
[48] Interview with Roberto Lavagna on Wednesday, July 25, 2012, in Buenos Aires.

efforts stand in stark contrast with those of President Alfonsín in the mid-1980s and Cristina Fernández de Kirchner in the mid-2000s, both of whom tried to bypass or manipulate Congress to achieve their objectives. They also contrast with Cavallo's own actions in 2000 when he initiated a wide range of economic policy changes with no virtually input from Congress. The consequences are clear. Even when the authority to make policy is uncontested, political support matters. High levels of political support facilitated the implementation of supporting legislation and increased confidence that the chosen policies would be successful. The lack of political support, in contrast, made implementing economic legislation more challenging and increased policy uncertainty.

Javier Corrales attributes Domingo Cavallo's ability to mobilize political support and build deference to his "linked interdependence" with those affected by Argentina's economic policy.[49] Cavallo's education at Harvard University, his writings on the problems of monetary stabilization without fiscal discipline, his role in the creation of the market-oriented think tank *Instituto de Estudios Económicos sobre la Realidad Argentina y Latinamericana* (IEERAL), and his appointment of like-minded individuals known as "the Cavallo Boys" to positions of power within the Menem administration all enhanced expectations that he would pursue liberal, market-oriented policies. Furthermore, his experience as foreign minister gave him international exposure, added credence to his desire for "rejoining rather than resisting the west," and increased the comfort level of international actors when negotiating with him.[50] His lack of a career in business or finance also freed him from the constraints and corruption that marred Néstor Rapanelli and Antonio Erman González.

The president's Peronist party scored major victories in legislative and provincial elections in the summer and fall of 1991. The PJ also gained a significant victory in the election of provincial governors, including the governor of the Province of Buenos Aires, where Vice President Eduardo Duhalde defeated his UCR rival. In addition, the market-oriented wing within the opposition UCR party gained relative to its more statist wing represented by Alfonsín.[51] As a consequence of this defeat, Alfonsín announced that he would not stand for reelection in the UCR.

---

[49] Corrales. "Why Argentines Followed Cavallo."   [50] Ibid., p. 61.

[51] R. Packenham (1994). *The Politics of Economic Liberalization: Argentina and Brazil in Comparative Perspective*. Notre Dame: Helen Kellogg Institute for International Studies, p. 14.

The electoral success signaled broad support for Menem and Cavallo, thus bolstering confidence that the Convertibility Plan would succeed politically and economically. As Robert Packenham argues:

The elections of August–September–October 1991 were a de facto plebiscite in favor of Menem's program of economic liberalization. Domingo Cavallo, who as economic minister was the main architect of that program, was referred to as "Santo Domingo." Menem was portrayed on the cover of the newsweekly magazine *Noticias* (12 September 1991) wearing a toga and a wreath on his head with the headline reading, *"Yo, El Supremo."* If one combined the electoral support for all the parties that supported Menem's policies – the PJ, the Angeloz factions of the UCR, the liberal UCeDe (whose leader was the very symbol of Argentine free-market thinking, Alvaro Alsogaray), and various other small and provincial parties – then one could safely conclude that at least 70 percent–80 percent of the Argentine electorate supported those policies.

The 1991 elections were not only an overwhelming mandate for Menem's policies but also a window on the profound changes within Argentine civil and political society. There was now more consensus on economic policies in Argentina than at any time since the first *Peronato* (1945–55), if not longer. This time the emerging consensus was not about intensifying state capitalism; it was about moving in liberalizing directions.[52]

This political validation continued in the 1993 legislative elections, as the PJ won 48 percent of the votes for national deputies compared with its second-place rival, the UCR, at 25.9 percent.[53]

The creation of the *Plan de Convertibilidad* (or simply "Convertibility") pegged the austral to the US dollar at a rate of 10,000:1, subsequently replaced the austral with the Argentine peso linked to the US dollar at a rate of 1:1, authorized contracts to be made in foreign currency, restricted the money supply to the level of hard-currency reserves, eliminated inflation-indexed accounts, reduced bank reserve requirements and implemented pension reform, public spending cuts and tax reforms. Cavallo also promoted the deregulation of wages, professional services, ports and transportation and domestic and foreign trade, as well as the elimination of regulatory offices. He nationalized the privatization process and accelerated the rate of privatizations.

---

[52] Ibid., p. 14.
[53] E. Cabrera & M. Victoria Murillo (1994). "The 1993 Argentine Elections." *Electoral Studies*, 13(2), 150–156. On November 14, President Menem further bolstered his capabilities by securing an agreement with former President Raul Alfonsín, who was once again head of the UCR, to accept constitutional reforms allowing the president to run for reelection in exchange for increased congressional constraints on the executive and the election, rather than appointment of the mayor of Buenos Aires. The agreement is known as the Olivos Pact.

The first significant test of the Convertibility Plan came in 1995 with the onset of the Mexican peso crisis, which generated widespread concern among investors in Latin America. With the onset of the Mexican peso crisis, foreign banks began to cancel lines of credit they had promised to large Argentine banks, which they, in turn, had lent to provincial banks or local governments. Provincial banks quickly became insolvent as depositors began withdrawing funds. Bank deposits ultimately fell 18 percent.[54]

After his initial efforts at promoting liquidity by easing bank reserve requirements and purchasing the assets of troubled banks, Cavallo sought the input of Gerry Corrigan, ex-president of the Federal Bank of New York. They developed a five-part solution to alter the rules on financing and give the Central Bank the authority to restructure financial institutions, develop an insurance system to guarantee deposits up to a certain limit, enforce mandatory reserve requirements, use long-term external loans for privatizations and to review the financial accounts of other financial institutions to assess their solvency.[55]

Cavallo sought congressional approval of the reform package just a few months before the 1995 elections. He succeeded in securing legislation by presenting what he called (and later titled his book) *el peso de la verdad* ("the weight of the truth"), in which he criticized President Menem for lessening his support for economic reform and for growing corruption and favoritism in the administration.

President Menem also lost some of his political clout as a result of push back during negotiations over constitutional reform and the Olivos Pact. Although his use of DNUs continued, his efforts to alter the constitution to allow for an additional term as president began to undermine his political base. The new constitution introduced checks and balances on presidential power and, exercising this newfound authority, Congress increasingly pushed back against the President's policy initiatives, making it harder for him to pursue his legislative agenda.

Menem's political fortunes improved dramatically following Argentina's successful response to the Mexican peso crisis. Cavallo's reform package – which effectively tightened bank regulation and encouraged stronger (often foreign) banks to take over weaker ones – succeeded in preserving the Convertibility Plan, restoring confidence in the economy, and rekindling economic growth.[56] President Menem was rewarded with

[54] D. Cavallo (1997). *El Peso de la Verdad (Espejo de la Argentina)*. Madrid: Planeta.
[55] Ibid.
[56] "A decline without parallel" (2002). *The Economist*, February 28. https://media.economist.com/news/special-report/1010911-1990s-argentina-was-latin-americas-star-how-did-it-become-basket-case.

a substantial political victory. On May 14, 1995, President Menem and Vice President Ruckauf of the PJ won 47.5 percent compared to 27.8 percent for the Bordon–Alvarez ticket of the Front for a Country in Solidarity (FrePaSo) and 16.2 percent for the Massaccesi–Hernandez ticket and the UCR.[57] The PJ also won a plurality in the Chamber of Deputies. This put Menem in a powerful political position. He praised Cavallo for his help in responding to the Mexican peso crisis, but tensions between them had worsened significantly as they exchanged accusations regarding deregulation, privatization and connections to the Mafia. Consequently, with the economic recovery underway, Menem replaced Cavallo with a more deferential Minister of the Economy, Roque Fernández.

In sum, in the face of economic and potential political collapse in 1990, President Menem shifted gears and fully embraced a change in strategy. He rebuilt his legislative capacity and he appointed, deferred to and bolstered a credible minister of the economy. Domingo Cavallo helped Menem improve his political relationships with Congress. Cavallo's history and credentials, combined with his lack of strong connections to the business community, gave him the ability to validate the President's policies. The combination of political capacity, deference to a credible economy minister and the uncontested authorization to create new economic institutions – especially the Convertibility Plan – generated a trifecta that enabled Cavallo to increase the predictability and likely efficacy of government policy. In contrast to the Austral Plan, the Convertibility Plan was an extraordinary success. Reflecting confidence that that low-inflation would persist, dollar-denominated debt held by Argentines grew dramatically as did the influx of foreign capital. Ironically, economic optimism gave President Menem an opportunity to replace Cavallo with a more deferential minister of the economy, which, in turn, enabled political exuberance and the crisis that followed.

3.2.4   Conclusion: Lessons from the Great War against Inflation for Constitutive Power

Concerns about inflation shaped much of the political and economic debate in Argentina from 1983 to 1996. As reflected in the RIC in Figure 3.2, policy flexibility was considered risky, while policy constraint was welcomed. The abilities of ministers of finance and presidents to reassure markets by shifting Argentina along the RIC toward further

---

[57] Edmund A. Walsh School of Foreign Service, Center for Latin American Studies, *Political Database of the Americas*. http://pdba.georgetown.edu/Elecdata/Arg/arg.html.

	The Power to Act			Prediction			Outcome	
	Authority to Act	Deference to Technocrats	Implementation Capacity of National Politicians	Impact of Technocrats		Behavior	Role of Technocrats	Market Behavior
5	High or Low	Low	High or Not Necessary	Confrontational technocrats likely to be replaced with sycophants	Cannot validate policy, targeted and broad strategies by politicians possible	No economic validation, political exuberance likely	1983–1985: Grinspun and Alfonsín collude, but have no alternative source of revenue	1983–1985: inflation grows, creditors demand payment
1	High	High	High or Not Necessary	Can constrain or expand policy flexibility	Can validate policy, targeted and broad strategies may be effective	Maximum bargaining power	1985–1986: Sourrouille briefly reinforces Alfonsín politically, constrains him economically	1985: Austral Plan successful briefly, inflation slows, investment grows, negotiations recommence
2	High	High	Low	Can constrain or expand policy flexibility if legislative support is unnecessary	Can validate policy, targeted strategies may be disruptive, broad strategies may be effective	Weak politicians appoint technocrats to bolster implementation capacity, but may abandon them	1987–1989: Sourrouille and team left unsupported, Alfonsín capitulates to domestic pressures	1987–89: Inflation returns
5	High or Low	Low	High or Not Necessary	Confrontational technocrats likely to be replaced with sycophants	Cannot validate policy, targeted and broad strategies by politicians possible	No economic validation, political exuberance likely	1989–1991: Rapanelli and González lack credibility	1988–1991: hyperinflation; FDI grows with privatizations potentially corrupt, other investors stay away
1	High	High	High or Not Necessary	Can constrain or expand policy flexibility	Can validate policy, targeted and broad strategies may be effective	Maximum bargaining power	1991–1996: Cavallo bolsters Menem politically, constrains him economically	1991–1996: Convertibility Plan quells inflation, growth and investment surge
2	High	High	Low	Can constrain or expand policy flexibility if legislative support is unnecessary	Can validate policy, targeted strategies may be disruptive, broad strategies may be effective	Weak politicians appoint technocrats to bolster implementation capacity, but may abandon them	1995–1996: Cavallo able to act as a substitute without Menem's support	1996: Argentina recovers quickly from contagion from Mexican peso crisis

Figure 3.3 Shaping policy and behavior in Argentina, 1983–1996.

policy constraint varied with shifts in deference and political capacity between the president, the economy minister and other technocrats, as specified in Figure 3.3.

From 1983 to 1985, Minister of the Economy Bernardo Grinspun had the authority to act and President Alfonsín was (at least initially) able to support him politically, yet they were unable to secure deference from international donors. As predicted by category 5 of Figure 3.3, they were politically exuberant, though the international community flatly rejected their efforts to invalidate debt obligations left by the previous military regime. Reflecting a similar pattern in 1989 and 1990, Economy Ministers Rapanelli and González had the authority to act and President Menem was (at least initially) able to support them politically, but they proved to be impotent, corrupt and unable to mobilize deference for their policies. As a result, all economic indicators responded poorly.

From 1985 to 1989, the Argentine government tried to instill market confidence by constraining their economic policy choices, most notably through the Austral Plan. Minister of the Economy Juan Sourrouille was granted the authority to act and was lauded by the President and international investors. The Austral Plan's early success empowered and was empowered by electoral success in the 1985 election. But as President Alfonsín's political capacity weakened and he capitulated to societal pressures for wage increases and other demands, the political viability of the Austral Plan evaporated. As predicted in category 2 of Figure 3.3, the combination of authority and deference without political support meant that the minister of the economy was left out on a limb. The minister's efforts to support the Austral Plan without political backing were insufficient, and the Austral Plan collapsed.

From 1991 to 1996, Minister of the Economy Cavallo was given the authority to create the Convertibility Plan, his background and lack of direct connections to the business community and willingness to work with and challenge the President gave him personal credibility. He and President Menem succeeded in rebuilding legislative support for their policies. Although his relationship with President Menem began to deteriorate in 1995–1996, Cavallo was able to mobilize his resources at home and abroad and develop a response to the Mexican peso crisis. He acted without political support from the President (i.e., as a substitute) and succeeded in doubling down on the Convertibility Plan and driving Argentina to the right on the RIC. Private capital flows and portfolio investment surged with the introduction of the Convertibility Plan portfolio in 1991, fell off during the Mexican peso crisis in 1994–1995 and then stabilized (see Figures 3.4 and 3.5).

3.3   Period II: The Prelude to Crisis and the Collapse, 1996–2002

With economic and political success in hand, President Menem consolidated power over economic policy by replacing Domingo Cavallo, who was increasingly seen as a political rival, with the more deferential Minister of the Economy Roque Fernández. The removal of a critical senior economic policymaker would normally be expected to raise doubts about the efficacy of economy policy; however, these concerns were likely counteracted by accolades from the IMF and World Bank praising Menem and declaring Argentina to be a poster child of economic liberalism in South America. Net inflows of foreign direct investment and public and publicly guaranteed debt surged. Portfolio investment and private non-guaranteed debt stabilized at around their 1993 levels, just prior to the Mexican peso crisis.[58]

---

[58] "World development indicators" (n.d.). *World Bank.* http://databank.worldbank.org/ ddp/home.do?Step=3&id=4. For a broader discussion of financial flows during this period, see: P. Blustein (2005). *And the Money Kept Rolling In (and Out): Wall Street, the IMF, and the Bankrupting of Argentina.* New York: Public Affairs.

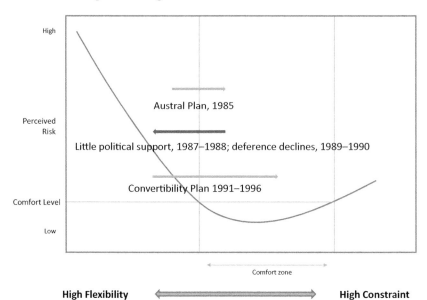

Figure 3.4 The great inflation battle.

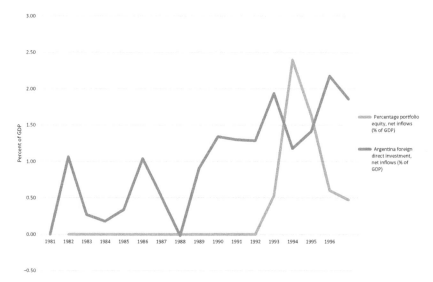

Figure 3.5 Net foreign investment into Argentina, 1981–1996.
Source: WB, 1981–1996. The World Bank, "World Development Indicators."
http://databank.worldbank.org/.

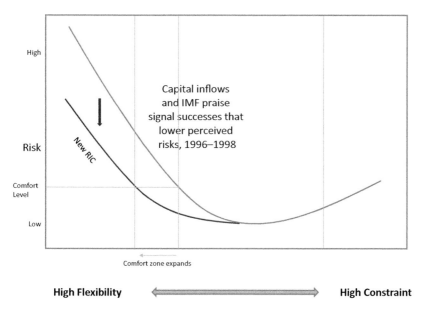

Figure 3.6 Argentina as poster child.

Continued capital inflows combined with IMF validation signaled a shift in investor expectations. As reflected in Figure 3.6, the risks of policy flexibility that had dominated inflation-fearing investors declined, thus lowering the level of risk associated with higher levels of policy flexibility. Although banks increasingly engaged in liability dollarization (a practice of transferring exchange risk to borrowers by requiring them to pay back peso loans in dollars), investor risk remained low (reflected in low bond spreads), and consumer behavior remained unchanged (reflected in continued borrowing in pesos with repayment required in dollars) until 2000.[59] The IMF also helped to create a sense of stability by continuing to provide financial

---

[59] Liability dollarization refers to the denomination of banking system deposits and lending in a currency other than that of the country in which they are held. It shifts exchange rate risk and inflation risk to the borrower. See: "What is domestic liability dollarization?" *Forex News*. www.forexnews.com/questions/whats-is-domestic-liability-dollarization. For its consequences, see: S. P. Berkmen & E. Cavallo (2009). "Exchange Rate Policy and Liability Dollarization: What Do the Data Reveal About Causality?" IMF Working Paper, WP/07/33, June.

assistance.[60] The combination of low perceptions of investor risk, unchanging consumer behavior, and continued access to liquidity at low costs (first from capital inflows and then from the IMF) reduced market pressure for economic reform and suggested that all was good.

Beginning in 1998, however, a perfect storm of internal and external events converged and ultimately shattered this permissive economic environment. An economic crisis in Russia in 1998 and the devaluation of Brazil's real in 1999 sparked fears of contagion. Generally, these circumstances would increase calls for greater policy flexibility. President Menem had a high degree of policy latitude, but rather than prioritizing the economy he used that freedom to attempt to build support for a third political term. In the absence of deference to a strong minister of the economy or the institutional constraints of the Convertibility Plan, government expenditures at the federal and provincial levels increased significantly. Consequently, while the peso remained legally fixed to the dollar, its real value declined. As expected, the risks that President Memem would react in unpredictable or politically-self serving ways increased. Therefore, as shown in Figure 3.7, the RIC during this period is expected to be steeper on both ends, and the comfort zone of market intervention is expected to shrink.

3.3.1   Economic Success and Political Exuberance

President Menem replaced Domingo Cavallo with Roque Fernández on August 6, 1996. Roque Fernández served as Minister of the Economy and Public Works through the end of Menem's Presidency on December 10, 1999. On paper, Minister Fernández looked like he would continue to pursue Cavallo's policies. He had been appointed by Cavallo to serve as the president of the Central Bank beginning in 1991 and, as such, had been principally responsible for managing the currency board which lies at the heart of the Convertibility Plan. He was a market-oriented "Chicago Boy" who had trained at the University of Chicago under Milton Friedman, and he was the founder of a neoliberal think tank. Thus, his economic philosophy closely matched Cavallo's. Unlike Minister

---

[60] G. A. Calvo, A. Izquierdo & E. Talvi (2003). *Sudden Stops, the Real Exchange Rate, and Fiscal Sustainability: Argentina's Lessons.* Cambridge, MA: National Bureau of Economic Research.

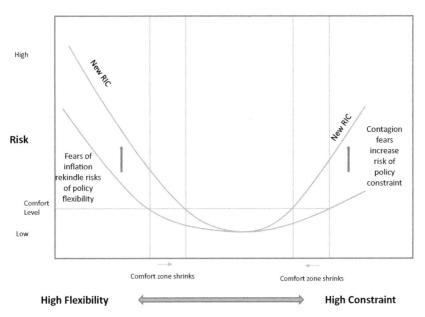

Figure 3.7 Argentina becomes a basket case, 1998–2001.

Cavallo, however, Minister Fernández was not successful in restraining President Menem and keeping him from using economic policy to reward supporters as he fought to secure a third term in office. Despite generally good economic conditions, unemployment levels in the provinces were increasing (as a result of both the privatizations and the gradual increase in the real exchange rate), utility prices were rising (though these increases were matched by significant improvements in the quality of water, phone and other services), and the government was bearing large costs associated with the privatization of social security. These headwinds were made worse by a series of political scandals and the poor Peronist showing in the 1997 legislative elections, which increased pressure on Menem to protect his political base and reward his supporters. To compensate, Menem doubled down on his efforts to build a coalition behind reforming the electoral system so that he could run for a third term. In the absence of a minister of the economy who was willing and able to persuade the president to change course, central government expenditure would be expected to rise even though the Convertibility Plan remained in place. Indeed, central government expenditure grew from less than 30 percent of GDP in 1992 to more than 50 percent in 2001.[61] As fiscal balances deteriorated, *The Economist* labeled Argentina's collapse "a decline without parallel," and lamented its transition from Latin America's star to a basket case.[62]

Despite these signals that domestic economic policy was increasingly coming unglued, global markets did not exert pressure on Argentina to correct its behavior in a timely manner. In markets, as in politics, behavior is relative. It mattered less that Argentina's policies were suspect than that Argentina looked relatively good – at least temporarily – when compared to other emerging market countries. Investors flocked to Argentina to escape crises in East Asia in 1997 and Russia in 1998. The run to Argentina was encouraged by the IMF and World Bank at their annual meeting in October 1998, when President Menem appeared jointly with US President Bill Clinton and Argentina was lauded as the poster child of the Washington Consensus. Michael Mussa, Chief Economist at the IMF in the 1990s, argues that the IMF made the situation worse by failing to press Argentina to pursue more responsible fiscal policies – especially during the growth period of the 1990s – and by extending financial support in the summer of 2001, after it was clear that the exchange rate would fail and default was inevitable.[63] Investors were further encouraged by ratings agencies which praised Argentina for its stability.[64]

3.3.2   The Return and Failure of the White Knights, 2001–2002

After Menem's attempt to run for a third term was ruled to be unconstitutional, the political fight shifted to a battle between Menem's party's candidate, Eduardo Duhalde, and Fernando de la Rúa. Political opposition to Duhalde increased with the creation of the Alliance for Work, Justice and Education (*Alianza para el Trabajo, la Justicia y la Educación*) in 1997. *Alianza* was a coalition party composed of the UCR, FrePaSo and some small provincial parties. Presenting themselves as moderate center-left politicians who would maintain Convertibility while ending corruption and raising employment levels, Fernando de La Rúa of the

[61] "A decline without parallel" (2002). *The Economist*, February 28. https://media .economist.com/news/special-report/1010911-1990s-argentina-was-latin-americas-star-how-did-it-become-basket-case.

[62] Ibid.

[63] M. Mussa (2002). *Argentina and the Fund: From Triumph to Tragedy*. Washington, DC: Institute for International Economics, p. 4.

[64] Veigel. *Dictatorship, Democracy and Globalization*, p. 171.

UCR and Carlos Álvarez of FrePaSo won election on October 24, 1999, with 48.5 percent of the vote.[65]

President de la Rúa faced a poor and deteriorating economic situation when he assumed office. Investor confidence was fragile, the economy was in recession and the government faced a large debt burden. Worst of all, Argentina's main trading partner, Brazil, had devalued its currency by 66 percent against the dollar in January of 1999. Argentina could not devalue its own currency in kind because of its fixed-exchange-rate regime. Consequently, Argentine prices could only be lowered relative to those in Brazil by lowering the costs of production, principally by cutting workers and lowering wages. This is why President de la Rúa promoted labor reform that allowed businesses to lay off workers and reduce salaries as needed. He also increased taxes and cut government spending in an effort to meet Argentina's debts.

President de la Rúa's ability to implement these reforms, which was already uncertain, was worsened by a political scandal in the fall of 2000 over allocations of corruption and bribery in the Senate with regard to a labor reform law. Eight senators in the Peronist party and three of *Alianza* were accused.[66] The dispute split *Alianza*, with FrePaSo backing Vice President Álvarez (who ultimately resigned) and the UCR backing President de la Rúa. Tensions increased in September. Silvia Sapag, a senator from the energy-rich province of Patagonia, told a federal judge that Senator Emil Caterer (who had already been accused as part of the bribery scandal) had offered her money for votes on a hydrocarbon bill. Investors responded negatively. The Spanish-owned energy company *Repsol Yacimientos Petrolíferos Fiscales* (Repsol YPF), for example, announced it was "considering canceling an $8 billion investment in Ineloquent province because of the lack of legal guarantees."[67] A spokesman from Repsol YPF noted further that, "Because of all the controversy with the senators and all that, all accusing each other of different things, the board has expressed its concern and told him that there are possibilities of investing in other places [such as Bolivia or Trinidad and Tobago]."[68] President de la Rúa's popularity dipped from 74 percent at its initial peak to 50 percent by the end of

---

[65] This compared to 38 percent for Eduardo Duhalde–Ramón Ortega and the PJ coalition who campaigned on a platform to modify Convertibility and renegotiate Argentine debt, and 10 percent for Domingo Cavallo–José Armando Caro Figueroa of the Partnership Action for the Republic, Union of Democratic Center and Santa Fe. Edmund A. Walsh School of Foreign Service, Center for Latin American Studies, *Political Database of the Americas*. http://pdba.georgetown.edu/Elecdata/Arg/arg.html.

[66] S. Brown (2000). "New bribe scandal hits Argentina's 'murky' Senate." *CNN*, September 21. http://archives.cnn.com/2000/WORLD/americas/09/21/argentina.bribes.reut.

[67] Ibid.   [68] Ibid.

2000, while approval of the government's economic policies reportedly declined from 35 percent to 13 percent.[69]

In order to rebuild his political position and instill confidence in the economy, President de la Rúa appointed a well-known conservative economist, José Luis Machinea, as minister of the economy. As noted earlier, Machinea had been president of the Central Bank under President Alfonsín and was responsible for developing the Spring Plan in 1986.

Once appointed, Minister Machinea acted quickly, securing a large credit line from the IMF in November of 2000.[70] The credit line was intended to be large enough to provide "armor" (*blindage*) against speculators by enabling Argentina to refinance and avoid defaulting on nearly US$40 billion of debt. In exchange for the armor, Argentina agreed to implement a series of reforms, including reducing pensions and deregulating labor union worker insurance.

The IMF loan was equivalent to Treasury Secretary Henry Paulson's request for a "bazooka" loaded with money in the summer of 2008. Unfortunately, foreshadowing Secretary Paulson's failure to calm markets and his inability to secure passage of the Troubled Asset Relief Program (TARP) in September of 2008, Machinea failed to secure sufficient political support to pass supporting legislation. Like President Alfonsín, President de la Rúa was unable to protect his economy minister or bring his policies to fruition. Machinea resigned on March 2, 2001. As seen in Figure 3.8, risk as reflected in the real interest rate and deposit rate stayed low until 2000, then increased significantly.

In response, President de la Rúa doubled down by appointing his former defense minister, Ricardo López Murphy, to the post on March 5, 2001. Economy Minister Murphy had the credentials of a conservative economist, but was not given any political armor. He was forced to resign almost immediately following a failed attempt to implement widely unpopular cuts in education spending. Murphy later argued that the crisis in 2001 was the result of a perfect storm of declining commodity prices, increasing interest rates due to the Asian financial crisis, and decreasing confidence due to the Russian crisis and the Brazilian devaluation. He said that he argued at the time that prices would eventually go up, Brazil would recover and grow and interest rates would go down. He

---

[69] The PRS Group (2000). "Country Risk Services, Argentina Country Report." November 1, p. 10.

[70] "Argentina: 2000 Article IV Consultation and First Review Under the Stand-By Arrangement, and Request for Modification of Performance Criteria – Staff Report and Public Information Notice Following Consultation" (2000). *International Monetary Fund*, December 19. www.imf.org/external/pubs/cat/longres.aspx?sk=3859.0.

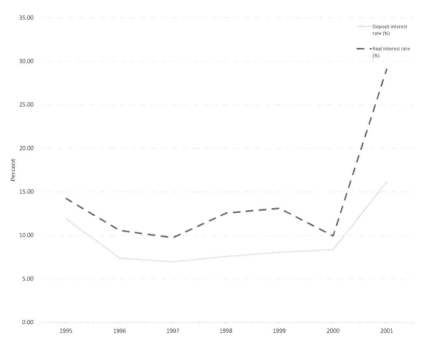

Figure 3.8 Precrisis risk in Argentina.
Source: The World Bank, "World Development Indicators." http://
databank.worldbank.org/.

declared, "All of this happened as I predicted, but it took time and the
public was not willing to accept a delay because de la Rúa did not exude
confidence. Instead, he was like Jimmy Carter, in that he talked about
economic malaise."[71]

On March 21, 2001, President de la Rúa called in Argentina's anti-
inflationary hero, Domingo Cavallo, to save the day. Congress
responded enthusiastically, treating Cavallo like a white knight who was
coming to the rescue. They awarded him "extraordinary powers" to fix
the economy without the need for consultation with the president or
Congress.[72]

In stark contrast to his efforts in the 1990s to build support for his
programs in congress, Cavallo enacted brash, dramatic economic policies

[71] Interview with Ricardo López Murphy (2012). Cordoba 637, Buenos Aires. July.
[72] C. Krauss (2001). "Argentina presses for ways to jolt its economy out of recession." *New
York Times*, March 25. www.nytimes.com/2001/03/25/world/argentina-presses-for-
ways-to-jolt-its-economy-out-of-recession.html.

without congressional involvement. He ran roughshod over the Convertibility Plan, the independence of the Central Bank and the regulation of the banking sector – all institutions that he had helped promote a decade earlier.[73] By acting on his authority without deference to existing institutions or securing validation from other individuals, Cavallo's actions sewed doubt rather than building confidence. This experience suggests that, left unchecked, unfettered power in the hands of technocrats is potentially as unsettling as it is in the hands of national politicians.

Cavallo began by breaking the tight link between the peso and the dollar and declaring that the Argentine peso would be pegged to a basket of dollars and euros. Instead of decreasing pressure on the peso, changing the program undercut investor confidence in the sustainability of the Convertibility Plan. This raised the prospect of inflation and rekindled fears among public and private debtors that they would be unable to pay their dollar-denominated loans. As a consequence, the spread between the interest rates paid for Argentina's bonds and US Treasury bonds rose by over 500 basis points (or 50 percent).

Cavallo then instituted a variety of harsh austerity measures. He increased taxes on financial transactions, removed exemptions on sales taxes and cut government spending and government services.[74] To counteract the recession-inducing effects of these policies, he simultaneously lowered the Central Bank's reserve requirements and allowed banks to use government bonds as reserves. When the president of the Central Bank, Pedro Pou, challenged these policies, Minister Cavallo accused him of corruption for failing to investigate charges of money laundering.[75] Congress backed Cavallo and began investigating Pou's activities. The investigation focused on a failed bank, *Banco República*, which was owned by an associate of President Menem and was allegedly involved in questionable international money laundering and other transfers of up to US$4 billion from 1992 to 2000.[76] Regardless of the validity of the corruption charges, policy disagreements between Cavallo and the president of the Central Bank highlighted significant internal turmoil and further undercut investor confidence in the efficacy of decisions made by the economic team.

---

[73] "Cavallo struggles to get a grip on Argentina's economy" (2001). *The Economist*, May 3. www.economist.com/node/612598.

[74] Ibid.

[75] "Argentina's banking scandal deepens" (2001). *BBC News*, February 21. http://news.bbc.co.uk/2/hi/americas/1182417.stm.

[76] R. Taylor (2001). "The dirty money war." *World Press Review*. www.worldpress.org/Americas/1175.cfm.

In order to quell investor fears of inflation, Cavallo then imposed a 13 percent cut in state-sector salaries and pension payments to those receiving more than US$500 a month, he required a large portion of national pensions to be converted into government bonds, he negotiated austerity measures with provincial governors and he declared a "zero deficit plan."[77] The IMF responded with an additional US$8 billion in loans.[78]

In short, Cavallo took dramatic action and demonstrated his ability to tap domestic and international sources of capital. Unfortunately, his ability to do so without any checks or balances made his policies unpredictable and raised uncertainty about their sustainability and consequences. Consequently, instead of calming public sentiment, the situation deteriorated. Nationwide protests erupted in July and September. On October 14, 2001, President de la Rúa and the *Alianza* government suffered a significant defeat in legislative elections in which the PJ took control of both houses of Congress. In the absence of any viable political support, investors interpreted Cavallo's flurry of activity as a sign of desperation and capital flight escalated.

In order to stop the flight of capital and runs on Argentine banks, Cavallo again doubled down by instituting the *corralito*, or "little fence," on December 1, 2001. The *corralito* initially froze all bank accounts, then forbade the withdrawal of US dollars and limited the withdrawal of pesos to 250–300 per week – this at a time when Buenos Aires was roughly as expensive as Washington, DC. The public responded by rioting in the streets with the popular cry, "*Que se vayan todos!*" meaning "Kick them all out!" Unable to withstand the public backlash against these policies, President de la Rúa declared martial law on December 19. This failed to slow the momentum of the collapse and he and Cavallo resigned.

During its collapse, Argentina was led by a series of very-short-term, temporary presidents. They included Ramón Puerta (who served for two days on December 21 and 22) and Adolfo Rodríguez Saá (who began on December 23, declared the country in default and left office one week later). On January 2, 2002, Eduardo Duhalde was appointed President by Congress for the duration of de la Rúa's official term. President Duhalde instituted the *corralón*, or "big fence," which forced the conversion of many accounts into peso-denominated bonds. He then ended Convertibility and first devalued the peso at a rate of 1:1.4 for savings and 1:1 for debt, then let it float freely.

---

[77] The PRS Group (2001). "Country Risk Services, Argentina Country Report." October 1, p. 1.
[78] Ibid.

The Power to Act			Prediction		Outcome	
Authority to Act	Deference to Technocrats	Implementation Capacity of National Politicians	Impact of Technocrats	Behavior	Role of Technocrats	Market Behavior
5 High or Low	Low	High or Not Necessary	Confrontational technocrats likely to be replaced with sycophants / Cannot validate policy, targeted and broad strategies by politicians possible	No economic validation, political exuberance likely	1996–1998: Minister of the Economy does not constrain Menem; IMF gives external validation	Capital inflows reduce market pressure, reforms stall
2 High	High	Low	Can constrain or expand policy flexibility if legislative support is unnecessary / Can validate policy, targeted strategies may be disruptive, broad strategies may be effective	Weak politicians appoint technocrats to bolster implementation capacity, but may abandon them	1999–2001: President reappoints Cavallo to save the day. Congress grants Cavallo complete policy flexibility. He acts quickly and unilaterally	Erratic economic policies worsen perceptions of policy uncertainty, trigger backlashes and suggest desperation

Figure 3.9 Shaping policy and behavior in Argentina, 1996–2001.

3.3.3   Conclusion to Period II: Prelude to Crisis and Constitutive Power

The period of 1996–2002 was one of exuberance when President Menem and then Domingo Cavallo concentrated authority over economic policy in their own hands. As a result, it was a period of high levels of political and policy uncertainty. With external validation and financial support from the IMF, Menem succeeded when external conditions were favorable. When the external situation changed, however, neither he nor Cavallo was able to reduce uncertainty about what the government was going to do and whether the chosen policy would succeed. Like Alan Greenspan and Hank Paulson, Domingo Cavallo had once been a hero of economic policy-making and then fell from grace. Now, he is widely criticized as one of the principal villains behind Argentina's subsequent economic crisis. Figure 3.9 summarizes these dynamics.

3.4   Period III: Recovery and Populist Resurgence

Argentina's recovery during the first decade after the crisis was remarkable. In a statement to the International Monetary and Financial Committee of the IMF in October of 2012, Hernán Lorenzino, Minister of Economy and Public Finance, describes this as an incomparable period:

Between 2003 and 2011, average annual economic growth was 7.7 percent, which constitutes the highest average growth rate in the country's economic history. During the same period, per capita GDP accumulative growth was 66.2 percent. Growth reached 9.2 percent in 2010 and 8.9 percent in 2011. This incomparable period of sustained growth has come hand in hand with a marked reduction in poverty, unemployment, and inequality.[79]

---

[79] H. Lorenzino (2012). Statement by Hernán Lorenzino, Minister of Economy and Public Finance, Argentina, to the International Monetary and Financial Committee of the International Monetary Fund at their twenty-sixth meeting, October 13, p. 10. www.imf.org/External/AM/2012/imfc/statement/eng/arg.pdf.

This outcome was the result of a combination of favorable market conditions mediated by a reduction in political and policy uncertainty resulting from the coordinated actions of President Néstor Kirchner and his Minister of the Economy, Roberto Lavagna. Together they succeeded in challenging both the IMF and international bondholders, securing a massive reduction in Argentina's debt, and rekindling economic growth that continued for nearly a decade after its crisis. Driven in part by a surge in soybean exports and the devaluation, export revenues grew from 11 percent of GDP just before the crisis to 28 percent of GDP in 2002; export revenues stayed above 20 percent of GDP until 2009, then began decreasing toward precrisis levels, reaching 13 percent in 2016.[80] This bolstered Argentina's growth, which rebounded from a −12 percent annual decline in GDP per capita in 2002 to an average of 7 percent every year from 2003 through 2007, before slowing dramatically in 2008.[81]

The added revenue enabled Argentina to pursue a tough bargaining position with bondholders and the IMF. At the same time, however, these successes also empowered President Néstor Kirchner and his wife and successor, Cristina Fernández de Kirchner, and diminished the political need for maintaining strong independently-minded ministers of the economy. Consequently, as the economy improved, they consolidated their authority over economic policy and increasingly demanded deference from their ministers. President Fernández de Kirchner fired economic technocrats who were critical of her agenda, and increasingly used economic policy to reward political supporters. When export revenues declined, she attempted to exploit other sources of revenue, including soy bean taxes and inflation financing. She then altered national statistics to lower the apparent level of inflation and cost of the debt. Mimicking efforts by President Alfonsín and Economy Minister Grinspun to take on the IMF and international investors in the 1980s, President Fernández de Kirchner and her Economy Ministers Hernán Lorenzino and Alex Kicillof took an increasingly confrontational approach to international investors – including nationalizing Repsol YPF in April of 2012,[82] and rejecting potential settlements with

---

[80] "World development indicators" (n.d.). *World Bank.* http://databank.worldbank.org/ddp/home.do?Step=3&id=4.

[81] Ibid.

[82] S. Romero & R. Minder (2012). "Argentina to seize control of oil company." *New York Times,* April 16. www.nytimes.com/2012/04/17/business/global/argentine-president-to-nationalize-oil-company.html.

bondholders in favor of a US\$20 billion default in July of 2014.[83] Since his election in 2015, President Mauricio Macri has taken steps to restore investor confidence, settle the outstanding disputes with holdout bondholders and remove many of these market-distorting policies. He retained political support though midterm elections in 2017, and Argentina successfully sold government bonds and secured new financing from the IMF. Despite these successes, his ability to reduce political and policy uncertainty has been weakened by a decline in confidence in the predictability and efficacy of Central Bank activity beginning in the summer of 2018. Like many before him, President Macri responded by appointing a new president of the central bank, Guido Sandleris. The ability of Sandleris and Minister of the Treasury and Public Finances Nicolás Dujovne to help President Marci restore confidence in the Argentine economy will likely vary as each attempts to assert authority over economic policy, secure deference to their policies and retain sufficient political support to implement needed policy changes.

3.4.1   Balancing Traumatized Constituents and the IMF, 2002–2003

Eduardo Duhalde was appointed as an interim president by the Argentine Congress on January 2, 2002. He and his Ministers of the Economy Jorge Remes Lenicov and Roberto Lavagna laid the foundation for Argentina's recovery. When President Néstor Kirchner was elected in 2003, he retained Roberto Lavagna and brought many of these programs to fruition. In the process, President Kirchner rebuilt the power of the presidency and Lavagna rebuilt the reputation of the minister of the economy.

President Duhalde's most critical challenges were rebuilding the IMF's confidence in Argentina's economic system in order to secure its financial support while also placating domestic constituents who had been hurt badly by the collapse. In his memoir, *Memory of the Fire*, President Duhalde describes being confronted with a wide range of demands from civil society, businesses and banks, the IMF, unions, provincial governors and Congress.[84] He highlights the eruption of massive country-wide protests against the *corralito* and the IMF in particular.

---

[83] M. Patton (2014). "Argentina defaults on its debt ... again." *Forbes.com*, August 1. www.forbes.com/sites/mikepatton/2014/08/01/argentina-defaults-on-its-debt-again/#2026910 74637.

[84] E. Duhalde (2007). *Memorias del Incendio (Memory of the Fire)*. Buenos Aires: Editorial Sudamericana.

The CGT union was incensed by the IMF's assertion that there were 420,000 "extra" workers in the provinces who should be fired before financial support would be granted. The CGT also criticized the IMF's demands that the government increase tax revenue, raise public utility rates (which were currently frozen) and foreclose on the quarter of a million mortgages that were in default.[85]

Javier Corrales sums up Duhalde's challenge of managing domestic constituents who were suffering from Argentina's economic collapse while also placating international investors who were looking to the IMF as an enforcer of economic orthodoxy:

Upon taking office in January 2002, Duhalde confronted two major problems: containing the rising unrest at home, and regaining the confidence of the IMF. His approach was schizophrenic. On the one hand, he embraced an anti-market rhetoric, thinking that this would placate the citizenry. In his acceptance speech, he lambasted the old economic model and the new business groups that had profited from privatization, ignoring the fact that it was his own party that had pursued the market reforms of the 1990s. He devalued the peso, thereby ending convertibility by presidential decree. By jettisoning the convertibility law, almost all contracts, which were written in dollars, became subject to renegotiation. In addition, all bank deposits and liabilities were "pesified" (i.e., converted to pesos, now devalued), giving rise to acrimonious legal conflicts about whose deposits and whose liabilities would be converted at which rate. This "massive destruction of property rights" has fueled financial speculation and forced many utilities and large companies into bankruptcy.

On the other hand, Duhalde began (gradually and almost secretly) to do as the IMF advised, not just devaluing, but also securing an agreement with the provinces to cut spending, unifying the exchange rate, and changing a bankruptcy law to match international standards.[86]

In short, Duhalde faced large and conflicting demands from international investors and domestic constituents. The IMF agreed to reschedule US$6.8 billion in debt, but made several specific, challenging legislative demands, including a fourteen-point plan for economic recovery.[87] To build domestic support for these reforms, Duhalde promised provincial governors that the needed fiscal adjustment would take

---

[85] B. Vann (2002). "Argentina defaults on loan to World Bank." *World Socialist Web Site*, November 16. www.wsws.org/articles/2002/nov2002/arg-n16.shtml.

[86] J. Corrales (2002). "The Politics of Argentina's Meltdown." *World Policy Journal*, 19(3), 29–42.

[87] L. Rohter (2003). "Argentina struggles to meet debt-relief terms." *New York Times*, February 11. www.nytimes.com/2003/02/11/world/argentina-struggles-to-meet-debt-relief-terms.html; Vann. "Argentina defaults on loan."

place through increased revenues from inflation rather than through layoffs.[88] He also promised opposition labor groups that he would replace Minister of the Economy Jorge Remes Lenicov, who had been severely criticized by the CGT for his efforts to push the government to comply with IMF directives, with Roberto Lavagna.[89] Having secured these compromises, Duhalde agreed to the IMF's fourteen-point plan. US Treasury Secretary Paul O'Neill, who had argued that the United States would not provide additional funding to Argentina until an agreement with the IMF had been reached, praised the action. He noted, "I am pleased that the President of Argentina and all provincial governors have expressed their intention to take serious action. This is a welcome expression of a national spirit of cooperation."[90]

Like Domingo Cavallo in the early 1990s, Lavagna was able to secure and exploit his institutional authority, retain a high degree of respect and deference from the president, and bolster and benefit from the president's electoral capacity. The combination of authority, deference and implementation capacity enabled the Argentine government to exploit the economic opportunities that resulted from its devaluation and market changes in the early 2000s and bargain from a position of strength with international lenders. Lavagna succeeded in both moderating and validating Kirchner's economic policies. By moderating Kirchner's populism, Lavagna kept Argentina from shifting to the left along the RIC (see Figure 3.10). In addition, the combination of Lavagna's credibility and President Kirchner's political capacity lowered the risks associated with default by enhancing the political and economic viability of Kirchner's policies throughout the debt negotiations.

3.4.2   The Kirchner–Lavagna Team, 2003–2005

President Néstor Kirchner entered office in a weak political position. He and Vice President Daniel Scioli and their Front for Victory Party came in second with only 21.9 percent of the vote on April 27, 2003.[91] Carlos Menem and Juan Carlos Romero and their Front for Loyalty Party had

[88] M. Obarrio (2002). "Apoyo condicionado de gobernadores aliancistas" (Conditional support from Alianza governors). *La Nación*, April 7. www.lanacion.com.ar/nota.asp?nota_id=386812.

[89] L. Rohter (2002). "Argentina partly opens banks and names an economy minister." *New York Times*, April 27. www.nytimes.com/2002/04/27/world/argentina-partly-opens-banks-and-names-an-economy-minister.html?ref=roberto_lavagna.

[90] J. Rosales (2002). "El Tesoro de EE.UU apoyó el acuerdo" (US Treasury Supports Agreement). *La Nación*, April 26. www.lanacion.com.ar/nota.asp?nota_id=391711.

[91] Edmund A. Walsh School of Foreign Service, Center for Latin American Studies. *Political Database of the Americas.* http://pdba.georgetown.edu/Elecdata/Arg/arg.html.

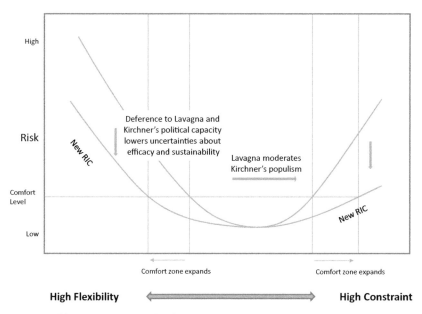

Figure 3.10 Argentina in recovery, 2003–2005.

won a plurality of the vote at 24.3 percent, while Ricardo López Murphy and Ricardo Gómez Díaz and their Recreate for Growth Party won 16.4 percent. Kirchner and Scioli won the office only after Menem and Romero withdrew from runoff elections.

President Kirchner attempted to build a political coalition by reappointing multiple ministers from the Duhalde administration, including Roberto Lavagna as minister of the economy. While serving under President Duhalde, Lavagna had gained widespread public support by eliminating the *corralito* in December of 2002, negotiating effectively with (i.e., defaulting on) the World Bank and for managing a two-year economic recovery with low inflation. Lavagna's positive public reputation enabled him to generate support for President Kirchner without appearing beholden to him.[92] Consequently, even though President Kirchner participated actively in economic policy-making, Lavagna retained his reputation for mediating the President's economic policy decisions. Throughout ongoing negotiations with the IMF, for example, Lavagna negotiated privately with US Secretaries of the Treasury John Snow and Paul O'Neill, as well as Undersecretary John Taylor. Lavagna recounted

---

[92] Interview with Roberto Lavagna on Wednesday, July 25, 2012, in Buenos Aires.

sending numerous faxes to President Kirchner's private line during the meetings. He commented that President Kirchner always responded quickly and remained intimately involved in negotiations. While such interactions were mutually reinforcing, Lavagna argued that he maintained ultimate control over economic policy by only agreeing to sign documents when he was confident that the government could fulfill the obligations.[93]

During the Duhalde administration, Lavagna bolstered his credibility with the IMF by not asking for additional financial support. He had instead argued that Argentina would have to resolve its problems internally and did not want to take on any more debt than it was able to pay.[94] He expressed concern that acting otherwise would create a situation like that of 1999, when the IMF gave Argentina ineffective "armor" against speculators, which made matters worse. Normal protocol enables those who wish to terminate their relationship with the IMF to repay their debt in five and a half years. Lavagna and Kirchner proposed following suit and paying off their debt. The United States and France strongly supported this idea (Lavagna remembers particularly welcoming remarks from US Secretaries of the Treasury O'Neill and Snow). José Octavio Bordón, Argentina's Ambassador to the United States, remembers US President George Bush replying to Lavagna with the appreciative comment that he had grown tired of negotiating with Yasser Arafat, who always promised all sorts of things but was never able to deliver on them, and would much prefer to negotiate a policy that could be reached and agreed to as he could with Lavagna.[95]

Minister Lavagna received strong support from provincial governors and members of the Peronist and *Alianza* parties in Congress during his term, but he occasionally faced opposition from other members of Kirchner's economic team.[96] In particular, Lavagna disagreed with Central Bank President Mario Blejer (who had been appointed by Lenicov) about Argentina's relationship with the IMF, the process of lifting constraints on the withdrawal of savings (the *corralito*), whether to provide loans to failing banks and Blejer's proposal to regain stability by fully dollarizing the Argentine economy.[97] Citing unresolvable differences,

[93] Interview with José Octavio Bordón, former Ambassador to the United States, in the Palermo section of Buenos Aires, Argentina, July 26, 2012.

[94] Interview with Roberto Lavagna on Wednesday, July 25, 2012, in Buenos Aires.

[95] Interview with José Octavio Bordón, former Ambassador to the United States, in the Palermo section of Buenos Aires, Argentina, July 26, 2012.

[96] M. Obarrio (2002). "Fuerte respaldo politico para Lavagna" (Strong political backing for Lavagna). *La Nación*, April 28. www.lanacion.com.ar/nota.asp?nota_id=392346.

[97] "Lavagna-Blejer, una relacion marcada por el desacuerdo" (2006). *Clarín*, June 22. http://edant.clarin.com/diario/2002/06/22/e-00403.htm.

Blejer resigned on June 24, 2002. Blejer's successor at the Central Bank, Aldo Pignanelli, resigned six months later, reportedly also because of differences with Lavagna.[98] Pignanelli's successor, Alfonso Prat-Gay, stayed in his position until the end of his term in September of 2004, but did not seek reappointment after complaining about a lack of influence in economic policy. Lavagna replaced Prat-Gay with Martín Redrado in September of 2004. Redrado worked in sync with Lavagna, focusing his efforts on promoting export competitiveness and building up foreign exchange reserves. Lavagna left office in November of 2005, but Redrado continued to pursue a comparable agenda as president of the Central Bank until January 7, 2010. At that point, he was dismissed by President Cristina Fernández de Kirchner for disagreements with her over the use of foreign exchange reserves to pay for increased government expenditures and foreign debt services. Based on the model presented in Chapter 2, Lavagna's ability to consolidate power among economic technocrats and Redrado's continuation as president of the Central Bank are expected to decrease perceptions of political and policy uncertainty. His dismissal and replacement with a more compliant central bank president in January of 2010, however, are expected to increase uncertainty by signaling an end to technocratic pushback against the administration.

In the decade following the collapse, the biggest challenges facing Argentina involved meeting its debt obligations to international creditors. The creditors included members of the Paris Club of creditor countries and private bondholders.[99] Normally, Paris Club countries do not negotiate debt restructuring unless the country has an IMF lending program in hand and has therefore undergone an Article IV review to assess its ability to repay its debts; furthermore, the IMF would generally not initiate a lending program until an agreement had been offered to all creditors.[100] Instead of following this practice, President Kirchner and Minister of the Economy Lavagna chose to negotiate with its creditors directly rather than use the IMF as an intermediary.

President Kirchner and Minister Lavagna took a hardline approach and filed a one-time offer with the US Securities and Exchange

---

[98] "Turmoil at the Argentine Central Bank" (2002). *New York Times*, December 7. www.nytimes.com/2002/12/07/business/turmoil-at-the-argentine-central-bank.html?ref= roberto_lavagna.

[99] See the official Paris Club website: www.clubdeparis.org.

[100] J. Hornbeck (2013a). "Argentina's Defaulted Sovereign Debt: Dealing with the 'Holdouts.'" *Library of Congress, Congressional Research Service*, p. 4.

Commission (SEC)[101] to settle Argentina's debt with 152 different bond series issued in seven currencies under multiple jurisdictions.[102] To compel the bondholders to accept the deal, President Kirchner encouraged the Argentine Congress to pass the Lock Law (*Ley Cerrojo*), which prohibited the government from reopening the exchange or making any kind of future offer on better terms and suspending payments on untendered debt after February 25, 2005.[103] Despite the threat of lawsuits from investors, President Kirchner stood firm on his assertion that, "*Es la última oferta que Argentina hace*," meaning that this was the last offer Argentina would make and it was unlawful to pay any "holdouts."[104] The bond exchange opened on January 14, 2005.[105] When the exchange closed, 76.1 percent of private bondholders had accepted the terms. Out of an outstanding debt of US$81.8 billion in bonds at face value, US$62.3 billion were exchanged for US$35.2 billion in new bonds.[106]

The success in negotiating this "haircut" in 2005 can be explained in part by the ability of President Kirchner and Economy Minister Lavagna to implement the Lock Law and Lavagna's ability to restrain the President from drawing down the country's reserves. Lavagna's success in this regard is reflected in the growth in Argentina's reserves from US$10 billion in January of 2003 to US$52 billion in 2011.[107] Combined with high export revenues, these actions sent a message that the Argentine government could hold out longer than the holdouts. In comparison to

---

[101] SEC Form 18-K, is also known known as the Annual Report for Foreign Governments and Political Subdivisions. It is used to update the Securities and Exchange Commission and investors regarding the status of a domestically traded foreign security and its issuer. The information required from a foreign issuer on this annual update includes anything that could materially affect the long-term solvency of the security or its issuer. See: www.investopedia.com/terms/s/sec-form-18-k.asp#ixzz3iXZV2B6M.

[102] The offer was presented in terms of a prospectus from the Republic of Argentina: See: Prospectus Settlement (to Prospectus Dated December 27, 2004), the Republic of Argentina. The prospectus is dated January 20, 2005. www.mecon.gov.ar/finanzas/download/us_prospectus_and_prospectus_supplement.pdf.

[103] "Argentina approves the 'lock law'" (2005). *BBCMUNDO.com*, February 10. http://news.bbc.co.uk/hi/spanish/business/newsid_4252000/4252425.stm; M. Murphy (2005). "Argentina: Debt Swap." *BBCMUNDO.com*, January 12. http://news.bbc.co.uk/hi/spanish/business/newsid_4168000/4168005.stm.

[104] "Kirchner, hard with creditors" (2005). *BBCMUNDO.com*, February 4. http://news.bbc.co.uk/hi/spanish/business/newsid_4237000/4237917.stm.

[105] Murphy. "Argentina: Debt Swap."

[106] Hornbeck. "Argentina's Defaulted Sovereign Debt," p. 5.

[107] Reserves declined thereafter as President Cristina Fernández de Kirchner drew them down to meet hard currency obligations, reaching US$31 billion at the end of her term in December of 2015. International Reserves of the Central Bank of Argentina BCRA (in millions of dollars). www.bcra.gov.ar/PublicacionesEstadisticas/Principales_variables_datos.asp.

the government, institutional bondholders tend to have short time horizons and are generally willing to accept a haircut rather than pursue prolonged and expensive litigation for uncertain returns; individual or retail investors similarly tend to sell their discounted bonds in secondary markets.[108]

Another area in which the Kirchner–Lavagna team exercised power over international investors involved the treatment of foreign companies that provided utility and transportation services. In 1999, Argentina froze the rate that utility companies could charge their consumers in pesos. The rate freezes remained in effect despite massive losses suffered by these companies during the economic collapse and recovery. Many foreign companies invested in Argentina in the early 1990s under the protection of bilateral trade agreements. Such agreements enable companies to file suits against Argentina for losses in the International Centre for the Settlement of Investment Disputes (ICSID) of the World Bank. Ten cases have been filed, but the Argentine authorities chose to ignore at least four rulings that were made in favor of the companies.[109]

Lavagna tried to convince Kirchner to allow the rates to rise and utility subsidies to fall. He argued that the short-term consequences of the rate freezes would be low, but that they would be costly in the medium to long term.[110] Over time, the cost of maintenance would shift to the government because the private companies were operating at a loss and would not be willing or able to sustain their services. Eventually, the shift in responsibilities from the companies to the government would lead to a de facto renationalization of basic services like water, electric power, gas and telephones. Until 2005, the subsidies amounted to US$1.6 billion (or 4.5 percent of gross national product). They were not problematic at the time because of trade surpluses in agriculture; however, between 2006 and 2011, they grew more than tenfold to US$18.1 billion.[111] As the costs of these programs grew, they became a major source of contention between Minister of Economy Lavagna and President Kirchner and others in his administration.[112]

[108] Hornbeck. "Argentina's Defaulted Sovereign Debt," p. 8.
[109] "Come and get me: Argentina is putting international arbitration to the test" (2012). *The Economist*, February 18. www.economist.com/node/21547836.
[110] Interview with Roberto Lavagna on Wednesday, July 25, 2012, in Buenos Aires.
[111] J. Hornbeck (2013b). *Argentina's Post-crisis Economic Reform: Challenges for U.S. Policy.* Washington, DC: Congressional Research Service, p. 5.
[112] Interview with Roberto Lavagna on Wednesday, July 25, 2012, in Buenos Aires.

In the face of growing friction and disagreements, Kirchner reduced Lavagna's authority. Rather than assigning sole authority over the commission responsible for negotiating rate hikes with utility companies (*Unidad de Renegociacion y Analisis de Contratos de Servicios Publicos*) to the minister of the economy – as had been the case since 2002 – President Kirchner divided the responsibility between the minister of the economy and the planning minister. Planning Minister Julio de Vido sided with the President against Lavagna. Lavagna described the resulting dispute as a policy difference rather than a confrontation between himself and President Kirchner.[113] Nonetheless, it marked a weakening of the minister of the economy's capacity to shape economic policy.

President Kirchner's faction of Peronism, the Front for Victory (*Frente para la Victoria*), won 54 percent of the vote in the House of Deputies on October 23, 2005. This victory gave President Kirchner the political mandate he had lacked when first elected. Just like President Menem, who replaced Domingo Cavallo with a less confrontational minister of the economy, Roque Fernández, when his economic and political circumstances improved, President Kirchner replaced Roberto Lavagna with a less confrontational minister of the economy, Felisa Miceli, on November 27, 2005. Miceli was described at the time as someone who is "a disciple of Mr. Lavagna but has none of his political clout."[114]

Lavagna's presence had given Kirchner's policies added legitimacy and political clout at home and abroad. Based on the model, his departure is expected to increase political and policy uncertainty. Policy uncertainty increased further on December 15, 2005, when Argentina paid off its debt of US$9.8 billion to the IMF. While Brazil had been praised for repaying its debt of US$15.56 billion to the IMF days earlier, Argentina's repayment was interpreted as a way for the government to further operate without IMF oversight or restrictions.[115] Consequently, two potential sources of validation and checks on the President's economic policies had been removed.

---

[113] Ibid.

[114] "After Lavagna, an uncertain tilt towards populism: the sacking of a successful economy minister suggests a turn away from the IMF and towards Chávez's Venezuela" (2005). *The Economist*, December 1. www.economist.com/the-americas/2005/12/01/after-lavagna-an-uncertain-tilt-towards-populism.

[115] C. Rush (2005). "Argentina, Brazil pay off debt to IMF; bankers nervous." *Executive Intelligence Review*, December 30. www.larouchepub.com/other/2005/3250arg_brazil_imf.html.

3.4.3   Political Consolidation, 2007–2015

President Cristina Fernández de Kirchner and Julio Cobos and their Victory Front Alliance (FPV-PJ) won the presidential elections on October 28, 2007, with 45.3 percent of the vote compared to Elisa Carrió and Héctor Rúben Giustiniani of the Civic Coalition Confederation which won 23.0 percent and Roberto Lavagna and Gerardo Morales of the An Advanced Nation Party which won 16.9 percent.[116]

President Fernández de Kirchner appointed Martín Lousteau as minister of the economy on December 10, 2007. Minister Lousteau stayed in the position for a little more than a year. During that time President Fernández de Kirchner diminished the authority of the minister of the economy relative to secretary of domestic trade (also known as the secretary of commerce) even though the latter officially reported to the minister of the economy. Ongoing conflicts between Secretary of Domestic Trade Guillermo Moreno, Minister of the Economy Lousteau and President of the Central Bank Martín Redrado undermined the credibility of the economic team. Lousteau complained of "permanent fights" with Moreno and accused him of providing faulty information to Central Bank President Redrado, which undermined the ability to make sound economic policy.[117] Even basic information about the economy including statistics by the *Instituto Nacional de Estadística y Censos* (INDEC) became suspect. According to Redrado, President Cristina Fernández de Kirchner ordered Guillermo Moreno to oversee the INDEC in order to ensure that the inflation rate was undervalued. Consequently, the Central Bank stopped using the INDEC's inflation numbers in 2009.[118] Investors interpreted the undervalued INDEC estimates as a technical default.[119] This increased tensions between Moreno and Lousteau who increasingly exchanged verbal insults in public.[120] These exchanges suggest that the economic team was dysfunctional and that the minister of the economy was unable to alter the dubious behavior of Moreno. Over time, Moreno gained a reputation

---

[116] Edmund A. Walsh School of Foreign Service, Center for Latin American Studies. *Political Database of the Americas.* http://pdba.georgetown.edu/Elecdata/Arg/arg.html.

[117] "Lousteau: 'Moreno le miente a la Presidenta'" (2008). *La Nación*, August 5. www.lanacion.com.ar/nota.asp?nota_id=1036736.

[118] I. Bermudez (2009). "El BCRA ya no usa el IPC." *Clarín*, January 25.

[119] M. Kiguel (2013). "Think tank 20: the G-20 and central banks in the new world of unconventional monetary policy." *Brooking Foundation*, August. www.brookings.edu/wp-content/uploads/2016/07/TT20-argentina_kiguel-2.pdf.

[120] "Cruces entre Moreno y Redrado por la manera de medir la inflación" (2009). *El Cronista*, January 31. www.treslineas.com.ar/cruces-entre-moreno-redrado-manera-medir-inflacion-n-54738.html.

as a thug who used intimidation tactics, extortion and even violence to keep companies from raising prices and trading with firms in line with the government's initiatives.[121]

Reflecting the centralization of power, an article in *Clarín* notes: "[Ministers of the Economy] Felisa Miceli, Miguel Peirano, Martín Lousteau, and Carlos Fernández were all overshadowed by the domineering presence of their supposed subordinate Guillermo Moreno. And they had to accept that economic decisions were made by Kirchner, first as President and later as an occupant of the Olivos residence."[122] Redrado argues further that Peirano resigned when it became clear that nothing would change at the INDEC and Moreno's influence would remain high under the new President Fernández de Kirchner.[123] In addition to the INDEC scandal, President Fernández de Kirchner's nationalized pension funds and created the Bicentennial Fund to pay down foreign debts. When president of the Central Bank Redrado pushed back, President Kirchner accused him of wrongdoing and demanded his resignation. Thus, the concentration of power in the executive had effectively eliminated the ability of the minister of the economy and president of the central bank to influence economic policy or control the institutions formally under their control.

On February 1, 2013, Argentina had become the first country to be sanctioned by the IMF for providing inaccurate national financial statistics. Many Argentine economists confirmed that the statistics were fraudulent but would only do so "off the record" because they or their friends had been threatened with tax audits and other legal actions for questioning official statistics regarding inflation.[124] According to *The Economist*, "The American Statistical Association has protested at the political persecution faced by its Argentine colleagues, and is urging the United Nations to act, on the ground that the harassment is a violation of the right to freedom of expression."[125]

---

[121] Ibid., p. 95.

[122] L. Ceriotto (2009). "Boudou apuesta a ser un ministro con peso propio" (Boudou positions himself as a strong minister). *Clarín*, July 12. http://edant.clarin.com/diario/2009/07/12/elpais/p-01956876.htm.

[123] "Respalda ATE los dichos de Bevacqua y busca neutralizar 'un maquillaje' en el Indec" (2009). *La Nación*, July 6. www.lanacion.com.ar/1147626-respalda-ate-los-dichos-de-bevacqua-y-busca-neutralizar-un-maquillaje-en-el-indec.

[124] Interviews with several economists in Buenos Aires in July of 2012, who asked to remain unnamed.

[125] "Argentina's inflation problem: the price of cooking the books" (2012). *The Economist*, February 25. www.economist.com/node/21548229.

The depth of economic incredulity is occasionally comical. An interview on Greek television went viral in April of 2013 during which Minister of the Economy Hernán Lorenzino denied knowledge of the inflation rate in Argentina, then tried to dodge questions about the INDEC altering its economic data to present an unrealistically rosy view of the Argentine economy. This was particularly poignant given that Greek Finance Minister Georgios Alogoskoufis admitted in 2004 that his country had reported bogus data regarding its budget deficits when applying for membership in the euro.[126] Flustered, Lorenzino ended the live interview by abruptly declaring he had to leave.[127] Though the interview is humorous, the consequences of losing economic credibility are not. The international banking community refused to service Argentine debts, the formerly hard-currency Argentine peso became nonexchangeable, access to international financing dried up, and the Argentine people could not get access to their savings.

President Fernández de Kirchner tried to compensate for the loss of access to international capital in other ways. In March of 2008, she declared an increase in Argentina's export taxes on soybeans on a sliding scale from 35 to 44 percent. Farmers and others responded with massive and violent protests. She narrowly got approval in the Chamber of Deputies for a package of agricultural taxes, but the bill failed in the Senate due to a tiebreaking vote in opposition by her Vice President, Julio Cobos. She then tried to sidestep Congress by exploiting the Economic Emergency Law. Her actions triggered a backlash from a wide range of people, including the urban middle class, the rural sector and right and left parties.

President Fernández de Kirchner likely overestimated her ability to raise agricultural taxes because she surrounded herself with loyalists and dismissed those who challenged her. While Minister Lousteau had played a central role in negotiating the soy tax with farm leaders, he resigned on March 24, 2008, following disputes with Guillermo Moreno. Absent direct contact with farm leaders, it is likely that Moreno did not recognize the transformation of agriculture in the postcrisis environment from one based on a provincial organizational structure to one that based on the leasing of agricultural land across multiple provinces by large, centrally located investors (like Grupo Lose Grobo, led

---

[126] D. Howden & S. Castle (2004). "Greece admits deficit figures were fudged to secure euro entry." *The Independent*, November 16. www.independent.co.uk/news/world/europe/greece-admits-deficit-figures-were-fudged-to-secure-euro-entry-533389.html.

[127] M. Kanaguiser (2013). "Lorenzino, en apuros por los datos del Indec." *La Nación*, April 26. www.lanacion.com.ar/1576401-lorenzino-en-apuros-por-los-datos-del-indec.

by the "Soybean King" Gustavo Grobocopatel).[128] The centralized management structure and geographic breadth of corporate links undermined the Kirchners' more traditional province-based sources of political influence. It also meant that agricultural groups from different regions across the country were easily mobilized in opposition to the government policy. Following the bruising fight over soy taxes, Minister of the Economy Carlos Fernández resigned and the President's party suffered a major legislative loss on July 28, 2009.[129]

The government's need for liquidity to make debt payments remained high. Most pressingly, Argentina was obligated to meet US$13 billion in maturing debt payments from the 2005 debt swap negotiations by the end of 2010. To generate additional revenue, President Fernández de Kirchner requested that the Central Bank release US$6.59 billion from national reserves to pay a portion of the debt due at the end of 2010. The head of the Central Bank, Hernán Martín Pérez Redrado, refused. He argued that the nationalization of the pension funds, the appropriation of Central Bank reserves and inflation were all used inappropriately to finance increases in government spending, noting that fiscal outlays increased by 35 percent in 2009.[130] In response, President Fernández de Kirchner asked Redrado to resign. Redrado again refused and filed a suit against the President, citing central bank autonomy. President Fernández de Kirchner issued a decree dismissing him for "misconduct and having failed in his official duties," appointing the Central Bank's vice president, Miguel Pesce, as his successor. The decree enabled President Fernández de Kirchner to bypass Congress, where her power had been diminished by the struggle over agricultural policy and the loss in midterm elections.

Given a pressing need for capital, Minister of Economy Carlos Fernández also began a process of reengaging international creditors. With President Fernández de Kirchner's support, he began by persuading Congress to suspend the Lock Law that had forbidden agreements with creditors who had not agreed to the terms of the 2005 debt swap. In December of 2009, Argentina then filed a prospectus with the SEC for a new bond issue. Minister Fernández announced the details on April 15

---

[128] J. Kennedy (2010). "Argentine farmer is global soybean king with 630,000 acres." *Corn +Soybean Digest*, February 15. www.cornandsoybeandigest.com/marketing/argentine-farmer-global-soybean-king-630000-acres.

[129] Edmund A. Walsh School of Foreign Service, Center for Latin American Studies. *Political Database of the Americas.* http://pdba.georgetown.edu/Elecdata/Arg/arg.html.

[130] I. Bermudez (2010). "El Gobierno es uno de los que más se beneficia con el aumento de precios." *Clarín*, November 15.

and an offer was made on April 30, 2010.[131] The bond exchange closed on June 22, with a second stage closing on December 31. More than two-thirds of the remaining investors accepted the terms. Thus, by the end of 2010, 91.3 percent of all creditors had accepted the terms of a debt swap.

An IMF analysis of the agreements revealed similarities between those who settled in 2005 and 2010.[132] Specifically, all of the Italian retail investors and all of the non-litigant investors from the 2005 agreements settled. These accounted for US$14 billion of the US$18.4 billion in outstanding bond claims. On the other hand, none of those pursuing legal action as a result of not participating in the 2005 debt swaps agreed to the terms in 2010. These holdouts were composed principally of hedge funds including Aurelius Capital Management and Elliott Management headed by Paul Singer. Singer's strategy was to force Argentina to pay the face value of its debt by withholding Argentine assets and pursuing legal action that forbade US mediating banks from paying any creditors unless the holdouts were paid.

President Fernández de Kirchner's political fortunes improved throughout 2010. She rallied her political base by taking credit for economic growth while promoting a variety of social programs for the poor and increasing subsidies designed to keep utility and food prices low. She also took on media conglomerates *Clarín* and *La Nación*, and she passed electoral reform that favored big political parties, such as the PJ.[133] *The Wall Street Journal* summarized her resurgent popularity as follows:

President Cristina Kirchner and her husband and predecessor, Néstor, are enjoying a political resurgence ahead of next year's presidential election, after more than two years in which Argentines had grown increasingly disenchanted with them. The Peronist power couple is benefiting from a brisk economic recovery, a surge of nationalism triggered by a bicentennial celebration and the country's strong early showing in the World Cup, as well as missteps by the deeply divided opposition. A June poll by the Management & Fit consultancy put Mrs. Kirchner's job-approval rating at 31.5 percent, up nearly nine points since September, a significant swing in a fragmented political environment.[134]

On October 28, 2010, former President Néstor Kirchner died unexpectedly from a heart attack. His death was met with an outpouring of

---

[131] Hornbeck. "Argentina's Defaulted Sovereign Debt," pp. 6–7.

[132] Hornbeck. "Argentina's Defaulted Sovereign Debt," p 7.

[133] Thanks to Kyle Yonker for his research on this topic.

[134] M. Moffett (2010). "Kirchners climb in Argentine polls." *Wall Street Journal*, July 1. http://online.wsj.com/article/SB10001424052748703374104575337091154159502.html.

sympathy and political support that, ironically, helped further rebuild President Fernández de Kirchner's political base. With what the opposition considered a sympathy vote on October 23, 2011, Cristina Fernández de Kirchner, Amando Boudou and the Victory Front Alliance won 53.9 percent of the vote compared to 16.8 percent for Hermes Juan Binner, Norma Elena Morandini and the Broad Progressive Front Alliance, and 11.1 percent going to Luis Ricardo Alfonsín and Javier González Fraga and the Union Alliance for Social Development.[135] The FPV-PJ alliance won 66.6 percent of the votes and 16 seats in the Senate and 38.46 percent of the votes and 50 seats in the Chamber of Deputies.

Following her electoral success, President Fernández de Kirchner took an increasingly nationalistic and hardline position toward foreign owners of formerly Argentine companies, often using them as scapegoats to distract public attention away from ever-increasing inflation and capital flight. The most striking example of this was the expropriation of a controlling stake in YPF S.A., an oil and gas company owned by the Spanish company Repsol, in May of 2012. The nationalization of 51 percent of YPF was orchestrated by Julio De Vido, Minister of Federal Planning Public Investment and Services, and Axel Kicilloff, Deputy Finance Minister. Congress enthusiastically supported the takeover by passing a bill that reflected its nationalistic sentiments entitled, "On Argentina's Hydrocarbon Sovereignty."[136]

While economic growth continued to be strong in 2011 (at 9.2 percent based on national statistics or 4.9 percent based on data from the World Bank), the expropriation of YPF reflected deeper problems in the Argentine economy.[137] YPF had been nationalized in part because of a shift from Argentina being a net exporter of energy prior to 2011 to a US$3.4 billion importer of oil and gas in 2012. One of the reasons given for the shift was that companies like YPF were thought to be underinvesting in energy production, especially given the recent discovery of significant shale reserves in Vaca Muerta. To increase local investment, the government instituted a variety of policies designed to make it more difficult for foreign investors to repatriate profits. These included asymmetric taxes

[135] Edmund A. Walsh School of Foreign Service, Center for Latin American Studies. *Political Database of the Americas.* http://pdba.georgetown.edu/Elecdata/Arg/arg.html.

[136] A. Fontevecchia (2012). "Shale gas wars: Argentina fracks Respol, Kirchner takes YPR." *Forbes,* April 17. www.forbes.com/sites/afontevecchia/2012/04/17/shale-gas-wars-on-argentinas-nationalization-of-repsol-ypf/#2ebd33613f05.

[137] "World development indicators" (n.d.). *World Bank.* http://databank.worldbank.org/ddp/home.do?Step=3&id=4; S. Romero (2012). "Move on oil company draws praise in Argentina, where growth continues." *New York Times,* April 26. www.nytimes.com/2012/04/27/world/americas/ypf-nationalization-draws-praise-in-argentina.html.

on imports and exports, capital controls and the suspension of convertibility between pesos to dollars.[138]

3.4.4   Reaching Out to Global Markets

By 2012, growth and export revenues were declining, while inflation and government expenditure were continuing to rise. As conditions deteriorated, President Fernández de Kirchner attempted to settle outstanding issues with YPF and reengage international investors.

First, in October of 2013, Minister of the Economy Hernán Lorenzino altered Argentina's long-standing policy of disputing arbitration claims filed by foreign companies as a result of the 2001 financial crisis. Settlements were reached with five companies, including the French media conglomerate Vivendi SA, British electricity and gas utility National Grid PLC, Continental Casualty Company (a subsidiary of the American financial and insurance company), the American water company Azurix and Blue Ridge Investments (a wholly owned subsidiary of Bank of America).[139] These companies had pursued arbitration under bilateral investment treaties using the World Bank's ICSID or the Rules of the United Nations Commission on International Trade Law (UNCITRAL Rules). While the ICSID convention requires member states to enforce its verdicts, Argentina has previously disputed automatic enforcement and instead claimed the right to submit the rulings to its domestic courts.

While the Argentine government argued that it would continue to give legal primacy to its domestic courts, the settlement enabled the IMF and World Bank to provide financial support to Argentina and both agreed to help it resolve ongoing disputes with holdout investors. On October 13, Minister of the Economy Lorenzino announced an agreement with the World Bank on a multiyear project to provide loans worth around US$3 billion to promote programs for the poor (he also announced that Argentina's Central Bank was seeking to bolster its reserves by negotiating a US$10 billion loan with

---

[138] "Respol expropriation: so who is eating Argentina's lunch now?" (2013). *EurActiv*, April 23. www.euractiv.com/section/trade-society/opinion/repsol-expropriation-so-who-is-eating-argentina-s-lunch-now.

[139] Herbet Smith Freehills (2013). "Argentina settles five outstanding investment treaty arbitration claims in historic break with its anti-enforcement Stance." *Arbitration Notes*, November 14. http://hsfnotes.com/arbitration/2013/10/14/argentina-settles-five-outstanding-investment-treaty-arbitration-claims-in-historic-break-with-its-anti-enforcement-stance.

China).[140] Settling outstanding disputes with Azurix and Blue Ridge Investments also opened up the possibility of reinstituting Argentina's trading privileges under the Generalized System of Preferences (GSP) with the United States.

Second, on January 21, 2014, Economy Minister Kicillof announced that the government "is willing to resolve 'inherited debt' from previous governments and was about to pay the Paris Club in 2008 before the collapse of Lehman Brothers Holdings Inc."[141] He met with negotiators in Paris the next day. In May, the Paris Club reported that it had reached an agreement with Argentina to repay US$9.7 billion over a five-year period and that the interest on the outstanding debt would be lowered from 7 percent to 3 percent if the amount was paid in full during this period. Kicillof announced an initial capital payment of US $650 million in July and US$500 million in May 2015. The agreement enabled export credit agencies in Paris Club countries to provide services to exporters interested in doing business in Argentina.[142] Taking on a populist tone, Kicillof declared that, "Today Argentina is on the path to regularizing and paying for the broken plates that 40 years of neoliberalism left us."[143]

Third, Argentina held talks with the IMF regarding its financial statistics and issued a new inflation index on February 13, 2014.[144] The IMF agreed that Argentina was making progress, but asked for more. More than two years after the initial request, on June 3, 2015, the IMF found again that remedial measures had "not been sufficient" and that Argentina was not yet in compliance with its obligations under Article VIII, Section 5 regarding the provision of these data.[145] Argentina was granted another extension, with a requirement to complete specified corrections by July 15, 2015.

Fourth, in February of 2014, Repsol announced that it had agreed to drop its legal claims against Argentina and accept US$5 billion in

---

[140] U. Rindebro (2013). "Partnership with World Bank could provide Argentina with US $3bn in loans." *BNamerica*, October 11.

[141] K. Parks (2014). "Argentina agrees to pay $9.7 billion to Paris Club." *Wall Street Journal*, May 28.

[142] Ibid.

[143] C. Devereux & P. Rosendo González (2014). "Argentina will repay Paris Club debt 13 years after default." *Bloomberg Business*, May 29. www.bloomberg.com/news/articles/2014-05-29/argentina-agrees-to-repay-9-7-billion-to-paris-club-creditors.

[144] S. Romig (2014). "IMF says Argentina needs to improve data more." *Wall Street Journal*, June 6. www.wsj.com/articles/imf-says-argentina-needs-to-improve-data-more-1402091563.

[145] International Monetary Fund (2015). Statement by the IMF Executive Board on Argentina, Press Release No. 15/252, June 3.

guaranteed Argentine bonds as compensation for the 51 percent expropriation of YPF.[146] The agreement also settled lawsuits pending in the United States and Spain against Chevron, which had invested with YPF in newly found shale gas reserves. The terms of the settlement represented a significant victory for Argentina given that it agreed to half of the amount that Repsol had been seeking through a World Bank tribunal. In addition, by settling the dispute, Argentina opened itself up to the international investments it needed to develop the Vaca Muerta shale gas reserves.

In short, after the Argentine economy began to falter in 2012, it tried a variety of domestic strategies to address shortages of foreign currency. Though outwardly defiant, it mended fences with international investors by settling outstanding arbitration claims, reaching a compensation agreement for the YPF nationalization, resolving the issue of economic statistics with the IMF and reaching a deal with Paris Club members.

The principal outstanding international financial problem involved the holdouts from the 2005 and 2010 debt renegotiations. The holdouts first sued for the right to place an "attach order" on assets held by the Argentine central bank in the Federal Reserve Bank of New York.[147] A district court found in favor of the investors, but an appellate court overturned its ruling on July 5, 2011, arguing that Argentina's Central Bank assets were immune from attachment. The case was appealed to the Supreme Court, but on June 25, 2012, the Supreme Court refused to hear the case.

The holdouts were more successful in suing for equal treatment under a policy based on the principle of *pari passu* which stipulates that all parties in a contract must be treated equally. No parties could be given preferential treatment, so Argentina could not use its funds in the Bank of New York Melon Bank Corporation to pay those who had accepted the exchange bonds in 2005 and 2010 without also paying the holdouts. In January of 2012, US District Judge Thomas Griesa blocked Argentina from paying holders of its restructured debt unless it also paid US$4.65 billion to a group of holdouts led by Paul Singer's NML Capital.[148] According to Martin Guzman and Joseph Stiglitz, the net return for NML would be 1,500 percent of its initial investment due to the debt

---

[146] S. Reed & R. Minder (2014). "Repsol in $5 billion settlement with Argentina." *New York Times*, February 25. www.nytimes.com/2014/02/26/business/international/repsol-said-to-reach-settlement-with-argentina.html.

[147] For a review of these cases, see: Hornbeck. "Argentina's Defaulted Sovereign Debt."

[148] B. Van Voris (2015). "Argentina 'me-too' bond holdouts seek equal-treatment ruling." *Bloomberg Business*, May 29. www.bloomberg.com/news/articles/2015-05-29/argentina-me-too-bond-holdouts-seek-equal-treatment-ruling.

and a "compulsory" interest rate of 9 percent under New York law.[149] An appellate court concurred on October 26, 2012, as did a district court on November 21, 2012. An appellate court then stayed the filing on February 27, 2013, just prior to the next payment due to the exchange bondholders, but it left in question the prospect that Argentina would have to pay the holdouts US$1.3 billion. In June of 2014, the US Supreme Court refused to hear an appeal against Judge Griesa's ruling. This created chaos and uncertainty. As summarized by *The Economist*:

Argentine behaviour since the Supreme Court decision has been erratic, to put it mildly. President Cristina Fernández de Kirchner and Axel Kicillof, her economy minister, have both expressed willingness to negotiate in certain circumstances, only to blast the court ruling and NML in others. They have taken out full-page adverts in American newspapers lambasting Judge Griesa's decision; Mr. Kicillof has delivered impassioned diatribes against vulture funds to the United Nations (UN) and Organisation of American States (OAS).[150]

Complicating the situation, approximately 500 additional companies are seeking comparable compensation.[151] Under a "Rights upon Future Offers" (RUFO) clause written into the restructured bond contracts, no offers better than those negotiated in 2005 and 2010 can be extended to anyone without being extended to all.[152] The RUFO was set to expire on December 31, 2014. Consequently, when the Supreme Court refused to consider Argentina's appeal, negotiations effectively halted until January 1, 2015, since RUFO could completely overturn the previous debt swap agreements at huge expense. Economy Minister Axel Kicillof responded that Argentina was willing to offer the holdouts similar terms to the 2005 and 2010 debt swaps and was interested in finding a solution to pay all creditors, including the "me too" holdouts, but could not afford to pay everybody the face value plus interest of the original debt.[153]

The judge had set the deadline of July 10 for a deal. On July 30, 2014, Economy Minister Alex Kicillof said that investors had rejected his terms

---

[149] M. Guzman & J. Stiglitz (2016). "How hedge funds held Argentina for ransom." *New York Times*, April 1. www.nytimes.com/2016/04/01/opinion/how-hedge-funds-held-argentina-for-ransom.html.

[150] "Argentina and the holdouts: tick tock" (2014). *The Economist*, July 17. www.economist.com/americas-view/2014/07/17/tick-tock.

[151] NML Capital Ltd. v. Republic of Argentina, 14-cv-08601, US District Court, Southern District of New York (Manhattan).

[152] "Argentina and the holdouts: tick tock" (2014). *The Economist*, July 17. www.economist.com/americas-view/2014/07/17/tick-tock.

[153] C. Russo (2015). "Argentine bonds rally after holdout proposal to resume talks." *Bloomberg Business*, February 20.

and the government would "immediately be in default" on about US$20 billion worth of debt.[154] In effect, Argentina defaulted on its debt because it was forbidden by a New York judge from paying bondholders with whom it had reached a debt restructuring agreements in 2005 and 2010. Judge Grieca has no jurisdiction over Argentina, but does have jurisdiction over the Bank of New York Mellon Corporation which holds Argentine funds.[155] In October of 2015, a US appeals court upheld the 2014 ruling and refused to force the Bank of New York Mellon Corporation to pay any of the bondholders using the funds on deposit from the government of Argentina.[156]

In April 2015, YPF issued a ten-year bond, the Bonar 2024, in an attempt to raise capital to invest in the Vaca Muerta shale reserve (and make up a disappointing bond issued in February that raised only a third of its desired revenue).[157] It sold US$1.4 billion worth of bonds. Argentina claimed that the Bonar 2024 bonds were domestic and therefore not subject to the rules imposed in 2012 by US District Judge Griesa. The holdouts, led by NML, argued that the Bonar 2024 bonds were subject to the ruling because they were being traded by Deutsche Bank and therefore demonstrated that Argentina had access to international capital even though it defaulted in July of 2014. US District Judge Griesa agreed to consider NML's request that "Argentina's BONAR 2024 Bonds and its other External Indebtedness also are subject to the Equal Treatment Provision."[158] Minister of the Economy Kicillof argued that the Bonar 2024 was "issued to address compensation for Repsol and is not related to the restructuring of debt, or with those who enter the exchange or with the holdouts. So it's a bonus that has nothing to do with vultures."[159] With that, President Fernández de Kirchner and Minister of the Economy Kicillof held out against the holdouts they called "vultures" and

---

[154] "Argentina defaults for second time" (2014). *BBC News*, July 31. www.bbc.com/news/business-28578179.

[155] M. O'Brien (2014). "Everything you need to know about Argentina's weird default." *Washington Post*, August 3. www.washingtonpost.com/news/wonk/wp/2014/08/03/everything-you-need-to-know-about-argentinas-weird-default/?utm_term=.f5cafc5bb1db.

[156] J. Ax (2015). "U.S. court rejects creditors' bid for Argentine funds held by BNY Mellon." *Reuters*, October 5. www.reuters.com/article/us-argentina-debt-court/u-s-court-rejects-creditors-bid-for-argentine-funds-held-by-bny-mellon-idUSKCN0RZ1K 120151005.

[157] "Argentina's YPF wants to issue new 10-yr bond – sources" (2015). *Reuters*, April 22. www.reuters.com/article/argentina-ypf/argentinas-ypf-wants-to-issue-new-10-yr-bond-sources-idUSL5N0XJ5D920150422.

[158] B. Van Voris & K. Porzecanski (2015). "Argentina bondholders may seek to block Bonar 2024 payments." *Bloomberg Business*, July 16. www.bloomberg.com/news/articles/2015-07-16/holders-of-argentine-bonds-may-seek-to-block-bonar-24-payments.

[159] "Kicillof: 'Griesa cannot block the charging of the BONAR 2024'" (2015). *The Chronicler*, August 16. www.cronista.com/economiapolitica/Kicillof-Griesa-no-puede-bloquear-el-cobro-del-Bonar-2024-20150816-0001.html.

"financial terrorists" through the presidential elections in October 25, 2015. They left the newly elected President Mauricio Macri and his Minister of the Economy Alfonso Prat-Gay with a fragile economy, low foreign exchange reserves and a legacy of difficult and unfinished negotiations with foreign investors.

3.4.5   Prudence and Graduate Adaptation

President Mauricio Macri and his Republican Proposal party entered the presidency in a relatively weak position following a runoff election on November 22, 2015. Upon entering office, he attempted to reestablish trust in Argentina's economic institutions and those leading them, and build sufficient political capacity to address Argentina's underlying problems. As a step forward in that process, he appointed Alfonso Prat-Gay as minister of the economy. Prat-Gay had been president of the Bank of Argentina from December 2002 to September 2004, during which time he gained a reputation for promoting Central Bank independence, anti-inflationary policies and debt restructuring. He was recognized as the Central Bank Governor of the Year by *Euromoney*.[160]

On February 2, 2016, Prat-Gay reached an agreement with a group of Italian bondholders who settled for US$1.35 billion.[161] He then reached an agreement with two hedge funds, Montreux Capital and EM Ltd., who settled for US$1.1 billion on February 17. On February 29, he agreed to a settlement of US$4.65 billion with the largest holdout creditors – NML Capital (a subsidiary of Elliott Management led by Paul Singer), Aurelius Capital and Dart Management.[162] On April 13, 2016, a federal appeals court in New York upheld a decision by Judge Griesa on February 19, to lift his injunction blocking Argentina's access to international creditors if Argentina repealed laws barring payments to the holdouts and pays them.[163] On May 31, the Argentine Senate ratified the settlement and lifted its prohibition against paying the holdouts.[164]

---

[160] F. Salmon (2004). "Central bank governor of the year 2004: Alfonso Prat-Gay." *Euromoney*, September 1. www.euromoney.com/Article/1001457/Title.html.
[161] "Why Argentina is ending its long debt battle" (2016). *The Economist*, March 3. www.economist.com/the-economist-explains/2016/03/03/why-argentina-is-ending-its-long-debt-battle.
[162] Ibid.
[163] "The green light" (2016). *The Economist*, April 16. www.economist.com/finance-and-economics/2016/04/16/the-green-light.
[164] U. Goni (2017). "Argentina settles creditor dispute with $4.6 billion deal after marathon session." *The Guardian*, February 29. www.theguardian.com/world/2016/feb/29/argentina-settles-creditor-dispute-deal.

The resolution provided NML capital with a payment of US$2.28 billion, approximately half of its original demand, for an effective rate of return of 1,180 percent.[165] Court-appointed mediator Daniel Pollock described President Macri and Minister of the Economy Prat-Gay's "course correction ... [as] nothing short of heroic."[166] This settled the battle with vulture funds who refused to accept the terms of the debt negotiations in 2005 and 2010 and had sued Argentina in US federal court.

The settlement was part of plan to restore Argentina's access to international credit markets.[167] President Macri and Minister of the Economy Alfonso Prat-Gay also dismantled exchange controls, ended most export taxes, devalued the peso and begun to remove subsidies for electricity, gas, water and transportation.[168] President Macri has also tried to reduce labor costs, loosen labor laws, and shrink the public sector. All of these efforts have required political and legislative support. Macri benefited from strong resentment by labor and other groups in society against President Fernández de Kirchner. His coalition also won strong victories in midterm elections in October of 2017.

President Macri's successes have, however, been undermined by political uncertainty resulting from confusion and turnover within his economic team. In the face of capital outflows in June of 2018, Central Bank President Sturzenegger first announced that the Central Bank would do less in the future to sustain the peso except in "disruptive situations," but then he sold reserves in an effort to hold the peso steady, then he stopped selling reserves and let the peso slide.[169] These swings in behavior generated high levels of uncertainty about what the Central Bank would do in the future. To restore confidence, President Macri replaced Sturzenegger with Nicolás Caputo, the current minister of the economy and a former central banker, and made Nicolás Dujovne, the new minister of the economy.

---

[165] Guzman & Stiglitz. "How hedge funds held Argentina for ransom."

[166] Goni. "Argentina settles creditor dispute."

[167] "How Mauricio Macri is trying to rehabilitate Argentina's economy" (2016). *The Economist.* September 23. www.economist.com/the-economist-explains/2016/09/23/how-mauricio-macri-is-trying-to-rehabilitate-argentinas-economy.

[168] "At mid-term elections, Argentina chooses between sobriety and Peronism" (2017). *The Economist,* October 21. www.economist.com/the-americas/2017/10/21/at-mid-term-elections-argentina-chooses-between-sobriety-and-peronism.

[169] "Why countries like Argentina and Turkey fret about exchange rates" (2018). *The Economist,* June 21. www.economist.com/finance-and-economics/2018/06/21/why-countries-like-argentina-and-turkey-fret-about-exchange-rates.

In September of 2018, Dujovne announced that he had secured an agreement with the IMF to increase a US$50 billion loan negotiated in June by US$7.1 billion. In Christine Lagarde's words, "This is the biggest loan in the history of the IMF."[170] The IMF loan requires the Argentine government to balance the government budget by 2020 and reach a fiscal surplus in the near future. It also prohibits the central bank from intervening in the economy unless the peso falls below 44 pesos to the dollar (being currently at about 39 pesos to the dollar). Everything looked like it was heading in the right direction until one day before the announcement when Nicolás Caputo resigned as president of Argentina's Central Bank over disagreements pertaining to the IMF guidelines limiting Central Bank intervention.[171] So, it appears that uncertainty will continue to be high and the Argentine tango with international financial markets will continue to be dramatic.

3.4.6   Lessons from the Postcrisis Period

The postcrisis era can be divided into four periods. During the first period, from 2002 to 2005, authority, deference and implementation capacity were all high (category 1, row 1 in Figure 3.11). President Néstor Kirchner and Roberto Lavagna were able to rebuild local and international confidence in Argentina's leadership. Though their policy agenda was populist, Lavagna was able to limit political excesses and rebuild the economy while decreasing government expenditure as a percentage of GDP and holding inflation in check. He exploited his institutional authority, secured deference from the President and international community, and secured sufficient political support to keep Argentina in the low-risk sweet spot on the RIC as it recovered from the crisis. They were also aided by a surge in global demand and an increase in prices for soybeans. Agricultural exports provided a substantial boost to the economy. Despite accepting an enormous haircut, investor risk diminished dramatically following the conclusion of debt negotiations in 2005.

In the second period from 2005-2015, authority and implementation capacity varied while deference declined (category 5). Presidents

---

[170] U. Goni (2018). "Argentina gets biggest loan in IMF's history at $57bn." *The Guardian*, September 26. www.theguardian.com/world/2018/sep/26/argentina-imf-biggest-loan.

[171] D. Gallas (2018), "Argentina's central bank boss Luis Caputo quits after three months." *BBC News*, September 25. www.bbc.com/news/business-45643974.

The Power to Act			Prediction		Outcome	
Authority to Act	Deference to Technocrats	Implementation Capacity of National Politicians	Impact of Technocrats	Behavior	Role of Technocrats	Market Behavior
1 High	High	High or Not Necessary	Can constrain or expand policy flexibility	Can validate policy, targeted and broad strategies may be effective	Maximum bargaining power	2002–2005: Lavagna builds credibility of Finance Minister and bolsters Kirchner	Negotiates debt default and haircut
5 High or Low	Low	High or Not Necessary	Confrontational technocrats likely to be replaced with sycophants	Cannot validate policy, targeted and broad strategies by politicians possible	No economic validation, political exuberance likely	2005–2015: Cristina Fernández de Kirchner centralizes authority, dismisses challenging technocrats, appoints loyalists and thugs	Soybean tax backfires, holdouts sue in New York courts
1 High	High	High or Not Necessary	Can constrain or expand policy flexibility	Can validate policy, targeted and broad strategies may be effective	Maximum bargaining power	2015–2017: Prat-Gay rebuilds credibility of Finance Minister and bolsters Marci	Debt with holdouts is resolved, distorting policies are resolved, successful reentry into bond markets
5 High or Low	Low	High or Not Necessary	Confrontational technocrats likely to be replaced with sycophants	Cannot validate policy, targeted and broad strategies by politicians possible	No economic validation, political exuberance likely	2018: chaotic actions by Central Bank and internal transitions undercut confidence in economic team, Marci attempts to compensate through personnel changes	Inflation builds, IMF assistance secured

Figure 3.11 Shaping policy and behavior in Argentina, 2002–2017.

Néstor Kirchner and Cristina Fernández de Kirchner began consolidating power, reducing the authority of the economy minister and replacing economic technocrats who challenged them with loyalists. Their legislative capacity waxed and waned, but they often compensated by asserting executive authority. The presidents engaged in a wide variety of strategies to extract revenue from other sources (including export taxes and the nationalization of pension funds and foreign companies), imposed a variety of restrictive policies in order to control capital flight (including capital controls on local Argentines as well as importers and exporters) and manipulated basic economic information. When alternative sources of revenue proved insufficient, President Cristina Fernández de Kirchner and her ministers of the economy reached agreements with the IMF, the Paris Club, corporate litigants and over 91 percent of bondholders.

In the third period, from 2015-17, authority, deference and legislative capacity were all high (category 1). Newly elected President Mauricio Macri attempted to reestablish trust in Argentina's economic institutions. He appointed Alfonso Prat-Gay, a well-known and highly respected minister of the economy, and worked closely with him in securing Argentina's reentry into global financial markets. They succeeded in resolving the payments disputes with bondholders left over from the 2001 crisis and the 2005 and 2010 debt restructuring negotiations, selling a government bond and securing financing from the IMF. Macri also bolstered his political stature following successful midterm elections in 2017.

In 2018, however, confidence in the economic team declined following seemingly disparate responses by the Central Bank to capital flight and the resignation of the president of the Central Bank over the conditions associated with the IMF bailout. With technocratic influence increasingly unclear, uncertainty about the direction and efficacy of Argentina's future policies increased. As expected, investor risk responded in kind. Between January of 2006 and May of 2018, interest rates were high but steady at about 30 percent; in May they jumped to 40 percent, in August they jumped to 60 percent and in October they passed 71 percent.[172]

3.5   Conclusion: Lessons from the Argentine Tango

What can we learn from the dramatic dance among Argentine Presidents, economic technocrats and foreign investors?

- **Lesson 1: The ability of the minister of the economy and other economic technocrats to be oracles, heroes and villains varies over time as a function of the levels of authority, deference and implementation capacity they are able to sustain.**

The economic team in Argentina is formally led by the minister of the economy, who is appointed by the president and serves as head of the Ministry of Economy and Public Finance. The governor of the Central Bank of Argentina (BCRA) reports to the minister of the economy. Since Argentina's transition to democratic rule in 1983, ministers of the economy and central bankers have promoted wide-ranging institutional innovations to manage economic policy and alter market behavior at home and abroad. While many failed, some succeeded for multiple years.

Some ministers of the economy were selected for their expertise or heroic reputations and are (or at least were) highly respected by the president and investors at home and abroad.[173] Others were selected because they were loyalists (or at least nonthreatening) to the president. Many of the latter are considered sycophants and are commonly described as either inept or corrupt. Some presidents had the political will and capacity to protect their economic team and bring supporting legislation to fruition; others were unwilling or unable to do so.

---

[172] LEBAC interest rates and adjustment coefficients established by the BCRA, Monetary Statistics Department, Central Bank of the Argentina Republic. www.bcra.gob.ar/ PublicacionesEstadisticas/Cuadros_estandarizados_series_estadisticas_i.asp?prevPage=stat.

[173] Argentina has the paradoxical reputation of being home to great economists and an awful economy. N. Smith (2015). "Argentina: great economists, awful economy." *Bloomberg*, August 4. www.bloomberg.com/view/articles/2015-08-04/argentina-is-land-of-great-economists-awful-economy.

Deference from the private sector as well as the president also shifted over time. Indeed, some ministers who were considered oracles and praised as heroes have fallen from grace and are now considered villains by many. Former Minister of the Economy Domingo Cavallo is the most prominent fallen hero of economic policy in Argentina.

- **Lesson 2: Everybody manipulates authority.**

The ability of international bond holders and foreign companies to bargain with Argentina varied with the degree to which they were able to assert their authority, generate deference and/or exploit electoral capacity to their advantage. Like the several European politicians who used their domestic authorities and institutions to challenge the European Central Bank – by, for example, calling for a referendum on austerity measures or asserting the jurisdiction of national courts and legislatures over international agreements – bondholder holdouts asserted their contractual authority and the jurisdiction of a US court to keep Argentina from completing debt-reduction agreements.

- **Lesson 3: Institutions rely on continued support and deference.**

Even seemingly strong laws and institutions weaken when deference to them declines or their supporters lack the political will and capacity to bring reinforcing legislation to fruition. After its initial success in lowering inflation in 1985, for example, the economic program known as the Austral Plan faltered when President Raúl Alfonsín succumbed to societal pressures to raise military and public-sector wages. Even the famed Convertibility Plan – which beat inflation throughout the 1990s by pegging the peso to the dollar at 1:1 and imposing rigid restrictions on Argentine monetary policy – required ongoing support. It is highly unlikely that the Convertibility Plan would have survived the Mexican peso crisis in 1994–1995 without Minister of the Economy Cavallo's intervention. Yet, rather than acknowledging the crucial role played by Cavallo and other individuals, many praised the resilience of the institution itself. Arguing that the Convertibility Plan would last "forever," President Menem replaced Cavallo with a more deferential minister of the economy. In doing so, he doing so weakened the government's commitment to the tight fiscal policies at the federal and provincial levels that were needed to sustain the Convertibility Plan. Consequently, "forever" turned out to be six years. Those who consider the European institutions to be self-sustaining or the existence of a fixed-exchange-rate regime or independent central bank or other institutions as bulwarks against inflation should take note.

- **Lesson 4: Prevailing conditions affect political as well as economic behavior.**

Argentine presidents tend to defer to strong ministers of the economy and accept limits on their economic policy-making authority when the economy is poor or they are weak politically. For example, President Fernando de la Rúa reappointed the famed inflation warrior Cavallo as minister of the economy in March of 2001 to restore market confidence in Argentina's economic policy. The Argentine *Congreso* doubled down on the President's bet by granting Cavallo "superpowers" to act without consultation. In contrast, national politicians tend to challenge constraints on their authority and demand greater deference from others when political and economic conditions improve. President Menem dismissed Minister of the Economy Cavallo in 1996 following his reelection and Argentina's quick recovery from the Mexican peso crisis; similarly, President Néstor Kirchner replaced Minister of the Economy Roberto Lavagna in 2005 after Argentina's postcrisis recovery and debt negotiations were well underway. In each case, the presidents appointed more deferential and less politically competitive ministers of the economy. Absent deference, economic technocrats have little influence over whether their policies will be sustained and whether economic policies beyond their control – including fiscal spending, taxation, subsidies and others – will support or contradict their efforts.

- **Lesson 5: Permissive economic conditions can empower political leaders, but they also create perverse incentives.**

In the early 1990s, revenues generated from the privatization of public utilities enabled President Menem to placate potential union and business critics of the Convertibility Plan. In the early 2000s, surging export earnings from soybean production lessened Argentina's dependence on global financial markets and enabled President Kirchner and Economy Minister Lavagna to take a hardline bargaining position with foreign investors and the IMF.

At the same time, permissive economic conditions can encourage perverse behavior. Net financial inflows are often treated as rewards for good behavior and permission to engage in less prudent behavior – even when they are the result of exogenous factors.[174] For example,

---

[174] Argentina is not the only country to fall prey to the seduction of net capital inflows or permissive market conditions. The same type of behavior took place in 2001 when European investors, especially from Germany and France, poured money into Greece. The Greeks had not become paragons of good economic policy; rather, Greece had just adopted the euro and was therefore considered as safe an investment as the rest of the

the success of the Convertibility Plan in buffering Argentina from the Mexican peso crisis in 1995 combined with recognition of Argentina as the poster child of economic development during the annual meeting of the IMF and World Bank in 1998 led to a dramatic increase in foreign capital inflows from 1995 through the first quarter of 1999. This diminished market pressure on President Menem to maintain fiscal discipline. It did not matter that the inflow was driven more by the collapse of economies in Asia than it was by "good" behavior in Argentina. By the second quarter of 1999, Argentina and much of South America experienced a "sudden stop" in capital inflows (a fall from over 5 percent of GDP in the second quarter of 1999 to 1 percent a year later), while the risk spread of the Emerging Market Bond Index rose in the same period (from less than 500 basis points to more than 1,600 basis points).[175]

To offset contagion fears, the IMF approved a three-year Stand-By agreement worth US$7.2 billion. IMF Managing Director Stanley Fischer compounded the illusion of economic soundness by praising Argentina for having "embarked on a strong economic program aimed at promoting the recovery and sustained growth of the economy, with continued price stability."[176] As a result, when the crash came in 2001, Argentina owed private bondholders US$81.8 billion, the Paris Club countries US$6.3 billion and the IMF US$9.5 billion.[177]

Of course, permissive economic conditions also generate perverse incentives for investors, domestic borrowers and consumers. The perverse incentives of foreign investors and brokers associated with the emerging market index in Argentina are well documented.[178] Similar dynamics appeared domestically in consumer banking following the creation of the Convertibility Plan. Pent-up consumer demand led to an increase in

---

Eurozone. Market pressure for economic reform in Greece evaporated as money sloshed in. A similar dynamic also took place in the United States in 2010 and 2011 when inflows of skittish European investors shifted their portfolios to US markets, thereby reducing market pressure on Congress and the president to reach an accord on debt limits and the federal budget. Despite repeated bloviating by American politicians that investors would surely flee the United States unless it got its budget and debt in order, money surged inward and interest rates remained low. Thus, rather than disciplining political behavior in Argentina, Greece or the United States, markets were permissive and let national politicians off the hook.

[175] Calvo, Izquierdo & Talvi. *Sudden Stops*.

[176] "IMF approves $7.2 billion three-year Stand-By credit for Argentina" (2000). *IMF Survey*, 29(6), March 20. www.imf.org/external/pubs/ft/survey/2000/032000.pdf. For an internal criticism of IMF policy with regard to Argentina, see: Mussa. *Argentina and the Fund*.

[177] Hornbeck. "Argentina's Defaulted Sovereign Debt," p. 3.

[178] Blustein. *And the Money Kept Rolling In*.

borrowing for a wide range of goods, from washing machines to cars and homes. This trend continued throughout the 1990s despite a shift in lending from pesos to dollars which passed the risk of a currency devaluation from lenders to borrowers. The perception among borrowers that the pegged exchange rate would go on forever is similar to the so-called "irrational exuberance" of US and European borrowers and investors who assumed that home values would always continue to go up. The rise of store-specific credit cards in Argentina in the late 2000s created an additional surge in consumer borrowing that paralleled the buildup of consumer credit in the United States and elsewhere in the same time period.

In sum, Argentina's experiences demonstrate repeatedly that national politicians tend to become politically exuberant when they are not matched with strong ministers of the economy or central bankers. They are also empowered – yet misdirected by – permissive economic conditions. Lack of validation by a strong and credible minister of the economy or central banker increases uncertainty regarding the direction and likely success of national economic policy; similarly, lack of political leadership and implementation capacity increase uncertainty that economic policies will be sustainable and promises will be kept.

At the same time, despite its tumultuous history, Argentina's experiences over the past thirty years provide a glimmer of optimism for the United States and Europe. Authority, deference and political capacity are highly variable. Under the right circumstances, strong economic leaders can empower and substitute for weak politicians. When matched with strong yet deferential politicians, strong ministers of finance – like Cavallo, Lavagna, and perhaps Dujovne – can build confidence in their economies and drive their countries forward. Their success also suggests that the nationalist rhetoric that has come to dominate European and American politics is not necessarily long lasting nor fatally destructive. Even if the current situation is turbulent, it is not permanent. New leaders and new circumstances will bring new possibilities.

4   The Federal Reserve Goes Political

4.1   The Federal Reserve Goes Political

> Monetary policy can be a powerful tool, but it is not a panacea for the problems currently faced by the U.S. economy. Fostering healthy growth and job creation is a shared responsibility of all economic policymakers, in close cooperation with the private sector.
>
> Ben Bernanke, Chairman of the Federal Reserve[1]

In the wake of the recent financial crisis, Federal Reserve Chairman Ben Bernanke argued repeatedly that fostering healthy growth and job creation required legislative action.[2] He warned that continued political battles over fiscal and monetary policy, financial regulation and the debt ceiling were "deeply irresponsible" and would have "catastrophic consequences for the economy that could last for decades."[3] At the same time, like Alan Greenspan before him, Bernanke joined secretaries of the Treasury and other technocrats in guiding and enabling legislation, helping presidents outmaneuver critics and compensating for political uncertainty when political battles between the President and Congress stalled economic legislation. Far from being apolitical actors, these technocrats manipulated authority, exploited deference from politicians and business leaders, and alternately bolstered and challenged national politicians in order to shape US economic policy, manage market behavior and coordinate global activities before, during and after the recent financial crises.[4]

---

[1] B. Bernanke (2011b). "Economic Outlook and Recent Monetary Policy Actions." Before the Joint Economic Committee, US Congress, Washington, DC. October 4. www.federalreserve.gov/newsevents/testimony/bernanke20111004a.htm.

[2] Ibid.

[3] Bernanke, B. S. (2012a). "The economic recovery and economic policy." Speech at the Economic Club of New York. New York, November 20. www.federalreserve.gov/newsevents/speech/bernanke20121120a.htm.

[4] G. Shambaugh (2013). "States and Markets in the Age of Globalization: Is Intervention by the Federal Reserve a Substitute for Political Action?" Presented at the 2013 Annual Meeting of the International Studies Association, San Francisco. See also: Financial

The ability of central bankers and Treasury secretaries to mediate the impact of political and economic change on investor behavior varied with shifts in authority, deference and political capacity. As in Argentina, the willingness of national politicians to delegate authority or defer to economic technocrats increased in times of crisis and tended to decline when economic or political contexts improved. For example, President Bush's willingness to defer to Alan Greenspan declined when his popularity surged following the 9/11 attacks. Similarly, immediately following electoral victories and when the urgency of a crisis subsided, congressional critics often attempted to reign in the authority of the Federal Reserve and Treasury.

In addition to using traditional monetary policy tools to manage price stability and employment, the chairs of the Federal Reserve worked with the Treasury secretaries and other technocrats to shape the overall trajectory of economic policy. In the precrisis era, from 1992 to 2007, Greenspan joined forces with Robert Rubin, Larry Summers and Arthur Levitt to promote the use of monetary over fiscal policy, prioritize self-regulation of the financial sector and prohibit the regulation of derivatives. During the peak of the crisis, from 2008 through 2010, Bernanke, Henry Paulson and Timothy Geithner were first responders, lenders of last resort and coordinators of the domestic and international policy responses. To minimize specific-actor risks, they targeted firms whose condition or behavior had potentially negative systemic consequences while also developing broad-based programs so that other firms could seek assistance without the stigma associated with seeking a bailout. In the postcrisis era, from 2011 to today, central bankers Bernanke, Janet Yellen and Jarome Powell worked with counterparts in the Treasury to compensate for political uncertainty by managing policy flexibility and creating permissive market conditions while guarding against inflation. Through September of 2014, they did so by keeping interest rates close to zero and purchasing investors' mortgages and Treasury bonds at above market rates through a series of quantitative easing (QE) programs. In December of 2015, the Federal Reserve's Federal Open Market Committee (FOMC) announced that economic conditions had improved sufficiently to warrant "normalizing" its economic policies by

Crisis Inquiry Commission (2011). *The Financial Crisis Inquiry Report: Final Report of the National Commission on the Causes of the Financial and Economic Crisis in the United States.* Washington, DC: Government Printing Office. www.gpo.gov/fdsys/pkg/GPO-FCIC/pdf/GPO-FCIC.pdf. Two memoirs are also particularly informative: H. Paulson (2010). *On the Brink: Inside the Race to Stop the Collapse of the Global Financial System.* New York: Hachette Publishing; A. Greenspan (2007). *The Age of Turbulence.* New York: Penguin Publishing.

selling the bonds that it had purchased in the QE programs and raising interest rates as needed. Nonetheless, under Chair Yellen's guidance, the FOMC continued supporting "accommodative" economic conditions until October 2017. It did so by leaving the US$4.5 trillion portfolio intact and relying on traditional policy tools like the discount rate to manage the economy as needed.[5] Since then, the Federal Reserve has been gradually "unwinding" its balance sheet by selling the bonds it had accumulated since 2008.[6] As of October 2018, the Federal Reserve balance sheet has declined to US$4.17 trillion.[7] Under the leadership of Jarome Powell, the Federal Reserve has continued this process of "policy normalization" by gradually unwinding the balance sheet and manipulating interest rates to manage the money supply and market expectations.

This chapter evaluates how shifts in authority, deference and implementation capacity among economic policymakers and national politicians affected their abilities to shape economy policy and mediate the impact of political and economic changes on investor behavior. It analyzes action taken in the precrisis period from 1992 to 2008, during the peak of the crisis from 2008–2010 and in the postcrisis recovery period since 2010.

4.2   Precrisis Dynamics: Deference, Political Capacity and the Authority to Deregulate

The period from President Clinton's election in November of 1992 through September of 2008 was characterized by an ever-present vigilance against inflation and a widespread belief that excessive regulation was inhibiting the competitiveness of the US financial industry. Thus, the risk intervention curve (RIC) for this period reflects high levels of risk associated with both excessive policy flexibility on the part of the President and policy rigidity associated with excessive regulation (see Figure 4.1).

In the precrisis era, chairmen of the Federal Reserve, Treasury secretaries and other economic technocrats were lauded as oracles who

---

[5] "Credit and liquidity programs and the balance sheet: the Federal Reserve's balance sheet" (n.d.). *US Federal Reserve*. www.federalreserve.gov/monetarypolicy/bst_fedsbalance sheet.htm.

[6] "Policy normalization" (n.d.). *US Federal Reserve*. www.federalreserve.gov/monetary policy/policy-normalization.htm.

[7] "Credit and liquidity programs and the balance sheet: recent balance sheet trends" (n.d.). *US Federal Reserve*. www.federalreserve.gov/monetarypolicy/bst_recenttrends.htm.

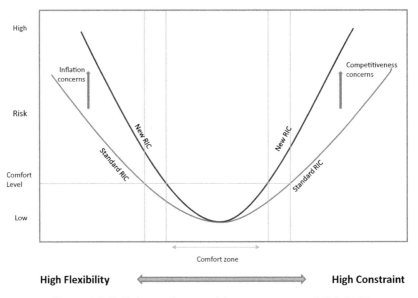

Figure 4.1 Inflation and competitiveness concerns, 1992–2007.

understood the market and could manage competing concerns regarding inflation, growth and competitiveness. Their prowess seemed to be confirmed by the so-called "Great Moderation" of the late 1990s and early 2000s that was characterized by moderate inflation, low volatility and consistent growth.[8] In terms of the RIC in Figure 4.1, they succeeded in maintaining levels of policy flexibility within investors' narrow comfort zone given prevailing concerns about both inflation and the competitiveness of the financial sector.

The age of Federal Reserve activism in the United States began with Chairman Paul Volcker who raised interest rates in 1979 to slay the two-headed dragon of high unemployment and inflation – so-called stagflation – that had tormented the United States in the 1970s. His success heralded the golden era of central bank independence by bolstering the theory that the inflationary cycle of rational expectations could be broken if policy discretion over monetary policy was delegated to technocrats or technocratic institutions that were willing to tighten the money supply despite the potentially negative political consequences associated with

[8] "The Great Moderation" (n.d.). *Federal Reserve History*. www.federalreservehistory.org/essays/great_moderation.

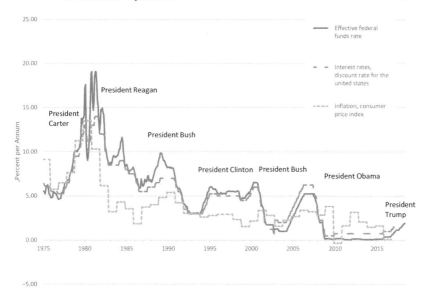

Figure 4.2 The federal funds rate, the discount rate and inflation.
Sources: "Effective Federal Funds Rate [FEDFUNDS]," "Interest Rates, Discount Rate for United States [INTDSRUSM193N]," "Inflation, Consumer Prices for the United States [FPCPITOTLZGUSA]" (n.d.). *World Bank, Federal Reserve Bank of St. Louis.* https://fred.stlouisfed.org/.

the subsequent slowing the economy. Following Volcker's example, Federal Reserve Chairmen Greenspan, Bernanke, Yellen and Powell each repeatedly demonstrated the courage to manipulate interest rates in pursuit of stable prices, full employment and lower long-term interest rates regardless of the political consequences for the president or his party. Under their leadership, the FOMC raised rates in 1994, 1999 and 2015 despite the likely negative effects of doing in subsequent elections for those in power. It also lowered rates to stimulate the economy in response to the recession of 1990, the terrorist attacks and subsequent recession in 2001, and the great recession of 2007–2015 (see Figure 4.2).[9]

In addition to using traditional monetary policy tools to manage the economy, the chairs of the Federal Reserve, secretaries of the Treasury and other technocrats exploited their authority and capitalized on the

---

[9] "Effective Federal Funds Rate [FEDFUNDS]" (n.d.). *Board of Governors of the Federal Reserve System (US), Federal Reserve Bank of St. Louis.* https://fred.stlouisfed.org/series/FEDFUNDS.

high levels of deference to shape the trajectory of national economic policy. Two instances of this behavior were particularly consequential in the precrisis period.

The first involved efforts by the Federal Reserve chairman, Treasury secretary and other technocrats to promote deregulation and the use of monetary policy rather than fiscal policy as the principal means of managing the economy. They employed new policy-making institutions (especially the National Economic Council [NEC]) and engaged in a broad range of public efforts to validate President Clinton's 1993 Economy Plan which was based on these principles. They also promoted legislation that limited the authority of regulators who challenged their agenda. Their legislative strategy culminated in the repeal of the Glass–Steagall Act that had separated investment and commercial banking, the passage of the Commodity Futures Modernization Act of 2000 that prohibited the regulation financial products known as over-the-counter (OTC) derivatives by the US Commodity Futures Trading Commission (CFTC), and the promotion of the principle of self-regulation by the Security and Exchange Commission in 2003.

The second involved efforts by the Treasury and Federal Reserve to overcome policy rigidities generated by political battles between the president and Congress. They enabled the provision of US assistance to Mexico during its 1994 financial crisis despite congressional opposition. They also added flexibility when fighting between President Clinton and Congress that stalled legislation and led to shutdowns of the government from November 14 to 19, 1995 and from December 16, 1995 to January 6, 1996. Their efforts succeeded, but Congress retaliated by restricting the Treasury Department's authority.

4.2.1   Changing the Trajectory of US Economic Policy

Driven by the mantra, "It's the Economy, Stupid!" then-presidential candidate William J. Clinton promised to prioritize economic policy and invest in America through fiscal stimulus, a middle-class tax cut and by providing basic health care for all Americans.[10] Ironically, like Argentine President Menem, he reversed course once in office. Instead of fiscal stimulus and tax cuts, President Clinton's 1993 Economic Plan focused on reducing the deficit by raising taxes, cutting spending and

---

[10] M. Kelly (1992). "The 1992 campaign: The Democrats – Clinton and Bush compete to be champion of change; Democrat fights perceptions of Bush gain." *New York Times*, October 31. www.nytimes.com/1992/10/31/us/1992-campaign-democrats-clinton-bush-compete-be-champion-change-democrat-fights.html.

promoting fiscal restraint. Three sets of events appear to have motivated this change from fiscal expansion to fiscal discipline. The first was a meeting between the president-elect and Federal Reserve Chair Alan Greenspan in Little Rock, Arkansas, on December 3, 1992, which focused on the interdependence of fiscal policy, budget deficits, the bond market and the US economy.[11] The second was a Domestic Economic Summit in Little Rock on December 14 and 15[12] and a subsequent meeting of senior economic advisors on December 30.[13] The third was a projection by the Congressional Budget Office that showed a far worse budget deficit than had been anticipated, and a related memo from Gene Sperling to the President that outlined the challenges this posed to the President's agenda.[14] Combined, these events shifted the President's focus from fiscal stimulus to deficit reduction, the use of monetary policy and an increased reliance on the Federal Reserve to stimulate/slow the economy.[15] These policies became part of the 1993 Economic Plan.

The shift in focus to debt and interest rates can be summed up by James Carville's musing: "I used to think if there was reincarnation, I wanted to come back as the President or the Pope or a .400 baseball hitter. But now I want to come back as the bond market. You can intimidate everyone."[16] Carville's musing reflects a recognition that the United States has been a debtor nation since 1985. Although approximately two-thirds of US debt is held domestically, net claims and assets abroad have outweighed foreign claims and assets in the United States

[11] B. Woodward (1994). *The Agenda: Inside the Clinton White House*. New York: Simon & Schuster, pp. 68–70; B. Woodward (2000). "Behind the boom." *Washington Post*, November 12. www.washingtonpost.com/archive/lifestyle/magazine/2000/11/12/behind-the-boom/418c4dd0-36fc-40fb-ab22-f5ae14090782/?utm_term=.0229a48a58e7; Interview with Robert Rubin conducted by Chris Bury for *Frontline*, July 2000. www.pbs.org/wgbh/pages/frontline/shows/clinton/interviews/rubin.html.

[12] T. Friedman (1992). "The transition; experts gather for conference on the economy." *New York Times*, December 14. www.nytimes.com/1992/12/14/us/the-transition-experts-gather-for-conference-on-the-economy.html.

[13] G. Ifill (1993). "Clinton's economic plan; economic plan grew slowly out of marathon of debate." *New York Times*, February 21. www.nytimes.com/1993/02/21/us/clinton-s-economic-plan-economic-plan-grew-slowly-out-of-marathon-of-debate.html.

[14] G. Sperling (1992). "Economic overview." Memorandum to the President of the United States, Office of the Presidential Transition, December 23, p. 1. See also: G. Shambaugh & P. Weinstein (2016). *The Art of Policymaking: Tools, Techniques and Processes in the Modern Executive Branch*. Washington, DC: CQ Press, pp. 196–198.

[15] "The transition; excerpts from Clinton's conference on state of the economy" (1992). *New York Times*, December 15. www.nytimes.com/1992/12/15/us/the-transition-excerpts-from-clinton-s-conference-on-state-of-the-economy.html?pagewanted=all.

[16] J. Greenwald (1994). "Greenspan's rates of wrath: the Fed jacks up borrowing costs, but the move is too much for Main Street and not enough for Wall Street." *Time Magazine*, November 28. http://content.time.com/time/magazine/article/0,9171,981879,00.html.

since then. With the exception of four years of budget surpluses during the Clinton administration from 1998 to 2001, the US government has relied on selling bonds in domestic and foreign markets to meet its budgetary obligations.[17] This has repeatedly raised fears that debt payments could eat up an increasingly large portion of GDP and crowd out other investments. In a worst-case scenario, the Federal Reserve could be forced to raise rates and thus sacrifice domestic economic growth in order to sell government bonds, much like Argentina and Turkey are doing today.

The reality of debt costs has been mixed. On one hand, the cost of debt to the United States has declined from a high of 15.2 percent for ten-year Treasury bonds in 1981 to 1.53 percent – one-tenth the cost – in July of 2012 during the height of the European debt crisis (See Figure 4.2). On the other hand, access to cheap financing enabled debt levels to rise across the economy. The federal debt grew from 30 percent of GDP in 1981 (approximately US$1 trillion) to 100 percent of GDP in 2012 (approximately US$16 trillion).[18] In the first quarter of 2018, the Federal Debt reached 105.2 percent of GDP (US$21 trillion).[19]

4.2.1.1 Deference, Validation and the Success of the 1993 Economic Plan
The 1993 Economic Plan was a striking policy-making success, especially in comparison to welfare and health care reform.[20] Robert Rubin, the director of the NEC, used his position to broker negotiations among multiple economic policy stakeholders including Secretary of the Treasury Lloyd Bentsen, Council of Economic Advisors Chair Laura Tyson, US Trade Representative Mickey Kantor and Office of Management and Budget Director Leon Panetta. He built deference by promoting the NEC as an effective conduit for getting messages to the President and eliciting a presidential decision.[21]

---

[17] The US Department of the Treasury provides statistics on US external debt. See: "U.S. gross external debt" (n.d.). *US Department of the Treasury.* www.treasury.gov/resource-center/data-chart-center/tic/Pages/external-debt.aspx.
[18] "Federal Debt: Total Public Debt as Percent of Gross Domestic Product [GFDEGDQ188S]" (n.d.). *Federal Reserve Bank of St. Louis, US Office of Management and Budget.* https://fred.stlouisfed.org/series/GFDEGDQ188S.
[19] "Federal Debt: Total Public Debt [GFDEBTN]" (n.d.). *Board of Governors of the Federal Reserve System (US), Federal Reserve Bank of St. Louis.* https://fred.stlouisfed.org/series/GFDEBTN.
[20] Shambaugh & Weinstein. *The Art of Policymaking,* pp. 198–199.
[21] Ibid. See also: I. M. Deslter (1996). *The National Economic Council: A Work in Progress.* Washington, DC: Institute for International Economics, pp. 9–18.

Greenspan also played an important role in validating President Clinton's 1993 Economic Plan.[22] He testified in Congress that Clinton's strategy was a "serious" proposal based on "credible" economic assumptions.[23] He also sent broad signals of support to the public at large by sitting between Hillary Clinton and Tipper Gore at the President's first State of the Union address when the economic plan was announced.[24] As a result, prominent scholars and practitioners have argued that the NEC and the budget process were "island(s) of effective White House process in the 'madhouse' of the early Clinton Administration."[25]

The degree to which President Clinton internalized these policies and continued to defer to Alan Greenspan is reinforced by three facts.[26] The first is his non-reaction to Greenspan's raising of interest rates beginning in February of 1994. Despite the perception by some in the Clinton administration that Alan Greenspan had broken an implicit agreement to keep interest rates low and that raising interest rates when he did likely contributed to the "Republican Revolution" in the midterm elections in November of 1994, neither President Clinton nor Chairman Greenspan publicly criticized the other.[27] Second, President Clinton nominated Greenspan for a third term as chairman of the Federal Reserve in February of 1996.[28] Third, despite increased political capacity following his very successful reelection campaign in 1996 (in which he won 379 electoral votes and 55 percent of the popular vote), President Clinton continued to support efforts by Greenspan, Summers and Rubin to promote deregulation. He lobbied for the implementation of a series of complementary economic policies focused on fiscal

[22] "Clinton's Economic Plan" (1983). *New York Times*, February 18. www.nytimes.com/1993/02/18/us/clinton-s-economic-plan-the-details-clinton-s-plan-austerity-and-change.html.

[23] S. Greenhouse (1993). "Greenspan the politician." *New York Times*, February 1. www.nytimes.com/1993/02/01/business/greenspan-the-politician.html.

[24] J. Berry (1993). "The Fed chief's unlikely alliance." *Washington Post*, March 21. www.washingtonpost.com/archive/business/1993/03/21/the-fed-chiefs-unlikely-alliance/798698c4-cfb3-4a7a-8314-0c8f76681aab.

[25] Deslter. *The National Economic Council*, p. 2; J. Birnbaum (1996). *Madhouse: The Private Turmoil of Working for the President.* New York: New York Times Books; J. Orszag, P. Orszag & L. Tyson (2001). "The process of economic policy-making during the Clinton administration." Prepared for the conference on American Economic Policy in the 1990s, Center for Business and Government, John F. Kennedy School of Government, Harvard University, June 27–30, pp. 1–86.

[26] "The Clinton presidency: Historic economic growth" (n.d.). *The White House Archives.* https://clintonwhitehouse5.archives.gov/WH/Accomplishments/eightyears-03.html.

[27] B. Woodward, "Behind the boom"; Interview with Robert Rubin conducted by Chris Bury for *Front Line.* www.pbs.org/wgbh/pages/frontline/shows/clinton/interviews/rubin.html.

[28] Alan Greenspan was first nominated by President Ronald Reagan in June of 1987.

responsibility. These included the Deficit Reduction Plan of 1993 and the Balanced Budget Agreement of 1997. In his 1998 and 1999 State of the Union addresses, President Clinton dedicated budget surpluses to enhancing social security and reducing the national debt.[29] He also signed a series of regulatory reforms that liberalized financial markets. These included the Gramm–Leach–Bliley Act of 1999 (Pub. L. 106-102, 113 Stat. 1338, enacted November 12, 1999) that repealed the Glass–Steagall Act, the Commodity Futures Modernization Act of 2000 (Pub. L. 106-554, enacted on December 21, 2000) that forestalled regulation of credit default swaps and the Voluntary Regulation policy passed by the Securities and Exchange Commission (SEC) under the Consolidated Supervised Entities program, which lowered the reserve requirements for investment banks and allowed an increase in leverage.[30]

4.2.1.2 Promoting Deregulation by Restricting Authority In addition to maintaining anti-inflation vigilance, Greenspan joined Robert Rubin (first as NEC Director and then Secretary of the Treasury), Lawrence Summers (first as Deputy Secretary and then Secretary of the Treasury) and others in driving US economic policy towards financial liberalization.[31] For their efforts, *Time Magazine* lauded them as the "Three Musketeers" and "The Committee to Save the World – so far."[32]

Their tactics included a notorious confrontation with Brooksley Born, head of the CFTC, in the spring of 1998.[33] Born argued that the collapse of Long-Term Capital Management in September of 1998, which had used derivatives to leverage more than US$1 trillion in debt, demonstrated the dangers associated with derivatives and the importance of

---

[29] "The Clinton presidency: Historic economic growth" (n.d.). *The White House Archives.* https://clintonwhitehouse5.archives.gov/WH/Accomplishments/eightyears-03.html.

[30] M. Sherman (2009). *A Short History of Financial Deregulation in the United States.* Washington, DC: Center for Economic and Policy Research.

[31] For the legislation, see the US Commodity Futures Trading Commission website: www.cftc.gov/index.htm. See also: Testimony of Patrick Parkinson, Deputy Director, Division of Research and Statistics, "Commodity Futures Modernization Act of 2000," before the Committee on Banking, Housing, and Urban Affairs, US Senate, September 8, 2005. www.federalreserve.gov/boarddocs/testimony/2005/20050908/default.htm.

[32] J. Cooper Ramo (2000). "The three marketeers." *Time Magazine*, February 15. http://content.time.com/time/world/article/0,8599,2054093,00.html.

[33] Interview with Brooksley Born, *Front Line: The Warning.* August 28, 2009. www.pbs.org/wgbh/pages/frontline/warning; J. Carney (2009). "The warning: Brooksley Born's battle with Alan Greenspan, Robert Rubin and Larry Summers." *Business Insider*, October 21. www.businessinsider.com/the-warning-brooksley-borns-battle-with-alan-greenspan-robert-rubin-and-larry-summers-2009-10.

transparency and regulatory oversight of OTC transactions.[34] In the face of vigorous opposition, she asserted that the CFTC had the expertise and authority to provide this oversight. Meetings between Born, Greenspan, Rubin and SEC Chairman Arthur Levitt on the President's Working Group on Financial Markets have been described as adversarial.[35] The Presidential Working Group did not accept Born's recommendation and instead recommended changes to the Commodity Exchange Act that were designed to "promote innovation, competition, efficiency and transparency in over-the-counter derivative markets" by eliminating them from the Commodity Exchange Act.[36] The degree of contestation between Born and the others quickly became public.[37]

In his memoir, Timothy Geithner argues that this was more an instance of "turf and interests than substance or ideology."[38] The turf battles were between the Federal Reserve and New York banks that dominated the derivatives markets on one side and the CFTC and the Chicago-based commodities markets on the other. He noted that Born's concerns were prescient, but had little chance of getting approved by Congress – where Summers' and Greenspan's arguments about the usefulness of derivatives in hedging and distributing risk were persuasive, fear that government interference could stifle this complex and quickly evolving business was widespread, and the incentives of self-regulation in the industry were popular.[39] Lobbying by Summers and Greenspan helped to promote the adoption of the Commodity Futures Modernization Act of 2000, which specified that most derivatives would not be regulated under the Commodity Exchange Act or by the CTFC.[40] Following suit just three years

---

[34] B. Born (1998). "The lessons of long-term capital management L.P." Remarks at the Chicago Kent IIT Commodities Law Institute, October 15. www.cftc.gov/sites/default/files/opa/speeches/opaborn-37.htm.

[35] Interview with Brooksley Born, *Front Line: The Warning*. August 28, 2009. www.pbs.org/wgbh/pages/frontline/warning; A. Faiola, E. Nakashima & J. Drew (2008). "What went wrong." *Washington Post*, October 15. www.washingtonpost.com/wp-dyn/content/story/2008/10/14/ST2008101403344.html.

[36] "Report of the President's Working Group on Financial Markets" (2009). *US Department of the Treasury*, November. www.treasury.gov/resource-center/fin-mkts/documents/otcact.pdf.

[37] Testimony of Patrick Parkinson, Deputy Director, Division of Research and Statistics, "Commodity Futures Modernization Act of 2000," before the Committee on Banking, Housing, and Urban Affairs, US Senate, September 8, 2005. www.federalreserve.gov/boarddocs/testimony/2005/20050908/default.htm.

[38] T. Geithner (2014). *Stress Test: Reflections on Financial Crises*. New York: Random House, p. 131.

[39] Ibid., pp. 133–134.

[40] For a review of Greenspan's legacy, see: P. Goodman (2008). "Taking hard new look at a Greenspan legacy." *New York Times*, October 8. www.nytimes.com/2008/10/09/business/economy/09greenspan.html?pagewanted=all.

before the financial crisis hit, the SEC announced its support for establishing a voluntary program for reporting financial information. Obligatory reporting requirements were avoided in order to "improve the timeliness, accuracy and analysis of financial disclosure in Commission filings."[41]

This case demonstrates the political activism of the Federal Reserve and other economic policymakers. It highlights how individual technocrats can shape economic policy by exploiting deference, mobilizing political support and manipulating authority. By doing so, they increased policy flexibility by deregulating the financial industry. Unfortunately, their policies had tragic consequences and the accolades of "oracle" and "hero" proved to be temporary.

4.2.1.3   Tax Cuts and 9/11 President George W. Bush entered office in a weak political position having lost the popular vote to Al Gore (47.9 percent to 48.4 percent). Consequently, he sought validation from his economic team to build political support for his principal policy goal: passing US$1.3 trillion in tax cuts. Treasury Secretary O'Neill was chosen to be the administration's primary advocate, but a series of gaffs – including O'Neill's reporting that future budget deficits would be large and tax increases would be necessary, his insinuation that the administration was not pursuing a strong dollar policy as promised, and his positing the war in Iraq was not connected to the attacks on September 11 – raised concerns that his views did not fully align with the President's.[42] Chairman Greenspan was more supportive.[43] On January 25, 2001, he testified before Congress that "budget surpluses are growing so big that taxes can be reduced even while eliminating the national debt at the end of the decade," adding that the economy was slowing down, so simulative actions may be warranted and the Fed might lower interest rates.[44] With Greenspan's support, the Economic

---

[41] "SEC Proposes Rule to Establish Voluntary Program for Reporting Financial Information on EDGAR Using XBRL" (2004). *US Securities and Exchange Commission*, September 27. www.sec.gov/news/press/2004-138.htm.

[42] R. Suskind (2004). *The Price of Loyalty: George W. Bush, the White House, and the Education of Paul O'Neill.* New York: Simon & Schuster; J. Dickerson (2004). "Confessions of a White House insider." *Time Magazine*, January 10. http://content.time.com/time/magazine/article/0,9171,574809,00.html.

[43] P. Krugman (2002). "The quiet man." *New York Times*, January 8. www.nytimes.com/2002/01/08/opinion/the-quiet-man.html.

[44] "Greenspan on tax changes" (2001). *C-Span*, January 25. www.c-span.org/video/?c4177086/greenspan-tax-changes. See also: F. Pellegrini (2001). "Greenspan's brave new world has room for Bush's tax cut." *Time Magazine*, January 25. http://content.time.com/time/nation/article/0,8599,96747,00.html; C. Lochhead (2001). "Greenspan endorses a cut in tax rate/budget surpluses will erase national debt, he says." *SF Gate*, January   26.   www.sfgate.com/news/article/Greenspan-Endorses-A-Cut-in-Tax-Rate-

Growth and Tax Relief Reconciliation Act of 2001 passed through Congress and was signed into law on June 7, 2001 (Pub. L. 107-16, 115 Stat. 38).

In the aftermath of the economic slowdown following the terrorist attacks on September 11, 2001, President Bush pushed to make his tax cuts permanent. Following the tragic attacks, popular support for President Bush soared to 90 percent, the highest presidential approval rating ever recorded by Gallup.[45] This gave him extraordinarily high levels of legislative capacity on counterterrorism policy and other legislative agenda items. One of these was a second round of tax cuts. He first consolidated power by securing resignations from Treasury Secretary Paul O'Neill and NEC head Lawrence Lindsay.[46] Markets responded positively, with the Dow Jones Industrial average rallying by 22.49 points, seemingly expressing a desire for increased policy flexibility so the President could address sluggish growth, rising joblessness and the terrorist threat as needed.[47] Once again, President Bush sought Chairman Greenspan's validation and support for his tax cut.[48] Greenspan initially sat on the sidelines as debate about the tax cuts heated up.[49] He then offered a highly qualified opinion, noting that "It would probably be unwise to unwind the long-term tax cut, because it is already built into the system," but that this would provide almost no stimulus to the economy.[50] His argued that budget discipline was needed and that tax cuts and other stimulus efforts should be put off until the economic uncertainties pertaining to the war in Iraq had dissipated.[51] Even though he did not receive Greenspan's

Budget-2959985.php; "Greenspan eyes tax cuts" (2001). *CNN Money*, January 25. https://money.cnn.com/2001/01/25/economy/greenspan.

[45] "Bush job approval highest in Gallup history" (2001). *Gallup News*, September 24. https://news.gallup.com/poll/4924/bush-job-approval-highest-gallup-history.aspx.

[46] M. Allen & J. Weisman (2002). "Bush ousts O'Neill and a top advisor." *Washington Post*, December 7. www.washingtonpost.com/archive/politics/2002/12/07/bush-ousts-oneill-and-a-top-adviser/89cd55b1-417f-4b65-941b-ca508ad9f122/?utm_term=.001f223655d0.

[47] J. Gerstenzang (2002). "Bush fires his top economic advisors." *Los Angeles Times*, December 7. http://articles.latimes.com/2002/dec/07/nation/na-bushecon.

[48] "The economic effects of 9/11: a retrospective assessment" (2002). *Congressional Research Service*, September 27. www.fas.org/irp/crs/RL31617.pdf.

[49] Krugman. "The quiet man."

[50] E. Andrews (2002). "Fed Chief says he supports Bush tax cuts." *New York Times*, November 14. www.nytimes.com/2002/11/14/business/fed-chief-says-he-supports-bush-tax-cut.html.

[51] "Greenspan 1, Bush 0: warning of growing budget deficits, Fed chairman undercuts Bush, GOP arguments for tax cuts" (2003). *CNN Money*, February 11. https://money.cnn.com/2003/02/11/news/economy/greenspan/index.htm; J. Weisman (2002). "Greenspan throws damper on permanent tax-cut plan." *Washington Post*, November 14. www.washingtonpost

endorsement, President Bush continued to ride a wave of high approval ratings and signed the Jobs and Growth Tax Reconciliation Act of 2003 (Pub. L. 108-27, 117 Stat. 752) into law on May 28, 2003. Then, like President Clinton before him, President Bush signaled his support for Alan Greenspan by asking him to continue to serve as chair of the Federal Reserve on May 18, 2004.[52]

4.2.2   The Success and Consequences of Outmaneuvering Congress

The chair of the Federal Reserve and secretary of the Treasury can also expand policy flexibility by helping the president overcome institutional constraints and outmaneuver political opponents. Examples in the pre-crisis era took place during the Mexico peso crisis of 1994–1995 and the budget battles and government shutdowns of 1995–1996. These experiences provide insights into similar problems later faced by the Obama administration.

4.2.2.1   Using Plan B to Help Mexico, 1994–1995 Coordinated efforts by the Federal Reserve, Treasury and congressional leaders to rescue the Mexican economy in 1994 demonstrate the highly integrated and political roles played by economic technocrats across the government. In January of 1995, Secretary of the Treasury Rubin and Federal Reserve Chairman Greenspan proposed a rescue plan for Mexico through which the United States would supplement a $2.6 billion loan from the International Monetary Fund (IMF) with a $40 billion "wall of money" to restore confidence in Mexico.[53] They initially received bipartisan support in Congress as well as the backing of President Clinton, four former presidents, five former secretaries of commerce and six former secretaries of the treasury.[54] However, newly elected members of Congress – who were fresh from a landslide midterm electoral victory in November of 1994 – opposed the deal.

Opponents of the Mexican bailout were motivated by their criticism of the recently negotiated North American Free Trade Agreement and fears that tax payers would end up financing loan guarantees to a

---

.com/archive/politics/2002/11/14/greenspan-throws-damper-on-permanent-tax-cut-plan/38a44685-056a-4af2-9d4d-33e5058dfc6a/?utm_term=.a265708df101.

[52] K. Gilpin (2004). "Bush re-nominates Alan Greenspan for Fed." *New York Times*, May 18.   www.nytimes.com/2004/05/18/business/bush-renominates-alan-greenspan-for-fed.html?_r=0.

[53] Geithner. *Stress Test*, p. 70.

[54] C. R. Henning (1999). *The Exchange Stabilization Fund: Slush Money or War Chest.* Washington, DC: Institute for International Economics, p. 63.

foreign government that many perceived to be unstable and unable or unwilling to make needed economic policy reforms.[55] Despite lobbying by Greenspan, a promise of US$7.5 billion in credits to Mexico from the IMF, and support from President Clinton and Vice President Al Gore, vote counts by the end of January suggested that passage was unlikely.[56]

Fearing a potential rejection by Congress, Treasury Secretary Rubin changed strategy. Under Plan B, rather than requesting additional funding authority, the Treasury would get the needed financing from the Exchange Stabilization Fund (ESF).[57] The ESF was established in 1934 to enable the Treasury Department to "promote exchange rate stability and counter disorderly conditions in the foreign exchange market" by buying and selling foreign currency and providing "shorter-term credit to foreign governments and monetary authorities."[58] Though ESF activities are subject to congressional oversight, no legislative action is needed to tap these funds. In short, Rubin was able to exploit the Treasury's statutory authority over the ESF to bypass Congress. By doing so, he enabled the United States to respond despite the inability of the President and congressional leaders to mobilize legislative support. On January 31, 1995, President Clinton announced that he would authorize the secretary of the Treasury to extend US$20 billion in credits to Mexico using the ESF.[59] The agreement was implemented on February 21. The ESF funds were supplemented by US$17.8 billion from the IMF and US$10 billion from the Bank for International Settlements, plus additional support from Canada and other Latin American countries.[60]

Congressional leaders affirmed the President's and Treasury's authority to take action, but rank-and-file members fought back by attempting to limit the Treasury Department's ability to use the funds in the future. Beginning on February 23, the House began passing

[55] "Clinton Leads Mexico Bailout Effort." In *CQ Almanac 1995, 51st edn.*, 10-16-10-17. Washington, DC: Congressional Quarterly, 1996. http://library.cqpress.com/cqalmanac/cqal95-1099614.

[56] Henning. *The Exchange Stabilization Fund*, p. 63.   [57] Ibid.

[58] "FEDPOINT: Exchange Stabilization Fund" (n.d.). *Federal Reserve Bank of New York*. www.newyorkfed.org/aboutthefed/fedpoint/fed14.html. See also: "Exchange Stabilization Fund" (n.d.). *US Department of the Treasury*. https://home.treasury.gov/policy-issues/international/exchange-stabilization-fund.

[59] Henning. *The Exchange Stabilization Fund*, p. 64.

[60] "Clinton Leads Mexico Bailout Effort." In *CQ Almanac 1995, 51st edn.*, 10-16-10-17. Washington, DC: Congressional Quarterly, 1996. http://library.cqpress.com/cqalmanac/cqal95-1099614.

resolutions demanding documentation about US assistance to Mexico. On March 30, Senator Alfonse D'Amato (R-NY), chairman of the Senate Banking Committee, offered a proposal barring the Clinton administration from using more than US$5 billion from the ESF per year without congressional approval.[61] He eventually withdrew that proposal, but soon tried again. On August 5, he added an amendment to the Treasury, Postal Service and General Appropriations Act of 1996. The "D'Amato Amendment" restricted the authority of the Department of the Treasury to make any loan or extension of credit in excess of US$1 billion for more than 180 days without an Act of Congress.[62]

The D'Amato Amendment was too late to affect the rescue package for Mexico, but it effectively delayed the US government's response to an economic crisis in Thailand in 1997. The delay had several economic and geopolitical consequences that likely motivated some in Congress to reinstate the Treasury Department's authority. On the home front, the US stock market plummeted as the crisis spread from Thailand to Indonesia, South Korea, Malaysia, the Philippines and Hong Kong.[63] Internationally, the Japanese minister of finance suggested that Japan could create an Asian Monetary Fund to fill the void left by the absence of the United States in the Pacific.[64] Legislative support of the "D'Amato Amendment" weakened and it was not renewed. During the summer and fall of 1998, critics including Senator Lauch Faircloth (R-NC) and Representatives Jim Saxton (R-NJ), Bernie Sanders (I-VT) and Max Baucus (D-MT) tried again but failed to restrict the Treasury's authority over the ESF.

The Treasury took advantage of the shifting congressional sentiment to provide "contingent additional financial support" in conjunction with the IMF to Korea, Brazil and Argentina.[65] In 1998, Secretary Rubin, Larry Summers and Timothy Geithner secured a "second line of defense" of US$20 billion to complement a US$55 billion rescue package for Korea from the IMF.[66]

The battle over ESF funding reflects how shifts in legislative capacity and battles over authority can alter the flexibility of economic policy. The

---

[61] Ibid.

[62] Congressional Record, 104th Congress (1995–1996), Congressional Record article 69 of 195, D'AMATO (AND OTHERS) AMENDMENT NO. 2229 (Senate – August 5, 1995), proposed Amendment to bill H.R. 2020. www.congress.gov/104/crec/1995/08/05/CREC-1995-08-05-pt1-PgS11521-2.pdf.

[63] Henning. *The Exchange Stabilization Fund*, p. 78.   [64] Geithner. *Stress Test*, p. 83.

[65] Henning. *The Exchange Stabilization Fund*, p. 78.   [66] Geithner. *Stress Test*, p. 91.

Treasury used its statutory authority to bypass congressional critics; congressional critics in turn exploited public angst and their newfound legislative capacity to limit the Treasury's authority to take similar actions in the future. As the Asian financial crisis spread, economic and political conditions changed and congressional challenges to the Treasury's authority declined.

4.2.2.2 Outmaneuvering Veto Players in the 1995 Budget Battles President Bill Clinton suffered a substantial midterm electoral loss in 1994 in the so-called "Republican Revolution" led by Republic Speaker of the House Newt Gingrich.[67] In an effort to exploit this political victory, Speaker Gingrich threatened to prevent the House from voting on extending the debt ceiling unless President Clinton agreed to a series of demands including US$245 billion in tax cuts, welfare reform, restraints on Medicare and Medicaid growth and a balanced budget in seven years.[68] Congress had last raised the debt ceiling on August 10, 1993. The debt limit of US$4.9 trillion was expected to be hit in November.

The US Congress is responsible for passing appropriations bills that specify US government expenditures. If expenditures exceed revenues, Congress has constitutional authority "To borrow money on the credit of the United States" (Article I, Section 8) and is obligated to pay its debts. Section 4 of the Fourteenth Amendment notes, "The validity of the public debt of the United States, authorized by law, including debts incurred for payment of pensions and bounties for service in suppressing insurrection or rebellion, shall not be questioned."[69] Since 1917, Congress has also imposed a limit on the amount that the Treasury Department is authorized to pay for the debt. Thus, Congress follows a two-step process: passing a budget, then raising the debt ceiling as needed to accommodate its associated debt obligations. As noted by the General Accounting Office:[70]

The debt limit does not control or limit the ability of the federal government to run deficits or incur obligations. Rather, it is a limit on the ability to pay obligations already incurred. While debates surrounding the debt limit may

---

[67] Shambaugh & Weinstein. *The Art of Policymaking*, ch. 13.

[68] This forsakes the "Gephardt Rule" of 1979 that the House would raise the debt limit when budget resolutions were approved.

[69] "Constitution of the United States" (n.d.). *National Archives*. www.archives.gov/exhibits/charters/constitution_transcript.html.

[70] "DEBT LIMIT: Delays Create Debt Management Challenges and Increase Uncertainty in the Treasury Market." GAO-11-203: Published: February 22, 2011. Publicly Released: February 22, 2011. Washington, DC: US Government Accountability Office.

raise awareness about the federal government's current debt trajectory and may also provide Congress with an opportunity to debate the fiscal policy decisions driving that trajectory, the ability to have an immediate effect on debt levels is limited. This is because the debt reflects previously enacted tax and spending policies.

In 1979, Richard Gephardt authored a rule to resolve uncertainty associated with the debt limit by linking the passing of a budget resolution to a parallel increase in the debt limit to pay for it.[71] The Gephardt Rule was not contested until 1994, when newly elected congressional members of the "Republican Revolution" attempted to exploit the debt ceiling as a source of leverage to constrain the President's policy agenda.[72]

Foreshadowing a sentiment that he would repeatedly express in 2011, Representative John Boehner (R-OH) warned in November of 1995 that "Nobody should assume we're going to have a debt-limit extension. If the vote were held today, it would not pass."[73] Nonetheless, President Clinton refused to give in to what he termed "economic blackmail," and subsequently vetoed congressional bills that would increase the debt limit for a month in exchange for higher Medicare premiums and other benefits and spending cuts.[74] When the continuing resolution that had kept the government operating expired on November 13, all nonessential government services were shut down. On November 19, the President and Congress reached a general agreement to balance the budget in seven years and reopened the government using another continuing resolution. Negotiations broke down again and the government shut down again when that continuing resolution expired on December 16.[75] The government reopened once more on January 6 after the

---

[71] K. Mahnken (2013). "Dick Gephardt, where art thou?" *New Republic*, October 9. https://newrepublic.com/article/115084/dick-gephardt-rule-how-he-could-have-avoided-debt-crisis.

[72] B. Heniff Jr. (2008). "Developing debt-limit legislation: The House's 'Gephardt Rule.'"*Congressionalresearch.com*, July 1. http://congressionalresearch.com/RL31913/document.php.

[73] K. Brandiesky (2011). "How Clinton handled his debt ceiling crisis better than Obama." *New Republic*, August 2. https://newrepublic.com/article/93043/obama-clinton-debt-ceiling-crisis.

[74] Ibid.

[75] "Slaying the dragon of debt" (n.d.). *Regional Oral History Office, The Bancroft Library, University of California, Berkeley.* http://bancroft.berkeley.edu/ROHO/projects/debt/governmentshutdown.html. See also: "The budget battle" (n.d.). *CNN.* www.cnn.com/US/9512/budget/budget_battle/index.html; E. Drew (1997). *Showdown: The Struggle between the Gingrich Congress and the Clinton White House.* New York: Touchstone; C. Jones (1999). *Clinton and Congress, 1993–1996: Risk, Restoration, and Reelection.* Norman: University of Oklahoma Press; S. Gillon (1999). *The Pact: Bill*

President and Congress reached an agreement on a budget that included a seven-year balanced budget plan. The question of raising the debt limit, however, remained unresolved.

President Clinton was highly constrained by congressional opponents throughout this episode. Secretary of the Treasury Rubin attempted to compensate by developing strategies to increase policy-making flexibility. His began by exploiting authority granted to the Treasury by Congress following a debt ceiling crisis in 1985. In 1985, Congress authorized the Treasury Secretary to temporarily manipulate its intergovernmental debt obligations in order to meet its public debt obligations.[76] It also granted the secretary of the treasury the authority to determine a "debt issuance suspension period" if debt obligations cannot be met without exceeding the debt limit. Rubin engaged in a series of actions to manipulate the duration of the negotiations.[77] On November 15, 1995, he declared a debt issuance suspension period.[78] On January 22, he announced a series of measures to postpone the debt crisis until the end of February. He also sent a letter to House Speaker Newt Gingrich warning that he only had the capability to extend debt payments until March 1.[79] As they would again in 2011, Moody's rating agency reacted by announcing that it was considering downgrading its rating on US Treasury bonds due to a fear that a political stalemate would lead to a government default.[80]

To avoid default until March 1, Secretary Rubin engaged in a series of unorthodox strategies including redeeming securities held by the Civil Service Fund before maturity to prevent the amount of public debt from exceeding the debt ceiling, suspending investments to the Civil Service Retirement and Disability Trust Fund, and suspending investments to

---

Clinton, Newt Gingrich, and the Rivalry That Defined a Generation. Norman: University of Oklahoma Press.

[76] G. Dodaro (1996). "Debt ceiling: analysis of actions during the 1995–1996 crisis." *United States General Accounting Office*, B-270619, August 30, p. 15; "Reaching the Debt Limit: Background and Potential Effects on Government Operations" (2013). *Congressional Research Service*, September 19, p. 3.

[77] The Treasury took extraordinary actions during debt-limit negotiations to meet its federal obligations to pay its creditors in 1985, 1995–1996, 2002, 2004, 2011 and 2013. See: "Reaching the Debt Limit" (2013). *Congressional Research Service*, September 19.

[78] Dodaro. "Debt ceiling."

[79] J. Hook & J. Gerstenzang (1996). "Rubin details measures to postpone debt crisis." *Los Angeles Times*, January 23. http://articles.latimes.com/1996-01-23/news/mn-27721_1_debt-crisis.

[80] A. Clymer (1996). "G.O.P. lawmakers offer to abandon debt-limit threat." *New York Times*, January 25. www.nytimes.com/1996/01/25/us/gop-lawmakers-offer-to-abandon-debt-limit-threat.html.

the Government Securities Investment Fund, (G-Fund).[81] Rubin's strategies extended President Clinton's bargaining window and ultimately enabled the President to build public support for his position regarding the government shutdown. Rubin summarized the situation as follows:[82]

The basic threat was, "We will not raise the debt ceiling, therefore, you will not be able to pay the debt, and you'll be in default," as a way of pressuring the president to sign a budget that he basically believed was unsound. At the Treasury Department, we found a means of drawing on federal trust funds – something that'd never been done before, at least in the way that we did it – to continue paying the debt, even though they wouldn't raise the debt ceiling. ... That trumped the Republicans' hand, and took that strategy off the table. So then they moved to the strategy of forcing a showdown over shutting down the government, and that, ultimately, is what happened.

On February 8, Congress relented partially by passing PL 104-104, which gave the Treasury the authority to issue securities from the G-Fund equal to the March 1996 social security payments without them counting against the debt ceiling until March 15, 1996.[83] On March 28, 1996, Congress sent the President a bill raising the debt ceiling to US $5.5 trillion while also reducing regulation on small businesses and altering taxes on social security. The President signed the bill on March 30.

Markets responded positively to Rubin's interventions, suggesting that they helped mitigate political and policy risks associated with legislative rigidity. Interest rates on three-month Treasury bills declined from 5.3 percent when Rubin intervened in November of 1995 to 4.9 percent in March of 1996 when the debt limit was increased.[84] A comparison to international interest rates suggests that the interventions also kept international markets calm. The spread between the London Interbank Offer Rate (LIBOR) and Treasury bills during this period remained relatively stable, ranging from 51 basis points when Rubin first intervened to 54 basis points when the issue was resolved.[85]

Although Congress had authorized the Treasury secretary to take these actions in 1985, that authority had never been exercised.[86]

---

[81] Authorized by Congress in 5 U.S.C. 8438 – Civil Service Retirement and Disability Fund.

[82] Interview with Robert Rubin conducted by Chris Bury for *Front Line*, July 2000. www.pbs.org/wgbh/pages/frontline/shows/clinton/interviews/rubin.html.

[83] Dodaro. "Debt ceiling"; Hook & Gerstenzang. "Rubin details measures."

[84] "FRED Economic Data" (n.d.). *Federal Reserve Bank of St. Louis*. http://research.stlouisfed.org/fred2.

[85] Ibid.   [86] Dodaro. "Debt ceiling," p. 15.

Consequently, Representatives Gerald Solomon (R-NY) and Christopher Cox (R-CA) threatened to impeach Secretary Rubin on the grounds that he was ignoring the will of Congress by borrowing more money for the Treasury.[87] In a postcrisis review, the General Accounting Office cleared the Treasury of exceeding its authority. The GAO argued:

> During the 1995–1996 debt ceiling crisis, Treasury used its normal investment procedures for 12 of the 15 major government trust funds included in our review. ... Treasury departed from its normal procedures in handling the investments and redemptions for the remaining three major trust funds (Civil Service fund, G-Fund, and Exchange Stabilization Fund) and took other actions to stay within the $4.9 trillion debt ceiling established in August 1993. These departures and other actions were proper and consistent with legal authorities the Congress has provided to the Secretary of the Treasury.[88]

Nonetheless, congressional leaders attempted to forestall future actions by the Treasury by limiting the resources at its disposal. The Contract with America Advancement Act of 1996 (Pub. L. 104-121) increased the debt limit, but it also stipulated that social security and Medicare trust funds cannot be used to meet public debt obligations.[89]

Despite these prohibitions, the Treasury remained active. During the George W. Bush administration, it engaged in "extraordinary measures" in 2002, 2003, 2004 and 2006.[90] During the Obama administration, the Treasury Department did so during the debt ceiling debates in 2011–2012 and 2015. These experiences often mimic the 1995–1996 pattern in which the Treasury secretary asserts his authority to help the president overcome political opposition and Congress retaliates by attempting to reduce that authority.

4.2.3   Conclusion: Lessons from the Precrisis Era

As reflected in the RIC presented in Figure 4.3, economic policies during the precrisis era were focused on reducing risk by maintaining

---

[87] S. Pearlstein (1996). "Republicans threaten to impeach Rubin if he borrows again to avoid default." *Washington Post*, January 5. www.washingtonpost.com/archive/politics/1996/01/05/republicans-threaten-to-impeach-rubin-if-he-borrows-again-to-avoid-default/2b74386c-66 6d-4a51-82a0-6e1afdd2341f/?utm_term=.feb367521abf.

[88] Dodaro. "Debt ceiling," p. 5.

[89] "Contract with America Advancement Act of 1996." Pub. L. 104-121–March 29, 1996, 110 Stat. 847.

[90] "Understanding the Federal debt limit" (2015). *Concord Coalition*, October 8. www.concordcoalition.org/issue-briefs/2015/1008/understanding-federal-debt-limit.

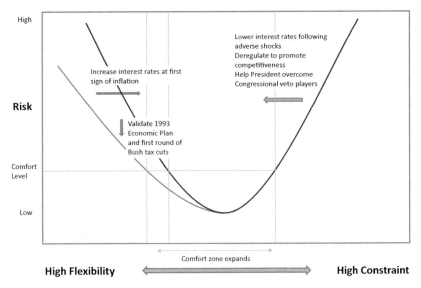

Figure 4.3 Inflation and competitiveness concerns, 1992–2007.

inflation vigilance while reducing the policy rigidities associated with excessive regulation and debilitating power struggles between the President and Congress. Greenspan, Rubin, Summers and others also altered the trajectory of US economic policy by validating the 1993 Economic Plan and the first round of President Bush's tax cuts. Their interventions increased the comfort zone reflected in Figure 4.3.

The ability of the Federal Reserve, Treasury and other economic policymakers to shift the US position along these RICs to achieve these objectives varied with shifts in authority, deference and implementation capacity. The expected variations and outcomes are shown in Figure 4.4.

When the authority to act was uncontested, deference was high and implementation capacity was high or unnecessary (as in the case of traditional open-market operations), economic policymakers are expected to be able to shift the United States along the RICs to decrease risk (category 1 in row 1 in Figure 4.4). This pattern fits the Federal Reserve's manipulation of interest rates. Though often politically disruptive, the Federal Reserve's authority was not challenged. As reflected in President Clinton's willingness to reappoint Greenspan and implement

	The Power to Act			Prediction		Outcome	
Authority to Act	Deference to Technocrats	Implementation Capacity of National Politicians	Impact of Technocrats		Behavior	Role of Technocrats	Market Behavior
1 High, Uncontested	High, Deference Granted	High or Not Necessary	Can constrain or expand policy flexibility	Can validate policy, targeted and broad strategies may be effective	Maximum bargaining power	1992–2008: Fed manipulates interest rates in response to changing circumstances	Markets generally respond as expected to shifts in federal funds rate
2 High, Uncontested	High, Deference Granted	Low	Can constrain or expand policy flexibility if legislative support is unnecessary	Can validate policy, targeted strategies may be disruptive, broad strategies may be effective	Weak politicians appoint technocrats to bolster implementation capacity, but may abandon them	1993: Clinton seeks and secures Fed validation for economic plan; 1996, 2000: reappoints Greenspan	Markets rally
2 High, Uncontested	High, Deference Granted	Low	Can constrain or expand policy flexibility if legislative support is unnecessary	Can validate policy, targeted strategies may be disruptive, broad strategies may be effective	Weak politicians appoint technocrats to bolster implementation capacity, but may abandon them	June 2001: Bush seeks and secures Fed validation for tax package	Markets rally
5 High or Low	Low, Deference Demanded	High or Not Necessary	Confrontational technocrats likely to be replaced with sycophants	Cannot validate policy, targeted and broad strategies by politicians possible	No economic validation, political exuberance likely	September 2001: presidential popularity and legislative capacity surge, deference to others declines; Fed lowers rates to stimulate economy through 2004, then begins raising rates to decrease "froth" in the market May 2003: Bush enacts second round of tax cuts with reluctant support from the Fed	The notional value of mortgage-backed securities and related financial instruments increases significantly, bubbles begin to form

Figure 4.4 Shaping policy and behavior in the United States, 1992–2007.

complementary legislation, as well as his and President Bush's efforts to secure Greenspan's validation of their economic policies, deference remained high.

Deference to constraining economic technocrats – both the Treasury secretary and the director of the NEC – declined in the fall of 2001. This period is characterized by a dramatic surge in President Bush's popularity and legislative capacity. It also likely reflects a broader shift resulting from the 9/11 attacks after which people placed a higher value on the government's ability to adapt to changing circumstances than on policy stability. As a consequence, it is not surprising that President Bush felt empowered to fire naysaying technocrats.

When authority is uncontested, deference is high and political capacity is low, the model predicts that national politicians will seek validation for economic policymakers. As predicted, President Clinton and President Bush both sought validation from the chairman of the Federal Reserve (category 2 in rows 2 and 3 in Figure 4.4). In contrast to President Clinton, who continued to support Greenspan, Rubin and Summers' promotion of financial liberalization even after rebuilding his political clout by winning reelection in 1996, President Bush chose to ignore Greenspan's concerns about his second round of tax cuts and dismissed Treasury Secretary O'Neill for not fully supporting the administration's positions once his own political fortunes had improved (category 5 in row 4 in Figure 4.4). As expected, markets responded positively to the former and negatively to the latter.

4.3   Financial and Political Crisis Management, 2008–Present

The 2008 financial crisis has been described as "the largest financial shock since the Great Depression, inflicting heavy damage on markets and institutions at the core of the financial system."[91] During peak periods of the crisis, the Federal Reserve, Executive Branch and Congress all played active roles in stimulating the economy, providing financial support to failed or failing companies, engaging in regulatory reform and working with other countries to coordinate global policy responses.[92] Between December of 2007 and July of 2010, the Federal Reserve and Treasury engaged in extensive institutional innovations.[93] Congress enacted the Troubled Asset Relief Program (the second time around) and approved bailouts for the auto industry as well as for major financial firms.[94] The American Recovery and Reinvestment Act of 2009 and the Tax Relief, Unemployment and Insurance Reauthorization, and Job Creation Act of 2010 (which extended the Bush-era tax cuts) were enacted and, after much political infighting, the Dodd–Frank Wall Street Reform and Consumer Protection Act was signed.[95] During this period, national governments coordinated stimulus programs, central banks around the world

---

[91] "Global prospects and policies" (2008). *International Monetary Fund*, April, p. 4. www.imf.org/external/pubs/ft/weo/2008/01/pdf/c1.pdf.

[92] Shambaugh. "States and Markets." See also: Financial Crisis Inquiry Commission (2011). *The Financial Crisis Inquiry Report: Final Report of the National Commission on the Causes of the Financial and Economic Crisis in the United States*. Washington, DC: Government Printing Office. www.gpo.gov/fdsys/pkg/GPO-FCIC/pdf/GPO-FCIC.pdf.

[93] Federal Reserve System (2011). "Opportunities Exist to Strengthen Policies and Processes for Managing Emergency Assistance." Report to Congressional Addressees. GAO-11-696. *United States Government Accountability Office*, p. 3 (table 1). www.gao.gov/new.items/d11696.pdf.

[94] On TARP, see: www.federalreserve.gov/bankinforeg/tarpinfo.htm. On its relationship to the automobile bailouts, see: B. Canis & B. Webel (2013). "The Role of TARP Assistance in the Restructuring of General Motors," *Congressional Research Service*, May 9. https://digitalcommons.ilr.cornell.edu/key_workplace/991.

[95] Dodd–Frank Wall Street Reform and Consumer Protection Act (Pub. L. 111-203, H.R. 4173, signed on July 21, 2010). www.gpo.gov/fdsys/pkg/PLAW-111publ203/content-detail.html. Policy actions also included the Economic Stimulus Act of 2008 (Pub. L. 110-185, 122 Stat. 613, enacted on February 13, 2008), the American Recovery and Reinvestment Act of 2009 (ARRA) (Pub. L. 111-5, enacted on February 17, 2009), the Tax Relief, Unemployment Insurance Reauthorization, and Job Creation Act of 2010 (Pub. L. 111-312, H.R. 4853, 124 Stat. 3296, enacted on December 17, 2010, which extended the Bush tax cuts), the Small Business Lending Fund Act of 2010, (H.R. 5297, enacted on September 27, 2010), the Budget Control Act of 2011 (Pub. L. 112-25, S. 365, 125 Stat. 240, enacted on August 2, 2011), the Temporary Payroll Tax Cut Continuation Act of 2011 (Pub. L. 112-78, enacted on December 23, 2011), the Middle Class Tax Relief and Job Creation Act of 2012 (Pub. L. 112-96, H.R. 3630, 126 Stat. 156, enacted on February 22, 2012) and the American

created swap lines, multilateral fora grew in scale and representativeness, and multilateral economic reforms were implemented.[96]

The interventions were widely successful. By the end of 2010, uncertainty and investor risk had declined from their stratospheric levels and most crisis-related assistance programs had concluded and even generated profits. In short, during the peak of the crisis, "The System Worked!"[97]

Ironically, as happened in Argentina, when economic and political conditions improved, deference to economic technocrats declined and domestic political conflict intensified. Almost immediately following the signing of the Dodd–Frank financial reform legislation on July 21, 2010, political brinksmanship between the US Congress and President Obama generated increasing political uncertainty on a range of issues including whether the United States would default on the national debt or shut down due to policy disputes over health care policy and the deficit.[98] Political uncertainty led to a downgrading of the US economy by credit-rating agencies and a self-imposed draconian austerity program known as "the sequester" when no agreement was reached on the budget.[99]

With President Obama constrained by Congress and legislation stalled, economic policymakers took on the roles of enablers and substitutes. Much as its predecessors had done, the Treasury Department helped President Obama outmaneuver congressional opponents during their prolonged budgetary battles. The Federal Reserve, meanwhile, often intervened to stimulate the economy when political uncertainty was high.

Echoing Bernanke's warning, however, the Federal Reserve's interventions were imperfect substitutes, and the benefits of its actions were not distributed evenly within society. Consequently, while the Fed and other economic regulators were technocrats remained heroes for some, for others they fell from grace and were derided as villains. Complaints of favoritism, unevenness of the recovery and ties to Wall Street have fueled political polarization and public criticism of the Federal Reserve, the Treasury and other economic institutions and experts.

Taxpayer Relief Act of 2012 (Pub. L. 112-240, H.R. 8, 126 Stat. 2313, enacted on January 2, 2013).

[96] Federal Reserve System. "Opportunities Exist."

[97] D. Drezner (2012). "The irony of global economic governance: the system worked." *Tufts University*. https://politics.utoronto.ca/wp-content/uploads/2012/10/The-Irony-of-Global-Economic-Governance.pdf.

[98] For a useful timeline of these events, see: "Washington's budget fiasco: a timeline" (n. d.). *CNN Money*. https://money.cnn.com/interactive/economy/budget-follies-timeline/?iid=EL.

[99] Ibid.

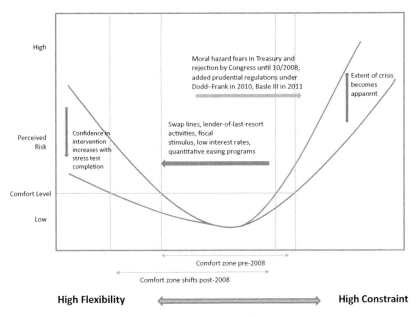

Figure 4.5 The US financial crisis and beyond.

The RIC during the crisis is reflected in Figure 4.5. As the extent of the crisis became apparent in September of 2008, the risks of policy rigidity and private-sector paralysis increased. Initially, Treasury Secretary Paulson's protestations against intervention and Congress's aversion to supporting the Troubled Asset Relief Program (TARP) increased risk by signaling rigidity and driving the United States to the right along the RIC. After the collapse of Lehman Brothers, the Treasury, Federal Reserve, Federal Deposit Insurance Corporation (FDIC) and others changed course and pursued a wide range of innovative strategies to increase economic policy flexibility and encourage market activity. While most crisis-related lender-of-last-resort activities concluded in 2010, the Federal Reserve continued to encourage market activity by keeping interest rates close to zero and using QE to stimulate the economy.

4.3.1   Using Appointments to Compensate for Limited Political Capacity

President George W. Bush's popularity peaked at the extraordinarily positive 90–6 percent approval–disapproval based on a Gallup poll conducted on September 21 and 22, 2001. As noted above, this gave him high levels of implementation capacity and led to a decline in the level of deference granted to technocratic critics. As the wars in Afghanistan and Iraq dragged on, however, the President's popularity declined. By the onset of the financial crisis seven years later, the President's approval-disapproval rating had declined to 27–69 percent.[100] The significance of that drop was driven home when President Bush failed to deliver support from his own political party and only a third of Republicans in the House of Representative voted in favor of TARP. The President's political weakness was compounded by the inability of Henry Paulson and Ben Bernanke to convince Congress to approve their request. Lacking implementation and deference from congress, the technocrats and the President appeared impotent as the measure failed on September 29. Markets reacted violently.[101]

On October 3, 2008, Congress relented and passed with Emergency Economic Stabilization Act which authorized the Treasury to spend up to US$700 billion to buy mortgage-backed securities and other distressed assets. The Treasury interpreted this authority broadly, but ultimately did not cost the tax payers much money. As of December 31, 2012, it had received US$405 billion in returns on US$418 billion in funds that were eventually allocated through the program.[102]

President Obama began his term with a relatively high approval–disapproval rating of 67–13 percent based on a Gallup poll conducted between January 19 and 25, 2009. His popularity declined thereafter, reaching 44–48 percent on a Gallup poll conducted between November 1 and 4, 2010. The significance of this drop was driven home by severe electoral losses for the Democratic Party during midterm elections on November 2, which President Obama derided as a "shellacking." President Obama's approval rating stayed in the same range throughout the intense and drawn-out budget battles that led to a downgrading of the US credit rating in August of 2012, the imposition of draconian cuts though a self-imposed sequester in February of 2013, and a shutdown of the federal government in September and October of 2013 orchestrated by Senator Ted Cruz. Thus, President Obama had limited implementation capacity throughout the majority of his presidency.

[100] "Presidential job approval center" (n.d.). *Gallup*. www.gallup.com/poll/124922/presidential-job-approval-center.aspx.

[101] C. Isidore (2008). "Bailout plan rejected – supporters scramble." *CNN Money*, September 29. https://money.cnn.com/2008/09/29/news/economy/bailout.

[102] A. Glass (2013). "Bush signs bank bailout, Oct. 3 2008." *Politico*, October 3. www.politico.com/story/2013/10/bush-signs-tarp-legislation-oct-3-2008-097742.

4.3.1.1 Linked Interdependence When political leaders are weak, they often appoint particular economic policymakers to increase market confidence and generate support for their economy policies. Appointees may signal policy continuity or change. Appointees may also provide particular areas of expertise or access to specific networks. Theories of central bank autonomy emphasize the degree of independence between the head of the central bank and the executive branch, but generally do not address the fact that many central bankers and finance ministers are drawn from or have strong ties to the private sector. Indeed, many senior economic policymakers are chosen because of their close connections with the private sector or other government bureaucracies.

Connections with the business world may signal an understanding and appreciation of business concerns, but they can also be interpreted as a source of potential corruption and patronage. As a consequence, Javier Corrales argues that economic leaders who demonstrate "linked interdependence" with those affected by their policies may be preferable to those who come directly from the business world.[103] Such leaders have expertise and strong reputations in their professions, but lack direct association with the businesses and others who will be affected by their policies. Financial leaders like these include Federal Reserve Chairmen Alan Greenspan and Ben Bernanke and Treasury Secretary Timothy Geithner.

Others come directly from the business world. These include Treasury Secretaries Robert Rubin and Hank Paulson, who were former co-chairman and chairman of Goldman Sachs, respectively. Their knowledge of the financial industry and close relations with other financial executives proved critical during their respective political and financial crises. This was demonstrated on October 13, 2008, when Paulson, Bernanke and Geithner convened a meeting of the CEOs of the nine largest financial companies in Washington, DC. Largely for fear of being identified as needing assistance, none wanted to accept a bailout. Nonetheless, Paulson, Bernanke and Geithner used their regulatory authority and reputations to persuade them all to accept a capital infusion of US$125 billion so that no individual company would be stigmatized and the banking system would be recapitalized.[104]

---

[103] J. Corrales (1997b). "Why Argentines Followed Cavallo: A Technopol between Democracy and Economic Reform." In J. I. Domínguez, ed., *Technopols: The Role of Ideas and Leaders in Freeing Politics and Markets in Latin America in the 1990s.* University Park: Penn State Press, pp. 49–93.

[104] "'Good number' of banks seeking federal capital, Paulson says" (2008). *New York Times*, October 16. http://dealbook.nytimes.com/2008/10/16/good-number-of-banks-

President Obama sought to reassure the markets by reappointing Ben Bernanke as chairman of the Fed; by appointing Timothy Geithner, who had been the president of the Federal Reserve Bank of New York during the Bush administration, as Treasury secretary; and by appointing Larry Summers as director of the NEC.[105] Unfortunately, confidence in Geithner as a "reliable and respected voice on financial issues" faded when the public became aware that he had failed to pay his social security taxes for several years.[106] Geithner was further undermined by ongoing congressional criticism of TARP, a public outcry regarding US$165 million in bonuses paid by AIG after getting bailed out,[107] complaints that he failed to explain the Obama administration's Financial Stability Plan during his debut as secretary of the Treasury on February 10, 2009,[108] and anxiety regarding the seemingly prolonged waiting period for the release of his initial stress tests in the spring of 2009. Though President Obama said that he had confidence in Geithner and would not allow him to resign, Geithner's appointment did little to bolster confidence in US economic policy until the release of his first stress test on April 24, 2009.[109] Even after that, he continued to face calls for his resignation by opponents in Congress.[110]

seeking-federal-capital-paulson-says; R. Farley (2012). "The problems with limiting large banks." *New York Times*, May 23. http://dealbook.nytimes.com/2012/05/23/the-problems-with-limiting-large-banks.

[105] E. Andrews (2009). "Obama to nominate Bernanke to 2nd term at Fed." *New York Times*, August 24. www.nytimes.com/2009/08/25/business/25bernanke.html; R. Schroeder (2008). "Obama taps Geithner, Clinton, Richardson, Summers." *Wall Street Journal*, November 23. www.marketwatch.com/story/geithner-clinton-summers-to-take-senior-obama-posts.

[106] "Geithner's tax troubles are serious" (2008). *Forbes*, January 13. www.forbes.com/2009/01/13/treasury-geithner-obama-biz-beltway-cx_bw_0113geithner2.html; C. O'Brien (2009). "Timothy Geithner's tax problems." *Washington Post*, January 19. www.washingtonpost.com/wp-dyn/content/article/2009/01/18/AR2009011802070.html.

[107] Congressional Oversight Panel for Economic Stabilization (2008). "The first report of the Congressional Oversight Panel for Economic Stabilization." *CNN*, December 10. http://money.cnn.com/news/specials/storysupplement/bailout_report; see also: D. Goldman (2008). "Congress demands answers on bailout House panel hears testimony from Treasury and key bailout oversight administrators on government's handling of funds." *CNN Money*, December 10. http://money.cnn.com/2008/12/10/news/economy/bailout_oversight_hearing/index.htm?postversion=2008121013.

[108] J. Calmes (2009). "For Geithner's debut, a lukewarm reception." *New York Times*, February 10. www.nytimes.com/2009/02/11/business/economy/11geithner.html.

[109] Board of Governors of the Federal Reserve System (2009). "The Supervisory Capital Assessment Program: Overview of results." *US Department of the Treasury*, May 7. www.treasury.gov/initiatives/financial-stability/TARP-Programs/bank-investment-programs/scap-and-cap/Pages/default.aspx.

[110] A. Sorkin (2004). "What Timothy Geithner really thinks." *New York Times Magazine*, May 8. www.nytimes.com/2014/05/11/magazine/what-timothy-geithner-really-thinks.html?_r=2; see also: M. Jaffe (2009). "Echoing Democrat's comments,

Geithner stepped down on January 21, 2013, just after the December 31 agreement between President and Congress to extend the Bush-era tax cuts and establish a March 1 deadline for negotiations to avoid automatic cuts through the "sequester."[111] Given the continued salience of the budget negotiations, President Obama appointed Jack Lew, who had served as director of the Office of Management and Budget under both Presidents Clinton and Obama.

4.3.1.2 Deference and Division Unity among policymakers and regulators was generally high during the crisis, but not universally so. Fed Chairman Bernanke met regularly with Secretaries of the Treasury Hank Paulson and Timothy Geithner. Their relationships developed during March of 2008 while working to resolve the collapse of Bear Stearns. They grew tighter still in September and October as the crisis exploded. From September 16 through February of 2010, the Federal Reserve and Treasury coordinated their lender-of-last-resort functions. On September 16, for example, the Federal Reserve provided US$85 billion to support the Treasury Department's efforts to forestall the collapse of AIG. In addition, it provided a large amount of additional lending to support TARP. As reported by Bloomberg based on a Freedom of Information lawsuit filed against the Fed, "Bank of America and New York-based Citigroup each received $45 billion from TARP [initiated on October 3, 2008]. At the time, both were tapping the Fed. Citigroup hit its peak borrowing of $99.5 billion in January 2009, while Bank of America topped out in February 2009 at $91.4 billion."[112]

In contrast, when jurisdictional lines are unclear or policy disagreements persist among regulators within or across the various agencies, private-sector actors are often uncertain about who might intervene and what they are likely to do. These dynamics are particularly noticeable in the United States because of the diffuse nature of its economic policy-making and regulatory structures.[113] Economic policy-making in the

---

two Republicans call for Geithner to go." *ABC News,* November 19. http://abcnews.go.com/Politics/house-republicans-treasurys-geithner-resign/story?id=9127162.

[111] "Geithner's planned departure puts Obama in tough spot" (2013). *CNBC,* January 4. www.cnbc.com/id/100354135.

[112] B. Ivry, B. Keoun & P. Kuntz (2011). "Secret Fed loans gave banks $13 billion undisclosed to Congress." *Bloomberg,* November 27. www.bloomberg.com/news/2011-11-28/secret-fed-loans-undisclosed-to-congress-gave-banks-13-billion-in-income.html.

[113] E. Murphy (2015). *Who Regulates Whom and How? An Overview of U.S. Financial Regulatory Policy for Banking and Securities Markets. CRS Report, R43087.* Washington, DC: Congressional Research Service, p. 2.

executive branch[114] is divided among the Department of the Treasury,[115] the NEC,[116] the Council of Economic Advisors[117] and the Office of Management and Budget.[118] To complicate matters further, the United States does not have a single central bank. Instead, the Federal Reserve System is composed of twelve regional Federal Reserve Banks, a seven-member Board of Governors (of which the chairman is the first among equals), a twelve-member FOMC, and member banks throughout the country.[119] Regulatory responsibility for commercial banking is divided among the Federal Reserve, the FDIC,[120] the National Credit Union Administration and state regulators.[121] Before being abolished in 2010, banks and thrifts that focused on mortgage markets were managed by the Office of Thrift Supervision (OTS).[122] Currently, thrifts are overseen by the Office of the Comptroller of the Currency (OCC),[123] while thrift-holding companies are regulated by the Federal Reserve. The Dodd–Frank Act also created an interagency Federal Stability Oversight Council to monitor systemic risk across the banking system.[124]

Different regulators have different objectives and use different strategies for reducing uncertainty and risk. The principal objective of banking regulators is to reduce systemic risk to the financial system as a whole by monitoring the safety, soundness and diversity of lending practices by member banks.[125] They manage risk by providing lender-

---

[114] Shambaugh & Weinstein. *The Art of Policymaking*, chs. 2, 13 and 14.

[115] The Treasury Department is the executive agency responsible for promoting economic prosperity and ensuring the financial security of the United States. See: https://home.treasury.gov/about/general-information/role-of-the-treasury.

[116] The NEC was established in 1993 to advise the president on US and global economic policy. See: www.federalregister.gov/agencies/national-economic-council.

[117] The Council of Economic Advisers is charged with offering the president objective economic advice on the formulation of both domestic and international economic policy. See: www.whitehouse.gov/cea.

[118] For the Office of Management and Budget, see: www.whitehouse.gov/omb.

[119] "About the Fed" (n.d.). *US Federal Reserve*. www.federalreserve.gov/faqs/about-the-fed.htm.

[120] To learn more about the Federal Deposit Insurance Corporation, see: www.fdic.gov/about/learn/symbol.

[121] Murphy. *Who Regulates Whom and How?* p. 2.

[122] To learn more about the Office of Thrift Supervision in the Department of the Treasury, see: www.treasury.gov/about/history/Pages/ots.aspx.

[123] To learn more about the Office of the Comptroller of the Currency in the Department of the Treasury, see: www.occ.gov/about/what-we-do/mission/index-about.html.

[124] To learn more about the Financial Stability Oversight Council, see: www.treasury.gov/initiatives/fsoc/Pages/home.aspx.

[125] F. Allen & R. Herring (2001). *Banking Regulation versus Securities Regulation.* Philadelphia: Wharton Financial Institutions Center. Cited in: Murphy. *Who Regulates Whom and How?*

of-last-resort services to banks and deposit insurance and other guarantees to borrowers. They also focus on making sure that banks have adequate capital to sustain normal operations and to withstand the pressure of an economic downturn. In his memoir on the financial crisis, Secretary Geithner argues that the preferred strategies and reputations for stringency varied across different agencies. He notes, for example, that Sheila Bair at the FDIC initially disagreed with him regarding the extent to which the FDIC should expand the scope and domain of its borrower protections in the fall of 2008. He also argues that the OTS was known for weak enforcement and that the OTS and OCC had inherent conflicts of interest because they were both funded by fees collected by member banks and were therefore encouraged to woo clients by offering potentially weaker enforcement.[126]

Regulators in the securities and derivatives markets include the SEC,[127] which supervises investment banks, and the CFTC,[128] which monitors futures contracts. Rather than reduce the risk of default, their principal roles are to protect investors from unscrupulous brokers and to enhance the efficiency of financial exchanges by monitoring and requiring the disclosure of information pertaining to the exchange of financial contracts. This is important because although money-market mutual funds and money-market accounts provided by investment banks look and operate like commercial bank accounts, they are not covered by the capital requirements or deposit insurance associated with the commercial banking system.[129]

Consequently, there was no deposit insurance on the Primary Fund – a money-market fund with US$65 billion in assets – when it "broke the buck" on September 16, 2008, due to its exposure to securities issued by Lehman Brothers Holdings which had declared bankruptcy on September 15. "Breaking the buck" means that its shares fell below their face value of one dollar (e.g., their value fell to 97 cents on the dollar).[130] In response, the Federal Reserve created multiple facilities to stabilize short-term debt markets, including commercial paper that was

---

[126] Geithner. *Stress Test*, p. 166.
[127] To learn more about the SEC, see: www.sec.gov/about/whatwedo.shtml.
[128] To learn more about the CFTC, see: www.cftc.gov/about/missionresponsibilities/index.htm.
[129] Geithner. *Stress Test*, p. 166.
[130] "Money-Market Fund 'Breaks the Buck'" (2008). *New York Times: DealBook*, September 17. http://dealbook.nytimes.com/2008/09/17/money-market-fund-says-customers-could-lose-money.

purchased by individual investors using money-market accounts and money-market mutual funds.[131] In order to stem the panic, the Federal Reserve created the Asset-Backed Commercial Paper Money Market Mutual Fund Liquidity Facility on September 19, the Commercial Paper Funding Facility on October 7 and the Money Market Investor Funding Facility on October 21, 2008.[132] No other mutual fund "broke the buck," but uncertainty in general market conditions remained high through mid-2009.

4.3.1.3 Budget Battles Revisited, 2011, 2013 and 2015 Like their predecessors in 1995, Republicans elected in the midterm elections on November 2, 2010 (i.e., the "Tea Party Revolution"), tried to compel the President to make deep spending cuts and other policy changes by threatening not to raise the debt ceiling.[133] Prolonged and tumultuous negotiations over the six years that followed created high levels of political uncertainty and risk. Repeated failures to reach an agreement led to repeated last-minute actions to avoid variety of calamities including default, a downgrading of the US credit rating in August of 2011, a self-imposed austerity program known as the sequester in March of 2013 and a government shutdown for 16 days in October 2013.

Throughout the ordeal, President Obama and Federal Reserve Chairs Bernanke and Yellen joined Treasury Secretaries Geithner and Lew in emphasizing the dangers of defaulting or even potentially defaulting on US debt obligations.[134] They repeatedly chastised Congress for invoking the debt limit as a bargaining chip, reminding them that protecting the full faith and credit of the United States was one of their constitutional mandates. Per his mandate, the secretary of the Treasury repeatedly notified Congress when debt limits would be breached.[135] These letters

---

[131] Commercial paper is short-term debt with maturities of less than 270 days that is purchased with little or no collateral.

[132] B. Webel & M. Labonte (2010). *Government Interventions in Response to Financial Turmoil.* Washington, DC: Congressional Research Service.

[133] P. Wallsten, L. Montgomery & S. Wilson (2012). "Obama's evolution: behind the failed 'grand bargain' on debt." *Washington Post,* March 17. www.washingtonpost.com/politics/obamas-evolution-behind-the-failed-grand-bargain-on-the-debt/2012/03/15/gIQAHyyfJS_story.html.

[134] "Debt Limit" (2016). *US Department of the Treasury,* January 29. https://home.treasury.gov/policy-issues/financial-markets-financial-institutions-and-fiscal-service/debt-limit; see also: "The Potential Macroeconomic Effect of Debt Ceiling Brinksmanship" (2013). *US Department of the Treasury,* October. www.treasury.gov/initiatives/Documents/POTENTIAL%20MACROECONOMIC%20IMPACT%20OF%20DEBT%20CEILING%20BRINKMANSHIP.pdf.

[135] "Debt Limit" (2016). *US Department of the Treasury,* January 29. www.treasury.gov/initiatives/Pages/debtlimit.aspx.

generally provided detailed information regarding what "extraordinary means" the Treasury would use and how long they would last before the debt limit was breached again.[136]

The Treasury Department exercised the same basic authority it had in 1995, but the nature of the contestation had changed. In 1995, members of Congress were surprised by Rubin's use of "extraordinary measures" to extend the payment period. Although the authority existed, it had not been exercised before. In particular, members did not expect the Treasury to tap the Social Security Fund as a source of revenue. They contested that practice and, once the crisis was over, removed the Social Security Fund from the set of trusts that could be used to meet debt obligations.

In contrast, in the budget battles of 2011 through 2015, Secretaries Geithner and Lew were widely expected to use "extraordinary means" to avoid default. Indeed, rather than contesting the use of extraordinary means, critics protested that they did not go far enough. Some argued, for example, that Treasury could avoid default with less money if it paid some of its public obligations immediately but delayed payments on others.[137] This strategy of prioritizing debt repayments is similar to the Treasury's use of other "extraordinary means," except that it infringed on debt held by the public rather than internal government agencies and trusts. On January 21, 2011, Deputy Secretary of the Treasury Neal Wolin argued against the proposal, noting:[138]

While well-intentioned, this idea is unworkable. It would not actually prevent default, since it would seek to protect only principal and interest payments, and no other legal obligations of the U.S., from non-payment. Adopting a policy that payments to investors should take precedence over other U.S. legal obligations would merely be default by another name, since the world would recognize it as a failure by the U.S. to stand behind its commitments. It would therefore bring about the same catastrophic economic consequences Secretary Geithner has warned against, including sharp rises in mortgage interest rates and other borrowing costs for families; reductions in the value of homes, 401(k) plans and other retirement savings; and negative effects on the dollar and the safe haven status of Treasury bonds and other Treasury securities. Such a policy

---

[136] This letter contains an appendix with specific details about the funds that would or could be tapped and how much revenue doing so would generate. Letters written by the secretaries of the Treasury are maintained by the Department of the Treasury online; see: "Debt Limit" (2016). *US Department of the Treasury*, January 29. www.treasury.gov/initiatives/Pages/debtlimit.aspx.

[137] 114th Congress, First Session. H.R. 692 (Report No. 114-265) To ensure the payment of interest and principal of the "Default Prevention Act."

[138] "Debt Limit" (2016). *US Department of the Treasury*, January 29. www.treasury.gov/initiatives/Pages/debtlimit.aspx.

would also be unacceptable to American servicemen and women, retirees, and all other Americans, who would rightly reject the notion that their payment has been deemed a lower priority by their government. For these reasons, the Department of Treasury has always emphasized – regardless of which party has held the White House or either house of Congress – that the only way to prevent default and protect America's creditworthiness is to enact a timely increase in the debt limit.

The Chairman of the Federal Reserve concurred that, "This approach is extremely dangerous. By appearing to make a default legitimate and manageable, it would heighten the risk that one will actually occur."[139]

Nonetheless, a group of newly elected and highly ideological Republicans in the House of Representatives chose not to defer to this advice. In the spring of 2011, negotiations broke down when John Boehner was unable to generate sufficient support from within his own party for his "grand bargain" with President Obama.[140] Distrust of Boehner from inside the party grew as rumors spread that Boehner had been negotiating without their input.[141] The last-minute breakdown of negotiations, in turn, fueled distrust of Boehner by administration officials.[142]

As the crisis progressed, Republicans criticized the Treasury for not using all of the tools available to it and of intentionally underestimating the time it could keep the country from going into default. The Treasury Department rebutted that its resources were far more limited than they had been in 1995. Rubin had been able to secure about US$40 billion in debt ceiling headroom in 1995. Using the same techniques, Geithner

[139] J. Friedman (2015). "Congress shouldn't play politics with the debt ceiling." *Center on Budget and Policy Priorities*, October 20. www.cbpp.org/blog/congress-shouldnt-play-politics-with-the-debt-ceiling.

[140] M. Bai (2012). "Obama vs. Boehner: who willed the debt deal?" *Washington Post*, March 12. www.nytimes.com/2012/04/01/magazine/obama-vs-boehner-who-killed-the-debt-deal.html?_r=0.

[141] M. Leahy (2011). "Is the biggest threat to Speaker of the House John Boehner the 'Young Guns' in his own party?" *Washington Post*, May 19. www.washingtonpost.com/lifestyle/magazine/is-the-biggest-threat-to-speaker-of-the-house-john-boehner-the-young-guns-in-his-own-party/2011/04/29/AFJhYU7G_print.html; see also: J. Bouie (2015). "The revolution devours its own." *Slate*, September 25. www.slate.com/articles/news_and_politics/politics/2015/09/john_boehner_devoured_by_the_gop_revolution_his_right_wing_rhetoric_came.html.

[142] L. Montgomery & P. Kane (2011). "Debt-limit vote is canceled in House as Boehner, GOP leaders struggle to gain votes." *Washington Post*, July 28. www.washingtonpost.com/business/economy/boehner-other-gop-leaders-ramp-up-pressure-on-republicans-to-pass-debt-plan/2011/07/28/gIQARD5veI_story.html; see also: E. Wasson (2011). "Boehner rebuts Obama's criticism, says the president moved the goal posts." *The Hill*, July 23. https://thehill.com/policy/finance/173099-boehner-rebuts-obama-criticism-says-president-moved-goal-post.

raised about US$150 billion in 2011.[143] Unfortunately, this fourfold increase in funds was overwhelmed by an eightfold increase in the annual budget deficit that had grown from US$164 billion in 1995 to US$1.3 trillion in 2011. Members of Congress rebutted that other options were available. The House Financial Services Committee began a probe in 2013 and issued a subpoena for documents in May 2015. On February 1, 2016, they released a report highlighting consultations and strategy sessions between the Treasury and Federal Reserve regarding how to prioritize payments.[144] The Treasury acknowledged the possibility of prioritizing debt payments, but maintained its refusal to do so because it would lead the country into that "uncharted territory that's fraught with risk."[145]

In short, like Secretary Rubin, Treasury Secretaries Geithner and Lew tried to use their authority to employ "extraordinary means" to extend the time available to the President and Congress to negotiate. That authority was insufficient, rank-and-file members of Congress refused to defer to their recommendations, and neither President Obama nor Speaker Boehner had the capacity to mobilize supporting legislation. Consequently, the debt negotiations collapsed. Ironically, the mistaken presumption that the Treasury had the capacity to intervene appears to have emboldened congressional critics by creating an expectation that they would be bailed out or could at least shift the blame for the failure to the Treasury. These expectations generated a classic moral hazard problem.

4.3.2   The Federal Reserve as an Enabler and Substitute

The Federal Reserve responded to the financial crisis of 2007–2015 through a series of targeted and broad-based lender-of-last-resort initiatives, by stimulating the economy using traditional open-market operations to lower the federal funds rate, and through a series of

---

[143] E. Pianin (2011). "Treasury's bag o' tricks may not avert catastrophe." *Fiscal Times*, February 4. www.thefiscaltimes.com/Articles/2011/02/04/Treasurys-Bag-of-Tricks-May-Not-Avert-Catastrophe.

[144] P. Schroeder (2016). "GOP investigation: treasury misled Congress, public about the debt limit." *The Hill*, February 1. http://thehill.com/policy/finance/267711-gop-probe-treasury-misled-congress-public-on-debt-limit.

[145] D. Watson (2015). "There is only one solution to the debt limit." *US Department of the Treasury*, October 16. www.treasury.gov/connect/blog/Pages/one-solution-debt-limit.aspx.

"extraordinary" QE measures.[146] Between August of 2007 and December of 2008, the Federal Reserve tried to stimulate the economy through traditional means.[147] It lowered the federal funds rate from 5.25 percent to 0.25 percent, decreased the spread between its primary lending rate at the discount window and the federal funds rate in August of 2007 and again in March of 2008, and extended the lending period from one to thirty days. Once the federal funds rate had effectively reached zero, the Fed exploited an innovative strategy known as quantitative policy that it had developed during the US savings and loan crisis in the 1990s. The strategy involved a series of three QE initiatives (QE1, QE2 and QE3) that were designed to stimulate borrowing by increasing the money supply and lowering interest rates through the purchase of mortgage-backed securities and Treasury bonds. The QE initiatives were complemented by Operation Twist, a program that was designed to lower long-term interest rates by shifting the balance of long-term and short-term debt in the Federal Reserve's portfolio. The Bank of England later followed a similar strategy of expanding their monetary base by purchasing bonds. The European Central Bank and Bank of Japan also developed QE programs, though their programs were designed to provide direct lending to banks rather than providing liquidity through bond purchases.[148]

On May 22, 2013, Chairman Bernanke reported to Congress that the Federal Reserve would slow down its asset purchase program in the next few months.[149] He reiterated his comments in June, announcing that the Federal Reserve could taper its bond-buying program later in 2013 if the economy continued to improve. On September 18, 2013, however, he changed course and signaled that the Federal Reserve would put off any decision to taper until later in the year.[150] The Fed only restarted the taper following the reopening of the government, the passage of a budget agreement and the passage of a clean debt-limit bill.

---

[146] For a review of these policies, see: Federal Reserve System. "Opportunities Exist"; see also: B. Fawley & C. Neely (2013). "Four Stories of Quantitative Easing." *Federal Reserve Bank of St. Louis Review* 95(1), 51–88.

[147] For a review of these policies, see Federal Reserve System. "Opportunities Exist"; see also: J. Felkerson (2011). *$29 Trillion: A Detailed Look at the Fed's Bailout by Funding Facility and Recipient, Working Paper No. 698.* Annandale-On-Hudson: Levy Economics Institute of Bard College.

[148] For a comparison of QE as practiced by the Federal Reserve, Bank of England, European Central Bank and the Bank of Japan, see: Fawley & Neely. "Four Stories of Quantitative Easing."

[149] B. Bernanke (2013a). "The economic outlook." *Federal Reserve*, May 22. www.federalreserve.gov/newsevents/testimony/bernanke20130522a.htm .

[150] Bernanke, B. S. (2013b). Press conference. *Federal Reserve*, September 18. www.federalreserve.gov/mediacenter/files/FOMCpresconf20130918.pdf.

In total, the Federal Reserve intervened by announcing, implementing, extending or withdrawing its QE and Operation Twist programs ten times between the beginning of QE1 on November 25, 2008 and its decision to begin scaling back the magnitude of its QE program on December 18, 2013. These interventions took place on November 25, 2008(QE1), March 18, 2009 (QE1 extended), November 3, 2010 (QE2), September 21, 2011 (Operation Twist), June 20, 2012 (Operation Twist extended), September 13, 2012 (QE3), December 12, 2012 (QE3 and Operation Twist extended), May 22, 2013 (likelihood of taper announced to Congress), June 18, 2013 (second taper announcement), September 18, 2013 (taper suspended), December 18, 2013 (taper begun), and October 29, 2014 (taper ends). Finally, on December 16, 2015, the Federal Reserve raised interest rates for the first time since 2006.[151]

Ongoing political tensions between Congress and Presidents Bush and Obama during the crisis were punctuated by several significant points of conflict. These include: (1) the congressional rejection of the first TARP proposal on September 29, 2008; (2) the Republican landslide victories in midterm elections in November of 2010; (3) the budget and debt ceiling showdowns of June and July of 2011, and the subsequent downgrade of US credit by Standard and Poor's from AAA to AA+ on August 5, 2011 (despite the passage of the Budget Control Act);[152] (4) September through November of 2011 when budget negotiations collapsed and a "Super Committee" tasked with developing a budget plan quit amid scandals and the government approached the "Fiscal Cliff";[153] (5) February through March of 2013 between the passage of the "No Budget, No Pay Act" as a last-ditch effort to avoid the coming budget sequester that hit on March 1;[154] and (6) September through October of

---

[151] "The Federal Reserve's response to the financial crisis and actions to foster maximum employment and price stability" (2018). *US Federal Reserve*. www.federalreserve.gov/monetarypolicy/bst_crisisresponse.htm.

[152] "United States of America long-term rating lowered to 'AA+' due to political risks, rising debt burden; Outlook negative" (2011). Official Statement, *Standard and Poor's*, August 5. www.washingtonpost.com/wp-srv/politics/documents/spratingreport_080611.pdf.

[153] "Statement from co-chairs of the Joint Select Committee on Deficit Reduction" (2011). *US Senate*, November 21. www.murray.senate.gov/public/index.cfm/2011/11/statement-from-co-chairs-of-the-joint-select-committee-on-deficit-reduction.

[154] The act is intended "To ensure the complete and timely payment of the obligations of the United States Government until May 19, 2013, and for other purposes." H.R.325, see: http://thomas.loc.gov/cgi-bin/query/z?c113:H.R.325.

2013 when Senator Cruz rallied opposition to the Affordable Care Act that culminated in a shutdown of the federal government.[155]

The Federal Reserve often intervened when political uncertainty was high. For example, the Federal Reserve enacted the second round of QE on November 3, 2010, the day before the midterm elections in which critics of the President's policies were expected to – and did – win a large number of seats.[156] On August 9, 2011, in response to the political turmoil and resulting downgrade by Standard and Poor's, the Federal Reserve announced its intention to keep interest rates exceptionally low until 2013.[157] Similarly, the Federal Reserve expanded QE3 on December 12, 2012 disagreements escalated and it appeared that the US was to go over the so-called Fiscal Cliff. Echoing the earlier theme, Bernanke warned again that the failure of Congress and the President to resolve their differences "could have a very negative effect on hiring, jobs, wages, economic activity, investment. And of course, the consequences of that will be felt by everybody."[158] At the same time, however, he again acted to mitigate political uncertainty by increasing monthly bond purchases under QE3 to US\$85 billion while extending Operation Twist. Leaving the end point open, he announced that the Federal Reserve would keep interest rates low "at least as long as the unemployment rate remains above 6½ percent," which could last "at least through mid-2015."[159] Noting that "the economic recovery has certainly come a long way, although it is not complete," Federal Reserve Chairwoman Janet Yellen announced the first-quarter point rise in the federal funds rate since 2008 on December 16, 2015.[160]

In another example, the Federal Reserve adjusted its plans to end its bond-buying program in response to the threat of a government shutdown. On May 22, 2013, Chairman Bernanke had reported to Congress that the Federal Reserve would slow down its asset-purchasing program

---

[155] For a transcript of Senator Cruz's filibuster, see: www.washingtonpost.com/sf/national/2013/09/25/transcript-sen-ted-cruzs-filibuster-against-obamacare.

[156] White House, Office of the Press Secretary, Press Conference by the President, November 3, 2010. www.whitehouse.gov/the-press-office/2010/11/03/press-conference-president.

[157] US Federal Reserve, Press Release, August 9, 2011. www.federalreserve.gov/newsevents/press/monetary/20110809a.htm.

[158] Bernanke, B. S. (2012b). Press conference. *Federal Reserve*, December 12. www.federalreserve.gov/mediacenter/files/FOMCpresconf20121212.pdf.

[159] Ibid.

[160] B. Appelbaum (2015). "Fed raises key interest rate for first time in almost a decade." *New York Times*, December 16. www.nytimes.com/2015/12/17/business/economy/fed-interest-rates.html.

in the next few months.[161] He reiterated his comments in June, announcing that the Federal Reserve could taper its bond-buying program later in 2013 if the economy continued to improve. On September 18, 2013, however, he changed course and signaled that the Federal Reserve would put off any decision to taper until later in the year.[162] He did so to calm market reactions when congressional Republicans began mobilizing support for a shutdown of the government unless the administration agreed to repeal the Affordable Care Act. Tensions peaked with a twenty-one-hour filibuster led by Senator Ted Cruz on September 24, 2013 and the closing of the government in October.[163] The Federal Reserve waited to begin reducing its QE program until after the government reopened and an agreement among the parties was reached.

4.3.3   Expectations

Expectations regarding crisis interventions are summarized in Figure 4.6. In the spring of 2008, the Federal Reserve and Treasury maintained high levels of deference, but had limited authority to engage with Bear Stearns or Sally Mae and Freddy Mac, and President Bush was weak. This is reflected in category 4 in row 1 in Figure 4.6 (low authority, high deference, and low implementation capacity). As predicted, they succeeded when legislative support was not necessary (Bear Stearns) but ran into difficulty when Congressional support was needed. By September, with mixed signals emanating from the Treasury Secretary and Federal Reserve about bailouts and fear following the collapse of Lehman Brothers, deference had declined and the situation shifted to category 6 (low authority, low deference, and low implementation capacity). Given this, it is not surprising that Congress rejected the first TARP proposal. Legislative capacity increased momentarily with the passage of the second TARP proposal on October 3, and reliance on (and begrudging deference to) the technocrats increased as the extent of the crisis apparent (category 3). Although the authority to provide bailouts remained contested, the Federal Reserve and Treasury were able to secure the cooperation of large financial companies in October (category 4) and the Federal Reserve was able to begin its QE programs in November without significant challenges to its authority (category 2). President Obama attempted to build confidence in his economic plans by

---

[161] B. Bernanke (2013a). "The economic outlook." *Federal Reserve*, May 22. www.federalreserve.gov/newsevents/testimony/bernanke20130522a.htm.

[162] Bernanke, B. S. (2013b). Press conference. *Federal Reserve*, September 18. www.federalreserve.gov/mediacenter/files/FOMCpresconf20130918.pdf.

[163] For a transcript of Senator Cruz's filibuster, see: www.washingtonpost.com/sf/national/2013/09/25/transcript-sen-ted-cruzs-filibuster-against-obamacare.

	The Power to Act			Prediction		Outcome	
	Authority to Act	Deference to Technocrats	Implementation Capacity of National Politicians	Impact of Technocrats	Behavior	Role of Technocrats	Market Behavior
4	Low, Contested	High, Deference Granted	Low	Can constrain or expand policy flexibility if additional authority and legislative support are not necessary / Can validate policy, targeted strategies may be effective, broad strategies may be effective	Technocrats can help leaders outmaneuver political opponents, but long-term uncertainty remains	March–September 2008: Federal Reserve and Treasury expand authority under Article 13(3) to resolve Bear Stearns' collapse. Paulson secures authority to manage Freddie Mac and Fannie Mae, but argues that the government remains opposed to bailouts. Does not support Lehman Brothers, but uses 13(3) to assist AIG	Markets become increasingly jittery in August. Nationalizing Fannie Mae and Freddie Mac is insufficient to calm growing political and policy uncertainties. Failure to bail out Lehman Brothers triggers market panic
6	High or Low	Low, Deference Demanded	Low	Technocrats are impotent / Cannot validate policy, broad strategies by politicians may be effective	Minimum bargaining power, maximum uncertainty	September 29, 2008: House of Representatives fails to support Wall Street bailout package	Markets tumble, private-sector liquidity freezes
3	Low, Contested	High, Deference Granted	High or Not Necessary	Can constrain or expand policy flexibility if additional authority is not needed / Can validate policy, targeted and broad strategies may be effective	Technocrats will attempt to expand authority	October 3, 2008: TARP passes. Temporary political victory, but legislative capacity expected to remain	Market tumble subsides
4	Low, Contested	High, Deference Granted	Low	Can constrain or expand policy flexibility if additional authority and legislative support are not necessary / Can validate policy, targeted strategies may be disruptive, broad strategies may be effective	Technocrats can help leaders outmaneuver political opponents, but long-term uncertainty remains	October 13, 2008: Fed and Treasury compel large financial companies to accept capital infusion, then engage in wide-ranging innovations	Market confidence gradually returns
2	High, Uncontested	High, Deference Granted	Low	Can constrain or expand policy flexibility if legislative support is unnecessary / Can validate policy, broad strategies may be disruptive, broad strategies may be effective	Weak politicians appoint technocrats to bolster implementation capacity, but may abandon them	November 2008–October 2014: QE timed to reduce political as well as market uncertainties	Interventions compensate for increase political uncertainty generated by budget battles between the President and Congress
2 → 6	High or Low	High → Low	Low	Technocrats are impotent / Cannot validate policy, broad strategies by politicians may be effective	Minimum bargaining power, maximum uncertainty	November 2009: Obama announces he will reappoint Geithner and others from previous administration, but Geithner mishandles personal taxes and has difficulty explaining policy	Criticisms of bailouts and administration policies increase even as markets recover
4	Low, Contested	High, Deference Granted	Low	Can constrain or expand policy flexibility if additional authority and legislative support are not necessary / Can validate policy, targeted strategies may be effective, broad strategies may be effective	Technocrats can help leaders outmaneuver political opponents, but long-term uncertainty remains	2011–2015: Treasury Secretaries Geithner and Lew exercise "extraordinary measures" to avoid default but their tools are weaker than in 1995	Debt negotiations collapse repeatedly

Figure 4.6 Shaping policy and behavior in the United States, 2008–2010.

appointing Timothy Geithner, who had been president of the New York Fed under President Bush, as Treasury Secretary. Unfortunately, the benefits of doing so were undercut by disagreements among regulators, a kerfuffle regarding AIG bonuses and several missteps. This helped shift the United States from category 2 to 6 in row 4 in Figure 4.6. Confidence in Geithner increased after the release of the stress test results in May of 2009, but legislative capacity and congressional challenges to the Fed and Treasury's authority to intervene persisted.

The political dynamics in the Obama administration reflected category 4 dynamics from the Spring of 2009 through the end of his term (the bottom row in Figure 4.6). The Treasury and Federal Reserve interpreted their lender-of-last resort authority broadly (expanding the scope of TARP and invoking Article 13(3)). They successful assisted failing companies, but challenges to their authority persisted even after the "bailouts" had ended. Critics similarly contested Geithner and Lew use (and lack of us) of "extraordinary measures" to avoid default throughout the debt-limit fights. The entire QE program was considered extraordinary, though it was not challenged to the degree that its Article 13(3) operations had been. President

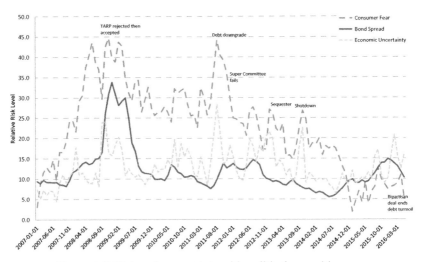

Figure 4.7 Risk and uncertainty with political opposition.

Obama also continually deferred to and defended his economic team. This suggests that the Federal Reserve should have been able to validate policy and help leaders outmaneuver political opponents, but some political uncertainty will remain until implementation capacity improves.

4.3.4   Outcomes

The consequences of Federal Reserve interventions are presented in Figures 4.7 and 4.8. Each figure tracks uncertainty and risk using three variables: policy uncertainty, consumer fear and investor risk. Policy uncertainty is operationalized using the Policy Uncertainty Index created by Scott Baker, Nick Bloom and Steven Davis, which is an index of search results from ten large newspapers for clusters of keywords referring to uncertainty, the economy and policy.[164] This index is used as an indicator of perceptions of risk and uncertainty among the attentive public, meaning those who are well informed about economic and political events.

Consumer fear is operationalized using the University of Michigan/ Thomson Reuters Consumer Sentiment Index, which is a composite of national survey responses to five questions pertaining to respondents' families' well-being compared to last year, their anticipated future well-being, the trajectory of business in the next year and broader economic

---

[164] S. Baker, N. Bloom & S. J. Davis (n.d.). "Economic Policy Uncertainty." www.policy uncertainty.com/us_monthly.html.

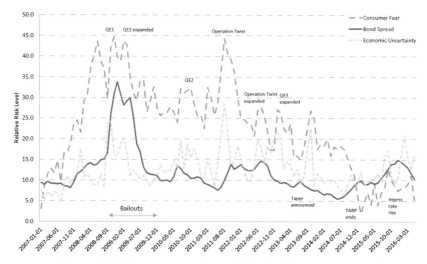

Figure 4.8 Risk and uncertainty with Federal Reserve interventions.

conditions over the next five years and personal spending expectations.[165] Higher values on the Consumer Sentiment Index represent greater optimism. The index is normalized to a value of 100 in 1966. The Consumer Fear Index is 100 minus the Consumer Sentiment Index. I present consumer fear rather than consumer sentiment to clarify the visual comparisons with the policy uncertainty and consumer risk indicators in Figures 4.7 and 4.8. Higher levels of the Consumer Fear Index indicate higher levels of perceived risk and uncertainty by the general public.

Investor risk is operationalized as the difference between Moody's Seasoned AAA and BAA corporate bond yields.[166] The use of corporate bond spreads as an indicator of risk and uncertainty is bolstered by the finding that less than half of the difference in these spreads can generally be explained by the financial health of the specific companies involved, and the remainder is attributed to a variety of factors, including expectations regarding future economic activity.[167] Absent a specific policy that

---

[165] For more information, see: Curtin, R. (n.d.). "Surveys of Consumers, University of Michigan." www.sca.isr.umich.edu; "University of Michigan: Consumer Sentiment" (n.d.). *Economic Research, Federal Reserve Bank of St. Louis.* http://research.stlouisfed .org/fred2/series/UMCSENT.

[166] Not seasonally adjusted. *Source:* "FRED Economic Data" (n.d.). *Federal Reserve Bank of St. Louis.* http://research.stlouisfed.org.

[167] S. Gilchrist & E. Zakrajlek (2011). "Credit Spreads and Business Cycle Fluctuations." NBER Working Paper No. 17021, May, p. 2.

affects AAA and BAA companies or bonds differently, the price levels of AAA and BAA are likely to be affected similarly by other economic shifts and shocks. As a consequence, the spread between them approximates the amount of risk in the economy by comparing "safe" (AAA) and slightly less safe (BAA) assets while controlling for general economic and political conditions that would affect both classes of bonds. Using corporate bond spreads is preferable to analyzing the shift in the spread between corporate bonds and US Treasury securities or the TED rate (i.e., the Treasury–EuroDollar rate, which is the difference between the federal funds rate and the London Interbank Offer Rate) because US Treasury securities, the federal funds rate and the TED rate are more likely to be affected by turmoil in European and other global markets as investors seek the safety of US government bonds.[168]

The specific effects of veto-player actions by Congress on risk and uncertainty are presented in Figure 4.7. The rejection of TARP, prolonged debt negotiations, Standard and Poor's downgrade in 2011 and implementation of the sequester each created peaks in consumer fear, investor risk and economic policy uncertainty. As expected, there is an immediate (though short-term) drop in risk across all of the indices that correspond to the passage of TARP in the second round in October of 2008. Investor risk and economic policy uncertainty tend to return to a general baseline after spiking, though economic uncertainty is much more volatile and tends to both spike and decline rapidly. Consumer fear, in contrast, remained elevated substantially above its starting level in January of 2007 from the peak of the crisis in September of 2008 until the effective return to normality in January of 2015. Investor risk was the least affected by the government shutdown in 2013. Signs of cooperation tended to have positive effects, but none other than the passage of the TARP legislation appear at a minimum or peak in risk.

The Federal Reserve often intervened when risk was peaking (see Figure 4.8). Investor risk, consumer fear and economic policy uncertainty generally decreased after the implementation and extension of QE programs. Declines also followed the commencement of Operation Twist and the suspension of the taper. Economic policy uncertainty is more volatile than consumer fear or investor risk, but it also appears to decline for short periods following the interventions. Periods of highly

---

[168] The values of each variable are modified to make their comparison more visually apparent. Specifically, the value of investor risk plotted is ten times the value of the actual BAA–AAA bond spread, and the value of policy uncertainty plotted is one-tenth the value found in the Policy Uncertainty Index. These conversions are used simply to make the changes in each variable more apparent in a single image.

public political confrontations – especially the tumultuous summer of 2011 in which the United States was downgraded from AAA to AA+, there were budget disputes late in 2012 and Obamacare was linked to the debt limits in the fall of 2013, subsequently leading to a government shutdown – are associated spikes in uncertainty.

4.4   Conclusion: Lessons Learned from the US Experience

Four lessons from all of these events are particularly noteworthy.

- **Lesson 1: Economic policymakers respond to political as well as economic uncertainty and risk.**

The Federal Reserve, Treasury and other regulators intervened repeatedly to enable as well as constrain economic policy-making and market activity. Reflecting the ideal of central bank independence, chairs of the Federal Reserve often adjusted monetary policies at times that were not optimal for the president and other national politicians. Operating beyond this ideal, chairs of the Federal Reserve also worked in close cooperation with the secretaries of the Treasury and other regulators by providing supplemental resources and helping manage policy and market behavior. Secretaries of the Treasury across multiple administrations helped their presidents outmaneuver political opponents, while the chairmen of the Federal Reserve and other technocrats altered the authorities of regulatory institutions and lobbied legislators in order to promote their preferred policy agendas.

- **Lesson 2: Authority matters, but the delegation of authority is not equivalent to the ability to shape policy or alter market behavior.**

The US experiences add three corollaries to this proposition.

  - **2a: National politicians and economic technocrats can expand their authority strategically. While often successful in the short run, assertions of authority beyond existing norms are often met by retaliatory legislation designed to restrict such assertions in the future.**

Members of Congress often retaliated against what they considered to be extraordinary actions by the Federal Reserve and Treasury by tightening limits on what they could do, who they could regulate and what resources they had at their disposal. These restrictions can limit the ability of the Fed and Treasury to respond to future crises. Congressionally imposed limits on the Department of the Treasury after it intervened in the Mexican peso crisis of 1994–1995 constrained the US government's response to the Asian Financial Crisis in 1997.[169] More recently, Congress has restricted the authority of the Federal Reserve to "bail out" failing companies as part of the Dodd–Frank Wall Street Reform and Consumer Protection Act.[170]

- ○ **Lesson 2b: The ability of economic policymakers to reduce perceptions of risk and uncertainty declines when lines of authority are unclear and/or deference to those in positions of authority declines.**

These dynamics are particularly noticeable in the United States because of the diffuse nature of its economic policy-making and regulatory structures.[171] Different regulators have different objectives and use different strategies to reduce uncertainty and risk. When jurisdictional lines are unclear or policy disagreements persist among regulators within or across the various agencies, private-sector actors are often uncertain about who might intervene and what they are likely to do. Under such circumstances, targeted interventions may appear ad hoc and fail to send clear signals about the likelihood of future interventions to other actors.

- ○ **Lesson 2c: Changes in political capacity can have a significant impact on the level of deference granted to economic policymakers by the president or members of Congress.**

Some presidents generally defer to the policy recommendations made by the chairman of the Federal Reserve and members of their economic teams. Several presidents have reappointed economic technocrats from administrations to signal economic policy continuity. President Clinton reappointed Alan Greenspan in 2000; similarly, President Obama reappointed Timothy Geithner in 2009. At the same time, when their political circumstances improve, presidents tend demand greater deference from their advisors and disregard or dismiss those with whom they disagree.[172] Members of Congress act in a similar manner, often

---

[169] As discussed below, once the consequences of the limitations became apparent, the president was able to convince enough members of Congress to let the constraints expire.

[170] "The Dodd–Frank Act" (n.d.). *US Commodity Futures Trading Commission,* www.cftc.gov/LawRegulation/DoddFrankAct/index.htm.

[171] Murphy. *Who Regulates Whom and How?* p. 2.

[172] President Nixon's influence over Chairman of the Federal Reserve Arthur Burns is perhaps the most striking example of a president who demanded deference from a supposedly politically independent central banker. B. Abrams (2006). "How Richard Nixon Pressured Arthur Burns: Evidence from the Nixon Tapes." *Journal of Economic Perspectives* 20(4), 177–188.

asserting their authority and seeking to reduce the authority of others following electoral victories.

- **Lesson 3: Individual leaders matter. The actions of individual leaders can have a significant impact on economic policy and market behavior.**

President Clinton renewed Alan Greenspan's appointment on January 4, 2000 despite animosity between many in the administration and Greenspan over his decision to raise interest rates several months ahead of the 2004 midterm elections. Reappointing Greenspan sent a message of economic policy continuity that was well received, with the Dow Jones index increasing 124 points.[173] President Bush's appointment of Hank Paulson, the former chairman of Goldman Sachs, as Treasury secretary was similarly well received by Wall Street. Following the same pattern, President Obama sought to reassure the markets by reappointing Ben Bernanke as chairman of the Fed, by appointing Timothy Geithner as Treasury secretary and by appointing Larry Summers as director of the NEC.[174]

The priorities and strategic choices made by individual decision-makers can have a significant impact on economic policy and market behavior. Chairman of the Federal Reserve Alan Greenspan, Director of the NEC and then Treasury Secretary Robert Rubin and Secretary of the Treasury Larry Summers played central roles in promoting financial liberalization at home while fighting economic crises in Mexico, Asia and Russia in the 1990s. Chairman of the Federal Reserve Ben Bernanke and Treasury Secretaries Henry Paulson and Timothy Geithner were first responders during the onset of the crisis in December of 2007 through 2010. Paulson's concerns about the dangers of "moral hazard" had a significant negative impact on the US response in the early phases of the crisis. Geithner's commitment to "stress tests" had a significant positive impact on the administration's actions as the crisis progressed. Federal Reserve Chair Ben Bernanke's decisions regarding when to end the QE program and Chair Janet Yellen's decisions regarding when to raise interest rates have had profound impacts. It is also important to recognize that

---

[173] "Should President Clinton have reappointed Alan Greenspan as Fed chairman?" (2000). *Crossfire*, January 5. http://transcripts.cnn.com/TRANSCRIPTS/0001/05/cf.00.html.

[174] Andrews. "Obama to nominate Bernanke."

disagreements among technocrats had and continue to have significant impacts on policy actions and market behavior. In short, rather than simply inferring policy and behavior based on the presence or absence of particular institutions, it is important to recognize the individuals who run them.

- **Lesson 4: Economic statecraft and market pressures create perverse incentives in highly interdependent environments.**

Market forces can be empowering. Indeed, the scale and durability of the US economy and global trust in the dollar as a store of value gave and continues to give US policymakers substantial leverage in international markets. At the same time, however, this attraction also reduces market pressures on US politicians to correct poor behavior. Since 1980, the cost of debt has continued to decline for the national government and consumers. The reputation of the dollar as a safe store of value in an otherwise turbulent world meant that foreign capital kept flowing into the United States despite legislative gridlock. Thus, rather than promoting policy discipline, the market enabled political infighting, government shutdowns and the draconian sequester to take place by not demanding higher interest rates on US bonds.

In sum, the chairs of the Federal Reserve, secretaries of the Treasury and key members of Congress exhibited exceptional creativity and responsiveness as they navigated the United States through turbulent economic and political circumstances. They often wrestled with one another as they struggled to figure out what to do, who should do it and how to pay for it. While members of Congress often tried to limit the activities of the president, Treasury and the Federal Reserve, they also enabled bailouts, passed economic stimulus programs, crafted economic policy reforms and eventually allowed debt management to take place. While the secretaries of the Treasury and chairs of the Federal Reserve often attempted to outmaneuver their critics, they also enabled and promoted legislation and intervened to reduce the consequences of political and policy risks. Along the way, national politicians and economic policymakers demonstrated the malleability of political institutions and the significance of the people who lead them.

Today, Federal Reserve Chair Jerome Powell is continuing along the path chosen by his predecessors Ben Bernanke and Janet Yellen by gradually raising interest rates to keep inflation at bay. President Trump's criticisms that the decision to raise rates is "crazy" and that the Federal Reserve is "out of control" are reminiscent of President Richard Nixon's efforts to compel Federal Reserve Chairman Arthur Burns to keep interest rates low so as to keep employment high despite the danger of inflation.[175] The high turnover among technocrats in the Trump administration suggests that the President could follow the Argentine pattern of replacing Powell with a more compliant central banker. As of now, however, Chairman Powell retains the support of Treasury Secretary Steven Mnuchin and continues to demonstrate the will to reduce political uncertainty and policy uncertainty by gradually slowing the economy.[176] The lack of deference from President Trump suggests that Powell's impact will be minimal in areas that extend beyond his traditional purview – like tax and trade policy – but that he will be able to affect monetary policy where the Federal Reserve's authority is uncontested and legislative support is not necessary.

---

[175] W. Martin & B. Bryan (2018). "An ugly economic lesson from the Nixon era proves why Trump's criticisms of the Fed are so worrying." *Business Insider*, July 20. www.businessinsider.com/trump-federal-reserve-interest-rate-attacks-echo-nixon-disaster-2018-7; B. White (2018). "Trump channels Richard Nixon on the Fed." *Politico*, August 29. www.politico.com/story/2018/08/29/trump-federal-reserve-jerome-powell-richard-nixon-799209.

[176] S. Lane (2018). "Mnuchin defends 'phenomenal' Powell after Trump criticism." *The Hill*, August 28. https://thehill.com/policy/finance/403965-mnuchin-defends-phenomenal-powell-after-trump-criticism.

5   A Greek Tragedy

5.1   The European Odyssey

Europe's journey toward the ideal of ever-denser integration, peace and prosperity has been buffeted by repeated trials of temptation, frustration and risk. Like Odysseus, who bound himself to the mast of his ship to avoid the seductive songs of the Sirens, political leaders of Europe bound themselves by treaty and fealty to the principle of fiscal discipline in order to protect themselves from the alluring yet fickle flows of global capital. As they discovered, such constraints are neither always effective nor always desirable. Consequently, also like Odysseus, economic policy-makers and national politicians continue to employ a wide range of strategies to steer Europe past the twin challenges posed by a modern-day Scylla (i.e., a multiheaded monster of sluggish economic growth, resurgent nationalism and social unrest that threatens to yank politicians out of office and cast countries out of the European Union [EU]) and Charybdis (i.e., a whirlpool of financial capital energized by expansive monetary policy and conditional bailouts that threatens to pull individual countries and perhaps the EU itself underwater).

The gods often encouraged, aided and relied on Odysseus, yet they readily penalized him for not conforming to their expectations. In parallel, European political leaders have supported and relied on the European Central Bank (ECB); yet they have also been quick to reprimand undesired assertions of authority. Like Odysseus, ECB Presidents Jean-Claude Trichet and Mario Draghi have overcome many challenges successfully, but their actions have not satisfied everybody. Consequently, while considered oracles or heroes by some, they, the ECB and other institutions like it have come to be seen as the embodiment of overbearing villains by others.

Like its counterpart in the Americas, the ECB has attempted to reduce market uncertainty by managing price stability and general market conditions. It has attempted to reduce political uncertainty by working with national leaders to develop effective policy responses and taking supplemental action when necessary, reduce policy uncertainty by validating certain actions and challenging others, and reduce specific-actor uncertainty by offering conditional assistance and compelling wayward actors to alter their behavior. The ECB's ability to accomplish these objectives varied with shifts in the constitutive power dynamics among economic technocrats and national politicians as they battle over the authority, deference and political capacity to shape economic policy in Europe. In Argentina, the key players in the politics of economic policy-making are the minister of the economy (in various permutations) and the president. In the United States, they are the chairman and Board of Governors of the Federal Reserve, the Treasury secretary, the president and Congress. In Europe, they include the president and members of the Governing Council of the ECB, the prominent political actors in the European Commission, and leaders in countries who need or whose banks need assistance. Like the Federal Reserve, the ECB is formally "independent in the exercise of its powers" from member states and other European institutions, yet it is also a strategic political actor that influences policy decisions and manages their consequences.[1]

This chapter analyzes the effects of shifts in constitutive power dynamics among economic technocrats and national politicians on the ECB's ability to manage investor risks during three overlapping periods: the precrisis era of banking and political exuberance from 1999 to 2009; the sovereign debt crisis period from 2010 to 2015; and the postcrisis era of rejuvenation from 2014 to 2018. In the precrisis period, investors placed a high level of trust in European institutions and the protective armor that Eurozone membership provided against the turmoil of the US financial crisis. ECB efforts to stimulate economic growth while monitoring inflation were welcomed. At the same time, like their counterparts in the Americas whose acceptance of policy constraints declined when times were good, European leaders did not adhere to the fiscal limits and other policy constraints they had formally agreed to. Low levels of deference by member governments to Eurozone institutions help to explain why the ECB was less successful in influencing national policies than it was in altering bank behavior or in coordinating international responses to the financial crisis with other central bankers from 2007 through 2009.[2]

---

[1] "Consolidated Version of the Treaty of the Functioning of the European Union," Section 6, Article 282 in *Official Journal of the European Union*, C 202, vol. 59, June 7, 2016, p. 167. www.ecb.europa.eu/ecb/legal/pdf/oj_c_2016_202_full_en_txt.pdf.

[2] D. Drezner (2014). *The System Worked: How the World Stopped Another Great Depression*. Oxford: Oxford University Press.

The level of contestation and the intensity of policy disagreements among national politicians and economic technocrats rose as they wrestled over how to respond to banking and sovereign debt crises and related specific-actor risks posed by Ireland, Greece, Spain, Italy and others. During this second period of the crisis between 2010 and 2015, the ECB attempted to restore investor confidence by providing liquidity and by working with European governments to develop a crisis management regime. It also attempted to bolster the credibility of the new crisis management institutions and reduce specific-actor risks by compelling wayward countries to participate in them and adopt the requisite policy reforms. In addition, though Trichet and Draghi repeatedly called on national governments to take greater responsibility for crisis management, the ECB intervened to compensate policy rigidity when national leaders were unwilling or unable to act. On July 26, 2012, in the most famous and consequential of such interventions, ECB President Mario Draghi famously declared that "the ECB is ready to do it takes to preserve the euro. And believe me it will be enough."[3]

Draghi's promise and the ECB Governing Council's announcement two days later that it would undertake the Outright Monetary Transactions (OMT) program were remarkably successful in restoring investor confidence and reducing the cost of financing for national governments across the Europe. Yet, even though the OMT was never implemented, Draghi's actions sparked intense criticism from those who argued that the ECB had once again exceeded its purview. The level of contestation peaked in June of 2013 when the Federal Constitutional Court of Germany (FCC) expressed opposition to the ECB's OMT program. The level of contestation began to decline in February of 2014 when the FCC referred the matter to the Court of Justice of the European Union (CJEU) for a preliminary ruling. It declined further when the CJEU ruled in favor of the ECB in June of 2015, and faded in June of 2016 when the FCC rejected the challenge to the OMT and placed only minor limitations on the German Central Bank's participation in the program.

In the third period of the crisis, the ECB shifted focus to rekindling economic growth and bolstering the institutional structures of the EU. Beginning in June of 2014, the ECB embarked on a stimulus program that included lowering interest rates, the expansion of targeted longer-term refinancing operations (LTROs) and an asset purchase program

---

[3] M. Draghi (2012). "Verbatim of the remarks made by Mario Draghi at the Global Investment Conference in London." *European Central Bank*, July 26. www.ecb.europa.eu/press/key/date/2012/html/sp120726.en.html.

(APP).[4] Ironically, like the US Congress, which sought to limit the authority of the Federal Reserve after the financial crisis had subsided, the German courts are again challenging the ECB's authority to conduct its quantitative easing policies. Rulings on these actions could constrain the ability of the ECB to take similar action in the future, but their current impact will be minimal since these policies are being unwound as economic growth gradually returns to Europe.

Based on the model presented in Chapter 2, variations in the contestation of authority, deference and implementation capacity are expected to have specific consequences for political and market behavior. Each of the sections that follow concludes with an assessment of the degree to which these expectations are met.

5.2   Birth to Adolescence, 1999–2009

The first decade of the Eurozone was a golden era for the interactions among markets, institutions and investors in Europe. On January 1, 1999, eleven countries willingly adopted the euro, delegated authority over monetary policy to the ECB and committed to conforming their fiscal policies to specified guidelines as needed to sustain their common currency. The effectiveness of this confluence of uncontested authority, policy deference and commitments to implement supporting legislation in shaping investors' expectations is reflected in the convergence and collective decline of bond yields as governments prepared to join the Eurozone (see Figure 5.1). This effect was repeated for Greece, whose bond yields converged with the others as it prepared to join the Eurozone two years later.

The strength of the protective armor that Eurozone membership provided from the economic uncertainties in international markets is reflected in the comparison of the persistently low and steady bond yields within the Eurozone despite dramatic shifts in European news coverage of economic uncertainty elsewhere. The Economic Policy Uncertainty Index tracks reporting on economic policy uncertainty in newspaper articles across Europe. It shows spikes in media reports about economic uncertainty following the Russian financial crisis in September of 1998, the terrorist attacks against the United States in September of 2001, the US invasion of Iraq in March of 2003 and the Lehman Brothers collapse in September of 2008 (see Figure 5.2).[5] Despite local press coverage of

---

[4] "Press Release: Monetary policy decisions" (2016). *European Central Bank*, March 10. www.ecb.europa.eu/press/pr/date/2016/html/pr160310.en.html.
[5] The Economic Policy Uncertainty Index tracks the reporting of economic policy uncertainty in newspaper articles across Europe. S. R. Baker, N. Bloom & S. J. Davis.

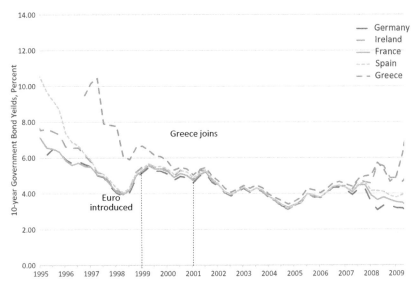

Figure 5.1 Convergence and adoption of the euro.
Sources: Organisation for Economic Co-operation and Development, Long-Term Government Bond Yields: 10-year: Main (Including Benchmark) for Germany, Ireland, France, Spain, and Greece. Retrieved from FRED, Federal Reserve Bank of St. Louis. https://fred.stlouisfed.org.

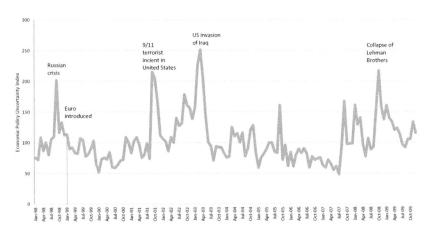

Figure 5.2 European media coverage of economic policy uncertainty.
Source: S. R. Baker, N. Bloom & S. J. Davis. Economic Policy Uncertainty Index for Europe [EUEPUINDXM]. Retrieved from FRED, Federal Reserve Bank of St. Louis. https://fred.stlouisfed.org/.

these events, bond yields across the Eurozone remained low and continued to move in tandem with one another. In short, for almost ten years, Eurozone membership served as a shield against global shocks for investors in Europe, much like the Convertibility Plan had done for investors in Argentina a decade earlier.

Eurozone members share a common currency and accept a common monetary policy, but do not share a common fiscal policy and have not established formal mechanisms for transferring money from more to less productive member countries. Instead, each Eurozone member country is responsible for maintaining a de facto peg between its notional national currency and the euro. Since members have delegated monetary policy-making authority to the ECB, maintaining the peg requires them to adjust their fiscal policies so that the real value of national prices (e.g., their notional national currencies) align with the euro. Failing to do so could create economic distortions and generate significant movements in capital and labor across the Eurozone. In the absence of a system of cross-national financial transfers, managing these imbalances while maintaining the peg may require adjusting national prices and reallocating national income internally in socially disruptive and politically difficult ways. During the crisis, for example, countries in distress were often compelled to undergo internal devaluations (e.g., lowering national prices by reducing government expenditure on public benefits and services, reducing public sector employment, and reforming labor regulations to make it easier for private sector employers to fire workers and reduce wages) while reallocating national income to pay creditors. While some countries guaranteed their bank's debt during the crisis, fiscal limits (as well as fairness concerns) led to the practice of private-sector involvement (PSI) through which investors had to accept less than the expected return on their investments (e.g., they get a haircut). To avoid these challenges, Eurozone members committed themselves to maintaining their government deficits and national debts to within limits specified in the Stability and Growth Pact (SGP) of 1999. To ensure market discipline and reduce the prospect of moral hazard created by expectations that the ECB would bail out countries who got into financial difficulty,[6] Eurozone members prohibited the ECB from using monetary policy to finance their countries' debts. The prioritization of fiscal discipline and economic restraint is reflected in the pre-2008 risk intervention curve

Economic Policy Uncertainty Index for Europe [EUEPUINDXM]. Retrieved from FRED, Federal Reserve Bank of St. Louis. https://fred.stlouisfed.org/.
[6] Moral hazard results when the provision of a safety net or the prospect of being bailed out creates an incentive for national governments to engage in excessive risk-taking or otherwise imprudent behavior.

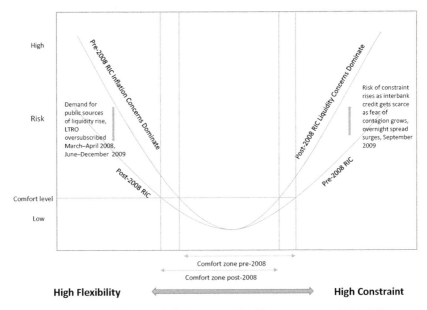

Figure 5.3 Europe: inflation control with easy money, 1999–2009.

(RIC) in Figure 5.3, which shows relatively low levels of risk associated with greater policy constraints and relatively high levels of risk associated with greater policy flexibly.

As the exposure of European banks to mortgage-backed securities and the fallout from the financial crisis in the United States spread, investor preferences for intervention shifted to the left along the policy flexibility-constraint spectrum. Concerns about the responsiveness of the ECB and European Commission to shortfalls in private-sector liquidity, the banking crisis and the burgeoning sovereign crisis increasingly took precedence over concerns about the credibility of national commitments to fiscal constraint and fears of inflation. Signs of this shift include the oversubscription of the ECB's LTROs in March and April of 2008 and June, September and December of 2009, and the rise in overnight spreads in the interbank market from September of 2008 through September of 2009.[7] In stylized form, this is reflected in a shift from the pre-2008 RIC to the post-2008 RIC in Figure 5.3. With the caveat that

[7] J. Beirne (2010). "The EONIA spread before and during the crisis of 2007 to 2009: the role of liquidity and credit risk." *European Central Bank*, August 2. http://macro.soc.uoc.gr/docs/Year/2011/papers/paper_3_4.pdf; D. Bowman (2010). "The ECB's use of term refinancing operations." *Federal Reserve*, August 3. www.federalreserve.gov/monetarypolicy/files/FOMC20100805memo02.pdf.

the risk tolerance of investors can vary widely, the comfort level of a stylized investor is included to suggest how the changing curve would affect the desired balance between policy flexibility and constraint.

5.2.1 Managing Growth and Inflation in the Golden Era

The European economic boom of 2000 faltered in 2002 and 2003 due to a combination of shocks including the terrorist attacks in the United States, rising tensions in Afghanistan and Iraq and the collapse of the dot-com bubble. These shocks hit Europe's three largest economies hard. Germany's GDP growth rate fell from 2.96 percent in 2000 to −0.71 percent in 2003, France's growth rate fell from 3.88 percent to 0.82 percent and Italy's growth rate fell from 3.71 percent to 0.15 percent.[8] In an effort to rekindle growth, the ECB pursued a relatively lax monetary policy. From August of 2001 through June of 2003, it gradually decreased its main refinancing rate from 4.75 percent to 2 percent and its marginal lending rate from 5.75 percent to 3 percent.[9]

Much like the federal funds rate in the United States, the main refinancing rate sets the minimum price at which that banks in the Eurozone can loan money to or borrow money from one another on a short-term basis in what is known as the interbank market.[10] The ECB manages these rates by auctioning capital to member banks through its main refinancing operations (MROs).[11] Unlike the Federal Reserve, the ECB does not purchase bonds directly; rather, it establishes short-term repurchase contracts (REPOs) with banks. The REPOs enable the banks to borrow money for a short period of time (generally two weeks to three months) in exchange for collateral held by the ECB. Eligible collateral

---

[8] "Indicators: Agriculture and Rural Development" (n.d.). *World Bank Data.* https://data.worldbank.org/indicator.

[9] S. Micossi (2016). "The Monetary Policy of the European Central Bank (2002–2015)." CEPS Special Report No. 109, May, p. 6.

[10] "Monetary policy decisions" (n.d.). *European Central Bank.* www.ecb.europa.eu/mopo/decisions/html/index.en.html.

[11] The actual overnight interbank market rate at which financial firms lend to and borrow from each other on an overnight basis is known as the Euro Overnight Index Average (EONIA). The difference between the main lending rate and the EONIA is often used as an indicator of the effectiveness of monetary policy across the broader economy – the smaller the difference, the more effective the monetary policy transmission process. The rate for interbank transactions for up to a year in maturities is known as the Euribor rate. In October 2019, the ECB began providing the euro short-term rate (ESTER), a euro unsecured overnight rate reflecting the wholesale borrowing costs of euro area banks. See: "Why are benchmark rates so important?" (2018). *European Central Bank,* September 21, 2017, updated October 31. www.ecb.europa.eu/explainers/tell-me-more/html/benchmark_rates_qa.en.html.

consists of high-quality tradable securities. If financial institutions are unable to secure funding at a desirable rate in the interbank market or through MROs, they can borrow directly from the ECB on an overnight basis using its marginal lending facility. The rate at which banks may do so is known as the marginal lending rate. The marginal lending rate is set at a higher level than the MRO. The rate at which banks may deposit surplus funds with the euro system on an overnight basis is known as the deposit rate. The deposit rate is set at a lower level than the MRO. Under normal circumstances, interbank lending is conducted at rates that are greater than the deposit rate and less than the marginal rate.[12]

Prior to the economic crisis, the ECB auctioned preset amounts of credit to banks through the MRO process. It encouraged banks to rely on private-sector liquidity by setting the marginal lending rate at 1 percent (e.g., 100 basis points) higher than the minimum bid rate in the interbank market, thus making overnight borrowing from the ECB more expensive than borrowing from other banks. Following the Lehman Brothers collapse and the failure of the US congress to pass the initial Troubled Asset Relief Program (TARP), the ECB changed strategy.[13] On October 15, 2008, citing downside risks of turmoil in financial markets affecting energy and food prices and potentially sparking protectionism, Trichet and the Board of Governors announced that they would drop interest rates and shift MROs to a "fixed-rate tender procedure with full allotment."[14] "Fixed-rate tender" means that the ECB would target a fixed interest rate for interbank transactions rather than set a minimum bid level for interbank auctions.[15] "Full allotment" means that banks could be granted the full amount they requested against a broad range of collateral. Thus, the fixed-rate full allotment policy was designed to provide banks with full access to all of the liquidity they asked for. Furthermore, their bids would be satisfied at a specific interest rate. This was a significant change from the previous practice of forcing banks to bid against another for a limited pool of funds, as had been done before October 15.

---

[12] For an excellent summary of ECB policy tools, see: "ECB policy – understanding the European Central Bank" (2009). ForEx, August 24. www.forexfraud.com/forex-articles/ecb-policy-european-central-bank.html.

[13] "Key ECB interest rates" (2018). European Central Bank. www.ecb.europa.eu/stats/policy_and_exchange_rates/key_ecb_interest_rates/html/index.en.html.

[14] Prior to October 15, 2008, the MROs were used to establish a minimum bid rate for transactions among banks in the interbank market. These transactions were known as variable-rate tenders because the rate was set by banks competing for the money through auctions.

[15] Since October 15, 2008, the ECB has used MROs to target a fixed rate for interbank transactions. These are known as fixed-rate tenders. They have durations of one week.

José Manuel González-Páramo, member of the Executive Board of the ECB, proclaimed that this policy provided "a very flexible tool, as counter parties can themselves control the amount of liquidity they demand ... The fixed-rate full allotment policy is probably the most significant non-standard measure the ECB is implementing."[16]

The new policy was designed to bolster confidence by enabling the ECB to act as a lender of last resort for banks without limiting the available funds. In addition to providing liquidity as needed, the policy increased confidence by giving the ECB an added means of monitoring private sector activity.[17] Low demand for ECB funds would signal that liquidity in the interbank market had become sufficiently plentiful and inexpensive. The cost of private sector liquidity is estimated using a weighted average of lending on the interbank market in the EU and European Free Trade Association known as the Euro Overnight Index Average (EONIA).[18] A small spread between the EONIA and the ECB's discount rate suggests that the ECB's monetary tools are working effectively; when the EONIA greatly exceeds the ECB rate – as happened in the fall of 2008 – the financial system is under stress and the ECB's monetary tools are not working properly.[19]

In addition, the policy gave the ECB an added source of leverage over private-sector lending in the interbank market.[20] If private-sector liquidity was insufficient to meet demand and the costs of borrowing in the interbank market rose above the ECB's marginal lending rate, banks would have an incentive to shift their financing to the ECB marginal facility. This would exert downward pressure on interbank lending rates by lowering demand in the interbank market until the interbank market rate fell below the ECB's fixed discount rate.

The ECB's policies were relatively successful in managing market expectations. Interest rate decreases in the early 2000s led to a dramatic increase in the money supply (M3) across the Eurozone beginning in about 2004 (see Figure 5.4).[21] When signs of inflation began to appear,

---

[16] I. Kaminska (2011). "On the ECB's 'most significant non-standard measure.'" *Financial Times*, December 8. https://ftalphaville.ft.com/2011/12/08/785211/on-the-ecbs-most-significant-non-standard-measure/?mhq5j=e1.

[17] Ibid.　　[18] See: Euribor-rates.edu. www.euribor-rates.eu/eonia.asp.

[19] T. Linzert & S. Schmidt (2008). "What Explains the Spread between the Euro Overnight Rate and the ECB's Policy Rate?" *European Central Bank*, Working Paper Series, No. 983, December.

[20] Kaminska. "On the ECB."

[21] The ECB defines monetary aggregates as follows: "M1 is the sum of currency in circulation and overnight deposits; M2 is the sum of M1, deposits with an agreed maturity of up to two years and deposits redeemable at notice of up to three months; M3 is the sum of M2, repurchase agreements, money market funds shares/units and debt

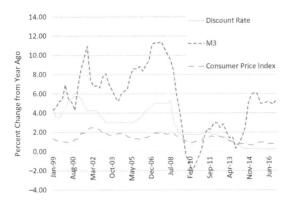

Figure 5.4 Interest rates, the money supply and inflation in the euro area.
Source: International Monetary Fund. Interest Rates, Discount Rate for Euro Area and M3 for Euro Area, Organisation for Economic Co-operation and Development, Consumer Price Index: Harmonized Prices: Total All Items Less Food, Energy, Tobacco, and Alcohol for the Euro Area. Retrieved from FRED, Federal Reserve Bank of St. Louis. https://fred.stlouisfed.org.

the ECB Board of Governors began raising interest rates. The anti-inflation focus of Jean-Claude Trichet and the ECB Board of Governors is reflected in the decisions to increase interest rates beginning in December of 2005 and continuing to do so until they peaked at 5.25 percent on July 9, 2008, at about the same time that Secretary Henry Paulson was promising to fend off a future economic crisis with his economic bazooka.[22] Even on October 2, 2008, just two weeks after Lehman Brothers collapsed, when explaining the ECB's decision to promote flexibility via the expansion of several lending facilities, Trichet kept an eye on inflation, noting that "annual inflation rates are likely to remain well above levels consistent with price stability for some time."[23]

On October 8, 2008, the ECB joined other central banks in a coordinated rate reduction, lowering its discount rate from 5.25 percent to 4 percent (see Figure 5.4). It continued to lower the

securities with maturity of up to two years." See: "Monetary aggregates" (n.d.). *European Central Bank.* www.ecb.europa.eu/stats/money_credit_banking/monetary_aggregates/html/index.en.html.

[22] J.-C. Trichet & L. Papademos (2008). Introductory Statement with Q&A, July 3. www.ecb.europa.eu/press/pressconf/2008/html/is080703.en.html.

[23] Ibid. For a similar perspective, see: C. Bastasin (2015) *Saving Europe: Anatomy of a Dream.* Washington, DC: Brookings Institution, p. 26.

discount rate until reaching 1.75 percent in April of 2009. In April and July of 2011, the ECB increased the discount rate, reaching 2.25 percent. As deflation set in, the ECB dropped the interest rate again, reaching 0.3 percent in July of 2014 and 0.25 percent in January of 2016.[24]

European bond yields provide a similarly positive picture through the spring of 2008 (see Figure 5.1). Reflecting the added risk associated with the first signs of the financial crisis in Europe with PNB Paribas in August of 2007, bond rates across Europe rose in unison from about 4 percent in January of 2007 to about 4.5 percent in August of 2007. From that point through the spring of 2008, they declined again, almost in unison and almost reaching precrisis levels.

5.2.2   *Low Deference and the Prelude to Crisis*

The money supply across Europe as a whole remained relatively stable from 1999 through 2008, however, the combination of the lax monetary policy of the early 2000s and the confidence-building benefits of joining the euro had significantly different impacts across member countries. Growth in the money supply was faster and more volatile in Greece, Ireland, Portugal and Spain than in Germany. The changes in Greece were perhaps the most dramatic, with a surge in liquidity in 2001 when it joined the euro and a dramatic decline in liquidity in 2010 and 2011 after its real economic situation became known. This is important because it shows that the needs and experiences of individual countries differed substantially from the European "average." The European "average" matters because the ECB's mission is to maintain price stability in the Eurozone rather than in any particular country, yet policies designed to address the Eurozone as a whole are often not optimal for the needs of a particular member state. Although the European Commission and ECB made many country-specific policy adjustments during the financial crisis, monetary policy remains generalized even though its impact is highly country specific.

Figure 5.5 shows clearly that Greece, Ireland, Spain, Portugal and Germany experienced liquidity booms and busts even as the Eurozone as

[24] "Key ECB interest rates" (2018). *European Central Bank*. www.ecb.europa.eu/stats/ policy_and_exchange_rates/key_ecb_interest_rates/html/index.en.html.

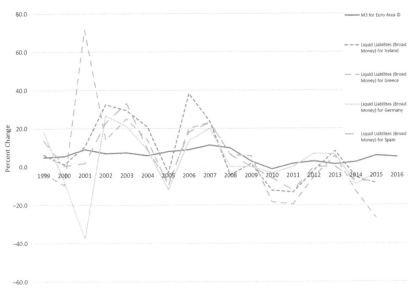

Figure 5.5 Broad money in the euro area.
Sources: International Monetary Fund. M3 for Euro Area, World Bank. Liquid Liabilities (Broad Money) for Ireland, Liquid Liabilities (Broad Money) for Greece, World Bank. Liquid Liabilities (Broad Money) for Germany, World Bank. Liquid Liabilities (Broad Money) for Spain. Retrieved from FRED, Federal Reserve Bank of St. Louis. https://fred.stlouisfed.org.

a whole remained stable. The surges in liquidity between 2002 and 2003 and between 2006 and 2007 were greater in peripheral countries than in Germany, while the interim drop in liquidity in 2005 was less in the peripheral countries than in Germany. This suggests that until 2009 at least, membership in the Eurozone had a greater stabilizing impact for peripheral countries. After 2009, membership in the EU no longer provided as effective a buffer. Government bond rates across Europe soared and the money supply collapsed in peripheral countries. In short, the Eurozone armor had begun to crack.

The ECB's decisions to raise interest rates in May of 2006, July of 2008 and April and July of 2011 also had differential effects on member countries. Critics argue, for example, that the decision to raise interest rates in 2006 was well timed to fight potential inflation in Germany, where the money supply and credit had begun to grow quickly, but it was too late to forestall credit booms in Ireland and Spain, which were

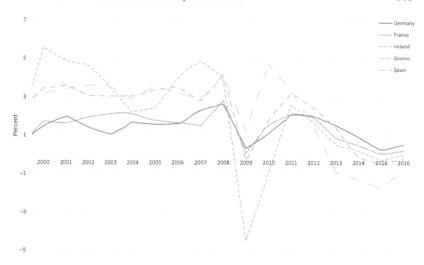

Figure 5.6 Inflation in Germany, France, Ireland, Greece and Spain.
Sources: World Bank. Inflation, consumer prices for Germany, consumer prices
for France, consumer prices for Ireland, consumer prices for Greece and
consumer prices for Spain. Retrieved from FRED, Federal Reserve Bank of St.
Louis. https://fred.stlouisfed.org.

already well underway (see Figure 5.6).[25] Similarly, the interest rate
hikes in 2008 and 2011 reflected concerns about inflation in Germany,
France or the EU overall, but worsened access to credit and slowed
growth in Ireland and others in the periphery. Figure 5.6 also shows that
interest rate declines in 2011 and 2012 succeeded in quelling inflation in
Germany and France, but went too far for Ireland, Spain and Greece,
which became deflationary. The differential effects of monetary policy
across the core and peripheral countries highlight the blunt nature of
monetary policy.

The surges in liquidity in Greece and Spain in 2000–2004 and
2006–2007 also show the enabling market conditions that led to over-
spending in Greece and real-estate bubbles in Spain. European bond
rates began to diverge after the ECB raised interest rates in July of 2008.
They split further following the Greek crisis in 2010. As uncertainty rose,
investors sought safety, money flowed out of smaller European countries.
Bond rates in peripheral European countries soared, while bond rates in
German subsided.

---

[25] Micossi. "The Monetary Policy," p. 9.

5.2.3   Expanding Authority to Add Liquidity

Prior to the financial crisis, the ECB offered Eurozone banks access to inexpensive credit through LTROs that had to be repaid in three months. During the crisis, the ECB expanded the amounts and durations of the loans.[26]

LTROs are designed to encourage banks to lend (and thus promote increased economic activity) by providing banks with inexpensive access to liquidity. To the extent that sovereign bonds can be used as collateral, LTROs also increase demand for sovereign debt and thereby lower the rates that governments must pay to sell their bonds. LTROs supplemented the ECB's MROs by offering increasingly longer-term financing. The maturities on LTROs were extended from three months to six months in April of 2008, to one year in June of 2009 and to three years in December of 2012.

From the beginning, the LTROs were highly popular and oversubscribed. The initial auction of €25 billion on April 3, 2008 drew bids of €103.1 billion from 177 European banks.[27] On May 7, 2009 the ECB announced that it would extend the maturity of LTROs to one year with full allotment at the same rate as MROs with allotments taking place in June, September and December of 2009.[28] This meant that interest rates would be fixed and reduced from 4.25 percent to 1 percent.[29] The interest-rate reduction was part of a broader strategy employed by the ECB to encourage banks to purchase government bonds and thus bypass the de jure prohibition against them purchasing government bonds directly. The prohibition in Article 104 of the Maastricht Treaty states:

Overdraft facilities or other type of credit facility with the ECB ... in favour of Community institutions or bodies, central governments, regional local or other public authorities, other bodies governed by public law or public understanding

---

[26] T. Linzert, D. Nautz & U. Bindseil (2004). "The Longer Term Refinancing Operations of the ECB." Working Paper Series. *European Central Bank*. www.ecb.europa.eu/pub/pdf/scpwps/ecbwp359.pdf?b822e3758edd79c03daf72200fd7470f.

[27] J. Wooley (2008). "ECB offers longer-term finance via six month LTROs." *Euromoney*, May 2. www.euromoney.com/article/b1322cm2dyyprq/ecb-offers-longer-term-finance-via-six-month-ltros.

[28] €25 billion of LRTOs with six-month maturities were allocated on July 9, 2008; the first twelve-month LTRO was offered in June of 2009. In response to the debt crises in Greece, Ireland, Italy and Spain, the first thirty-six-month LTROs were offered in December of 2011; the second thirty-six-month LTRO (LTRO2) was offered in February of 2012. "Press Release: Longer-term refinancing operations" (2009). *European Central Bank*, May 7. www.ecb.europa.eu/press/pr/date/2009/html/pr090507_2.en.html.

[29] "Key ECB interest rates" (2018). *European Central Bank*. www.ecb.europa.eu/stats/policy_and_exchange_rates/key_ecb_interest_rates/html/index.en.html.

of Members states should be prohibited, as shall the purchase directly from them by the ECB or national central banks of debt instruments.[30]

In short, the ECB is forbidden from bailing out Eurozone countries or their governments. Since it could not do so directly, the ECB designed the LTRO program to encourage banks to support national governments, thus helping both while remaining in compliance with the letter if not the spirit of Article 104. As Carlo Bastasin notes, this "Grand Bargain" had three components:[31]

- The ECB would provide financing by offering inexpensive liquidity directly to the banks through the LTROs.
- Banks would be incentivized to purchase sovereign bonds due to the interest-rate differentials between the relatively high returns on sovereign bonds and the low cost of LTRO debt. Note that the return on sovereign bonds ranged from 4 percent in Germany to over 5.5 percent in Greece and Ireland (see Figure 5.3), while the cost of LTROs had fallen to 1 percent.
- National governments would be able to sell their debt and, in exchange, would agree not to expand their fiscal deficits beyond reasonable limits as specified in the SGP.

The ECB and bank components of the bargain were successful. The twelve-month LTRO auctioned on June 25, 2009, attracted a record 1,100 bidders and €442 billion being allotted at 1 percent.[32] National governments benefited substantially: by December of 2009, the banking sector had absorbed as much as 70 percent of the debt of their home countries. Two years later, to compensate for a credit crunch and to decrease policy risk, the ECB announced two additional LTROs with a maturity of three years. On December 21, 2011, the first three-year LTRO provided €489.2 billion to 523 credit institutions; on February 29, 2012, the second three-year LTRO provided €529.5 billion to 800 credit institutions.[33]

The third component of the grand bargain was, however, less successful. As early as 2003, France and Germany had violated their

---

[30] "Treaty on European Union, as signed in Maastricht on 7 February 1992." https://europa.eu/european-union/sites/europaeu/files/docs/body/treaty_on_european_union_en.pdf.

[31] Bastasin. *Saving Europe*, p. 96.

[32] "Annual report: 2009" (2010). *European Central Bank*. www.ecb.europa.eu/pub/pdf/annrep/ar2009en.pdf?30d90321a98348b879be2a56fa28c055.

[33] "Economic and monetary developments: monetary and financial developments" (2012). *ECB Monthly Bulletin*, March. www.ecb.europa.eu/pub/pdf/other/mb201203_focus03.en.pdf?633af8e40f98a75808996a7857cbbd93.

commitments to the SGP and their deficits went above 3 percent of GDP.[34] Although threatened with sanctions, neither France nor Germany paid any penalties for their noncompliance.[35] Concerns were also raised about SGP violations by Portugal in 2002 and Greece in 2005. In the face of increasing violations and ridicule by European Commission President Romano Prodi, the European Commission attempted to increase deference to the SGP in 2005 by adding exceptions to the fiscal criteria and changing the process for rectification.[36] None-theless, in July of 2007, French President Nicolas Sarkozy announced that France would not meet its balanced budget objective by 2010.[37]

As long as economic conditions remained positive, investors did not respond negatively to the lack of compliance with the SGP. Interest rates for France, Germany, Portugal and Greece remained low and did not fluctuate with the announcements that the SGP targets would not be met. As the crisis evolved, however, country-specific differences became more significant. By 2012, 23 out of 27 member states had failed either to keep their budget deficits below 3 percent of GDP or their government debts below 60 percent of GDP.[38] The list of violators facing excessive deficit procedures grew to include Portugal, France, Germany, the Netherlands, Greece, Italy, Spain, Ireland, Belgium, Austria and Finland. The reasons for failure varied for different countries from exuberant fiscal expenditure to the absorption of bank debt, but the signal it sent was clear: the SGP protocols did not constrain government expenditures.[39]

Consequently, while this "grand bargain" enabled the ECB to bypass institutional restrictions on its ability to purchase sovereign debt, neither

---

[34] K. Stacey (2011). "Who originally broke the EU fiscal rules? France and Germany." *Financial Times*, December 6. www.ft.com/content/dfb8adf7-7ca4-384c-a737-f28c0dc46924.

[35] In 2003, Germany and France voted against an excessive deficit procedure that would have automatically triggered noncompliance cases, despite breaking the 3-percent debt ceiling. Speech by González-Páramo, J. M. (2011). Member of the Executive Board of the ECB, at the XXIV Moneda y Crédito Symposium, Madrid, November 4. www.ecb.europa.eu/press/key/date/2011/html/sp111104_1.en.html.

[36] J. Creel & F. Saraceno (2010). "European Fiscal Rules after the Crisis." *Journal of Innovation Economics & Management* 6(2), 95–122.

[37] C. Secchi & A. Villafranca, eds. (2009). *Liberalism in Crisis? European Economic Governance in the Age of Turbulence*. Cheltenham: Edward Elgar, p. 157.

[38] Bastasin. *Saving Europe*, p. 101; H. Kube (2012). "The EU Financial Crisis – European Law and Constitutional Law Implications." Center for International Studies, Working Paper Series, No. 1–12, June.

[39] Speech by González-Páramo, J. M. (2011). Member of the Executive Board of the ECB, at the XXIV Moneda y Crédito Symposium, Madrid, November 4. www.ecb.europa.eu/press/key/date/2011/html/sp111104_1.en.html.

the ECB nor the SGP succeeded in securing government compliance with their fiscal commitments. Consequently, in the words of Carlo Bastasin, the "ECB became – willing or not – the main policy actor in the euro zone."[40]

The lack of deference by national governments to their fiscal commitments was highlighted succinctly by José Manuel González-Páramo, member of the Executive Board of the ECB, at a symposium on the ECB and the debt crisis. He argued:[41]

The EU's economic governance framework failed to prevent and correct unsustainable national policies that contributed to the build-up of major imbalances in euro area countries. This applies in particular to the weak implementation of policy recommendations, the inadequacy of enforcement measures taken to discourage or correct deficit infringements, and the insufficient recognition by national policy-makers of the need to ensure mutual consistency between national policies in a monetary union, especially with regard to the issue of competitiveness.

In November of 2011, the EU doubled down on the SGP by adopting a more comprehensive package of EU rules designed to monitor budgets and economic policies known as the Six Pack. The program is organized under the European Semester Procedure, which requires member states to get approval for their budget plans from the European Commission. In January of 2013, a Fiscal Compact that put a lower cap on public deficits and required a reduction in public debt entered into force.[42] Though these changes were substantial, they have not been effective at reducing political and policy uncertainties because their recommendations have been implemented unevenly and it is unclear whether member countries will sustain sufficient reforms.[43]

[40] Bastasin. *Saving Europe*, p. 27.
[41] Speech by González-Páramo, J. M. (2011). Member of the Executive Board of the ECB, at the XXIV Moneda y Crédito Symposium, Madrid, November 4. www.ecb.europa.eu/press/key/date/2011/html/sp111104_1.en.html.
[42] "History of the Stability and Growth Pact" (2015). *European Commission*. https://ec.europa.eu/info/business-economy-euro/economic-and-fiscal-policy-coordination/eu-economic-governance-monitoring-prevention-correction/stability-and-growth-pact/history-stability-and-growth-pact_en#2011; Kube. "The EU Financial Crisis," p. 3.
[43] European Political Strategy Centre (2018). "The Euro Plus Pact." European Commission, Strategic Note #3. *The Euro Plus Pact*, Issue 3, May 8. https://ec.europa.eu/epsc/file/strategic-note-3-euro-plus-pact_en; D. Papadimoulis (2016). "The Stability and Growth Pact has failed." *Social Europe*, July 11. www.socialeurope.eu/stability-growth-pact-failed.

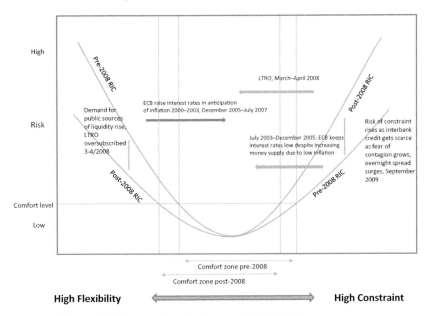

Figure 5.7 Interventions in Europe, 1999–2009.

5.2.4   Insights for Power from the Precrisis Era

The ECB's actions are summarized in Figure 5.7. In the precrisis era, the ECB had uncontested authority and high levels of deference, and European governments promised to implement supporting legislation. It manipulated interest rates to both ward off high inflation and spur economic activity when inflation was low. As the crisis evolved, the ECB coordinated currency swaps with the Federal Reserve to provide access to dollars, engaged in coordinated interest rate reductions with the Federal Reserve and other central banks, and pursued a variety of strategies to increase liquidity in euros. The latter included the adoption of a fixed-rate full allotment policy and the auctioning of LTROs to provide financing and encourage banks to purchase government bonds.

Investors and banks responded enthusiastically and treated the ECB as if its constitutive power reflected the conditions in category 1 in the first three rows to Figure 5.8. Yet, while the ECB's authority was generally uncontested before 2010, deference from national politicians wavered (category 5 in row 4 of Figure 5.8). As in the US and Argentine experiences, markets created perverse incentives. Easy access to capital following the adoption of the euro allowed for fiscal exuberance by national governments and financial exuberance by banks. Despite wide disparities in capital inflows and a lack of

	The Power to Act			Prediction		Outcome	
	Authority to Act	Deference to Technocrats	Implementation Capacity of National Politicians	Impact of Technocrats	Behavior	Role of Technocrats	Market Behavior
1	High	High	High or Not Necessary	Can constrain or expand policy flexibility	Can validate policy, targeted and broad strategies may be effective	Maximum bargaining power	1999–2007: ECB intervened using monetary policy to manage inflation and growth	Adoption of Eurozone inspires investor confidence, interest rates conform and drop
1	High	High	High or Not Necessary	Can constrain or expand policy flexibility	Can validate policy, targeted and broad strategies may be effective	Maximum bargaining power	2007–2008: ECB coordinates responses with other central banks	Confidence in Eurozone remains high, interest rates in Eurozone remain low
1	High	High	High or Not Necessary	Can constrain or expand policy flexibility	Can validate policy, targeted and broad strategies may be effective	Maximum bargaining power	April 2008, June 2009: ECB lengthened the maturities on its LTRO programs to 6 months, then to 1 year	Banks highly responsive, LTROs oversubscribed
5	High or Low	Low	High or Not Necessary	Confrontational technocrats likely to be replaced with sycophants	Cannot validate policy, targeted and broad strategies by politicians possible	No economic validation, political exuberance likely	2002–2011: ECB is unable to improve government compliance with SGP	Bond rates remain low across Eurozone. Rates do not diverge until Greek announcement in October 2009

Figure 5.8 Shaping policy and behavior in Europe, 1999–2009.

compliance by European governments with their SGP obligations, investors continued to trust the protective armor of Eurozone institutions to protect them against country-specific and market risks.

The ECB demonstrated a high degree of institutional adaptation. For example, while operating within guidelines specified by its statute – specifically, to prioritize price stability and not to bail out national governments – the ECB exploited its constitutive power to create incentives for banks to do what it could. Half of the ECB's grand bargain worked. Banks purchased government bonds, but national governments did not respond as desired. As predicted, the ECB was highly effective when its authority was uncontested, deference was high and implementation capacity was either high or not necessary – as was true with monetary policy in the pre-1999 period. When deference declined, neither technocrats in the ECB nor the European Commission was willing or able to constrain or validate behavior and, as predicted, political exuberance was prevalent (see category 5 in the bottom row of Figure 5.8).

5.3 Mitigating Specific-Actor Risk and the Sovereign Debt Crisis, 2010–2015

The intense period of the European crisis from 2010 through 2015 began and ended with concerns about specific-actor risk, political risk and market risk. Specific-actor risk involved the fates of Greece, Ireland, Portugal, Spain and Italy (and others outside of the Eurozone) and the spillover effects of their difficulties. Political risk involved whether and how European governments would intervene. Market risk involved shortfalls in private-sector liquidity, contagion and the extent of private sector involvement (PSI) in bearing the costs of the sovereign debt crisis.

The sovereign debt crisis burst onto the European scene immediately following the collapse of Lehman Brothers when the Irish government decided to provide two-year guarantees to prevent a run on its banks. The Irish government's guarantees highlighted the scale of bank debt, the fickleness of private-sector liquidity and the speed at which bank guarantees can overwhelm national finances. In its postcrisis evaluation, the European Commission marked Ireland's bailout as the pivot point in the transition from a European banking crisis to a sovereign debt crisis:[44]

In practice in September 2008, the authorities issued a two-year guarantee on existing banks' liabilities (Credit Institutions Financial Support Scheme – CIFS) amounting to €375bn (200 percent of GDP), in order to overcome banks' funding problems and address potential capital shortfalls. As a result, the solvency of the Irish sovereign and that of the banking system became directly intertwined. This eventually turned the banking crisis into a sovereign debt crisis ...

Despite the turbulence of the fall of 2008, the guarantees succeeded in mollifying investors. The yield on Irish bonds remained low, as did the yield on government bonds across Europe, until the Irish guarantees were about to expire and concerns about Greek finances rekindled fears of specific-actor risks.

The crisis escalated with a cascade of events following an announcement on October 19, 2009 by the finance minister for the newly elected Greek government, George Papaconstantinou, that Greece's budget deficit would likely hit 125 percent of GDP. This was double the previous government's estimate.[45] The rating agency Fitch responded by downgrading Greece's credit rating.[46] Prime Minister Papandreou acknowledged that the Greek economy was experiencing "without a doubt the worst economic crisis since the restoration of democracy."[47] Finance Minister Papaconstantinou attempted to calm markets by promising to increase transparency, restructure the economy and rationalize public finances, but Greek bond yields edged up from 4.57 percent in October to 5.49 percent in December suggesting that investors' perceptions of risk were rising.[48] In December, Fitch downgraded Greece's

---

[44] Houses of the Oireachtas (2013). "Ireland and the Troika programme." In *Report of the Joint Committee of Inquiry into the Banking Crisis*, pp. 329–356. https://inquiries.oireachtas.ie/banking/volume-1-report/chapter-10.

[45] K. Allan (2015). "Greek debt crisis: 20 key moments." *The Guardian*, June 25. www.theguardian.com/business/2015/jun/25/greek-crisis-20-key-moments-eurozone.

[46] A. Granitsas (2009). "Greece pledges reforms after Fitch downgrades ratings." *Wall Street Journal*, October 23. www.wsj.com/articles/SB125628478983803339.

[47] H. Smith (2009). "The new Iceland? Greece fights to rein in debt." *The Guardian*, November 30. www.theguardian.com/business/2009/nov/30/greece-iceland-debt.

[48] Organisation for Economic Co-operation and Development (n.d.). Long-Term Government Bond Yields: 10-year: Main (Including Benchmark) for Greece

credit rating again, noting "the weak credibility of fiscal institutions and the policy framework ... exacerbated by uncertainty" over the prospects for a balanced and sustained economic recovery."[49] Moody's and Standard & Poor's lowered their credit ratings as well.[50] Riots broke out. Investor risk continued to rise, with bond yields reaching 7.83 percent in April of 2010.[51]

Political uncertainty swirled around whether Ireland had the capacity to extend its guarantees and whether Greece could sustain its austerity measures in the face of a growing domestic backlash. Political uncertainty also swirled around whether the ECB, European Commission or International Monetary Fund (IMF) would come to their aid. The intensity of policy disagreement among political leaders over who was responsible for the crisis and who should shoulder the burden of responding to it is well documented.[52] At its core, the challenge involved balancing the belief that countries should be self-reliant and responsible for cleaning up their own messes with the more cosmopolitan notion that the crisis was, at its core, a European problem. Carlo Bastasin provides a particularly vivid account of how the nationalist sentiments generated political uncertainty about how the crisis would be managed. In the forward to Bastasin's book, Barry Eichengreen offers the following succinct summary of nationalist perspectives:[53]

In part, the problem stems from the fact that European leaders and their publics in different countries have fundamentally different views of who is to blame for the crisis and, therefore, who should take steps to resolve it. Germans analysts blame Southern European governments for borrowing recklessly and living beyond their means and for using statistical subterfuge to disguise this behavior while it was underway. In response, Southern European commentators note, not unreasonably, that someone lent their governments all that money. German and French banks, they observe, were in the vanguard of those snapping up high-yielding Greek and Spanish bonds.

For the purposes of this chapter, the specific nature of the policy disputes is less important than that their persistence generated political

---

[IRLTLT01GRM156N]. Retrieved from FRED, Federal Reserve Bank of St. Louis. https://fred.stlouisfed.org/series/IRLTLT01GRM156N.

[49] H. Smith & A. Seager (2009), "Financial markets tumble after Fitch downgrades Greece's credit rating." *The Guardian*, December 8. www.theguardian.com/world/2009/dec/08/greece-credit-rating-lowest-eurozone.

[50] "Greece debt rating downgraded by third agency." (2009) *BBC News*, December 22. http://news.bbc.co.uk/2/hi/business/8426085.stm.

[51] H. Smith (2010). "Greece struggles on after weak response to bond sale." *The Guardian*, March 29. www.theguardian.com/world/2010/mar/29/greece-bond-sale-weak-response.

[52] These disputes are documented in vivid detail in books by Carlo Bastasin and Neil Irwin. See: Bastasin. *Saving Europe*. See also: N. Irwin (2013). *The Alchemists: Three Central Bankers and a World on Fire*. New York: Penguin Group.

[53] Bastasin. *Saving Europe*, p. viii.

uncertainty about whether European leaders would be able to reach a consensus on a crisis response.

Against this backdrop, the ECB played a critical role in prodding the European Commission toward agreements on rescuing Greece and the creating of a crisis management regime. The success of these efforts is reflected in the creation of the European Financial Stability Facility (EFSF) and the European Financial Stabilisation Mechanism (EFSM) on May 10, 2010 and their successor, the European Stability Mechanism (ESM) on May 27, 2012. As complements, the ECB also announced the the creation of its Securities Markets Programme (SMP) on May 10, 2010, and its successor, the OMT program, on August 2, 2012.

To bolster the credibility of these crisis management institutions, Jean-Claude Trichet threatened to withhold the purchase of Italian and Spanish bonds through the SMP until each country agreed to implement a series of economic reforms. Trichet and Draghi also manipulated approval of emergency liquidity assistance (ELA) to compel Ireland and Greece to accept conditional lending from the European Commission and IMF, and they made OMT support conditional on participation in an EFSF/ESM program.

The ECB also pursued a variety of strategies to increase access to and lower the cost of capital. It provided liquidity and encouraged banks to purchase sovereign bonds by expanding its LTROs. The ECB offered LTROs in March of 2008 and June of 2009, and again in December of 2011 and February of 2012. In December of 2011, it also coordinated a reduction in the price of swap lines with the Federal Reserve and other central banks in order to increase access to dollars. And, with the exception of rate hikes in April and July of 2011, it maintained low interest rates.

Four sets of actions and reactions affecting the degree of policy flexibility and level of risk in the RIC are presented in Figure 5.9. Beginning in the bottom right, the sets depict: (1) the upward shift in the RIC resulting from specific-actor risk and the ECB's efforts to compensate by intervening in Greece and Ireland; (2) the adoption of the first Greek bailout and crisis response mechanism, a resignation in protest of the SMP and the ECB's efforts to bolster the SMP with letters to Italy and Spain; (3) Draghi's "whatever it takes" speech, the OMT program and movement toward the banking union, followed by contestation in the FCC and affirmation of the OMT program by the CJEU; and (4) recommitment to an enhanced SGP, liquidity enhancement through the enhanced LTROs and a series of broad stimulus measures that began in the summer of 2014.

As reflected in Figure 5.10, deference remained low until June of 2012 when Draghi declared that he would whatever it takes to preserve the euro. Before then, moments of legislation action and agreements were surrounded

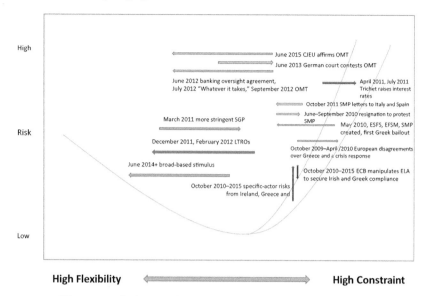

Figure 5.9 Actions and reactions in Europe, 2010–2015.

by ongoing policy disagreements and intransigence (reflecting shifts between categories 5 and 6 in the first four rows of Figure 5.10). When deference or implementation capacity was low, political uncertainty was high and markets remained skittish. When the ECB intervened to enforce compliance and implementation, political uncertainty decreased and markets reacted positively. The OMT program succeeded in part because it demonstrated the ECB's willingness to take action even when its authority was being contested. This shifted the ECB to category 3 in row 5 of Figure 5.10 as political uncertainty about emergency assistance declined. The GCC strongly contested the OMT program, but the court's rebuke came a year after the OMT program had been implemented. The OMT's dramatic success during that time generated widespread deference that was undaunted by the FCC ruling. The adoption of a more stringent SGP, the CJEU approval of the OMT, the granting of increased banking oversight responsibilities to the ECB, and acceptance of the ECB's broad-based stimulus programs suggest that authority, deference and implementation capacity have all increased and that the ECB's constitutive power shifted to category 1 in the bottom row of Figure 5.10. This bodes well for the future.

5.3.1   It's Greek to Me

European leaders took advantage of a prescheduled summit meeting on February 11, 2010, to focus on the growing turmoil in Greece. EU

The Power to Act			Prediction			Outcome
Authority to Act	Deference to Technocrats	Implementation Capacity of National Politicians	Impact of Technocrats	Behavior	Role of Technocrats	Market Behavior
5						
High or Low	Low, Deference Demanded	High or Not Necessary	Confrontational technocrats likely to be replaced with sycophants	Cannot validate policy, targeted and broad strategies by politicians possible	No economic validation, political exuberance likely	June 2010: agreements reached after extensive negotiations and bargaining. Disagreements about SMP lead to resignation and leaks. ECB bolsters SMP by linking access to economic reforms in Spain and Italy	EU markets are turbulent before resolution, but respond positively to agreements. Concerns about Greece and future European responses to troubled countries remain
6						
High or Low	Low, Deference Demanded	Low	Technocrats are impotent	Cannot validate policy, broad strategies by politicians may be effective	Minimum bargaining power, maximum uncertainty	November 2010: ECB attempts to compensate for lack of deference and capacity by compelling Ireland to accept bailout. ECB's authority is contested when letters become public	Markets in Ireland remain calm.
5						
High or Low	Low, Deference Demanded	High or Not Necessary	Confrontational technocrats likely to be replaced with sycophants	Cannot validate policy, targeted and broad strategies by politicians possible	No economic validation, political exuberance likely	April 2011, July 2011: ECB raises interest rates. Trichet notes potential for inflation in Europe	Markets roil. Concerns about specific-actor risks and potential for contagion rising
6						
High or Low	Low, Deference Demanded	Low	Technocrats are impotent	Cannot validate policy, broad strategies by politicians may be effective	Minimum bargaining power, maximum uncertainty	March 2012, July 2015: ECB attempts to compensate for lack of deference and capacity by manipulating ELA to compel Greece to accept second and third bailouts	Uncertainty spikes around second and third Greek bailout. Remains roiled after second bailout. Calms down after third bailouts accepted
3						
Low, Contested	High, Deference Granted	High or Not Necessary	Can constrain or expand policy flexibility if additional authority is not needed	Can validate policy, targeted and broad strategies may be effective	Technocrats will attempt to expand authority	June 2012: first steps towards banking union are taken. July 2012: Draghi issues "whatever it takes" pledge. September 2012: OMT specified. OMT contested immediately. June 2013: contestation peaks with FCC statement. June 2015 contestation decreases with CJEU approval of OMT	Markets respond positively. OMT never used, but ECB actions despite criticism decrease political uncertainty about a crisis response. Confidence rises. Recovery begins.
1						
High, Uncontested	High, Deference Granted	High or Not Necessary	Can constrain or expand policy flexibility	Can validate policy, targeted and broad strategies may be effective	Maximum bargaining power	March 2011: ECB and European Commission agreed to more stringent SGP to manage fiscal policy. November 2012, February 2012 ECB initiates large LTRO programs to provide liquidity. June 2014: ECB begins broad-based stimulus program to promote recovery after debt crisis	Markets respond positively. Renewed SGP increases confidence in EU institutions. Banks take advantage of LTRO program. Stimulus programs reinvigorate stalled talks in 2011 and help restore growth.

Figure 5.10 Shaping policy and behavior in Europe, 2010–2015.

President Herman Van Rompuy attempted to calm market fears by declaring, "Euro area member states will take determined and coordinated action if needed to safeguard stability in the Europe area as a whole."[54] The Greek government, however, had not made a formal request for assistance and no specific proposal was agreed upon. Uncertainty about whether the European Commission would intervene increased on March 17, 2010, when, in a speech to the Bundestag, Chancellor Merkel described the Greek debt crisis as the "biggest challenge ever" and speculated, "It would even be possible to exclude a country from the euro

---

[54] I. Traynor & G. Wearden (2010). "EU leaders reach Greek bailout deal." *The Guardian*, February 11. www.theguardian.com/business/2010/feb/11/eu-summit-greece-bailout-imf.

zone when over the long term it no longer fulfills the conditions."[55]
On March 26, she softened her position somewhat by suggesting the
possibility that Germany would support a Greek bailout as a "last resort,"
while also noting that Greece was not insolvent and had not requested
assistance.[56] Yield rates on ten-year Greek bonds briefly stopped escalat-
ing and even subsided slightly from 6.46 percent in February to 6.24
percent in March. Nonetheless, they shot up again in April, reaching
7.83 percent.[57]

Facing economic bankruptcy at home and increasing costs of raising
capital on international markets, Greek Prime Minister Papandreou
formally activated standby loans from the EU and IMF.[58] On May 2,
he accepted a three-year €110 billion financing agreement that included a
commitment by Greece to reduce its budget deficit to 3 percent of GDP
by 2014 by cutting salaries of public-sector workers, raising taxes on
cigarettes, fuel, gambling and luxuries, increasing value-added tax and
raising the retirement age for women in the public sector.[59] Despite
violent public protests and threats of strikes, Prime Minister George
Papandreou and Finance Minister Papaconstantinou committed themselves to implementing the reforms.[60]

Eurogroup President Jean-Claude Juncker said that the bailout would
"help restore confidence and safeguard financial stability in the Euro
area," yet many considered the bailout to be incomplete because it did
not include a crisis management system to address the possibility of
future crises in Greece or other Eurozone countries.[61] As noted by a
private investment company:[62]

[55] "Merkel wants scope to expel Eurozone troublemakers" (2010). *Euractiv*, March 18.
www.euractiv.com/section/eu-priorities-2020/news/merkel-wants-scope-to-expel-eurozone-
troublemakers; J. Ewing (2010). "Merkel urges tougher rules for Euro Zone." *New York
Times*, March 17. www.nytimes.com/2010/03/18/world/europe/18merkel.html.
[56] "Merkel says EU can back Greece as 'last resort'" (2010). *Euractiv*, March 25.
www.euractiv.com/section/eu-priorities-2020/news/merkel-says-eu-could-back-greece-
as-last-resort.
[57] Organisation for Economic Co-operation and Development. Long-Term Government
Bond Yields: 10-year: Main (Including Benchmark) for Greece
[IRLTLT01GRM156N]. Retrieved from FRED, Federal Reserve Bank of St. Louis.
https://fred.stlouisfed.org/series/IRLTLT01GRM156N.
[58] H. Smith (2010). "Greece activates €45bn EU/IMF loans." *The Guardian*, April 23.
www.theguardian.com/business/2010/apr/23/greece-activates-eu-imf-loans.
[59] D. Magnay et al. (2010). "Greece accepts bailout package." *CNN Money*, May 2. https://
money.cnn.com/2010/05/02/news/international/greece_bailout.
[60] Ibid.   [61] Ibid.
[62] D. Kyriakidou & M. Winfrey (2010). "Greece presses 'help' button, markets still wary."
Reuters, April 23. www.reuters.com/article/us-greece/greece-presses-help-button-
markets-still-wary-idUSTRE63M1LV20100423.

On the one hand it could be perceived a relief that Greece is taking the financial help but it does not address the systemic risk and begs the question as to whether countries like Spain may look for the same rescue package in the near future.

Trichet played a critical role in compelling European leaders to take the next step and create a crisis management regime. He did so by adopting a confrontational strategy that has been described as playing a "game of chicken" with the European Commission.[63] Rather than reassuring markets by promising to bolster the European Commission–IMF bailout package with an ECB-led crisis management regime, he remained noncommittal. At the regular monthly meeting of the ECB Governing Council that took place four days after the European Commission–IMF bailout package had been agreed to, Trichet simply noted that the issue of ECB involvement had not come up.[64] His unwillingness to commit to decisive action in the absence of EU agreement on a crisis management regime added to a perfect storm of political and market uncertainty on May 6. That day, Moody's issued a statement that emphasized the risk of contagion, a "flash crash" on the New York stock exchange drove the Dow Jones Industrial Average down more than 1,000 points in half an hour, and David Cameron, who was known to be less favorable to the EU, became head of a new coalition government in Great Britain.[65] Economic and political uncertainties roiled markets and bond yields spiked for Greece, Spain, Portugal, Ireland and Italy. Eurozone leaders met to negotiate how much money would be mobilized, what mechanisms would be established for managing it and what role the ECB would play.[66] The meetings were reportedly highly contentious with France, Spain, Italy, Portugal and the European Commission on one side and Germany, the Netherlands, Austria and Finland on the other.[67] But, again, rather than offering a solution, Trichet demanded that the European Commission take the next

[63] "Two sides of the same coin? Independence and accountability of the European Central Bank" (2017). *Transparency International EU*. https://transparency.eu/wp-content/uploads/2017/03/TI-EU_ECB_Report_DIGITAL.pdf.

[64] J. Ewing (2010). "European bank's assurance fails to placate investors." *New York Times*, May 6. www.nytimes.com/2010/05/07/business/global/07ecb.html.

[65] J. Treanor (2015). "The 2010 'flash crash': how it unfolded." *The Guardian*, April 22. www.theguardian.com/business/2015/apr/22/2010-flash-crash-new-york-stock-exchange-unfolded.

[66] Bastasin. *Saving Europe*, p. 192.

[67] I. Traynor (2010). "How the euro – and the EU – teetered on the brink of collapse." *The Guardian*, May 14. www.theguardian.com/business/2010/may/14/nicolas-sarkozy-angela-merkel-euro-crisis-summit.

step. He argued, "We [the ECB] have done what we had to do. It is you, the member states, who have failed in your duty."[68] The combination of market panic and Trichet's brinksmanship worked. European leaders reached a compromise and announced the creation of a stabilization mechanism constituted by the EFSF (which would be replaced by the ESM in 2013), and the EFSM with the ability to lend €60 billion to countries in distress.[69] On May 9, Trichet convened another council meeting and finalized the SMP. On May 10, the ECB announced that it would conduct interventions in public and private securities markets under the SMP and had initiated purchases of government bonds from Ireland, Portugal and Greece. Furthermore, it would supplement its regular three-month LTRO with full allotment on May 26 and June 3 and with a six-month LTRO on May 12, 2010, and it would reactivate temporary liquidity swap lines with the Federal Reserve.[70] In short, immediately after the European leaders came through, the ECB responded with supporting actions designed to lower the cost of bonds in troubled countries and provide additional sources of liquidity in euros and dollars to Eurozone banks. Markets across Europe rallied in approval. Bond yields across Europe fell and remained low and steady throughout 2010 and the first half of 2011.

Unfortunately for Greece and other troubled countries, the most contentious aspect of the ECB's crisis response involved its efforts to assist troubled countries by purchasing their bonds through the SMP. On May 11, Axel Weber, president of the *Bundesbank* and member of the ECB's Governing Council, let it be known that he had opposed the SMP and the ECB's purchase of government bonds.[71] In October, he doubled down on his criticism, arguing, "As the risks associated with the SMP outweigh its benefits, these securities purchases should now be phased out permanently."[72]

---

[68] Bastasin. *Saving Europe*, p. 194.
[69] "EFSF FRAMEWORK AGREEMENT (as amended with effect from the Effective Date of the Amendments), consolidated version" (n.d.). www.esm.europa.eu/sites/default/files/20111019_efsf_framework_agreement_en.pdf.
[70] "Press Release: ECB decides on measures to address severe tensions in financial markets" (2010). *European Central Bank*, May 10. www.ecb.europa.eu/press/pr/date/2010/html/pr100510.en.html.
[71] J. Ewing (2010). "Central banker takes a chance by speaking out." *New York Times*, November 1. www.nytimes.com/2010/11/02/business/global/02weber.html.
[72] "Axel A Weber: monetary policy after the crisis – a European perspective" (2010). *BIS Review*. www.bis.org/review/r101018a.pdf.

5.3.2   Taming the Celtic Tiger, Spanish Bull and Italian Wolf

Like Argentina in the 1990s, Ireland had been a poster child of economic development before the crisis. From 1987 to 2007, the Celtic Tiger had a booming economy, with an average annual growth rate of 6.3 percent and a debt to GDP ratio was only 25 percent.[73] Unfortunately, the combination of rising incomes and low interest rates kindled a real-estate bubble that was larger than that of its US cousin. Between 1996 and 2007, housing prices quadrupled. Between 2003 and 2007 mort-gages increased threefold from €45 billion to €125 billion, while bank liabilities to international bondholders increased from €16 billion to €100.[74] Following the collapse of Lehman Brothers, private capital markets froze and Irish banks were unable to raise capital on inter-national bond markets to service their debts.

On September 29, 2008, the day after the US Congress rejected the first TARP proposal, Irish Minister of Finance Brian Lenihan inter-vened to protect Irish banks from a Lehman Brothers-like collapse. He did so by increasing existing protections for commercial deposits covered through the Deposit Guarantee Scheme from €20,000 to €100,000 and extending unlimited guarantees on all deposits in Allied Irish Banks, Bank of Ireland, Anglo Irish Bank, Irish Life and Perman-ent, Irish Nationwide and the EBS until September 29, 2010.[75] Extending unlimited guarantees to any money loaned to an Irish bank effectively guaranteed that creditors and bondholders would be paid back in full.

Other governments offered a mix of guarantees and asset purchases to reduce their banks' exposure to capital losses including liability guaran-tees for customer deposits, bond financing and capital injections.[76] Ireland was, however, much more exposed than others. Its guarantees reached 198.1 percent of GDP compared to the Netherlands at 33.9 percent, Denmark at 35.6 percent, Belgium at 26.4 percent, Sweden

---

[73] K. Whalen (2013). "Ireland's economic crisis: the good, the bad and the ugly." Presented at Bank of Greece Conference on the Europe Crisis, Athens, May 24. www.karlwhelan.com/Papers/Whelan-IrelandPaper-June2013.pdf.

[74] Ibid.

[75] The relevant policies include the Credit Institutions (Financial Support) Act 2008 (www.irishstatutebook.ie/eli/2008/act/18/section/1/enacted/en/html#sec1)   and   the Deposit Guarantee Scheme (www.centralbank.ie/consumer-hub/deposit-guarantee-scheme).

[76] A. Levy & S. Shich (2010). "The Design of Government Guarantees for Bank Bonds: Lessons from the Recent Financial Crisis." *OECD Journal: Financial Market Trends* 2010 (1). www.oecd.org/finance/financial-markets/45636972.pdf.

at 10.9 percent and the United Kingdom at 7 percent.[77] Despite their scale, the Irish two-year guarantees succeeded in calming investor fears.

The yield on Irish ten-year bonds remained low until July of 2010, just prior to the end of the two-year guarantees.[78] In September of 2008, the yield on Irish bonds were low and comparable to German bonds (at 4.09 percent and 4.56 percent, respectively). Irish bond yields remained low through July of 2010 when they reached 5.04 percent. The spread with German bond during that period grew, but this was because German bond yields had decreased to 3.10 percent.[79] While the yield on German bonds continued to decrease, the cost of Irish debt began increasing in August, reaching 6.57 percent in September of 2010 and peaking at 11.7 percent in June of 2011.[80]

As Irish banks ran out of capital, the ECB Governing Council gave the Central Bank of Ireland permission to provide them with emergency liquidity assistance (ELA).[81] The Anglo Irish Bank and Irish Nationwide Building Society, which were nationalized in January of 2009 and August of 2010 respectively,[82] borrowed large amounts of money under ELA programs.

ELA serves as a funding source for banks that do not have access to normal ECB funding operations.[83] While ELA is provided by national central banks, the ECB must be "informed or consulted" in advance "in order to ensure that ELA operations do not interfere with the single monetary policy of the Eurosystem."[84] Article 14.4 of the Statute of the European System of Central Banks grants the Governing Council of the ECB the authority to deny ELA that it assesses "interferes with the tasks

---

[77] Ibid.

[78] Organisation for Economic Co-operation and Development. Long-Term Government Bond Yields: 10-year: Main (Including Benchmark) for Germany [IRLTLT01DEM156N]. Retrieved from FRED, Federal Reserve Bank of St. Louis. https://fred.stlouisfed.org/series/IRLTLT01DEM156N; Organisation for Economic Co-operation and Development. Long-Term Government Bond Yields: 10-year: Main (Including Benchmark) for Ireland [IRLTLT01IEM156N]. Retrieved from FRED, Federal Reserve Bank of St. Louis. https://fred.stlouisfed.org/series/IRLTLT01IEM156N.

[79] Ibid. [80] Whalen. "Ireland's economic crisis." [81] Ibid.

[82] They were consolidated into the Irish Bank Resolution Corporation (IBRC) on July 1, 2011.

[83] "Emergency liquidity assistance (ELA) and monetary policy" (2017). *European Central Bank*, June. www.ecb.europa.eu/mopo/ela/html/index.en.html.

[84] "Agreement on emergency liquidity assistance" (2017). *European Central Bank*, May 17. www.ecb.europa.eu/pub/pdf/other/Agreement_on_emergency_liquidity_assistance_20170517.en.pdf?23bb6a68e85e0715839088d0a23011db.

and objectives of the ESCB."[85] The Governing Council of the ECB also has the authority to approve the maximum amount of ELA that can be provided for individual banks. The ECB exploited this authority to compel Ireland, Cyprus and Greece to accept conditional bailout programs.[86] It used threats to deny access to ELA or limit the increase of ELA as sticks and offered waivers to ELA collateral rules as carrots.[87]

On October 15, Ireland's Minister of Finance, Brian Lenihan received a letter from Jean-Claude Trichet emphasizing the *"extraordinarily large provision of liquidity by the Eurosystem to Irish banks* in recent weeks."[88] He noted that the Eurosystem "may limit, exclude or suspend counterparties' access to monetary policy instruments on the grounds of prudence," and that the assessment by the Governing Council of the appropriateness of its exposures to Irish banks depends very much on economic policy adjustment, enhancing financial structure capital and bank restructuring." On November 19, 2010, Jean-Claude Trichet sent another letter to Lenihan in which he emphasized the role of the Governing Council in assessing whether ELA might interfere with the objectives and tasks of the Eurozone. In it, he offered to authorize further provisions of ELA assistance to Irish banks only if "we receive in writing a commitment ... [that]:[89]

1. The Irish government send a request for financial support to the Eurogroup;
2. The request shall include the commitment to undertake decisive actions in the areas of fiscal consolidation, structural reforms and financial sector restructuring, in agreement with the European Commission, the International Monetary Fund and the ECB;
3. The plan for restructuring of the Irish financial sector shall include the provision of the necessary capital to those Irish banks needing it ...
4. The repayment of the funds provided in the form of ELA shall be fully guaranteed by the Irish government ...

---

[85] "Emergency liquidity assistance (ELA) and monetary policy" (2017). *European Central Bank*, June. www.ecb.europa.eu/mopo/ela/html/index.en.html.

[86] V. Boland & P. Spiegel (2014). "ECB threatened to end funding unless Ireland sought bailout." *Financial Times*, November 16. www.ft.com/content/1f4ed1fa-65ac-11e4-aba7-00144feabdc0.

[87] The ECB used ELA to reward Greece in May of 2010 and March and December of 2012, and again between March and May of 2015, as well as on July 16, 2015, four days after the third adjustment program was approved. Emphasis in the original. www.ecb.europa.eu/press/shared/pdf/2010-10-15_Letter_ECB_President_to_IE_FinMin.pdf?e19978a39fa112418947d2e16895009a.

[88] Ibid.

[89] Jean-Claude Trichet to Brian Lenihan, November 19, 2010. www.ecb.europa.eu/press/html/irish-letters.en.html.

The letter had an immediate effect. On November 21, Lenihan replied
to Trichet. He agreed to the bailout and described Irish actions to repair
the bank sector and reduce the dangers of financial stability to Ireland
and Europe. He also noted:[90]

> In relation to points (1) to (4) in your letter, I would like to inform you that the
> Irish Government has decided today to seek access to external support from the
> European and international support mechanisms. This grave and serious
> decision has been taken in light of the developments I have outlined above and
> informed by your recent communications, and the advice you have conveyed to
> me personally and courteously in recent days.

In November of 2010, the Irish government agreed on a funding
arrangement with the EU and IMF for €67.5 billion.[91] The financing
came from the EFSF and EFSM, the IMF's Extended Fund Facility and
bilateral loans from the United Kingdom, Sweden and Denmark. It also
included €17.5 billion from the National Pension Reserve Fund and
other domestic sources.[92] In exchange, Ireland agreed to enter into a
four-year program of economic austerity that included banking-sector
reform and fiscal adjustments that would be monitored every three
months by the EU and IMF. Irish Finance Minister Michael Noonan
announced that the guarantee program would end on March 28, 2013.[93]
The letters were, however, kept secret until November 6, 2014.[94]

The agreement stabilized the yield on ten-year Irish bonds, which had
risen from 5.5 percent in June of 2010 to 9.25 percent in November.
Following the agreement, the bond rate stabilized through February of
2011, then gradually increased to a peak of 11.7 percent in June of 2011,
and then began subsiding. International factors, including the introduction of the LTRO program in December of 2011 and the OMT program
announcement in September of 2012, likely helped to sustain domestic

---

[90] Brian Lenihan to Jean-Claude Trichet, November 21, 2010. www.ecb.europa.eu/press/
html/irish-letters.en.html.

[91] Whalen. "Ireland's economic crisis."

[92] Houses of the Oireachtas. "Ireland and the Troika Programme"; L. O'Carroll (2010).
"Ireland bailout: full Irish government statement." *The Guardian*, November 28.
www.theguardian.com/business/ireland-business-blog-with-lisa-ocarroll/2010/nov/28/
ireland-bailout-full-government-statement; "Press Release: Joint statement on Ireland
by EU Commissioner Olli Rehn and IMF Managing Director Dominique Strauss-
Kahn" (2010). *International Monetary Fund*, November 28. www.imf.org/en/News/
Articles/2015/09/14/01/49/pr10461.

[93] J.-C. Trichet & M. Draghi (2011c). "Trichet e Draghi: un'azione pressante per ristabilire la
giducia degli investitori." *Corriere della Sara*, September 29. www.corriere.it/economia/11_
settembre_29/trichet_draghi_inglese_304a5f1e-ea59-11e0-ae06-4da866778017.shtml.

[94] "Irish letters" (n.d.). *European Central Bank*. www.ecb.europa.eu/press/html/irish-
letters.en.html.

reforms and calm market expectations. By 2013, Ireland's sovereign debt rates had returned to precrisis levels.

The ECB used similar tactics in the summer of 2011 to compel Spain and Italy to alter their behaviors. On August 5, 2011, Jean-Claude Trichet and Mario Draghi wrote letters to Italian Prime Minister Silvio Berlusconi[95] and Spanish Prime Minister José Luis Rodríguez Zapatero[96] that linked the purchase of their sovereign bonds through the SMP program to economic reforms. The letter to Berlusconi was published on August 5 in *Corriere della Sara*.[97] Spanish Prime Minister José Luis Rodríguez Zapatero published the letter he received from the ECB in his memoirs.[98] It was later published by the ECB.[99] Both letters begin with a statement about the Governing Council's discussion on August 4. The letter to Zapatero asserts that the "Governing Council considers that for Spain pressing action by Spanish authorities is essential," and that "Spain needs to urgently underpin the standing of its sovereign signature and its commitment to fiscal sustainability and structural reforms with credible evidence."[100] These included significant measures to improve the functioning of the labor market, sustainability of public finances and market reforms. In parallel, the letter to Berlusconi stresses that "Italy urgently needs to strengthen the reputation of its sovereign signature and its commitment to fiscal sustainability and structure reforms."[101] It continues by asserting that recent Italian actions were not sufficient, and that significant measures to enhance potential growth, ensure the sustainability of public finances, improve administrative efficiency and business friendliness, and sustain public finances were necessary.

---

[95] J.-C. Trichet & M. Draghi (2011b). "Lettera della Bce all'Italia, testo integrale." *Wall Street Italia*, September 29. www.wallstreetitalia.com/lettera-della-bce-all-italia-testo-integrale.

[96] Jean-Claude Trichet and Miguel Fernández Ordoñez to José Luis Rodríguez Zapatero. December 19, 2014. www.ecb.europa.eu/pub/pdf/other/2011-08-05-letter-from-trichet-and-fernandez-ordonez-to-zapateroen.pdf.

[97] Trichet & Draghi. "Trichet e Draghi."

[98] V. Scarpetta (2013). "Where to publish an ECB letter setting your country's economic policy?" *Open Europe*, November 28. https://openeurope.org.uk/today/blog/ecb-letter-set-spain-economic-policy.

[99] Jean-Claude Trichet and Miguel Fernández Ordoñez to José Luis Rodríguez Zapatero. December 19, 2014. www.ecb.europa.eu/pub/pdf/other/2011-08-05-letter-from-trichet-and-fernandez-ordonez-to-zapateroen.pdf.

[100] Ibid.

[101] J.-C. Trichet & M. Draghi (2011a). "Letter of the European Central Bank to Silvio Berlusconi." *Voltaire Network*, August 5. www.voltairenet.org/article171574.html; Trichet & Draghi. "Lettera della Bce all'Italia."

In an interview with *Corriere della Sera*, Trichet argues that the letters were "not something extraordinary."[102] On August 7, 2011, however, the ECB declared victory by issuing a statement welcoming announcements from Italy and Spain concerning new measures and reforms in fiscal and structural policies, declaring that "it is on the basis of the above assessments that the ECB will actively implement its Securities Markets Programme."[103] In an interview with *EU News* published on January 14, 2014, Trichet justified his threat to withhold SMP access as necessary to protect Europe. He argued, "If the ECB had not bought the Italian bonds and Spanish bonds, the effect would have been dramatic," furthermore, these governments reformed in order to obtain ECB aid and the ECB "did not negotiate" the terms of the letters because, "We are going to intervene in order to prevent the ECB, Member States and the EU from losing their credibility."[104]

Berlusconi tried multiple times to pass legislation that supported the ECB's requests. Though an austerity package was eventually approved, it was considered deficient.[105] On October 22, 2011, Berlusconi was confronted by Merkel and Sarkozy, who accused him of not doing enough to address the debt problem. At a press conference two days later, Merkel and Sarkozy famously smirked when asked about whether they expected Silvio Berlusconi to carry out the expected reforms.[106] On November 12, Berlusconi resigned and President Giorgio Napolitano asked Mario Monti, who had been sworn in as a senator for life three days earlier, to form a government.

National politicians in the United States and Argentina often appoint or reappoint known economic technocrats to signal deference to particular policies. A parallel to this in Europe is the election or appointment of supporters of ECB policy like Mario Monti. Mario Monti is an economist who studied at Bocconi University in Milan and Yale University in the United States; he also taught economics at the University of Turin for fifteen years. In 1994, he was nominated by

[102] "ECB letter shows pressure on Berlusconi" (2011). *Financial Times*, September 29. www.ft.com/content/3576e9c2-eaad-11e0-aeca-00144feab49a.

[103] "Press Release: Statement by the president of the ECB" (2011). *European Central Bank*, August 7. www.ecb.europa.eu/press/pr/date/2011/html/pr110807.en.html.

[104] "Trichet, former ECB president: the letter sent to Berlusconi's government succeeded in saving Italy" (2014). *eunews*, January 14. www.eunews.it/en/2014/01/14/trichet-former-ecb-president-the-letter-sent-to-berlusconis-government-succeeded-in-saving-italy/11812.

[105] Bastasin. *Saving Europe*, p. 306.

[106] T. Kinton (2011). "Merkozy smirk at EU crisis summit boosts Berlusconi." *The Guardian*, October 24. www.theguardian.com/business/2011/oct/24/merkel-sarkozy-italy-berlusconi.

Italian Prime Minister Berlusconi. He was subsequently nominated by center-left Prime Minister Massimo D'Alema to serve on the European Commission, where he gained the moniker "Super Mario" for his willingness to pursue antitrust cases against corporate mergers by General Electric, Honeywell and Microsoft.[107] He also founded a European federalist organization known as the Spinelli Group in 2010. Gianfranco Fini, speaker of the lower chamber of the Italian parliament, noted that, "He has experience and, Europe-wide, is one of the most highly esteemed Italian personalities."[108] In short, Monti had a high degree of credibility. His appointment sent a strong signal that Italian policies would likely conform to those of the ECB and European Commission. Monti served as both prime minister and finance minister until July 2012. During his time in office, he implemented a series of austerity measures that included tax increases, raising the retirement age and pursuing structural reforms in the service sector. In December of 2012, he lost support from Berlusconi's People of Freedom party during two parliamentary confidence votes. Lacking political backing, he resigned so that a new government could be formed. Early elections were held on February 2013. Monti ran for office, but did not win enough parliamentary seats to form a coalition.[109]

Investor expectations that Monti was more likely than Berlusconi to defer to ECB and European Commission policies should be reflected in reduced level of policy risk. The yield on Italian bonds had been relatively low at 5.74 percent in August of 2011, then increased as tensions between Berlusconi, Merkel and Sarkozy increased, until it peaked at 7.05 percent in November of 2011. As expected, the yield began declining with Monti's appointment and fell to 4.49 percent in November of 2013.[110]

The letters sparked controversy among members of the ECB's executive board. On September 9, 2011, Jürgen Stark, the ECB's chief economist responsible for economic and monetary analysis, resigned in

[107] "Profile: Mario Monti" (2013). *BBC News*, February 18. www.bbc.com/news/world-europe-15695056.
[108] Ibid.
[109] Ibid.; J. M. Cunningham (n.d.). "Mario Monti." *Encyclopaedia Britannica*. www.britannica.com/biography/Mario-Monti.
[110] Organisation for Economic Co-operation and Development. Long-Term Government Bond Yields: 10-year: Main (Including Benchmark) for Italy [IRLTLT01ITM156N]. Retrieved from FRED, Federal Reserve Bank of St. Louis. https://fred.stlouisfed.org/series/IRLTLT01ITM156N.

protest.[111] His resignation was a public display of division on the ECB Board.[112] Daniel Grows, director of the Center for European Studies in Brussels, summarized the impact, noting:[113]

It's a very bad sign. It means that the split within the E.C.B. that we thought was far down the road is here now. It puts a shadow over the E.C.B. and risks financial markets asking, "How long can they go on buying these Italian bonds?" This indicates that the answer is, "Not as long as I had thought."

On October 23, 2011, however, Stark – who had been a strong opponent to ECB interventions – was replaced by Jörg Asmussen, a deputy finance minister who had a more conciliatory reputation and turned out to be a strong advocate for the SMP and OMT programs.[114] Consequently, while Stark's resignation initially raised political uncertainty, the appointment of Asmussen lowered uncertainty by suggesting that the ECB Governing Council was likely to be more unified than it had been.

5.3.3 *The Strong Do What They Will, the Weak Do What They Must*

The second Greek crisis began on April 23, 2011 with the European Commission's assessment that the Greek deficit was worse than anticipated. At a meeting on July 1, European governments agreed that PSI would be part of the second Greek bailout and that bondholders had to accept a "voluntary" 21-percent write-off of their bonds. Conditions in Greece had deteriorated by the time they met again on October 26, 2011 and the PSI was increased to a 50-percent haircut.[115] On October 31, Prime Minister Papandreou challenged to the revised terms by announcing that he would hold a referendum on the bailout agreement.[116]

---

[111] Boland & Spiegel. "ECB threatened to end funding."
[112] J. Ewing & N. Kulish (2011). "A setback for the Euro Zone." *New York Times*, September 9. www.nytimes.com/2011/09/10/business/global/a-top-ecb-official-to-resign.html.
[113] Ibid.   [114] Ibid.
[115] L. Baker & S. Sassard (2012). "Insight: how the Greek debt puzzle was solved." *Reuters*, February 29. www.reuters.com/article/us-europe-greece/insight-how-the-greek-debt-puzzle-was-solved-idUSTRE81S0NP20120229.
[116] H. Smith & D. Gow (2011). "Papandreou scraps Greek referendum as open warfare erupts in his party." *The Guardian*, November 3. www.theguardian.com/world/2011/nov/03/papandreou-scraps-greek-referendum-euro.

188 A Greek Tragedy

Papandreou's announcement caught negotiators by surprise and triggered dramatic downturns in US and European stock markets, market volatility increased significantly, and credit default swaps for Greece and Italy spiked.[117] However, rather than backing off, Chancellor Merkel called his bluff by arguing that, "in essence [the referendum] is about nothing else but the question, does Greece want to stay in the Eurozone, yes or no?"[118] Merkel and Sarkozy also agreed to suspend the next installment of aid – US$11 billion – until after the referendum.[119] Papandreou folded. Facing increasing opposition at home as well as pressure from abroad, he called off the referendum on November 3 and resigned on November 11.[120]

Papandreou was replaced by Lucas Papademos. Dr. Papademos had been a classmate of Mario Draghi's at the Massachusetts Institute of Technology and was a former ECB vice president.[121] On November 16, Prime Minister Papademos won a confidence vote with an overwhelming margin, securing 255 votes in the 300-seat Parliament.[122] This suggested that he was more likely to accept Troika guidelines and that he had the political capacity to implement necessary reforms. Like Mario Monti, who became the Italian prime minister on November 13, Papademos's appointment should have been reassuring to investors.[123] These potential benefits were, however, undercut by continued

---

[117] "Greek referendum spooks European stock markets" (2011). *Reuters*, November 1. www.reuters.com/article/markets-europe-stocks-idUSL5E7M11S420111101; "Greek referendum plan plunges markets into chaos" (2011). *ABC News*, November 1. www .abc.net.au/news/2011-11-02/greek-referendum-ignites-german-anger2c-hammers-mark ets/3614000.

[118] S. Erlanger & R. Donadio (2011). "Greek premier pledges vote in December on debt deal." *New York Times*, November 2. www.nytimes.com/2011/11/03/world/europe/ greek-cabinet-backs-call-for-referendum-on-debt-crisis.html.

[119] Ibid.

[120] "Greece PM Papandreou wins confidence vote" (2011). *BBC News*, November 5. www.bbc.com/news/world-europe-15586673; T. Vogel (2011b). "Papandreou wins vote of confidence." *Politico*, November 4. www.politico.eu/article/papandreou-wins-vote-of-confidence.

[121] T. Vogel (2011a). "Papademos set to take over from Papandreou." *Politico*, November 8. www.politico.eu/article/papademos-set-to-take-over-from-papandreou; "European debt crisis: Papademos named as Greece's new PM" (2011). *The Guardian Business Blog*, November 10. www.theguardian.com/business/blog/2011/nov/10/eurozone-crisis-italy-greece; S. Daley (2011). "Economist named to lead Greek unity government." *New York Times*, November 10. www.nytimes.com/2011/11/11/world/europe/greek-leaders-resume-talks-on-interim-government.html.

[122] Daley. "Economist named to lead Greek unity government."

[123] "Greece, Italy bet on technocrats to restore confidence" (2011). *EURACTIV.com with Reuters*, November 14. www.euractiv.com/section/elections/news/greece-italy-bet-on-technocrats-to-restore-confidence.

disagreements among other eurozone countries over how to respond to the Greek crisis. On November 1, Mario Draghi became president of the ECB and undertook a series of measures to increase liquidity and rejuvenate negotiations. On December 8, 2011 he announced two three-year LTROs. The first took place on December 21, 2011 and provided €489.2 billion to 523 banks; the second took place on February 29, 2012 and provided €529.5 billion to 800 banks and another €6.5 billion allotted in the regular three-month LTRO.[124] These programs were intended to provide sufficient liquidity to contain spillovers from the sovereign debt crisis broader financial markets. On February 9, 2012, Draghi said he expected the Eurozone "to recovery very gradually in the course of 2012."[125] To help restart negotiations among EU governments about the Greek crisis, he suggested that he might also return approximately €12 billion in profits the ECB had made on Greek government bonds so that European member governments could use that cash to supplement the Greek bailout.

The European governments responded well and reached an agreement on the terms of the second Greek bailout on February 21, 2012. It included a haircut of 53.5 percent for bondholders.[126] This was to be the world's largest debt-restricting deal in the world at €206 billion.[127] To compel the Greek government to agree to the new level of PSI, the ECB suspended the eligibility of using Greek bonds as collateral on February 28, 2012.[128] On March 9, the Papademos government announced that 85.8 percent of bond holders agreed to a haircut of 74 percent.[129] Yields on Greek bonds fell from 29.24 percent in February to 19.06 percent in March. In May, however, political uncertainty in Greece increased again as a result of the election of parties who rejected the terms of the Troika bailout. But no coalition was formed, and early elections in June of 2012 generated in a coalition government that agreed to implement the bailout

---

[124] "Economic and monetary developments: monetary and financial developments" (2012). *ECB Monthly Bulletin*, March. www.ecb.europa.eu/pub/pdf/other/mb201203_ focus03.en.pdf?633af8e40f98a75808996a7857cbbd93.

[125] H. Stewart (2012). "European Central Bank hints it may forgo profits on its Greek bonds." *The Guardian*, February 9. www.theguardian.com/business/2012/feb/09/ european-central-bank-may-forgo-profits-greek-bonds.

[126] Baker & Sassard. "Insight."   [127] Ibid.

[128] "Press Release: Eligibility of Greek bonds used as collateral in Eurosystem monetary policy operations" (2012). *European Central Bank*, February 28. www.ecb.europa.eu/ press/pr/date/2012/html/pr120228.en.html.

[129] K. Allen (2012). "Greece secures private-sector backing for crucial debt swap." *The Guardian*, March 9. www.theguardian.com/business/2012/mar/09/greece-private-sector-backing-debt-swap.

agreement. After rising to 27.82 percent in June, Greek bond rates began a gradual decline that continued until their reached 5.89 percent in September of 2014.

Uncertainty and interest rates were also increasing in Spain and Italy. Spain had been urging the ECB to purchase its bonds to decrease yields, but the ECB had instead been pushing for European governments to increase funding for the EFSF. Draghi had switched tactics and adopted a more confrontational approach in his efforts to get European leaders to take action. On May 31, 2012, Draghi argued to the European Parliament that the ECB had reached the limits of what it could do and that the structure of the Eurozone had become "unsustainable unless further steps were taken."[130] He criticized political leaders for taking half measures and argued that the ECB could not make up for a lack of decisive action by policymakers. He argued: "Can the E.C.B. fill the vacuum left by lack of euro area governance? The answer is no."[131]

Like Bernanke who argued that Congress had to take action to fix the economy, Draghi argued on June 6, 2012, that, "It is not right for monetary policy to fill other institutions' lack of action," a reference to the urgent need for Europe's leaders to resolve the euro crisis.[132] When legislative action was not forthcoming, however, both Bernanke and Draghi stepped forward to compensate. The Federal Reserve's response to congressional intransigence was engaging in quantitative easing as long as it was weak.[133] Draghi's response was a declaration heard around Europe: "Within our mandate, the ECB is ready to do whatever it takes to preserve the euro. And believe me, it will be enough."[134] Draghi's promise to fire his economic bazooka as needed finally remedied the instability caused by the sovereign debt crisis. It broke the hold of political uncertainty that had plagued the Eurozone for months.

---

[130] J. Ewing (2012). "A tense warning for euro states: do something now." *New York Times*, May 31. www.nytimes.com/2012/06/01/business/global/greek-banks-regain-access-to-european-central-bank-loans.html; B. Rooney (2012). "Draghi says euro is 'unsustainable' without action." *CNN Money*, May 31. https://money.cnn.com/2012/05/31/investing/ecb-draghi/index.htm.

[131] Ewing. "A tense warning."

[132] "ECB sees rising risks to Eurozone economy" (2012). *BBC News*, June 6. www.bbc.com/news/business-18339334.

[133] "Time for bankers to intervene" (2012). *New York Times*, June 26. www.nytimes.com/2012/06/27/opinion/time-for-bankers-to-intervene.html.

[134] "Verbatim of the remarks made by Mario Draghi" (2012). *European Central Bank*, July 26. www.ecb.europa.eu/press/key/date/2012/html/sp120726.en.html.

Date	Triggering Event	Waiver Granted	Waiver Revoked
May 2010	European Commission and Greece agree to first economic adjustment program	X	
February 2012	Anticipation of March 2012 debt restructuring		X
March 2012	Debt restructuring	X	
July 2012	Expiration of buy-back scheme for marketable debt issued or fully guaranteed by Greece		X
December 2012	Positive review of second economic adjustment program by Troika	X	
February 4, 2015	Syriza government threatens to leave program. Waiver was due to expire on February 28. Revoking earlier seen as "warning shot to Athens, and to Eurozone leaders, to agree to a new deal as soon as possible." Governing Council split		X
March–May 2015	Governing Council keeps raising the ceiling of ELA limits Governing Council decisions reported in the financial press, but not official. Lack of transparency creates uncertainty and leverage.	X	
June 2015	Troika makes a new program proposal on June 25, but negotiations break down with a call for a referendum to be held on July 5. Stock market closes on June 27. On June 28, Governing Council stops increasing ELA ceiling. Greek government closes banks on June 28 to avoid a run		X
July 2015	Governing Council reaffirms that it would not lift the ceiling. ECB instructs Bank of Greece to raise haircuts. On July 16, four days after acceptance of a third adjustment program, the Governing Council agrees to increase ceiling	X	

Figure 5.11 Manipulation of ELA to Greece.

5.3.4 The Strong Do What They Will, the Weak Do What They Must, Again

In the spring of 2015, the ECB again manipulated access to ELA to reduce specific-actor risk, this time to compel the Greek government to accept the terms of a third bailout package.[135] When its compliance improved, the ECB Governing Board extended waivers to the collateral requirements and financial limits of ELAs. When negotiations became problematic, it denied or rescinded them. With Greek banks losing about €2 billion a week,[136] access to ELA funding had a direct effect on Greek banks and, consequently, on the Greek government (see Figure 5.11).[137]

---

[135] "Two sides of the same coin? Independence and accountability of the European Central Bank" (2017). *Transparency International EU.* https://transparency.eu/wp-content/uploads/2017/03/TI-EU_ECB_Report_DIGITAL.pdf.

[136] J. Rankin & H. Smith (2015). "Eurozone chiefs strike deal to extend Greek bailout for four months." *The Guardian,* February 20. www.theguardian.com/business/2015/feb/20/eurozone-chiefs-meet-for-last-ditch-talks-to-avert-greece-cash-crunch.

[137] For a description of these events, see: "Two sides of the same coin? independence and accountability of the European Central Bank" (2017). *Transparency International EU.* https://transparency.eu/wp-content/uploads/2017/03/TI-EU_ECB_Report_DIGITAL.pdf.

Prime Minister Alexis Tsipras and the Syriza party were elected on January 25, 2015 on an anti-austerity platform. He and his finance minister, Yanis Varoufakis, were harsh critics of the Troika bailout conditions, repeatedly insisting that creditors support a bridge loan and drop demands for cuts in pensions and public-sector jobs as the price of additional support.[138] The ECB sent a warning shot of opposition to the Tsipras regime on February 4, 2015 by revoking a waiver on ELA collateral requirements three weeks earlier than originally planned. It announced that the "ECB Governing Council lifts its current waiver on minimum credit rating requirements for marketable instruments" and that liquidity needs "would have to satisfied by the relevant national central bank, in line with Eurosystem rules" because "it is currently not possible to assume a successful conclusion of the programme review."[139] In other words, special treatment was denied for failure to comply with program standards. On February 20, the government agreed to maintain its austerity measures and develop a list of policy reforms in exchange for an extension of the deadline for its €240 billion bailout payment for four months, to June 30. Jeroen Dijsselbloem called the agreement a "first step in this process of rebuilding trust."[140]

Following the agreement in February, the ECB Governing Council relented and gradually raised the limits on the amount of ELA that Greek banks could borrow. On June 18, twelve days before the deadline, Angela Merkel, François Hollande and Alexis Tsipras met to forestall a Greek bankruptcy, but the talks broke down acrimoniously with Christine Lagarde calling for "adults in the room" and warning that if Greece did not make its payment of €1.6 billion to the IMF on June 30, it would be declared to be in default and would disqualify itself from receiving any further IMF funds.[141] The next day, June 19, the ECB agreed to raise the cap on ELA available to Greek banks by €1.8 billion to €85.9 billion to forestall runs on Greek banks on Friday. But, as a signal of disapproval, the ECB said it would wait until Monday's meeting with the Troika to

[138] I. Traynor & P. Inman (2015). "Greece faces banking crisis after Eurozone meeting breaks down." *The Guardian*, June 18. www.theguardian.com/world/2015/jun/18/greece-faces-banking-crisis-after-eurozone-meeting-breaks-down.

[139] "Press Release: Eligibility of Greek bonds used as collateral in Eurosystem monetary policy operations" (2015). *European Central Bank*, February 4. www.ecb.europa.eu/press/pr/date/2015/html/pr150204.en.html.

[140] Rankin & Smith. "Eurozone chiefs strike deal."

[141] Traynor & Inman. "Greece faces banking crisis."

determine whether it would do more.[142] Prime Minister Tsipras responded defiantly, refusing to cut pensions and reaching out to Russia for financial assistance. Expressing concern about the political turmoil and failure to negotiate, Donald Tusk, Poland's prime minister and president of the European Council, argued:[143]

We are close to the point where the Greek government will have to choose between accepting what I believe is a good offer of continuing support, or head towards default. At the end of the day it can only be a Greek decision and a Greek responsibility ... The game of chicken needs to end and so does the blame game.

On Monday, June 22, EU leaders and the ECB met to negotiate a resolution to the crisis. In a show of support, the ECB Governing Council reinstated the waiver of minimum credit requirements for marketable instruments issued or guaranteed by Greece, subject to special haircuts, for one week.[144] This kept Greece afloat while negotiations were ongoing. At the same time, the Governing Council kept the pressure on by not adjusting the limits on ELA. Meanwhile, Lagarde, Draghi and Jeroen Dijsselbloem summoned Tsipras to Brussels on June 25 to offer €15.5 billion over the next five months in return for tax increases, pension cuts and other reforms. Their offer was set to expire on June 30.[145] Instead of accepting their terms, Tsipras called for a public referendum on the agreement. The Governing Council signaled its anger the next day by not increasing the ELA ceiling. This triggered a run on Greek banks and forced their closure. They would remain closed until July 20.[146] On June 30, Greece missed a scheduled €1.6 billion payment to the IMF.[147] Despite the protests of the European Commission, the referendum took place on July 5, 2015.[148]

---

[142] L. Elliott (2015). "ECB staves off collapse of Greek banking system with emergency funding." *The Guardian*, June 19. www.theguardian.com/world/2015/jun/19/ecb-greek-banking-system-emergency-funding-greece-creditors-monday-meetings.

[143] Ibid.

[144] "Press Release: ECB reinstates waiver affecting the eligibility of Greek bonds used as collateral in Eurosystem monetary policy operations" (2016). *European Central Bank*, June 22. www.ecb.europa.eu/press/pr/date/2016/html/pr160622_1.en.html.

[145] A. Nardelli (2015). "Three days that saved the euro." *The Guardian*, October 22. www.theguardian.com/world/2015/oct/22/three-days-to-save-the-euro-greece.

[146] G. Smith (2015). "Greece shutters its banks after the ECB turns off the taps." *Fortune*, June 28. http://fortune.com/2015/06/28/greece-capital-controls-bank-holiday-ecb.

[147] "Greece debt crisis: creditors press for new proposals" (2015). *BBC News*, July 6. www.bbc.com/news/world-europe-33413569.

[148] "Transcript of President Jean-Claude Juncker's press conference on Greece" (2015). *European Commission*, June 29. http://europa.eu/rapid/press-release_SPEECH-15-5274_en.htm.

The Greeks rejected the bailout conditions with a 61-percent no vote.[149] On July 6, the Governing Council retaliated by reaffirming that it would not increase ELA funding and asserting that ELA can only be provided with sufficient collateral.[150] Finance Minister Yanis Varoufakis resigned and was replaced by Euclid Tsakalotos. Bank closures were extended and ATM withdrawals were limited to to €60 per day.

Given market pressures and the denial of ELA from the ECB, the Tsipras government reversed course, and on July 8, 2015, it asked for a three-year bailout of €53.5 billion. On July 13, it accepted the terms, despite the fact that they involved larger pension cuts and tax increases than the bailout package that had been rejected in the referendum. On July 15, the Greek parliament approved austerity measures and Greece received a €86 billion loan. In response, the ECB backed an IMF recommendation to lengthen the terms of Greek debt to lessen its burden. On July 17, 2015, the ECB Governing Council signaled its approval by allowing the ELA ceiling to increase. The extension of ELA enabled banks to reopen on July 20.[151]

On July 20, Greece began to repay €4.25 billion to the ECB and €2.05 billion to the IMF.[152] When banks reopened, the €60 per day withdrawal maximum was replaced with a weekly one, capped at €420.[153] Tsipras succeeded in getting the austerity measures through parliament by working with opposition members in parliament. His implementation capacity continued to improve in September when he and the Syriza party won a snap election.[154]

Tsipras continued to maintain the promised austerity measures. In June of 2016, the ECB Governing Council again reinstated the waiver, acknowledging the Greek government's commitments to implementing reforms. A year later, Tsipras cut pensions and broadened the tax

---

[149] S. Daley (2015). "Greeks reject bailout terms in rebuff to European leaders." *New York Times*, July 5. www.nytimes.com/2015/07/06/world/europe/greek-referendum-debt-crisis-vote.html.

[150] "Press Release: ELA to Greek banks maintained" (2015). *European Central Bank*, July 6. www.ecb.europa.eu/press/pr/date/2015/html/pr150706.en.html.

[151] "The Daily Shot" (2015). *The Daily Shot Brief*, July 17. https://us10.campaign-archive.com/?u=451473e81730c5a3ae680c489&id=f69453a36e&e=3b53b92804.

[152] H. Ellyatt (2015). "ECB confirms it has been repaid by Greece." *CNBC*, July 20. www.cnbc.com/2015/07/20/greece-starts-paying-back-the-ecb-imf.html.

[153] "Greek debt crisis: banks reopen amid tax rise" (2015). *BBC News*, July 20. www.bbc.com/news/world-europe-33590334.

[154] K. Amadeo (2018). "Greek debt crisis explained." *The Balance*, November 8. www.thebalance.com/what-is-the-greece-debt-crisis-3305525.

base in return for another €86 billion in loans. And on July 25, 2017, Greece returned to capital markets by raising €3 billion through the sale of five-year government bonds.[155] Although half of the investors were swapping older Greek debt for the new bonds, the bond sale was a symbolic victory for Tsipras. The bailout program ended on August 20, 2018, though supervision will continue until the debt is repaid.

5.3.5 *Revitalizing Growth and the Suitors' Rebellion*

With the sovereign debt crisis under control and program countries able to raise capital on international markets at affordable rates, the ECB shifted its attention to revitalizing growth by providing access to credit and liquidity in the financial system. In June of 2014, Draghi laid out a quantitative easing strategy focused on lowering interest rates, expanding a series of targeted longer-term refinancing operations (TLTRO I and TLTRO II) and an asset purchase programme (APP).[156]

Interest rates fell into unprecedentedly low and negative territory. The ECB dropped the rates on its MROs from 0.25 percent on November 13, 2013, to 0.15 percent on June 11, 2014, to 0.05 percent on September 10, 2014, then to 0.00 percent on March 16, 2016. It also dropped its deposit facility rate from 0.00 percent on November 13, 2013, to –0.10 percent on June 11, 2014, to –0.20 percent on September 10, 2014, to –0.30 percent on December 15, 2015, and to –0.40 percent on March 15, 2016.[157]

The ECB announced the first round of eight targeted LTROs (TLTRO-I) on June 5, 2014, with maturities of up to four years at an average cost of 0.10 percent.[158] This was followed by a second round of four additional auctions announced on March 20, 2016 (TLTRO-II). In

[155] L. Alderman (2017). "In sign of progress for Greece, investors eagerly snap up new bonds." *New York Times*, July 25. www.nytimes.com/2017/07/25/business/dealbook/greece-debt-bonds.html.

[156] "Asset purchase programmes" (n.d.). *European Central Bank*. www.ecb.europa.eu/mopo/implement/omt/html/index.en.html.

[157] "Key ECB interest rates" (n.d.). *European Central Bank*. www.ecb.europa.eu/stats/policy_and_exchange_rates/key_ecb_interest_rates/html/index.en.html.

[158] "The targeted longer-term refinancing operations: an overview of the take-up and their impact on bank intermediation" (2017). *European Central Bank Economic Bulletin* (3), 42. www.ecb.europa.eu/pub/pdf/other/ebbox201703_05.en.pdf.

the final auction on March 23, 2017, 474 Eurozone banks borrowed an additional €233.5 billion.[159]

The TLTROs link the amount that banks can borrow and the interest rate they pay to the amount of loans they issue to nonfinancial corporations and households.[160] Specifically, banks could borrow up to 30 percent of the amount of their existing loans to nonfinancial corporations and households, other than loans to households for house purchases. As a further incentive to lend, banks that met their lending targets could borrow more in the final six TLTRO-I operations. Under TLTRO-II, banks that outperformed their benchmarks between February 1, 2016 and July 31, 2018 received additional rate reductions to as low as –0.40 percent interest.[161] Banks could also use TLTRO-II loans to repay TLTRO-I loans at 0.00 percent interest.

The targeted longer-term refinancing operations have been highly popular, with TLTRO and TLTRO-II credits reaching €761 billion as of March 2017.[162] The interest rates on loans to nonfinancial corporations declined across the euro area from about 3 percent before the TLTRO program began in 2014 to 2 percent in January of 2017. In addition, in 2014, lending rates in Italy (about 3.7 percent) and Spain (about 3.5 percent) had been substantially higher than in France (2 percent) and Germany (2.5 percent), yet by January of 2017 they had all converged to between approximately 1.7 and 2.2 percent.[163] The TLTROs also helped promote lending. While lending in vulnerable countries has declined since June of 2014, it declined less in those that bid on TLTROs (by 4 percent) than in those who did not (by 7 percent); in comparison, lending in less vulnerable countries increased by about 7 percent in those who bid on TLTROs and declined about 1 percent for those who did not.[164]

The APP consists of the Corporate-sector Purchase Programme (CSPP), Public-sector Purchase Programme (PSPP), Asset-backed Securities Purchase Programme (ABSPP) and third Covered Bond Purchase Programme (CBPP).[165] From March 2015 through March 2016, the Governing Council made €60 billion in monthly purchases under the APP. It increased its monthly purchases to €80 billion from April

[159] "Euro zone banks take more ultra-cheap ECB loans than expected" (2017). *Reuters*, March 23. www.reuters.com/article/eurozone-banks-ecb-tltro-idUSF9N1F8017.

[160] "Targeted longer-term refinancing operations (TLTROs)" (2018). *European Central Bank*. www.ecb.europa.eu/mopo/implement/omo/tltro/html/index.en.html.

[161] "The targeted longer-term refinancing operations: an overview of the take-up and their impact on bank intermediation" (2017). *European Central Bank Economic Bulletin* (3), 43. www.ecb.europa.eu/pub/pdf/other/ebbox201703_05.en.pdf.

[162] Ibid.   [163] Ibid.   [164] Ibid.

[165] "Asset purchase programmes" (n.d.). *European Central Bank*. www.ecb.europa.eu/mopo/implement/omt/html/index.en.html.

2016 until March 2017, then reduced them again to €60 billion from April 2017 through December 2017, and to €30 billion from January 2018 through September 2018. On October 25, 2018, the Governing Council announced that it would continue to make purchases of €15 billion under the APP until the end of December 2018 and then end the program.[166] As of November 2018, the total holdings under the APP were €2.56 trillion or about 11 percent of the euro area's nominal GDP. The PSPP accounts for 81 percent of total APP purchases. The ECB started purchasing public-sector securities under the PSPP on March 9, 2016. These included nominal and inflation-linked central government bonds and bonds issued by recognized agencies, regional and local governments, international organizations and multilateral development banks in the euro area.[167] Initial ECB analyses of the APP suggest that has had a significant short-term impact on GDP and could have a longer-term impact on inflation.

Other ECB actions include various security purchase programs including the CBPPs starting in 2009 (CBPP1) and 2011 (CBPP2) and an SMP starting in 2010, aimed at restoring the functionality of financial markets and supporting the banking sector, which plays a key role in the transmission of monetary policy in the euro area.[168]

5.4 Contesting Authority from the Two Pillars of Growth

On December 7, 1998, just prior to the introduction of the euro, President of the ECB Willem Duisenberg described monetary policy in the forthcoming Eurozone as "stability-oriented."[169] He operationalized the concept of monetary stability in the Eurozone in terms of the complementary objectives of maintaining price stability and economic vitality. Price stability of the euro is defined as "a year-on-year increase in the Harmonized Index of Consumer prices (HIPC) for the euro area of below 2 percent."[170] In 2003, the Governing Council signaled that neither inflation nor deflation were consistent with price stability by adding the clarification that "it aims to maintain inflation rates below,

---

[166] Ibid.   [167] Ibid.
[168] L. Gambetti & A. Musso (2017). "The Macroeconomic Impact of the ECB's Expanded Asset Purchase Programme (APP)." The European Central Bank Working Paper Series, No. 2017, June. www.ecb.europa.eu/pub/pdf/scpwps/ecb.wp.2075.en.pdf? b4cbbd6fdbec00f78c66a83b422de6e7.
[169] "The ESCB's stability-oriented monetary policy strategy" (1998). *European Central Bank*, December 7. www.ecb.europa.eu/press/key/date/1998/html/sp981207.en.html.
[170] Ibid.

but close to, 2 percent over the medium term."[171] Maintaining economic vitality "without prejudice to the objective of price stability" involves supporting "the general economic policies in the Union with a view to contributing to the achievement of the objectives of the Union."[172] Duisenberg emphasized that these two objectives were complementary. "By fulfilling its primary objective of maintaining price stability," he argued, "the ESCB will automatically also support the general economic policies in the European Community which are aimed at achieving the aforementioned objectives, namely non-inflationary growth and high employment."[173]

Duisenberg argued that the ECB's monetary objectives could be met by pursuing a two-pillar strategy. The first pillar emphasizes the money supply and prices. This pillar confirms the primacy of monetary policy in the ECB's charter. It aligns well with narrow interpretations of the role of central banks as inflation fighters in the economy. The second pillar emphasizes the broader set of economic and financial developments that could pose risks to prices and price stability in the euro area.[174] It reflects a more expansive interpretation of the role of central banks as financial shock absorbers responsible for managing economic and political factors that affect the functioning of the monetary transmission mechanism. It also recognizes that central banks have a unique ability to compensate for shortfalls in private-sector liquidity, serve as lenders of last resort and perform other important functions during a crisis.

The two-pillar approach provided flexibility in interpretation that helped generate the broad-based deference needed to secure the adoption of the euro. It also provided a framework for justifying more expansive interpretations of the ECB's mandate as the crisis developed. Early in the crisis, Jean-Claude Trichet maintained a reputation as an inflation hawk. His infamous decisions to raise interest rates in the summer of 2011 despite growing uncertainties regarding the European debt crisis bolstered expectations that he would continue to prioritize price stability in ways that were consistent with the first pillar. At the same time, Trichet's other actions (e.g., his pursuit of a lax monetary policy prior to the crisis,

[171] "The definition of price stability" (n.d.). *European Central Bank.* www.ecb.europa.eu/mopo/strategy/pricestab/html/index.en.html.

[172] "Protocol No (4) On the Statute of the European System of Central Banks and of the European Central Bank" (2012). *Official Journal of the European Union. European Central Bank,* October 26. www.ecb.europa.eu/ecb/legal/pdf/c_32620121026en_protocol_4.pdf.

[173] "The ESCB's stability-oriented monetary policy strategy" (1998). *European Central Bank,* December 7. www.ecb.europa.eu/press/key/date/1998/html/sp981207.en.html.

[174] Ibid.

his use of a fixed-rate tender procedure with full allotment to bolster the ECB's role as a lender of last resort, his use of LTROs to encourage banks to purchase government bonds and the purchase of government bonds under the SMP program) reflected a shift toward broader engagement reflected in the second pillar. José Manuel González-Páramo, member of the Executive Board of the ECB, articulated the broadening perspective by Trichet, Draghi and members of the ECB's Board as follows:[175]

> The ECB reacted to the financial turmoil in full accordance with both its mandate and with key principles of modern central banking practice. First of all, the ECB's policies were always guided by its primary objective, which is to maintain price stability. However, we have learned from the financial crisis that while price stability is certainly a necessary condition for financial stability, it is not a sufficient one. The materialization of systemic risk and financial instability triggered deep recessions with great economic costs. These developments carried risks for medium-term price stability which called for bold decisions by central banks around the world.

Several prominent members of the ECB's Governing Council rebelled against this shift. On September 9, 2011, for example, Jürgen Stark resigned in what was widely perceived to be a protest over the ECB's decision to buy Italian and Spanish government bonds.[176] His departure came six weeks before the end of Jean-Claude Trichet's term and his replacement by Mario Draghi. To the consternation of critics like Stark, Mario Draghi extended Trichet's more expansive behavior, and Stark's replacement, Jörg Asmussen, became a defender of ECB interventions.[177]

5.4.1 Challenging "Whatever It Takes"

The ECB's authority is delineated by the Treaty of Lisbon, which was approved by the European Parliament on February 20, 2008.[178] To go into effect – as it eventually did on December 1, 2009 – the Treaty of Lisbon required ratification by its 27 member countries. Initially rejected by referendum in Ireland in June of 2008; it was revised and then

---

[175] Speech by González-Páramo, J. M. (2011). Member of the Executive Board of the ECB, at the XXIV Moneda y Crédito Symposium, Madrid, November 4. www.ecb.europa.eu/press/key/date/2011/html/sp111104_1.en.html.

[176] Ewing & Kulish. "A setback for the Euro Zone."

[177] A. Breidthardt (2013). "Berlin defends ECB bond plan, casts doubt on court's power." *Reuters*. June 11. www.reuters.com/article/uk-germany-court-idUKBRE95A0CA20130611.

[178] The Treaty of Lisbon amends the Maastricht Treaty of 1993 and its successor, the Treaty of the European Union of 2007, as well as the Treaty of Rome of 1957 and its successor, the Treaty on the Function in of the European Union of 2007. The Lisbon Treaty is available online at: www.lisbon-treaty.org/wcm.

approved in a second referendum in October of 2009. In the interim, in June of 2009, the Federal Constitutional Court of Germany (FCC) confirmed its position that the Treaty of Lisbon was compatible with German law. The Karlsruhe Lissabon–Urteil decision by the GCC was praised by Chancellor Merkel and President of the European Commission José Manuel Barroso as an indication that the treaty would soon enter into force.[179] Yet, the court's decision also reasserted the primacy of German law over European law. Highlighting concerns about a "democratic deficit" within the EU, the FCC argued that any delegation of German law to the EU would require a waiver to or change in the German Basic Law.[180] Any actions by the German government within Europe and any European actions that affected German citizens would have to be submitted to the German parliament for approval.[181]

The Karlsruhe Lissabon–Urteil decision highlights the potential for national institutions to constrain the actions of the ECB and other European institutions.[182] Although the FCC ultimately accepted the European Court of Justice's interpretation that the ECB's actions were justified, contestation of the ECB's authority affected its ability to manage market expectations.

On September 6, 2012, the ECB released technical features of the OMT program. These included the opportunity for countries in EFSF/ESM programs to purchase unlimited amounts of sovereign bonds.[183] The OMT program was contested by members of the ECB's Governing Council, led by Germany. The challenge was spearheaded by Jens Weidmann, the president of the *Bundesbank*, who, with Jürgen Stark, had opposed the purchase of Irish and Portuguese bonds in August of 2011.[184]

Weidmann supported a narrow interpretation of the ECB's mandate, and he described ECB assistance to troubled countries as a Faustian

[179] U. Knapp (2009). "All losers have won." *Frankfurter Runschau*, June 6. www.fr.de/politik/bundesverfassungsgericht-zum-eu-vertrag-alle-verlierer-haben-gewonnen-a-1097387.

[180] "Urteil des Bundesverfassungsgerichts zum Vertrag von Lissabon" (2007). *Bundeszantrale für politische Bildung*, December 13. www.bpb.de/politik/hintergrund-aktuell/69361/urteil-zum-vertrag-von-lissabon-30-06-2009.

[181] Bastasin. *Saving Europe*, p. 111.

[182] Bundesverfassungsgericht (n.d.). "Judgement of the Second Senate of 30 June 2009." www.bundesverfassungsgericht.de/SharedDocs/Entscheidungen/EN/2009/06/es20090630_2bve000208en.html.

[183] "Press Release: Technical features of Outright Monetary Transactions" (2012). *European Central Bank*, September 6. www.ecb.europa.eu/press/pr/date/2012/html/pr120906_1.en.html.

[184] A. Framke & P. Carrel (2011), "Exclusive: Germans lead resistance to ECB bond buying." *Reuters*, August 5. www.reuters.com/article/us-ecb-bondbuys-exclusive-germans-lead-resistance-to-ecb-bond-buying-idUSTRE7741QJ20110805.

bargain.[185] He is the only member of the Governing Council to vote against the OMT program, which he derided as "tantamount to financing governments by printing banknotes,"[186] that "would lead to inflation and lesson pressure on governments to carry out reform."[187] He continued his opposition despite pressure from US President Barack Obama, French President François Hollande, British Prime Minister David Cameron, leaders of Germany's private banks, ECB Governing Council member Jörg Asmussen and a majority of monetary policy experts in northern Europe.[188]

The level of contestation peaked in June of 2013 when the GCC held its initial hearing on the OMT program. Weidmann argued that the OMT program blurred the line between monetary and fiscal policy, pushed the ECB beyond its narrow mandate to promote price stability and could impose large costs on German taxpayers if the ECB took on large amounts of risky debt. He also argued that the ECB's actions were undermining market discipline and fiscal autonomy.[189]

Representing the ECB, Jörg Asmussen argued that bond buying was within the ECB's purview.[190] To bolster Asmussen and build support for the ECB's actions, Draghi devoted part of his press conference on June 6 to highlighting the benefits of the OMT program and praising the German court:

When we all look back at what OMT has produced, frankly when you look at the data, it's really very hard not to state that OMT has been probably the most successful monetary policy measure undertaken in recent time. Before OMT we had some expectations of deflationary risks, and that's over. I think I see that as the greatest achievement of this monetary policy measure ... Ten-year sovereign bond yields declined spectacularly in several countries but went up in Germany. And that's very important for the saver, for the German saver, for insurance companies and pension funds ... OMT has brought stability, not only to the markets in Europe but also to the markets worldwide. ... So, I am saying that,

---

[185] M. Ygesias (2012). "Jens Weidmann implies Mario Draghi and the ECB are being manipulated by Satan." *Slate*, September 28. https://slate.com/business/2012/09/jens-weidmann-sites-goethe-to-imply-mario-draghi-and-the-european-central-bank-are-being-manipulated-by-the-devil.html.

[186] M. Steen (2012). "ECB bond buying likened to work of the Devil." *CNBC*, September 19. www.cnbc.com/id/49082034.

[187] C. Reiermann et al. (2012). "German Central Bank opposes euro strategy." *Spiegel*, August 27. www.spiegel.de/international/europe/german-bundesbank-opposes-euro-crisis-strategy-a-852237.html.

[188] Ibid.

[189] G. Wearden (2013). "Eurozone crisis as it happened: German court holds crucial hearing into ECB's bond-buying programme." *The Guardian*, June 11. www.theguardian.com/business/2013/jun/11/eurozone-crisis-switzerland-german-court-uk.

[190] "Bundesbank in court clash with ECB over bond-buying plan" (2013). *Financial Times*, June 11. www.ft.com/content/1ecb4826-d25f-11e2-aac2-00144feab7de.

looking back, one can only be quite satisfied with the results obtained by this operation.

About Karlsruhe, about the constitutional court, I'm absolutely confident that the court will decide in total independence and will analyse, will consider with thoroughness, fairness and competence all the advice from all sides.[191]

In short, while Weidmann was arguing on principle for a narrow interpretation of the ECB's mandate, while Draghi was focusing on outcomes. He emphasized that the program was highly successful, with Ireland, Spain and Portugal able to exit their financial support programs, leaving only Greece and Cyprus as ESM participants.

On January 14, 2014, the FCC in Karlsuhe issued its findings.[192] The FCC maintained an orthodox distinction between monetary policy as falling under the exclusive authority of the ECB and economic policy as remaining with the member states. It also asserted that unlimited purchasing of sovereign debt under the OMT program could neutralize the impact of market pressure on government bond yields, thereby reducing market pressure on national governments to alter their policies. Furthermore, the conditionality attached to the OMT program implied a requirement to change economic policy rather than monetary policy. Consequently, it did not accept the ECB's assertion that the OMT program was limited to monetary policy. Therefore, the OMT did not fall within its discretionary powers. At the same time, the FCC provided several caveats. It argued that the OMT program would be legal if the ECB exempted itself from debt restructuring, limited purchases ex ante and avoided price distortions on secondary markets.[193]

On February 7, the FCC distinguished the OMT issue from other concerns regarding the ESM and fiscal compact (both of which were dismissed on March 18, 2014, in favor of European integration).[194] It also suspended proceedings regarding the OMT program and referred the matter to the CJEU. It asked the GJEU to provide a preliminary

---

[191] M. Draghi & V. Constâncio (2013). "Introductory statement to the press conference (with Q&A)." *European Central Bank*, June 6. www.ecb.europa.eu/press/pressconf/2013/html/is130606.en.html.

[192] Ibid.; T. Beukers (2014). "The Bundesverfassungsgericht Preliminary Reference on the OMT Program: 'In the ECB We Do Not Trust. What about You?'" *German Law Journal* 15(2), 343–368.

[193] C. Schulz et al. (2016). "Germany economics focus." *Citi Research*, February 18. www.citivelocity.com/rendition/eppublic/uiservices/open_watermark_pdf?req_dt=cGRmTGluaz1odHRwcyUzQSUyRiUyRmlyLmNpdGkuY29tJTJGWXY1c1JxYmE3c3lHdzZnRzRONXRuZEtKcXdmJTI1MkZkd0pla1M3ajlEbE42V3c0VnVGT2ZLY0hXQlpRbzJLYWNVWmcmdXNlcl9pZD0xLTFFJNFJBQkMmdXNlcl90eXBlPUNTTQ.

[194] H. Siekmann & V. Wieland (2014). "Have markets misunderstood the German Court's decision on OMT?" *VOX CEPR Policy Portal*, October 3. https://voxeu.org/article/markets-and-german-court-s-decision-omt.

ruling on the compatibility of the OMT program and the prohibition against ECB involvement in the economic policies of member states under EU law and the monetization of sovereign debt.[195]

The OMT ruling and referral to the CJEU were seen by some as victories for Germany. The top economist at Morgan Stanley, Joachim Fels, noted that any arrangement under the OMT program would have to be approved by the German parliament. Consequently, even if the CJEU ruled that the ECB had acted appropriately, the FCC's ruling signaled that it would treat the plan as an *ultra vires* violation of the German constitution (e.g., an abuse of European powers resulting in an incursion into the authorities delineated for member states) and forbid German authorities from implementing it. Since the ESM requires mutual consent by the Board of Governors, linking the OMT program and the EFSF/ESM program effectively gave Eurozone governments potential veto capacity over participation in the OMT program.[196] Thus, Germany could veto bailouts triggered by the OMT program. Therefore, Fels declared, "The ECB's OMT is practically dead."[197] Investors, however, did not interpret the outcome this way. Instead, bond yields continued to decline. Why?

There are two potential explanations of this puzzle. Assuming that Fels' interpretation is broadly accepted and contestation remains high, the theory presented in Chapter 2 suggests that the OMT program is still likely to be successful as long as deference is high and implementation capacity is high or not needed. The widespread perception that the OMT program had been successful likely generated broad deference to the policy. Furthermore, it had succeeded without any supporting legislation. Unlike Henry Paulson, Draghi was able to keep his bazooka in his pocket. Consequently, the German threat to stop its implementation may not be considered relevant.

In addition, Fels' interpretation may be inaccurate because of investors' expected that the CJEU would likely support the ECB's actions. Thus, the referral could suggest that the level of contestation had decreased. Expectations that the CJEU would validate the ECB's authority were plausible

---

[195] S. Dahan et al. (2015). "Whatever It Takes? Regarding the OMT Ruling of the German Federal Constitutional Court." *Journal of International Economic Law* 18(1), 137–151.

[196] European Stability Mechanism (2014). "Frequently asked questions on the European Stability Mechanism." July 28. www.esm.europa.eu/sites/default/files/faqontheesm.pdf.

[197] M. Boesler (2013). "The ECB scheme that saved Europe from disaster last summer is practically dead." *Business Insider*, June 26. www.businessinsider.com/mario-draghis-omt-is-dead-2013-6.

based on the CJEU's decision in *Pringle* v. *Ireland* in 2012.[198] In *Pringle* it argued that "an economic policy measure cannot be treated as equivalent to a monetary policy measure for the sole reason that it may have indirect effects on the stability of the euro," and that the principal objective of the ESM was the stability of the Eurozone rather than to maintain price stability.[199] These interpretations suggest support for the German position. On the other hand, it also stipulated that the ESM programs did not violate the no-bailout clause (e.g., Article 125) of the Treaty on the Functioning of the European Union (TFEU) because they were bound by a principle of "strict conditionality" and the recipient remained subject to the budgetary discipline implied by the Maastricht Treaty.[200] In addition, the ECB's full allotment policy had set a precedent of providing access to unlimited loans to the banking system under certain policy conditions. In short, a liberal interpretation of the *Pringle* case suggests that, "although the Court of Justice acknowledges the importance of the formal distinction between economic and monetary policy, it has shown genuine flexibility in its willingness to align the ECB's mandate with those that are normally granted to a national central bank."[201] This liberal interpretation was validated on June 16, 2015, when the CJEU decided that the OMT program was consistent with its mandate and that "This program for the purchase of government bonds on the secondary markets does not exceed the powers of the ECB in relation to monetary policy and does not contravene the prohibition of monetary financing of member states."[202] On February 16, 2016, the FCC resumed its case against the OMT program with oral arguments, but on June 21, 2016, it rejected the challenge to the OMT program and placed only minor limitations on the German Central Bank's participation in the program.[203]

---

[198] Thomas Pringle v. Government of Ireland, CJEU, Case C-370/12, November 27, 2012. http://curia.europa.eu/juris/liste.jsf?num=C-370/12.

[199] Bundesverfassungsgericht (n.d.). "Judgement of the Second Senate of 21 June 2016." www.bundesverfassungsgericht.de/SharedDocs/Entscheidungen/EN/2016/06/rs20160621_2bvr272813en.html.

[200] S. Dahan et al. (2015). "Whatever It takes? Regarding the OMT Ruling of the German Federal Constitutional Court." *Journal of International Economic Law* 18(1), 137–151.

[201] Ibid.

[202] F. Siebelt & B. Koranyi (2015). "Top German court clears ECB's OMT scheme with minor limits." *Reuters*, June 21. www.reuters.com/article/us-ecb-policy-germany/top-german-court-clears-ecbs-omt-scheme-with-minor-limits-idUSKCN0Z725M; S. Brown (2015). "Mario Draghi can use his 'bazooka,'" *Politico*, June 16. www.politico.eu/article/ecb-legal-court-government-bonds.

[203] Ibid.

In sum, after several years of contestation, the legal battle was over. The ECB's authority was validated by the CJEU and accepted by the German federal constitutional court.

5.5   Return to Ithaca

The European odyssey provides a series of dramatic examples of second-order power as the ECB tried to reduce the destabilizing consequences of repeated battles among European leaders over economic policy. Success required reassuring investors that Europe's economic policies were flexible enough to respond to economic crises, but constrained enough to ward off fiscal exuberance and inflation. The ECB sought to increase policy flexibility by prodding the European Commission to resolve the Greek issue and establish a crisis response mechanism. The ECB complemented these initiatives with a variety of crisis response innovations of its own, demonstrating a willingness to take action even when policy disagreements were persistent and when member states contested its authority to do so. At the same time, the ECB sought to restore trust in the ability of European institutions to limit political exuberance. It did so by encouraging member governments to reestablish their commitments to fiscal restraint and to move forward on a banking union.

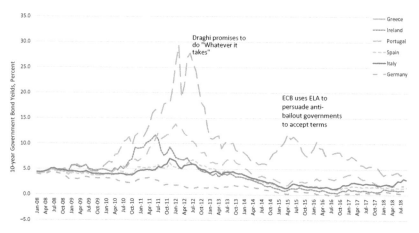

Figure 5.12 Intervention and investor risk in Europe.
Source: Organisation for Economic Co-operation and Development. Long-Term Government Bond Yields: 10-year: Main (Including Benchmark) for Germany, Italy, Spain, Portugal, Ireland and Greece. Retrieved from FRED, Federal Reserve Bank of St. Louis. https://fred.stlouisfed.org/.

Like their American cousins, however, European politicians tended to be less deferential to technocrats and their institutional commitments when times were either very good or very bad. Easy access to low-cost capital in the 1990s led to widespread shirking of fiscal commitments under the SGP. During the crisis, staunch domestic opposition to austerity programs similarly weakened the willingness of national politicians to conform to EU guidelines. When deference was low or implementation capacity was uncertain, the ECB manipulated incentives and threats to enforce compliance. Most infamously, it conditioned the purchase of Italian and Spanish bonds under the SMP on the implementation of policy reforms. It also manipulated ELA for Irish and Greek banks to compel their governments to accept conditional bailout programs.

The effectiveness of the ECB initiatives in shaping market expectations by intervening to reduce political and policy uncertainty is reflected in the general decrease of interest rates in Greece and across Europe to levels below what they had been when the euro was first adopted (see Figure 5.12). While angst about inequities in the economic recovery and concerns about illegitimate assertions of authority persist, these data suggest that the ECB succeeded in revitalizing the Eurozone.

6   Managing Markets in Turbulent Times

6.1   Markets Abhor Uncertainty

The rise of private-sector liquidity as a dominant component in global liquidity markets has created a penetrating web of financial interdependence that links the fates of investors, financial institutions and national governments to one another. The booms and busts of the last thirty years provide vivid evidence that the behavior of each of these actors can generate uncertainties that affect capital flows, credit dynamics and price levels, all of which have potentially significant social, economic and political consequences. The dynamics are ongoing. The newly released International Monetary Fund (IMF) *World Economic Outlook* celebrates a broad-based global recovery, but it also warns that the postcrisis economic expansion has not been balanced and may have peaked in several major economies.[1]

Perceptions that crisis and postcrisis interventions in the economy benefited some more than others have fanned popular resentment and encouraged political opposition, and they have led to the rise of extreme political parties on the left and right in the Americas and Europe. Ironically, the resulting rise in political polarization and hardening of political positions make corrective legislation at home less likely and greatly complicate multilateral coordination. Internal political battles in Great Britain over Brexit are generating waves of uncertainty that are rippling through Ireland and across Europe. European Union institutions appear strong, but the recovery has been uneven and EU-supporting politicians like German Chancellor Merkel and French President Macron are confronting increasingly populist and nationalist challengers from within their countries and from across Europe. In the Americas, Argentina is struggling with resurgent inflation and added uncertainties generated by

---

[1] International Monetary Fund (2018). *World Economic Outlook: Challenges to Steady Growth*. Washington, DC: IMF Publications. www.imf.org/en/Publications/WEO/Issues/2018/09/24/world-economic-outlook-october-2018.

turmoil in Venezuela, the election of a far-right president in Brazil and shifts in global demand for agricultural and energy exports. Meanwhile, President Trump's confrontational and unpredictable economic policies have wiped out a year's worth of profits in the US stock market as investors try to discern what might happen next in the US rows with China and others, and how shifting political currents in Washington will affect US policy.

In 2012, Managing Director of the IMF Christine Lagarde proclaimed central bankers to be the heroes for intervening to manage economic crises while political leaders squabbled.[2] Today, as before, political leaders are squabbling and markets are clearly demonstrating that they abhor uncertainty. Thus, the questions we began with remain critical: Under what conditions can central bankers and other economic technocrats save the day? When will they fail or, perhaps worse, when will they go too far?

The risk intervention curve (RIC) provides a tool that enables us to predict how the pulling and hauling of politics will affect market behavior. The second-order power model, in turn, enables us to predict whether central bankers and other economic policymakers will be able to manage market risks by reducing uncertainty about what national governments will do and whether their policies will be effective. In combination, these tools enable us to determine when central bankers, treasury secretaries and finance ministers are likely to be lauded as oracles, honored as heroes or fall from grace to be condemned as villains.

6.2   Second-Order Power

I argue that high levels of financial interdependence among investors, financial institutions and national governments create opportunities for the exercise of second-order power. One of the principal consequences of extensive financial connectivity is that the behavior of investors, financial institutions and governments is mediated by their expectations about what the others will do and what the consequences of their actions will be. This means that uncertainties generated by political turmoil can motivate changes in the behavior of investors and financial institutions with potential consequences for capital flows, credit dynamics and price levels. It also means that the ability of economic policymakers to reduce

---

[2] C. Lagarde (2012). "Promises to keep: the policy actions needed to secure global recovery," interview with K. Ryssdal. *American Public Media, Marketplace,* September 24. www.marketplace.org/topics/world/european-debt-crisis/imfs-christine-lagarde-urges-action-fiscal-cliff-euro-crisis.

political uncertainty and policy uncertainty gives them a source of leverage. Under the right conditions, they can reduce uncertainty about how national governments are likely to act (i.e., political uncertainty) by altering the discretion of national politicians over economic policy and by supplementing or limiting policy options. They can also reduce uncertainty about policy outcomes (i.e., policy uncertainty) by validating specific policies or policy agendas, altering market conditions and mitigating specific-actor risks. I define this as the exercise of second-order power because the ability of economic policymakers to change market behavior is a second-order effect of their power to reduce political and policy uncertainty.

Implementing second-order power strategies successfully is a two-step process. The first step is to specify the level of risk that investors or financial institutions are likely to attribute to particular policies under prevailing economic conditions. This can be doing using the RIC. The second step is to manage political uncertainty and policy uncertainty in ways that reduce risk. The ability of economic policymakers and institutions to do so varies with the extent to which their authority over economic policy is accepted or contested, deference is given to their policy recommendations, and supporting legislation is likely to be implemented and sustained. To the extent that economic policymakers can assert their authority, command deference or enforce policy compliance, and secure the implementation of supporting legislation as needed to shape economic policy they can reduce political uncertainty and policy uncertainty. All else being equal, this can reduce perceptions of risk and help to promote desirable market behaviors.

The effectiveness of second-order power is contingent on the ability of investors, financial institutions and other interested actors to make accurate assessments of political and policy uncertainties in countries of interest. This requires the ability to discern the degree to which authority over economic policy is accepted or contested, deference is high or low, and legislative capacity is high or low. As specified in Chapter 2, the following guidelines can be used to simplify and standardize these assessments:

- Authority: The level of authority over economic policy-making can be discerned by the clarity of lines of responsibility and accountability within a country's economic policy-making process and the frequency, spread and significance of manifestations and contrary manifestations of that authority. Authority can be considered highly contested if lines of responsibility and accountability are unclear or explicit legislative, political or legal actions are taken to challenge an assertion of authority or the promulgation of a regulation, or if such actions are taken to limit the future assertion of authority or regulatory action. Authority is often delineated with regard to its scope (i.e., issues of responsibility), domain (i.e., actors under jurisdiction), magnitude (i.e., how much can be done or demanded) and means (i.e., discretion over the use of particular tools and resources). One or more of these components may be respected while others are contested.

- Deference: The level of deference that national politicians are likely to grant to the policy guidance provided by economic technocrats and to the rules specified in economic agreements and institutions can be inferred by: (1) whether they appoint, retain or dismiss economic policymakers who are known for their expertise or policy successes and have shown a willingness to pursue prudent economic policies regardless of the political consequences, (2) the degree to which a policy consensus exists among senior policymakers, (3) the frequency, spread and significance of acts of compliance and noncompliance with existing protocols and agreements, and (4) the extent to which the policies are considered successful.

- Implementation capacity: The likelihood that governments will implement and sustain supporting economic policies can be discerned by the level of electoral success experienced by national politicians and the ability of national politicians to implement their legislative agendas. It is also reflected in the ability of policymakers to support their economic teams in the face of social and political backlashes.

6.3   Risk, Uncertainty and Intervention

The validity of the adage that markets abhor uncertainty has been reconfirmed many times over the past thirty years, yet, while the description is apt, it is not particularly helpful to investors or policymakers. The RIC enhances the utility of this adage by modeling the relationships among risk, political uncertainty and policy uncertainty. By doing so, it clarifies how political battles over economic policy can affect perceptions of risk. It also provides guidance to strategic actors seeking to manage market behavior by managing political and policy uncertainty.

The RIC builds on the pioneering work of Andrew MacIntyre, who posits that the policy preferences of investors reflect a trade-off between policy flexibility and policy constraint. *Ceteris paribus*, limiting the discretion of national politicians to shape economic policy increases the predictability and stability of economic policy decisions, but it can also inhibit the ability of politicians to adapt to changing circumstances. Alternatively, giving national politicians a freer hand to manage economic policy increases policy adaptability, yet it also potentially reduces the predictability and efficacy of future policy decisions. Consequently, the relationship between policy flexibility and risk is expected to be concave upward. Under normal conditions, high levels of either policy constraint or policy flexibility are riskier than moderate levels of both.

The RIC adds dynamism and agency to MacIntyre's model by treating the level of policy flexibility as variable and subject to strategic manipulation. It also considers the level of risk associated with a given level of policy flexibility to be variable and responsive to market conditions and specific-actor risks. Expectations about a country's position along the policy flexibility-constraint spectrum varies with political uncertainty about how the government is likely to act; the associated, level of risk varies with expectations about the consequences of the government's actions. Strategic actors can alter political uncertainty by expanding or reducing the available policy options and enabling or constraining the policy discretion of national politicians. They can alter the level of risk regarding policy outcomes by validating policy choices, altering market conditions and mitigating specific-actor risks.

As anticipated, the shape of the RIC varied significantly over the past thirty years in response shifting market conditions and specific-actor risks. When inflation concerns increased, the level of risk associated with high levels of policy flexibility increased as well. As expected under these conditions, indicators of investor risk generally declined when national politicians delegated authority over economic policy to credible economic policymakers and/or accepted other limits on their discretion over economic policy decisions. Also as expected, indicators of risk increased significantly when it became evident that these economic policymakers and institutions were not actually constraining policy decisions. For example, capital flooded into Argentina in the mid-1990s and Greece in the early 2000s when it appeared that their respective exchange rate regimes and other institutional commitments were disciplining economic policy decisions, but investors reversed course quickly when it became clear that these institutions were not constraining government expenditure sufficiently to keep prices from rising (see Figure 6.1). Investor confidence plummeted to its nadir in 2007 for Argentina and in 2009 for Greece when it was discovered that the governments in each country had been reporting inaccurate economic information. These revelations increased political uncertainty by demonstrating that national politicians were unconstrained by their national institutions and instead had been manipulating those institutions at will. Recognition of the unfettered nature of policy-making shifted both countries to the left on the flexibility–constraint spectrum of the RIC. Simultaneously, the fact that the economic data were fraudulent increased policy uncertainty

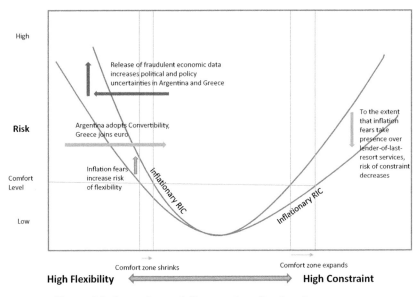

High

Release of fraudulent economic data
increases political and policy
uncertainties in Argentina and Greece

Risk

Argentina adopts Convertibility,
Greece joins euro

To the extent
that inflation
fears take
presence over
lender-of-last-
resort services,
risk of constraint
decreases

Comfort
Level

Inflation fears
increase risk
of flexibility

Inflationary RIC

Inflationary RIC

Low

Comfort zone shrinks   Comfort zone expands

High Flexibility   ⟵⟶   **High Constraint**

Figure 6.1 Argentina and Greece adopt fixed exchange rates.

about the true state of economic affairs. This increased the level of risk
for both countries, moving them into the upper-left corner of the inflationary RIC.

The shape of the RIC also changed significantly when private-sector
liquidity was scarce, fear of contagion was high or economic growth
stagnated. In these situations, increasing levels of policy constraint tend
to spook investors. Markets panicked, for example, when Secretary
Paulson chose not to bail out Lehman Brothers on September 15,
2008, and when the US House of Representatives rejected the first
bailout plan two weeks later. These actions were consistent with precrisis
efforts to reaffirm the government's commitments to enforcing market
discipline and fighting moral hazard by not bailing out failing companies.
By September of 2018, however, investors were more concerned
about liquidity shortfalls and specific-actor risks than the prospect
of moral hazard. Consequently, rather than restoring confidence,
these actions increased concerns that policy rigidity would inhibit the
government's ability to respond to the crisis in a timely manner (see
Figure 6.2). Investor risk began to subside after a bailout package was
approved on October 3, 2008 and it became clear that the Federal
Reserve and Treasury would do whatever it took to keep the economy
running.

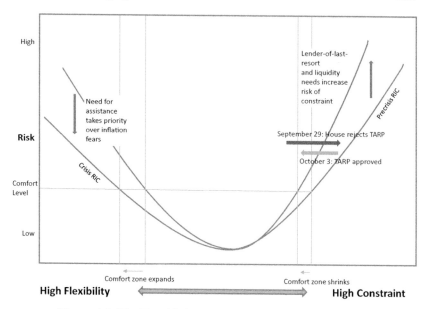

Figure 6.2 The Troubled Asset Relief Program (TARP) vote.

6.4   Managing Markets with Virtù

Once investor preferences for particular types of intervention have been
specified using the RIC, the next step in the exercise of second-order
power is to reduce uncertainty about how governments are likely to act
and what the consequences of their actions are likely to be. Over the past
thirty years, economic policymakers have asserted their authority and
created institutions to shape what political stakeholders can do in the
policy arena and what private-sector actors can do in domestic and global
markets. They have manipulated incentives and penalties to get other
actors to do things they would not otherwise do. And, when possible,
they have taken advantage of their reputations and positions (e.g.
exploited deference and authority) to promote particular policies and
policy agendas. In short, they have used and often combined aspects of
constitutive power (e.g., the power to determine who can do what),
relational power (e.g., the power to alter the behavior of specific actors),
and charismatic or ideational power (e.g., the ability to shape motivations
and preferences) to shape policy and alter market behavior.[3]

---

[3] M. Barnett & R. Duvall (2005). "Power in International Politics." *International
Organization* 59, 39–75; B. Hall (2010). *Central Banking as Global Governance:*

	The Power to Act			Prediction		
Authority to Act	Deference to Technocrats	Implementation Capacity of National Politicians		Impact of Technocrats		Behavior
Reflected in the degree to which the scope, domain, magnitude and tools of authority over economic policy are accepted	*Reflected in the appointment of politicians' critics with reputations for success or expertise and degree of unity or division of policymakers*	*Reflected in notional politicians' popularity, their ability to promote their legislative agendas and electoral outcomes*		*Reflected in the ability to manage political uncertainty by altering policy flexibility*	*Reflected in the ability to manage policy uncertainty by altering the likelihood of policy outcomes*	*Reflected in political and market behavior*
1 High, Uncontested	High, Deference Granted	High or Not Necessary		Can constrain or expand policy flexibility	Can validate policy, targeted and broad strategies may be effective	Maximum bargaining power
2 High, Uncontested	High, Deference Granted	Low		Can constrain or expand policy flexibility if legislative support is unnecessary	Can validate policy, targeted strategies may be disruptive, broad strategies may be effective	Weak politicians appoint technocrats to bolster implementation capacity, but may abandon them
3 Low, Contested	High, Deference Granted	High or Not Necessary		Can constrain or expand policy flexibility if additional authority is not needed	Can validate policy, targeted and broad strategies may be effective	Technocrats will attempt to expand authority
4 Low, Contested	High, Deference Granted	Low		Can constrain or expand policy flexibility if additional authority and legislative support are not necessary	Can validate policy, targeted strategies may be disruptive, broad strategies may be effective	Technocrats can help leaders outmaneuver political opponents, but long-term uncertainty remains
5 High or Low	Low, Deference Demanded	High or Not Necessary		Confrontational technocrats likely to be replaced with sycophants	Cannot validate policy, targeted and broad strategies by politicians possible	No economic validation, political exuberance likely
6 High or Low	Low, Deference Demanded	Low		Technocrats are impotent	Cannot validate policy, broad strategies by politicians may be effective	Minimum bargaining power, maximum uncertainty

Figure 6.3 Shaping policy and behavior.

I began with the proposition that the power to shape market behavior begins at home with the pulling and hauling of stakeholders vying for the authority, deference and implementation capacity needed to shape economic policy. I argued that variations in the degree to which authority over economic policy is accepted or contested, deference is given to those in positions of authority and extant agreements, and the implementation of supporting legislation are likely to generate six distinct patterns of behavior and outcomes. These correspond to the six enumerated rows in Figure 6.3. This focus on constitutive power dynamics builds on insights from Peter Bachrach and Morton Baratz and their contemporary counterparts like Michael Barnett, Raymond Duvall and Bruce Hall regarding power that comes from the ability to control an agenda, define and enforce the rules of the game and delineate the roles that actors play in the policy-making process and the economy. Barnett and Duvall provide a useful typology of

Constructing Financial Credibility. Cambridge: Cambridge University Press; D. Baldwin (1985). *Economic Statecraft.* Princeton: Princeton University Press; D. Baldwin (2016). *Power and International Relations: A Conceptual Approach.* Princeton: Princeton University Press; R. Dahl (1961). *Who Governs?* New Haven: Yale University Press; S. Lukes (1974) *Power: A Radical View.* London: MacMillan.

power based on the type and specificity of social relations. The model and cases presented here demonstrate how the direct and diffuse, specific and constitutive dimensions of power that they highlight interact. Bruce Hall, in turn, specifically highlights the power that central bankers derive from their authority to create and destroy money, allocate credit and define the rules that govern financial activity.[4] He reinforces the constructivist insight that this authority and the associated rules of the game are socially constructed and subject to contestation if central bankers fail to fulfill their expected roles. Given the rise of anti-globalist protest movements and the political backlash against central bankers and other economic policymakers since the recent economic crises, it is important to understand how the contestation of authority, declining deference or the loss of legislative support affect their power.[5]

The Argentine, US and European experiences confirm that battles over the authority to shape economic policy are often contentious, but that this contentiousness does not necessarily undermine the ability of economic policymakers or economic institutions to shape political or market behavior. The cases reveal that when authority, deference or implementation capacity is found wanting, economic technocrats can often manipulate incentives and threats and exploit their ideational capacities to limit the authority of critics, enforce compliance with desired policies and promote supporting legislation. This chapter concludes by highlighting several of these dynamics and their implications for the exercise of power in highly interdependent environments.

6.4.1   The Contingent Power of Authority and Institutions

The power of institutions and individuals in positions of authority within them are contingent on the degree to which others are willing to defer to their guidance and have the capacity to change their behavior or policies as directed. Without continued deference or legislative support, even formally influential institutions can become impotent. On the other hand, as long as deference remains high, the contestation of authority does not necessarily reduce the power of particular individuals or institutions to alter others' expectations and behavior.

The failure of the Stability and Growth Pact (SGP) to constrain the fiscal policies of its members is a classic example of this phenomenon. To mitigate the challenges associated with sharing a common monetary

---

[4] Hall. *Central Banking as Global Governance.*
[5] L. Pauly (2002). "Global Finance, Political Authority, and the Problem of Legitimation." In B. Hall & T. Biersteker, eds. *The Emergency of Private Authority in Global Governance.* Cambridge: Cambridge University Press, pp. 76–90.

policy but separate fiscal policies, Eurozone members committed themselves to maintaining their government deficits and national debts to within limits specified in the SGP of 1999. Despite its salience, however, compliance with the SGP has been notoriously poor. By the time the SGP was reformed in December of 2011, twenty-three out of twenty-seven member states had failed to meet their SGP obligations to keep their budget deficits below 3 percent of GDP and their government debts below 60 percent of GDP.[6] Though many criticized Greece and other program countries for profligate spending, the list of SGP shirkers included France, Germany, the Netherlands, Belgium, Austria and Finland, as well as Greece, Ireland, Portugal, Spain and Italy. The reasons for failure varied from exuberant fiscal expenditure in some countries to the absorption of bank debt in others, but the signal that the failures sent was clear and consistent: the SGP protocols did not constrain government policies or mitigate their consequences. In 2011, Eurozone members attempted to reduce political uncertainty by fortifying SGP with the Euro Plus Pact, which included more stringent rules, enhanced enforcement mechanisms and increased oversight.[7] In January of 2013, member countries also agreed to a Fiscal Compact that put a lower cap on public deficits and required a reduction in public debt.[8] Though these regulatory changes were substantial, implementation remains uneven, and it is unclear whether member countries have the will and capacity to maintain the specified reforms.[9]

The collapse of the Austral Plan provides a vivid example of how declining implementation capacity can undermine the power of institutions even when political leaders continue to agree with the policy recommendations of their advisors. With the backing of Argentine President Alfonsín, Minister of the Economy Sourrouille created a new currency, the austral, and implemented a series of significant economic

---

[6] C. Bastasin (2015). *Saving Europe: Anatomy of a Dream.* Washington, DC: Brookings Institution, p. 101; H. Kube (2012). "The EU Financial Crisis – European Law and Constitutional Law Implications." Center for International Studies, Working Paper Series, No. 1–12, June.

[7] L. Schuknecht, P. Moutot, P. Rother & J. Stark (2011). "The Stability and Growth Pact: Crisis and Reform." *European Central Bank*, Occasional Paper Series, 129, September. www.ecb.europa.eu/pub/pdf/scpops/ecbocp129.pdf.

[8] "History of the Stability and Growth Pact" (2015). *European Commission.* https://ec.europa.eu/info/business-economy-euro/economic-and-fiscal-policy-coordination/eu-economic-governance-monitoring-prevention-correction/stability-and-growth-pact/history-stability-and-growth-pact_en#2011; Kube. "The EU Financial Crisis," p. 3.

[9] European Political Strategy Centre (2018). "The Euro Plus Pact." *European Commission*, Strategic Note #3, May 8. https://ec.europa.eu/epsc/file/strategic-note-3-euro-plus-pact_en. D. Papadimoulis (2016). "The stability and growth pact has failed." *Social Europe*, July 11. www.socialeurope.eu/stability-growth-pact-failed.

reforms to fight inflation in 1985. The Austral Program was initially successful in reducing inflation. It also helped President Alfonsín's party win midterm elections in 1985. Over time, however, President Alfonsín's political strength declined, and he increasingly gave in to pressure from social groups who demanded wage hikes and other policies that undercut Sourrouille's economic reforms. Minister of the Economy Sourrouille and his economic team repeatedly took corrective actions, but they could not sustain their economic program in the face of countervailing policies. Without supporting legislation, the Austral Plan collapsed and hyperinflation returned.

The success of the European Central Bank's (ECB) bond-buying programs provides evidence that, if deference is high, contestation of authority does not necessarily reduce the power of particular individuals or institutions to alter market expectations. On May 11, 2010, one day after the Securities Markets Programme (SMP) was announced, Axel Weber, president of the *Bundesbank* and ECB Governing Council member, published a critique of the program and expressed his opposition to the ECB's purchase of government bonds.[10] On September 9, 2011, Jürgen Stark, the ECB's chief economist, resigned from the ECB Executive Board and Governing Council in protest over the SMP.[11] Combined with Weber's ongoing campaign against the SMP, Stark's resignation raised uncertainty about the sustainability of the program by suggesting that the ECB Governing Council was divided and that the German government did not support the program.[12] On October 23, 2011, however, Stark was replaced Jörg Asmussen, a deputy finance minister who had a more conciliatory reputation and who turned out to be an advocate for the SMP and Outright Monetary Transactions (OMT) programs.[13] Consequently, by resigning, Stark inadvertently improved the prospects of the bond-buying program by reducing divisions among policymakers within the ECB.

Contestation of the OMT program had a similarly paradoxical effect of bolstering the program's impact. In September 6, 2012, the ECB released the technical features of the OMT program. They included

[10] J. Ewing (2010a). "Central banker takes a chance by speaking out." *New York Times*, November 1. www.nytimes.com/2010/11/02/business/global/02weber.html.

[11] V. Boland & P. Spiegel (2014). "ECB threatened to end funding unless Ireland sought bailout." *Financial Times*, November 16. www.ft.com/content/1f4ed1fa-65ac-11e4-aba7-00144feabdc0.

[12] J. Ewing & N. Kulish (2011). "A setback for the Euro Zone." *New York Times*, September 9. www.nytimes.com/2011/09/10/business/global/a-top-ecb-official-to-resign.html.

[13] Ibid.

the authorization to purchase unlimited amounts of government bonds confidentially from member states in financial difficulty who were participating in a European Financial Stability Facility or Exchange Stabilization Fund program. In short, in a seeming direct contravention of its mandate, the ECB had become a lender of last resort in government bond markets. On September 12, 2012, in its ruling on German participation in the European Stability Mechanism, the German Federal Constitutional Court (FCC) noted that the acquisition of government bonds aiming at financing member's budgets was prohibited. Contestation peaked in June of 2013 when the FCC formally expressed its opposition to the OMT program, through January of 2014 when it deferred the OMT case to the European Court of Justice for a preliminary ruling. The level of contestation declined in June of 2015 when the European Court of Justice ruled that the ECB's actions were legal.

Rather than weakening the effect of the OMT program, the early and ongoing contestation combined with Mario Draghi's defense of the policy increased the credibility of his declaration that he would do "whatever it takes to preserve the euro," despite being challenged by courts in the most powerful country in Europe. Furthermore, as the calming effect of the OMT program became clear, deference to the program increased. During the hearings at the Court of Justice of the EU, for example, Mario Draghi and Jörg Asmussen were able to bolster their case by pointing to the dramatic drops in interest rates in Greece and across Europe.

6.4.2   *Deference, Authority and Implementation Capacity*

Economic policymakers who are able to command high levels of deference have also been able to exploit their ideational power to overcome political opposition.[14] Alan Greenspan's success in promoting liberalization provides a quintessential example of this phenomenon. As discussed in Chapter 4, Alan Greenspan played a pivotal role in persuading President Clinton and his senior advisors that the cost of servicing US debt could rise dramatically if investors lost faith in the ability of the

---

[14] This capability reflects the use of ideational power popularized by Steven Lukes in which power is derived from the ability to change others' preferences so that they choose to pursue particular courses of action because they want to do so. Though this aspect of power is often associated with the use of political or religious propaganda, commercial advertising and market-determined preferences, the cases presented above demonstrate that respected experts and trusted advisors can use their ideational power to generate deference toward particular policies and institutions, bolster legislative capacity to pass supporting legislation and augment authority. Lukes. *Power*.

government to fight inflation or thought that US regulations were inhibiting competitiveness. President Clinton agreed to forego fiscal stimulus and rely instead on monetary policy under the purview of the Federal Reserve. With the help of Robert Ruben and Larry Summers, Greenspan succeeded in implementing legislation that promoted deregulation and limited the authority of regulators who challenged his agenda.[15] These efforts led to the adoption of the 1993 Economic Policy that defined the economic policy trajectory for the remainder of the Clinton administration. They culminated in the passage of the Commodity Futures Modernization Act of 2000, which explicitly prohibited the US Commodity Futures Trading Commission from regulating financial products known as over-the-counter derivatives. President Clinton and President Bush affirmed their continued deference to Alan Greenspan and support for the policy agenda by reappointing him and repeatedly seeking his approval of their policies. The market consequences of these actions were profound. By reducing regulatory oversight, they shifted the United States to the far left on the policy–flexibility spectrum. This maximized policy flexibility and inspired technological and financial innovations that generated a twenty-year economic boom. As predicted by the RIC and reflected in the 2018 financial crisis, however, the lack of constraint generated economic exuberance and high levels of risk.

Domingo Cavallo similarly played a pivotal role in rationalizing Argentina's shift toward economic liberalism and in bolstering the government's commitment to fight inflation by creating the Convertibility Plan in 1991. The transformation succeeded in part because President Menem was willing to delegate economic authority and Cavallo was able to broaden Menem's political coalition. During the 1995 Mexican peso crisis, Cavallo further bolstered investor confidence by reinforcing the Convertibility Plan and working closely with an outside expert, Gerry Corrigan, ex-president of the Federal Bank of New York, to develop a response to the crisis. The success of his interventions had dramatic political and economic consequences. President Menem won the 1995 elections and investors flooded into Argentina.

Following the election, President Menem replaced Cavallo with Roque Fernández. As the 1990s progressed, neither Minister Fernández nor the Convertibility Plan were able to restrain President Menem, who increasingly asserted his discretion to reward supporters as he fought to secure a third term. In the absence of deference from the President, neither the existence of a credible minister of the economy nor strong institutions were

---

[15] J. Ramo (1999). "The three musketeers." *Time.* February 15. http://content.time.com/ time/world/article/0,8599,2054093,00.html.

insufficient to forestall practices that created fertile ground for the financial collapse. In March of 2001, as the Argentine crisis was beginning to explode, President de la Rúa called in Argentina's inflation-fighting hero, Domingo Cavallo, to save the day. The Argentine Congress responded enthusiastically, granting Cavallo "extraordinary powers" to fix the economy without the need for consultation with the President or Congress. In stark contrast to his efforts in the early 1990s, Cavallo ignored the Convertibility Plan and did not seek input from the President, the president of the Central Bank or Congress.[16] The chaotic nature of Cavallo's crisis response increased policy uncertainty and likely accelerated the onset of the crisis. As predicted by the RIC, unfettered policy-making is risky even if the policy-maker is an economic technocrat rather than a politician.

6.4.3   *The Contingent Power of Threats and Promises*

The exercise of relational power between actors in highly independent environments is also conditioned on how they believe others who are not party to the relationship will react. This second-order concern generates the paradox that targeted incentives are often shunned. For example, counter to the commonly expressed concern before the 2008 crisis that companies would exploit bailouts so that they could engage in ever-riskier behavior (i.e., engage in "moral hazard"), many tried to avoid bailouts because of the fear that accepting financial support would send a signal to their counterparties that the recipient was in financial distress. In a highly interdependent financial system in which survival depends on the ability to raise capital from private-sector actors, uncertainty about one's solvency can be devastating. Consequently, in order to get the nine largest financial institutions in the United States to accept a US$125 billion liquidity infusion, Paulson, Bernanke and Geithner had to convene a meeting of all of the CEOs and compel each one to accept part of the financing so that none would stigmatized.[17] The Irish government similarly only requested program funding from the EU and IMF under duress. In October and November of 2010, Jean-Claude Trichet sent Irish Minister of Finance Brian Lenihan letters that threatened to deny Irish banks access to emergency liquidity assistance if an agreement was

---

[16] "Cavallo struggles to get a grip on Argentina's economy" (2001). *The Economist*, May 3. www.economist.com/node/612598.

[17] "'Good number' of banks seeking federal capital, Paulson says" (2008). *New York Times*, October 16. http://dealbook.nytimes.com/2008/10/16/good-number-of-banks-seeking-

not reached and implemented.[18] The Irish government had overextended itself by guaranteed its banks' loans, so the fate of government finances was directly linked to the fate of Irish banks. Unsurprisingly, Ireland agreed to the ECB's terms. In order to avoid political backlash and improve the prospects for implementing the requisite legislation, the letters were initially kept secret.[19]

Economic technocrats often succeeded in compelling wayward countries to implement conditional bailouts and economic policy reforms, but the second-order effects of these interventions were contingent on the ability of the newly compliant government to sustain those reforms. For example, on August 5, 2011, Jean-Claude Trichet and Mario Draghi wrote a letter to Italian Prime Minister Silvio Berlusconi[20] that linked the purchase of Italian government bonds through the SMP program to the implementation of economic reforms. Berlusconi agreed to the conditions but had difficulty passing reform legislation.[21] In response to rising levels of political uncertainty, interest rates on Italian government bonds rose. In October, Prime Minister Berlusconi resigned and Mario Monti became prime minister and finance minister. In contrast to Berlusconi, "Super Mario" had a reputation as a strong mainline economist. His experience, expertise and dual appointment as prime minister and finance minister helped reduce political and policy uncertainty. Interest rates on Italy's bonds declined and remained low until Monti stepped down in July 2012.

6.5 Fortune and Financial Markets

Nevertheless, since our free will must not be eliminated, I think it may be true that fortune determines one half of our actions, but that she

federal-capital-paulson-says; R. Farley (2012). "The problems with limiting large banks." *New York Times*, May 23. http://dealbook.nytimes.com/2012/05/23/the-problems-with-limiting-large-banks.

[18] Jean-Claude Trichet to Brian Lenihan, October 15, 2010. www.ecb.europa.eu/press/shared/pdf/2010-10-15_Letter_ECB_President_to_IE_FinMin.pdf?e19978a39fa112418947d2e168 95009a.

[19] "Irish letters" (n.d.). *European Central Bank*. www.ecb.europa.eu/press/html/irish-letters.en.html.

[20] J.-C. Trichet & M. Draghi (2011b). "Lettera della Bce all'Italia, testo integrale." *Wall Street Italia*, September 29. www.wallstreetitalia.com/lettera-della-bce-all-italia-testo-integrale.

[21] T. Kinton (2011). "Merkozy smirk at EU crisis summit boosts Berlusconi." *The Guardian*, October 24. www.theguardian.com/business/2011/oct/24/merkel-sarkozy-italy-berlusconi.

leaves us to control the other half, or thereabouts. And I compare her to one of those torrential rivers ...[22]

Niccolò Machiavelli's guidance to princes seeking to master fortune offers a final bit of wisdom for modern-day policymakers seeking to shape market behavior. For Machiavelli, fortune is dynamic and ever-changing. Like a torrential river, it shapes our behavior in significant and often unexpected ways. Sometimes its waves lift us up and its currents drive us forward at great speed; sometimes its waves knock us down and its currents smash us on the rocks. And yet, fortune is not fully constraining. Building on insights from the past, a virtuous prince can learn to navigate the river and even tame its currents temporarily. Success requires a realistic understanding of how all those who are seeking to master fortune affect the river's flow. Virtù is reflected in leaders who, imbued with the cunning of a fox and the strength of a lion, are willing to use this knowledge and do whatever it takes to preserve the commonwealth. Machiavelli warns that constructing fortresses and following social institutions can be helpful, but the protections they provide are context specific and overreliance on them can generate hatred from the people one is seeking to protect. To reinforce this point, he muses prophetically:[23]

I shall praise both the prince who builds fortresses as well as he who does not. I shall blame the prince who relies on fortresses, but cares nothing about being hated by the people.

Like the torrential river of fortune, private-sector liquidity flows through a complex web of interdependent financial networks that permeate domestic and global economies. It shapes our behavior in significant and often unexpected ways, creating both great opportunities and great risks. And yet, it is not all-controlling. Like Machiavelli's virtuous princes, economic policymakers in Argentina, the United States and Europe continue to navigate the vagaries of financial markets strategically. Many have demonstrated the courage to do whatever it takes to preserve the commonwealth. They have built and fortified economic institutions to great advantage, but have found the utility of these institutions to be context specific and contingent on how others respond to their actions. To compensate, they have offered and denied vast amounts of public money to counterbalance variations in private sector liquidity, enabled and constrained national politicians, and cajoled and coerced

---

[22] N. Machiavelli (1995). *The Prince*, edited and translated by D. Wooton. Indianapolis: Hacket Publishing Company, ch. 24.
[23] Ibid., ch. 20.

recalcitrant countries and firms to alter potentially disruptive behavior. A few have also come to appreciate Machiavelli's caution against over-reliance on institutional defenses without also recognizing the consequences of doing so for the people whom they serve.

Following Machiavelli's advice, this book offer insights from the past to help today's leaders discern how best to exercise of power in highly independent and politically turbulent times. The RIC provides a tool to predict how the pulling and hauling of politics will affect market behavior. The second-order power model, in turn, suggests ways to manage market behavior by reducing uncertainty about what national governments will do and whether their policies will be effective. In combination, they help to identify the conditions under which central bankers, treasury secretaries and finance ministers will be lauded as oracles and hailed as heroes, and when they will fall from grace to be condemned as villains.

Bibliography

114th Congress, First Session. H. R. 692 [Report No. 114-265]. To ensure the payment of interest and principal of the "Default Prevention Act."

"A decline without parallel: In the 1990s, Argentina was Latin America's star. How did it become a basket case?" (2002). *The Economist*, February 28. https://media.economist.com/news/special-report/1010911-1990s-argentina-was-latin-americas-star-how-did-it-become-basket-case.

Abrams, B. A. (2006). "How Richard Nixon Pressured Arthur Burns: Evidence from the Nixon Tapes." *Journal of Economic Perspectives* 20(4), 177–188.

Ahamed, L. (2009). *Lords of Finance: The Bankers Who Broke the World.* New York: Penguin Group.

Alderman, L. (2017). "In sign of progress for Greece, investors eagerly snap up new bonds." *New York Times*, July 25. www.ft.com/content/c11daa34-711f-11e7-aca6-c6bd07df1a3c.

Allen, F. & Herring, R. (2001). *Banking Regulation versus Securities Regulation.* Philadelphia: Wharton Financial Institutions Center.

Allen, K. (2012). "Greece secures private-sector backing for crucial debt swap." *The Guardian*, March 9. www.theguardian.com/business/2012/mar/09/greece-private-sector-backing-debt-swap.

(2015). "Greek debt crisis: 20 key moments." *The Guardian*, June 25. www.theguardian.com/business/2015/jun/25/greek-crisis-20-key-moments-eurozone.

Amadeo, K. (2018). "Greek debt crisis explained." *The Balance*, November 8. www.thebalance.com/what-is-the-greece-debt-crisis-3305525.

"America's mortgage giants: Suffering a seizure" (2008). *The Economist*, September 8. www.economist.com/node/12078933.

Andrews, E. (2002). "Fed chief says he supports Bush tax cuts." *New York Times*, November 14. www.nytimes.com/2002/11/14/business/fed-chief-says-he-supports-bush-tax-cut.html.

(2009). "Obama to nominate Bernanke to 2nd term at Fed." *New York Times*, August 24. www.nytimes.com/2009/08/25/business/25bernanke.html.

"Annual report: 2009" (2010). *European Central Bank.* www.ecb.europa.eu/pub/pdf/annrep/ar2009en.pdf?30d90321a98348b879be2a56fa28c055.

Appelbaum, B. (2015). "Fed raises key interest rate for first time in almost a decade." *New York Times*, December 16. www.nytimes.com/2015/12/17/business/economy/fed-interest-rates.html.

Arend, A. C. (1999). *Legal Rules and International Society.* New York: Oxford University Press.

"Argentina: 1985 legislative elections" (n.d.). http://pdba.georgetown.edu/Elec
    data/Arg/cong85.html.
"Argentina: 1987 legislative elections" (n.d.). http://pdba.georgetown.edu/Elec
    data/Arg/cong87.html.
"Argentina: 2000 Article IV consultation and first review under the stand-by
    arrangement, and request for modification of performance criteria – Staff
    report and public information notice following consultation" (2000). Inter-
    national Monetary Fund, December 19. www.imf.org/external/pubs/cat/
    longres.aspx?sk=3859.0.
"Argentina cancels junta pardons" (2007). *BBC News*, August 27. http://news
    .bbc.co.uk/2/hi/americas/6594127.stm.
"Argentina's banking scandal deepens" (2001). *BBC News*, February 21. http://
    news.bbc.co.uk/2/hi/americas/1182417.stm.
"Argentina's inflation rate" (n.d.). https://tradingeconomics.com/argentina/infla
    tion-cpi.
Arnone, M., Laurens, B., Segalotto, J.-F. & Sommer, M. (2007). "Central Bank
    Autonomy: Lessons from Global Trends." IMF Working Paper, WP/07/88.
"Asset   purchase   programmes"   (n.d.).   *European   Central   Bank.*   www
    .ecb.europa.eu/mopo/implement/omt/html/index.en.html.
Associated Press (1989). "200 military officers are pardoned in Argentina." *New
    York Times*, October 8. www.nytimes.com/1989/10/08/world/200-military-
    officers-are-pardoned-in-argentina.html.
Bagehot, W. (1873). *Lombard Street: A Description of the Money Market* (1st edn.).
    New York: Scribner, Armstong & Co.
Bail, M. (2012). "Obama vs. Boehner: Who killed the debt deal?" *New York
    Times*, March 12. www.nytimes.com/2012/04/01/magazine/obama-vs-boeh
    ner-who-killed-the-debt-deal.html?_r=0.
Baker, L. & Sassard, S. (2012). "Insight: How the Greek debt puzzle was solved."
    Reuters, February 29. www.reuters.com/article/us-europe-greece/insight-
    how-the-greek-debt-puzzle-was-solved-idUSTRE81S0NP20120229.
Baker, S., Bloom, N. & Davis, S. (n.d.). "Economic Policy Uncertainty."
    www.policyuncertainty.com/us_monthly.html.
    (n.d.). Economic Policy Uncertainty Index for Europe [EUEPUINDXM].
    Retrieved from FRED, Federal Reserve Bank of St. Louis. https://fred
    .stlouisfed.org/series/EUEPUINDXM.
Baldwin, D. (1985). *Economic Statecraft.* Princeton: Princeton University Press.
    (2016). *Power and International Relations: A Conceptual Approach.* Princeton:
    Princeton University Press.
Barnett, M. & Duvall, R. (2005). "Power in International Politics." *International
    Organization* 59, 39–75.
Barr, C. (2008). "Fortune special report: Paulson readies the 'bazooka.'"
    CNNMoney, September 6. https://money.cnn.com/2008/09/06/news/econ
    omy/fannie_freddie_paulson.fortune/index.htm.
Bastasin, C. (2015). *Saving Europe: Anatomy of a Dream.* Washington, DC:
    Brookings Institution.
Beckner, S. (2011). "New York Fed study finds discount window stigma in
    crisis." *Market News International*, August 31. www.forexlive.com/blog/
    2011/08/31/new-york-fed-study-finds-discount-window-stigma-in-crisis.

Beirne, J. (2010). "The EONIA spread before and during the crisis of 2007 to 2009: The role of liquidity and credit risk." *European Central Bank*, August 25. http://macro.soc.uoc.gr/docs/Year/2011/papers/paper_3_4.pdf.

Berkmen, S. P. & Cavallo, E. A. (2009). *Exchange Rate Policy and Liability Dollarization: What Do the Data Reveal about Causality?* Washington, DC: International Monetary Fund.

Bernanke, B. S. (2006). "Reflections on the Yield Curve and Monetary Policy." Speech at the New York Economic Club, March 20. www.federal reserve.gov/newsevents/speech/bernanke20060320a.htm.

(2011a). "Dodd–Frank implementation: monitoring systemic risk and promoting financial stability." Speech before the Committee on Banking, Housing, and Urban Affairs, US Senate. Washington, DC, May 12. www.federal reserve.gov/newsevents/testimony/bernanke20110512a.htm.

(2011b). "Economic outlook and recent monetary policy actions." Speech before the Joint Economic Committee, US Congress. Washington, DC, October 4. www.federalreserve.gov/newsevents/testimony/bernanke2011 1004a.htm.

(2011c). "Implementation of the Dodd–Frank Act." Before the Committee on Banking, Housing, and Urban Affairs, US Senate. Washington, DC, February 17. www.federalreserve.gov/newsevents/testimony/bernanke20110217a.htm.

(2012a). "The economic recovery and economic policy." Speech at the Economic Club of New York. New York, November 20. www.federal reserve.gov/newsevents/speech/bernanke20121120a.htm.

(2012b). Press conference. *Federal Reserve*, December 12. www.federal reserve.gov/mediacenter/files/FOMCpresconf20121212.pdf.

(2013a). "The economic outlook." *Federal Reserve*, May 22. www.federal reserve.gov/newsevents/testimony/bernanke20130522a.htm.

(2013b). Press conference. *Federal Reserve*, September 18. www.federal reserve.gov/mediacenter/files/FOMCpresconf20130918.pdf.

(2015). *The Courage to Act: A Memoir of a Crisis and Its Aftermath.* New York: W. W. Norton.

Berry, J. (1993). "The Fed Chief's Unlikely Alliance." *Washington Post*, March 21. www.washingtonpost.com/archive/business/1993/03/21/the-fed-chiefs-unlikely-alliance/798698c4-cfb3-4a7a-8314-0c8f76681aab.

Beukers, T. (2014). "The Bundesverfassungsgericht Preliminary Reference on the OMT Program: 'In the ECB We Do Not Trust. What about You?'" *German Law Journal* 15(2), 343–368.

Birnbaum, J. (1996). *Madhouse: The Private Turmoil of Working for the President.* New York: New York Times Books.

Blustein, P. (2005). *And the Money Kept Rolling In (and Out): Wall Street, the IMF, and the Bankrupting of Argentina.* New York: Public Affairs.

Board of Governors of the Federal Reserve System (n.d.). Effective Federal Funds Rate [FEDFUNDS]. Retrieved from FRED, Federal Reserve Bank of St. Louis, June 14. https://research.stlouisfed.org/fred2/series/FEDFUNDS.

(n.d.). "About the Fed." www.federalreserve.gov/faqs/about-the-fed.htm.

(n.d.). "Credit and liquidity programs and the balance sheet." www.federalreserve.gov/monetarypolicy/bst_crisisresponse.htm.

(n.d.). "Federal Open Market Committee." www.federalreserve.gov/monetar
ypolicy/fomc.htm.

(n.d.). "Regulatory reform; Bear Stearns, J.P. Morgan Chase, and Maiden
Lane LLC." Last updated: February 12, 2016. www.federalreserve.gov/
newsevents/reform_bearstearns.htm.

(n.d.). "The Federal Reserve Act." www.federalreserve.gov/aboutthefed/
section13.htm.

Board of Governors of the Federal Reserve (2011). "Press release." August 9.
www.federalreserve.gov/newsevents/press/monetary/20110809a.htm.

Boesler, M. (2013). "The ECB scheme that saved Europe from disaster last
summer is practically dead." *Business Insider*, June 26. www.business
insider.com/mario-draghis-omt-is-dead-2013-6.

Boland, V. & Spiegel, P. (2014). "ECB threatened to end funding unless Ireland
sought bailout." *Financial Times*, November 16. www.ft.com/content/
1f4ed1fa-65ac-11e4-aba7-00144feabdc0.

Bonvecchi, A. (2014). "Organization and Management of Crisis Economic
Policy-Making: The United States in Comparative Perspective." Paper pre-
sented at the 2014 Annual Meeting of the American Political Science
Association.

Born, B. (2009). *Frontline: The Warning*. August 28. www.pbs.org/wgbh/pages/
frontline/warning.

Bouie, J. (2015). "The revolution devours its own." *Slate*, September 25. www
.slate.com/articles/news_and_politics/politics/2015/09/john_boehner_devoured_
by_the_gop_revolution_his_right_wing_rhetoric_came.html.

Bowman, A. et al. (2013). "Central Bank-Led Capitalism?" *Seattle University Law
Review* 36, 455.

Bowman, D. (2010). "The ECB's use of term refinancing operations." *Federal
Reserve*, August 3. www.federalreserve.gov/monetarypolicy/files/
FOMC20100805memo02.pdf.

Brandiesky, K. (2011). "How Clinton handled his debt ceiling crisis better than
Obama." *New Republic*, August 2. https://newrepublic.com/article/93043/
obama-clinton-debt-ceiling-crisis.

Braun, M. (2006). *The Political Economy of Debt in Argentina, or Why History
Repeats Itself*. Washington, DC: World Bank.

Brian Lenihan to Jean-Claude Trichet, November 21, 2010. www.ecb.europa.eu/
press/shared/pdf/2010-11-21_Letter_IE%20FinMin_to_ECB_%
20President.pdf?432af7ba36b71099b55893b819ae2502.

Brown, S. (2000). "New bribe scandal hits Argentina's 'murky' Senate." *CNN*,
September 21. www.cnn.com/2000/WORLD/americas/09/21/argentina
.bribes.reut.

(2015). "Mario Draghi can use his 'bazooka.'" *Politico*, June 16. www.politico
.eu/article/ecb-legal-court-government-bonds.

"Bundesbank in court clash with ECB over bond-buying plan" (2013).
Financial Times, June 11. www.ft.com/content/1ecb4826-d25f-11e2-aac2-
00144feab7de.

Bundesverfassungsgericht (n.d.). "Judgement of the Second Senate of 30 June
2009." www.bundesverfassungsgericht.de/SharedDocs/Entscheidungen/
EN/2009/06/es20090630_2bve000208en.html.

Bundesverfassungsgericht (n.d.). "Judgement of the Second Senate of 21 June 2016." www.bundesverfassungsgericht.de/SharedDocs/Entscheidungen/EN/2016/06/rs20160621_2bvr272813en.html.

Calmes, J. (2009). "For Geithner's debut, a lukewarm reception." *New York Times*, February 10. www.nytimes.com/2009/02/11/business/economy/11geithner.html.

Calvo, G. A., Izquierdo, A. & Talvi, E. (2003). *Sudden Stops, the Real Exchange Rate, and Fiscal Sustainability: Argentina's Lessons.* Cambridge, MA: National Bureau of Economic Research.

Carney, J. (2009). "The warning: Brooksley Born's battle with Alan Greenspan, Robert Rubin and Larry Summers." *Business Insider*, October 21. www.businessinsider.com/the-warning-brooksley-borns-battle-with-alan-greenspan-robert-rubin-and-larry-summers-2009-10.

"Cavallo struggles to get a grip on Argentina's economy" (2001). *The Economist*, May 3. www.economist.com/node/612598.

"Central bank independence in Japan – not what you would expect" (2013). *Reszat Online*, January 27. http://reszatonline.wordpress.com/2013/01/27/central-bank-independence-in-japan-not-what-you-would-expect.

"Charters of Freedom: Constitution of the United States." (n.d.). www.archives.gov/exhibits/charters/constitution_transcript.html.

Clark, W. R. (2002). "Partisan and Electoral Motivations and the Choice of Monetary Institutions under Fully Mobile Capital." *International Organization* 52(1), 725–749.

Clark, W. R. & Hallerberg, M. (2000). "Mobile Capital, Domestic Institutions, and Electorally Induced Monetary and Fiscal Policy." *American Political Science Review* 94(2), 323–346.

Clark, W. R., Reichert, U. N., Lomas, S. L. & Parker, K. L. (1998). "International and Domestic Constraints on Political Business Cycles in OECD Economies." *International Organization* 52(1), 87–120.

"Clinton leads Mexico bailout effort" (1996). *CQ Almanac 1995, 51, 10-16, 10-17.* Washington, DC: Congressional Quarterly. http://library.cqpress.com/cqalmanac/cqal95-1099614.

"Clinton's economic plan" (1993). *New York Times*, February 18. www.nytimes.com/1993/02/18/us/clinton-s-economic-plan-the-details-clinton-s-plan-austerity-and-change.html.

Clymer, A. (1996). "G.O.P. lawmakers offer to abandon debt-limit threat." *New York Times*, January 25. www.nytimes.com/1996/01/25/us/gop-lawmakers-offer-to-abandon-debt-limit-threat.html.

"Congress shouldn't play politics with the debt ceiling" (2015). *Center on Budget and Policy Priorities*, October 10. www.cbpp.org/blog/congress-shouldnt-play-politics-with-the-debt-ceiling.

Congressional Quarterly Almanac (n.d.). https://library.cqpress.com/cqalmanac.

Congressional Record, 104th Congress (1995–1996). Congressional Record article 69 of 195, D'AMATO (AND OTHERS) AMENDMENT NO. 2229 (Senate – August 5, 1995), proposed Amendment to bill H.R. 2020. www.congress.gov/104/crec/1995/08/05/CREC-1995-08-05-pt1-PgS11521-2.pdf.

"Consolidated version of the Treaty of the Functioning of the European Union" (2016). Section 6, Article 282. *Official Journal of the European Union*, C 202, 59, 167. www.ecb.europa.eu/ecb/legal/pdf/oj_c_2016_202_full_en_txt.pdf.

"Contract with America Advancement Act of 1996." Pub. L. 104-121 – Mar. 29, 1996 110 Stat. 847.

Corrales, J. (1997a). "Do Economic Crises Contribute to Economic Reform? Argentina and Venezuela in the 1990s." *Political Science Quarterly* 112(4), 617–644.

(1997b). "Why Argentines Followed Cavallo: A Technopol between Democracy and Economic Reform." In J. I. Domínguez (ed.). *Technopols: The Role of Ideas and Leaders in Freeing Politics and Markets in Latin America in the 1990s.* University Park: Penn State University Press, pp. 49–94.

(2002). "The Politics of Argentina's Meltdown." *World Policy Journal* 19(3), 29–42.

"Country List Government Debt to GDP" (n.d.). www.tradingeconomics.com/country-list/government-debt-to-gdp.

Country Risk Services (2000). Argentina country report. October 1.

"Credit and Liquidity Programs and the Balance Sheet." www.federalreserve.gov/monetarypolicy/bst_liquidityswaps.htm.

"Credit Institutions (Financial Support) Act 2008" (n.d.). www.irishstatutebook.ie/eli/2008/act/18/section/1/enacted/en/html#sec1.

Creel, J. & Saraceno, F. (2010). "European Fiscal Rules after the Crisis." *Journal of Innovation Economics & Management* 6(2), 95–122.

Crowe, C. & Meade, E. (2008). "Central Bank Independence and Transparency: Evolution and Effectiveness." IMF Working Paper, 08/119.

Cunningham, J. M. (n.d.). "Mario Monti." *Encyclopaedia Britannica.* www.britannica.com/biography/Mario-Monti.

Curtin, R. (n.d.). "Surveys of Consumers, University of Michigan." www.sca.isr.umich.edu.

Dahan, S. et al. (2018). "Whatever It Takes? Regarding the OMT Ruling of the German Federal Constitutional Court." *Journal of International Economic Law* 18(1), 137–151.

Daley, S. (2011). "Economist named to lead Greek unity government." *New York Times*, November 10. www.nytimes.com/2011/11/11/world/europe/greek-leaders-resume-talks-on-interim-government.html.

(2015). "Greeks reject bailout terms in rebuff to European leaders." *New York Times*, July 5. www.nytimes.com/2015/07/06/world/europe/greek-referendum-debt-crisis-vote.html.

"Debt 'Supercommittee': Statement from co-chairs of the Joint Select Committee on Deficit Reduction" (2011). *Washington Post*, November 21. www.washingtonpost.com/politics/statement-from-co-chairs-of-the-joint-select-committee-on-deficit-reduction/2011/11/21/gIQArEmsiN_story.html?utm_term=.4ee15494c31f.

"Debt Limit" (2016). *US Department of the Treasury*, January 29. https://home.treasury.gov/policy-issues/financial-markets-financial-institutions-and-fiscal-service/debt-limit.

"Deference" (n.d.). *Dictionary.com.* http://dictionary.reference.com/browse/deference.

"Deposit Guarantee Scheme" (n.d.). www.centralbank.ie/consumer-hub/deposit-guarantee-scheme.

"Derivatives Clearing Organization General Provisions and Core Principles" (n.d.). *US Commodity Futures Trading Commission.* www.cftc.gov/ucm/groups/public/@lrfederalregister/documents/file/2011-27536a.pdf.

Deslter, I. M. (1996). "The National Economic Council: A Work in Progress." In *Policy Analyses in International Economics*. Washington, DC: Institute for International Economics, pp. 9–18.

Dickerson, J. (2004). "Confessions of a White House insider." *Time Magazine*, January 10. http://content.time.com/time/magazine/article/0,9171,5748 09,00.html.

Dodaro, G. L. (1996). "Report to congressional requesters: 'debt ceiling: analysis of actions during the 1995–1996 crisis.'" *United States General Accounting Office, B-270619*, August 30. www.gao.gov/products/AIMD-96-130.

Draghi, M. (2012). "Verbatim of the remarks made by Mario Draghi at the Global Investment Conference in London." *European Central Bank*, July 26. www.ecb.europa.eu/press/key/date/2012/html/sp120726.en.html.

(2015). Introductory statement to the press conference [press release]. www.ecb.europa.eu/press/pressconf/2015/html/is150305.en.html.

Draghi, M. & Constâncio, V. (2013). "Introductory statement to the press conference (with Q&A)." *European Central Bank*, June 6. www.ecb.europa.eu/press/pressconf/2013/html/is130606.en.html.

Drew, E. (1997). *Showdown: The Struggle between the Gingrich Congress and the Clinton White House*. New York: Touchstone.

Drezner, D. (2014). *The System Worked: How the World Stopped Another Great Depression*. Oxford: Oxford University Press.

Dwyer, C. (2018). "Argentina hikes interest rate to 60 percent in bid to halt currency's fall." *NPR*, August 30. www.npr.org/2018/08/30/643264044/argentina-hikes-interest-rate-to-60-percent-in-bid-to-halt-currencys-fall.

Duhalde, E. (2002). "Argentina regrets." *Financial Times*, July 2.

(2007). *Memorias del incendio (Memory of the Fire)*. Buenos Aires: Editorial Sudamericana.

"Duties and Functions" (n.d.). *US Department of the Treasury*. https://home.treasury.gov/about/general-information/role-of-the-treasury.

"ECB hit by legal challenges over bond-buying programme" (2015). *Channel NewsAsia*, November 11.

"ECB letter shows pressure on Berlusconi" (2011). *Financial Times*. September 29. www.ft.com/content/3576e9c2-eaad-11e0-aeca-00144feab49a.

"ECB policy – understanding the European Central Bank" (2009). *ForEx*, August 24. www.forexfraud.com/forex-articles/ecb-policy-european-central-bank.html.

"ECB sees rising risks to Eurozone economy" (2012). *BBC News*, June 6. www.bbc.com/news/business-18339334.

"Economic and monetary developments: monetary and financial developments" (2012). *ECB Monthly Bulletin*, March. www.ecb.europa.eu/pub/pdf/other/mb201203_focus03.en.pdf?633af8e40f98a75808996a7857cbbd93.

"EFSF FRAMEWORK AGREEMENT (as amended with effect from the Effective Date of the Amendments), consolidated version" (n.d.). www.esm.europa.eu/sites/default/files/20111019_efsf_framework_agreement_en.pdf.

"El historial de los funcionarios que quedaron afuera del gabinete de Cristina Kirchner" (2013). *La Nación*, November 19. www.lanacion.com.ar/1639647-recambios-en-el-gabinete-con-la-marca-personal-de-cristina-kirchner.

Elliott, L. (2015). "ECB staves off collapse of Greek banking system with emergency funding." *The Guardian,* June 19. www.theguardian.com/world/2015/jun/19/ecb-greek-banking-system-emergency-funding-greece-creditors-monday-meetings.

Ellyatt, H. (2015). "ECB confirms it has been repaid by Greece." *CNBC,* July 20. www.cnbc.com/2015/07/20/greece-starts-paying-back-the-ecb-imf.html.

"Emergency liquidity assistance (ELA) and monetary policy" (2017). *European Central Bank,* June. www.ecb.europa.eu/mopo/ela/html/index.en.html.

"Euribor-rates.edu" (n.d.). www.euribor-rates.eu/eonia.asp.

"Euro zone banks take more ultra-cheap ECB loans than expected" (2017). *Reuters,* March 23. www.reuters.com/article/eurozone-banks-ecb-tltro-idUSF9N1F8017.

"European debt crisis: Papademos named as Greece's new PM" (2011). *The Guardian Business Blog,* November 10. www.theguardian.com/business/blog/2011/nov/10/eurozone-crisis-italy-greece.

European Stability Mechanism (2014). "Frequently asked questions on the European Stability Mechanism." July 28. www.esm.europa.eu/sites/default/files/faqontheesm.pdf

Ewing, J. (2010a). "Central banker takes a chance by speaking out." *New York Times,* November 1. www.nytimes.com/2010/11/02/business/global/02weber.html.

(2010b). "European bank's assurance fails to placate investors." *New York Times,* May 6. www.nytimes.com/2010/05/07/business/global/07ecb.html.

(2010c). "Merkel urges tougher rules for Euro Zone." *New York Times,* March 17. www.nytimes.com/2010/03/18/world/europe/18merkel.html.

(2012). "A tense warning for euro states: do something now." *New York Times,* May 31. www.nytimes.com/2012/06/01/business/global/greek-banks-regain-access-to-european-central-bank-loans.html.

(2016). "E.C.B.'s bold stimulus takes aim at Eurozone economy." *New York Times,* March 10. www.nytimes.com/2016/03/11/business/international/ecb-draghi-europe.html.

Ewing, J. & Kulish, N. (2011). "A setback for the Euro Zone." *New York Times,* September 9. www.nytimes.com/2011/09/10/business/global/a-top-ecb-official-to-resign.html.

"Exchange Stabilization Fund" (n.d.). *US Department of the Treasury.* https://home.treasury.gov/policy-issues/international/exchange-stabilization-fund.

"Extraordinary measures, simplified" (2015). *Bipartisan Policy Center,* March 13. http://bipartisanpolicy.org/library/extraordinary-measures-simplified.

Fannie Mae (n.d.). www.fanniemae.com/portal/index.html.

Farley, R. (2012). "The problems with limiting large banks." *New York Times,* May 23. http://dealbook.nytimes.com/2012/05/23/the-problems-with-limiting-large-banks.

Fawley, B. W., & Neely, C. J. (2013). "Four Stories of Quantitative Easing." *Federal Reserve Bank of St. Louis Review* 95(1), 51–88.

Federal Deposit Insurance Corporation (n.d.). www.fdic.gov/about/learn/symbol.

"Federal Reserve Board and Federal Open Market Committee release economic projections from the March 15–16 FOMC" (2016). *Federal Reserve Bank of New York,* March 16. www.federalreserve.gov/faqs/money_12848.htm.

"Federal Reserve System: Opportunities Exist to Strengthen Policies and Processes for Managing Emergency Assistance." GAO-11-696, July 2011.

"FEDPOINT: Exchange Stabilization Fund" (n.d.). *Federal Reserve Bank of New York*. www.newyorkfed.org/aboutthefed/fedpoint/fed14.html.

Felkerson, J. (2011). "$29 trillion: A Detailed Look at the Fed's Bailout by Funding Facility and Recipient." Working Paper No. 698. Annandale-on-Hudson: Levy Economics Institute of Bard College.

Fernández, R. B. (1991). "What Have Populists Learned from Hyperinflation?" In R. Dornbusch & S. Edwards (eds.). *The Macroeconomics of Populism in Latin America*. Chicago: University of Chicago Press, pp. 121–149.

Financial Crisis Inquiry Commission (2011). *The Financial Crisis Inquiry Report: Final Report of the National Commission on the Causes of the Financial and Economic Crisis in the United States*. Washington, DC: Government Printing Office. www.gpo.gov/fdsys/pkg/GPO-FCIC/pdf/GPO-FCIC.pdf.

"Financial regulation overhaul gives bank new powers" (2013). *The Herald*, April 1. www.heraldscotland.com/business/13098470.Financial_regulation_over haul_gives_Bank_new_powers.

Financial Stability Oversight Council (n.d.). www.treasury.gov/initiatives/fsoc/Pages/home.aspx.

"Fire the bazooka: it's time to nationalize America's mortgage giants – and then to dismantle them" (2008). *The Economist*, August 28. www.economist.com/node/12009702.

Foster, J. D. (2013). "The many real dangers of soaring national debt." *Heritage Foundation*, June 18. www.heritage.org/budget-and-spending/report/the-many-real-dangers-soaring-national-debt.

Framke, A. & Carrel, P. (2011). "Exclusive: Germans lead resistance to ECB bond buying." *Reuters*, August 5. www.reuters.com/article/us-ecb-bondbuys/exclusive-germans-lead-resistance-to-ecb-bond-buying-idUSTRE7741QJ20110805.

FRED (n.d.). Economic Data, *Federal Reserve Bank of St. Louis*. http://research.stlouisfed.org/fred2.

(2016). *Federal Reserve Bank of St. Louis*, June 13. https://research.stlouisfed.org/fred2/series/IRLTLT01USM156N.

Freddie Mac (n.d.). www.freddiemac.com.

Friedman, T. (1992). "The transition; experts gather for conference on the economy." *New York Times*, December 14. www.nytimes.com/1992/12/14/us/the-transition-experts-gather-for-conference-on-the-economy.html.

"Frontline: interview with Robert Rubin conducted by Chris Bury" (2000). www.pbs.org/wgbh/pages/frontline/shows/clinton/interviews/rubin.html.

Gambetti, L. & Musso, A. (2017). "The Macroeconomic Impact of the ECB's Expanded Asset Purchase Programme (APP)." *The European Central Bank Working Paper Series*, No. 2017, June. www.ecb.europa.eu/pub/pdf/scpwps/ecb.wp.2075.en.pdf?b4cbbd6fdbec00f78c66a83b422de6e7.

GAO-11-203 (2011). "DEBT LIMIT: Delays Create Debt Management Challenges and Increases Uncertainty in Treasury Market." Publicly released: February 22. www.gao.gov/products/GAO-11-203.

Geithner, T. (2014). *Stress Test: Reflections on Financial Crises*. New York: Random House.

"Geithner's planned departure puts Obama in tough spot" (2013). *Reuters*, January 4. www.cnbc.com/id/100354135.

"Geithner's tax troubles are serious" (2008). *Forbes*, January 13. www.forbes.com/2009/01/13/treasury-geithner-obama-biz-beltway-cx_bw_0113geithner2.html.

General Accounting Office, Report to Congressional Requestors (2011). "FEDERAL RESERVE SYSTEM: Opportunities Exist to Strengthen Policies and Processes for Managing Emergency Assistance." GAO-11-696, July.

Gilchrist, S. & Zakrajlek, E. (2011). "Credit Spreads and Business Cycle Fluctuations." NBER Working Paper No. 17021, May.

Gillon, S. (1999). *The Pact: Bill Clinton, Newt Gingrich, and the Rivalry That Defined a Generation.* Norman: University of Oklahoma Press.

Gilpin, K. (2004). "Bush renominates Alan Greenspan for Fed." *New York Times*, May 18. www.nytimes.com/2004/05/18/business/bush-renominates-alan-greenspan-for-fed.html?_r=0.

Goldman, D. (2008). "Congress demands answers on bailout House panel hears testimony from Treasury and key bailout oversight administrators on government's handling of funds." *CNN Money*, December 10. http://money.cnn.com/2008/12/10/news/economy/bailout_oversight_hearing/index.htm?postversion=2008121013.

González-Páramo, J. M. (2011). Member of the Executive Board of the ECB, at the XXIV Moneda y Crédito Symposium, Madrid, November 4. www.ecb.europa.eu/press/key/date/2011/html/sp111104_1.en.html.

"'Good number' of banks seeking federal capital, Paulson says" (2008). *New York Times*, October 16. http://dealbook.nytimes.com/2008/10/16/good-number-of-banks-seeking-federal-capital-paulson-says.

Goodman, P. (2008). "Taking hard new look at a Greenspan legacy." *New York Times*, October 8. www.nytimes.com/2008/10/09/business/economy/09greenspan.html?pagewanted=all.

Granitsas, A. (2009). "Greece pledges reforms after Fitch downgrades ratings." *Wall Street Journal*, October 23. www.wsj.com/articles/SB125628478983803339.

"Greece debt crisis: creditors press for new proposals" (2015). *BBC News*, July 6. www.bbc.com/news/world-europe-33413569.

"Greece debt rating downgraded by third agency" (2009). *BBC News*, December 22. http://news.bbc.co.uk/2/hi/business/8426085.stm.

"Greece PM Papandreou wins confidence vote" (2011). *BBC News*, November 5. www.bbc.com/news/world-europe-15586673.

"Greece, Italy bet on technocrats to restore confidence" (2011). *EURACTIV.com with Reuters*, November 14. www.euractiv.com/section/elections/news/greece-italy-bet-on-technocrats-to-restore-confidence.

"Greece's creditors allow a bit more money to flow" (2015). *The Economist*, July 16. www.economist.com/blogs/freeexchange/2015/07/ecb-and-greek-banks.

"Greek debt crisis: banks reopen amid tax rise" (2015). *BBC News*, July 20. www.bbc.com/news/world-europe-33590334.

"Greek referendum plan plunges markets into chaos" (2011). *ABC News*, November 1. www.abc.net.au/news/2011-11-02/greek-referendum-ignites-german-anger2c-hammers-markets/3614000.

"Greek referendum spooks European stock markets" (2011). *Reuters*, November 1. www.reuters.com/article/markets-europe-stocks-idUSL5E7M11S420111101.

Greenhouse, S. (1993). "Greenspan the politician." *New York Times*, February 1. www.nytimes.com/1993/02/01/business/greenspan-the-politician.html.

"Greenspan 1, Bush 0: warning of growing budget deficits, Fed chairman undercuts Bush, GOP arguments for tax cuts" (2003). *CNN Money*, February 1. https://money.cnn.com/2003/02/11/news/economy/greenspan/index.htm.

"Greenspan eyes tax cuts" (2001). *CNN Money*. January 25. https://money.cnn.com/2001/01/25/economy/greenspan.

"Greenspan on tax changes" (2001). *C-Span*, January 25. www.c-span.org/video/?c4177086/greenspan-tax-changes.

Greenspan, A. (1998). "Private-sector refinancing of the large hedge fund, Long-Term Capital Management." Before the Committee on Banking and Financial Services, US House of Representatives, October 1. www.federalreserve.gov/boarddocs/testimony/1998/19981001.htm.

(2007). *The Age of Turbulence: Adventures in a New World*. New York: Penguin Group.

Greenwald, J. (1994). "Greenspan's rates of wrath: the Fed jacks up borrowing costs, but the move is too much for Main Street and not enough for Wall Street." *Time Magazine*, November 28. http://content.time.com/time/magazine/article/0,9171,981879,00.html.

Grunwald, M. (2009). "Person of the Year 2009: Ben Bernanke." *TIME Magazine*, December 16. http://content.time.com/time/specials/packages/article/0,28804,1946375_1947251_1947520,00.html.

Hall, B. (2010). *Central Banking as Global Governance: Constructing Financial Credibility*. Cambridge: Cambridge University Press.

Harrison, D. (2015). "Fed adopts Dodd–Frank bailout limits." *Wall Street Journal*, November 30. www.wsj.com/articles/fed-set-to-adopt-final-emergency-lending-rule-1448889633.

Heniff Jr., B. (2008). "Developing debt-limit legislation: The House's 'Gephardt Rule.'" *Congressionalresearch.com*, July 1. http://congressionalresearch.com/RL31913/document.php.

Henning, C. (1999). *The Exchange Stabilization Fund: Slush Money or War Chest*. Washington, DC: Institute for International Economics.

Hirschman, A. (1945). *National Power and the Structure of Foreign Trade*. Berkeley: University of California Press.

"History of the Stability and Growth Pact" (2015). *European Commission*. https://ec.europa.eu/info/business-economy-euro/economic-and-fiscal-policy-coordination/eu-economic-governance-monitoring-prevention-correction/stability-and-growth-pact/history-stability-and-growth-pact_en#2011.

"History" (n.d.). *Office of Thrift Supervision in the Department of the Treasury*. www.treasury.gov/about/history/Pages/ots.aspx.

Hook, J. & Gerstenzang, J. (1996). "Rubin details measures to postpone debt crisis." *Los Angeles Times*, January 23. http://articles.latimes.com/1996-01-23/news/mn-27721_1_debt-crisis.

Hornbeck, J. (2013). *Argentina's Post-crisis Economic Reform: Challenges for U.S. Policy*. Washington, DC: Congressional Research Service.

Houses of the Oireachtas. (2013). "Ireland and the Troika programme." In *Report of the Joint Committee of Inquiry into the Banking Crisis*, pp. 329–356. https://inquiries.oireachtas.ie/banking/volume-1-report/chapter-10.

"How treasury auctions work" (n.d.). *TreasuryDirect*. www.treasurydirect.gov/instit/auctfund/work/work.htm.

"Indicators: agriculture and rural development" (n.d.). *World Bank Data*. https://data.worldbank.org/indicator.

International Monetary Fund (2018). *World Economic Outlook: Challenges to Steady Growth*. Washington, DC: IMF Publications. www.imf.org/en/Publications/WEO/Issues/2018/09/24/world-economic-outlook-october-2018.

"Introductory statement to the press conference (with Q&A)" (2013). *European Central Bank*. www.ecb.europa.eu/press/pressconf/2013/html/is130606.en.html.

"Irish letters" (n.d.). *European Central Bank*. www.ecb.europa.eu/press/html/irish-letters.en.html.

Irwin, N. (2013). "The Bank of Japan is coordinating policy with the Japanese government. That is a big deal." *Washington Post*, January 22. www.washingtonpost.com/blogs/wonkblog/wp/2013/01/22/the-bank-of-japan-is-coordinating-policy-with-the-japanese-government-that-is-a-big-deal.

(2014). *The Alchemists: Three Central Bankers and a World on Fire*. New York: Penguin Group.

Isidore, C. (2008). "Paulson in hot seat over Fannie, Freddie." *CNN Money*, July 15. https://money.cnn.com/2008/07/15/news/economy/Freddie_Fannie_Senate.

Ivry, B., Keoun, B. & Kuntz, P. (2011). "Secret Fed loans gave banks $13 billion undisclosed to congress." *Bloomberg*, November 27. www.bloomberg.com/news/2011-11-28/secret-fed-loans-undisclosed-to-congress-gave-banks-13-billion-in-income.html.

Jackson, H., Welker, K. & Alexander, P. (2018)."On the hunt for a betrayer, a 'volcanic' Trump lashes out." *NBC News*, September 6. www.nbcnews.com/politics/donald-trump/hunt-betrayer-volcanic-trump-lashes-out-n906941.

Jacobs, L. & King, D. (2016). *Fed Power: How Finance Wins*. Oxford: Oxford University Press.

Jaffe, M. (2009). "Echoing Democrat's comments, two Republicans call for Geithner to go." *ABC News*, November 19. http://abcnews.go.com/Politics/house-republicans-treasurys-geithner-resign/story?id=9127162.

"Japan's quantitative easing: A bigger bazooka" (2014). *The Economist*, October 31. www.economist.com/blogs/banyan/2014/10/japans-quantitative-easing.

Jean-Claude Trichet to Brian Lenihan, November 19, 2010. www.ecb.europa.eu/press/shared/pdf/2010-11-19_Letter_ECB_President_to%20IE_FinMin.pdf?31295060a74c0ffe738a12cd9139f578.

Jean-Claude Trichet and Miguel Fernández Ordoñez to José Luis Rodríguez Zapatero, December 19, 2014. www.ecb.europa.eu/pub/pdf/other/2011-08-05-letter-from-trichet-and-fernandez-ordonez-to-zapateroen.pdf.

Jones, C. O. (1999). *Clinton and Congress, 1993–1996: Risk, Restoration, and Reelection*. Norman: University of Oklahoma Press.

Kaminska, I. (2011). "On the ECB's 'most significant non-standard measure.'" *Financial Times*, December 8. https://ftalphaville.ft.com/2011/12/08/785211/on-the-ecbs-most-significant-non-standard-measure/?mhq5j=e1.

Kanter, J. & Kitsantonis, N. (2015). "E.C.B. agrees to extend lifeline to Athens." *New York Times*, June 19. www.nytimes.com/2015/06/20/business/international/ecb-greece-debt-meeting.html.

Kelly, K. (2009). "Inside the fall of Bear Stearns." *Wall Street Journal*, May 9. www.wsj.com/articles/SB124182740622102431.

Kelly, M. (1992). "The 1992 campaign: the Democrats – Clinton and Bush compete to be champion of change; Democrat fights perceptions of Bush gain." *New York Times*, October 31. www.nytimes.com/1992/10/31/us/1992-campaign-democrats-clinton-bush-compete-be-champion-change-democrat-fights.html.

Keohane, R. & Nye, J. (1977). *Power and Interdependence*. New York: Longman.

"Key ECB interest rates" (2018). *European Central Bank*. www.ecb.europa.eu/stats/policy_and_exchange_rates/key_ecb_interest_rates/html/index.en.html.

Kiensnoski, K. (2013). "Investing in Argentina? Get ready to cry." *CNBC*, December 20. www.cnbc.com/2013/12/20/investing-in-argentina-get-ready-to-cry.html.

Kiguel, M. A. (1989). *Inflation in Argentina: Stop and Go since the Austral Plan*. Washington, DC: World Bank.

Kim, J. Y. (2015). *Billions to Trillions: Ideas to Actions*. Washington, DC: World Bank. http://documents.worldbank.org/curated/en/144851468190446079/Billions-to-trillions-Ideas-to-actions-by-Jim-Yong-Kim-President-Addis-Ababa-Ethiopia.

King, M. (2000). "Balancing the Economic See-Saw." Speech to the Plymouth Chamber of Commerce and Industry's 187th Banquet, April 14. www.bis.org/review/r000417d.pdf.

Kinton, T. (2011). "Merkozy smirk at EU crisis summit boosts Berlusconi." *The Guardian*, October 24. www.theguardian.com/business/2011/oct/24/merkel-sarkozy-italy-berlusconi.

Kirchner, J. (2002). *Monetary Orders: Ambiguous Economics, Ubiquitous Politics*. Cornell: Cornell University Press.

Knapp, U. (2009). "All losers have won." *Frankfurter Runschau*, June 6. www.fr.de/politik/bundesverfassungsgericht-zum-eu-vertrag-alle-verlierer-haben-gewonnen-a-1097387.

Krugman, P. (2002). "The quiet man." *New York Times*, January 8. www.nytimes.com/2002/01/08/opinion/the-quiet-man.html.

Kube, H. (2010). "The EU Financial Crisis – European Law and Constitutional Law Implications." Center for International Studies, Working Paper Series, 1–12, June.

Kyriakidou, D. & Winfrey, M. (2010). "Greece presses 'help' button, markets still wary." *Reuters*, April 23. www.reuters.com/article/us-greece/greece-presses-help-button-markets-still-wary-idUSTRE63M1LV20100423.

Lagarde, C. (2012). "Promises to keep: the policy actions needed to secure global recovery," interview with K. Ryssdal. *American Public Media, Marketplace*, September 24. www.marketplace.org/shows/marketplace/marketplace-monday-september-24-2012.

(2014). *World Financial Growth Is Still Falling Short*. Washington, DC: Georgetown University.

Landau, J. P., ed. (2011). "Global Liquidity – Concept, Measurement and Policy Implications." *Committee on the Global Financial System (CGFS) Papers, No. 45: Bank of France, Bank for International Settlements.*

Landler, M. & Dash, E. (2008). "Drama behind a $250 billion banking deal." *New York Times,* October 14. www.nytimes.com/2008/10/15/business/econ omy/15bailout.html.

"Lapicera veloz: CFK firma un DNU cada mes y medio" (2014). *La Tecla,* December 8. www.latecla.info/3/nota_1.php?noticia_id=45923.

Lavagna, R. (2012). Interview with Roberto Lavagna. Interviewer: G. Shambaugh.

Leahy, M. (2011). "Is the biggest threat to Speaker of the House John Boehner the 'Young Guns' in his own party?" *Washington Post,* May 19. www .washingtonpost.com/lifestyle/magazine/is-the-biggest-threat-to-speaker-of-the-house-john-boehner-the-young-guns-in-his-own-party/2011/04/29/AFJhYU7G_ print.html.

"Letters to the editor: Timothy Geithner's tax problems" (2009). *Washington Post,* January 19. www.washingtonpost.com/wp-dyn/content/article/2009/01/ 18/AR2009011802070.html.

Levy, A. & Shich, S. (2010). "The Design of Government Guarentees for Bank Bonds: Lessons from the Recent Financial Crisis." *OECD Journal: Financial Market Trends* (2010), 1. www.oecd.org/finance/financial-markets/ 45636972.pdf.

Linzert, T. & Schmidt, S. (2008). "What Explains the Spread between the Euro Overnight Rate and the ECB's Policy Rate?" *European Central Bank,* Working Paper Series, No. 983, December.

Lochhead, C. (2001). "Greenspan endorses a cut in tax rate/budget surpluses will erase national debt, he says." *SF Gate,* January. www.sfgate.com/news/art icle/Greenspan-Endorses-A-Cut-in-Tax-Rate-Budget-2959985.php.

Lorenzino, H. (2012). Statement by Hernán Lorenzino, Minister of Economy and Public Finance, Argentina, to the International Monetary and Financial Committee of the International Monetary Fund at their twenty-sixth meeting, October 13. www.imf.org/External/AM/2012/imfc/statement/eng/arg.pdf.

Machiavelli, N. (1995). *The Prince,* edited and translated by D. Wooton. Indianapolis: Hacket Publishing Company.

MacIntyre, A. (2001). "Institutions and Investors: The Politics of the Economic Crisis in South East Asia." *International Organization* 55(1), 81–122.

Magnay, D. et al. (2010). "Greece accepts bailout package." *CNN Money,* May 2. https://money.cnn.com/2010/05/02/news/international/greece_bailout.

Mahnken, K. (2013). "Dick Gephardt, where art thou?" *New Republic,* October 9. https://newrepublic.com/article/115084/dick-gephardt-rule-how-he-could-have-avoided-debt-crisis.

Mallaby, S. (2010). *The Man Who Knew: The Life and Times of Alan Greenspan.* New York: Bloomsbury Publishing.

Manzetti, L. (1994). "Institutional Decay and Distributional Coalitions in Developing Countries: The Argentine Riddle Reconsidered." *Studies in Comparative International Development* 29(2), 82–114.

"Market risk" (n.d.). *Investopedia.* www.investopedia.com/terms/m/marketrisk .asp?layout=infini&v=5B&orig=1&adtest=5.

Marx, G. (1990). "Argentina's president pardons leaders of 'dirty war' on leftists." *Chicago Tribune*, December 30. http://articles.chicagotribune.com/1990-12-30/news/9004170832_1_pardoned-two-former-military-presidents-dirty-war.

McCracken, M. W. (2010). "Disagreement at the FOMC: the dissenting votes are just part of the story." *Regional Economist*. www.stlouisfed.org/~/media/Files/PDFs/publications/pub_assets/pdf/re/2010/d/FOMC.pdf October 2010.

"Menem: pardon our dirty war" (1991). *Los Angeles Times*, January 6. http://articles.latimes.com/1991-01-06/opinion/op-10843_1_dirty-war.

"Merkel says EU can back Greece as 'last resort.'" (2010). *Euractiv*, March 25. www.euractiv.com/section/eu-priorities-2020/news/merkel-says-eu-could-back-greece-as-last-resort.

"Merkel wants scope to expel Eurozone troublemakers" (2010). *Euractiv*, March 18. www.euractiv.com/section/eu-priorities-2020/news/merkel-wants-scope-to-expel-eurozone-troublemakers.

Micossi, S. (2016). "The Monetary Policy of the European Central Bank (2002–2015)." CEPS Special Report No. 109, May.

"Military uprisings" (n.d.). www.yendor.com/vanished/uprisings.html.

"Mission" (n.d.). *Office of the Comptroller of the Currency in the Department of the Treasury.* www.occ.gov/about/what-we-do/mission/index-about.html.

"Monetary aggregates" (n.d.). *European Central Bank.* www.ecb.europa.eu/stats/money_credit_banking/monetary_aggregates/html/index.en.html.

"Monetary policy decisions" (n.d.). *European Central Bank.* www.ecb.europa.eu/mopo/decisions/html/index.en.html.

"Money-market fund 'breaks the buck.'" (2008). *New York Times*, September 17. http://dealbook.nytimes.com/2008/09/17/money-market-fund-says-customers-could-lose-money.

Montgomery, L. & Kane, P. (2011). "Debt-limit vote is canceled in House as Boehner, GOP leaders struggle to gain votes." *Washington Post*, July 18. www.washingtonpost.com/business/economy/boehner-other-gop-leaders-ramp-up-pressure-on-republicans-to-pass-debt-plan/2011/07/28/gIQARD5veI_story.html.

Murphy, E. V. (2015). "Who Regulates Whom and How? An Overview of U.S. Financial Regulatory Policy for Banking and Securities Markets." *Congressional Research Service*, January 30.

Murphy, R. L. (2012). Interview with Ricardo López Murphy. Interviewer: G. Shambaugh.

Mussa, M. (2002). *Argentina and the Fund: From Triumph to Tragedy.* Washington, DC: Peterson Institute for International Economics.

"National Economic Council" (n.d.). *Federal Register.* www.federalregister.gov/agencies/national-economic-council.

O'Carroll, L. (2010). "Ireland bailout: full Irish government statement." *The Guardian*, November 28. www.theguardian.com/business/ireland-business-blog-with-lisa-ocarroll/2010/nov/28/ireland-bailout-full-government-statement.

"Obama taps Geithner, Clinton, Richardson, Summers" (2008). *Wall Street Journal*, November 23. www.marketwatch.com/story/geithner-clinton-summers-to-take-senior-obama-posts.

"Omnibus Budget Reconciliation Act of 1993" (n.d.). *The Free Dictionary.* http:// financial-dictionary.thefreedictionary.com/Omnibus+Budget+Reconciliation +Act+of+1993.

"Omnibus Budget Reconciliation Act of 1993" (1993). www.gpo.gov/fdsys/pkg/ BILLS-103hr2264enr/pdf/BILLS-103hr2264enr.pdf.

"Open Market Operations" (n.d.). *Federal Reserve Bank of New York.* www.federalreserve.gov/monetarypolicy/bst_openmarketops.htm.

Organisation for Economic Co-operation and Development (n.d.). Long-Term Government Bond Yields: 10-year: Main (Including Benchmark) for Germany [IRLTLT01DEM156N]. Retrieved from FRED, Federal Reserve Bank of St. Louis. https://fred.stlouisfed.org/series/IRLTLT01DEM156N.

Organisation for Economic Co-operation and Development (n.d.). Long-Term Government Bond Yields: 10-year: Main (Including Benchmark) for Greece [IRLTLT01GRM156N]. Retrieved from FRED, Federal Reserve Bank of St. Louis. https://fred.stlouisfed.org/series/IRLTLT01GRM156N.

Organisation for Economic Co-operation and Development (n.d.). Long-Term Government Bond Yields: 10-year: Main (Including Benchmark) for Italy [IRLTLT01ITM156N]. Retrieved from FRED, Federal Reserve Bank of St. Louis. https://fred.stlouisfed.org/series/IRLTLT01ITM156N.

Organisation for Economic Co-operation and Development (n.d.). Long-Term Government Bond Yields: 10-year: Main (Including Benchmark) for Greece [IRLTLT01GRM156N]. Retrieved from FRED, Federal Reserve Bank of St. Louis. https://fred.stlouisfed.org/series/IRLTLT01GRM156N.

Orszag, J., Orszag, P. & Tyson, L. (2001). "The Process of Economic Policy-Making during the Clinton Administration." Prepared for the conference on "American Economic Policy in the 1990s," Center for Business and Government, John F. Kennedy School of Government, Harvard University, June 27–30.

"Overview of Results" (2009). *US Department of Treasury,* May 7. www.treasury.gov/initiatives/financial-stability/TARP-Programs/bank-invest ment-programs/scap-and-cap/Pages/default.aspx.

Packenham, R. (1994). *The Politics of Economic Liberalization: Argentina and Brazil in Comparative Perspective.* Notre Dame: Helen Kellogg Institute for International Studies.

"Pardon of Argentine officers angers critics of military" (1989). *New York Times,* October 8. www.nytimes.com/1989/10/09/world/pardon-of-argentine-offi cers-angers-critics-of-the-military.html.

Parkinson, P. (2005). "Testimony before the Committee on Banking, Housing, and Urban Affairs." *US Senate,* September 8. www.federalreserve.gov/board docs/testimony/2005/20050908/default.htm.

    (2018). "Commodity Futures Modernization Act of 2000." Before the Committee on Banking, Housing, and Urban Affairs, US Senate, July 14. www.govinfo.gov/ content/pkg/CHRG-109shrg35904/pdf/CHRG-109shrg35904.pdf.

Paulson, H. (2010). *On the Brink: Inside the Race to Stop the Collapse of the Global Financial System.* New York: Hachette Book Group.

Pauly, L. (2002). "Global Finance, Political Authority, and the Problem of Legitimation." In B. Hall & T. Biersteker (eds.), *The Emergency of Private*

Authority in Global Governance. Cambridge: Cambridge University Press, pp. 76–90.

Pearlstein, S. (1996). "Republicans threaten to impeach Rubin if he borrows again to avoid default." *Washington Post*, January 5. www.washington post.com/archive/politics/1996/01/05/republicans-threaten-to-impeach-rubin-if-he-borrows-again-to-avoid-default/2b74386c-666d-4a51-82a0-6e1afdd234 1f/?utm_term=.5eb4982d3837.

Pellegrini, F. (2001). "Greenspan's brave new world has room for Bush's tax cut." *Time Magazine*, January 25. http://content.time.com/time/nation/art icle/0,8599,96747,00.html.

Pianin, E. (2011). "Treasury's bag o' tricks may not avert catastrophe." *Fiscal Times*, February 4. www.thefiscaltimes.com/Articles/2011/02/04/Treasurys-Bag-of-Tricks-May-Not-Avert-Catastrophe.

Plosser, C. I. (2015). "The veneer of consensus at the Fed." *Wall Street Journal*, December 9. www.wsj.com/articles/the-veneer-of-consensus-at-the-fed-1449705161.

"Policy tools" (n.d.). *Federal Reserve Bank of New York*. www.federalreserve.gov/monetarypolicy/taf.htm.

"Political risk" (n.d.). *Investopedia*. www.investopedia.com/terms/p/politicalrisk.asp?layout=orig.

Poole, W. (2005). "How Predictable is Fed Policy?" *Federal Reserve Bank of St. Louis Review* 87(6), 659–668.

Pop, V. & Blackstone, B. (2015). "EU court declares ECB's 2012 bond-buying plan legal." *Wall Street Journal*, June 16. www.wsj.com/articles/eu-court-declares-ecbs-2012-bond-buying-plan-legal-1434443230.

"Presidential job approval center" (n.d.). *Gallup*. www.gallup.com/poll/124922/presidential-job-approval-center.aspx.

"Press conference by the President" (2010). *White House*, November 3. www.whitehouse.gov/the-press-office/2010/11/03/press-conference-president.

"Press Release: ECB decides on measures to address severe tensions in financial markets." (2010). *European Central Bank*, May 10. www.ecb.europa.eu/press/pr/date/2010/html/pr100510.en.html.

"Press Release: ECB reinstates waiver affecting the eligibility of Greek bonds used as collateral in Eurosystem monetary policy operations" (2016). *European Central Bank*, June 22. www.ecb.europa.eu/press/pr/date/2016/html/pr160622_1.en.html.

"Press Release: ELA to Greek banks maintained" (2015). *European Central Bank*, July 6. www.ecb.europa.eu/press/pr/date/2015/html/pr150706.en.html.

"Press Release: Eligibility of Greek bonds used as collateral in Eurosystem monetary policy operations" (2012). *European Central Bank*, February 28. www.ecb.europa.eu/press/pr/date/2012/html/pr120228.en.html.

"Press Release: Eligibility of Greek bonds used as collateral in Eurosystem monetary policy operations" (2015). *European Central Bank*, February 4. www.ecb.europa.eu/press/pr/date/2015/html/pr150204.en.html.

"Press Release: Joint statement on Ireland by EU Commissioner Olli Rehn and IMF Managing Director Dominique Strauss-Kahn" (2010). *International Monetary Fund*, November 28. www.imf.org/en/News/Articles/2015/09/14/01/49/pr10461.

"Press Release: Longer-term refinancing operations" (2009). *European Central Bank*, May 7. www.ecb.europa.eu/press/pr/date/2009/html/pr090507_2.en.html.

"Press Release: Monetary policy decisions" (2016). *European Central Bank*, March 10. www.ecb.europa.eu/press/pr/date/2016/html/pr160310.en.html.

"Press Release: Statement by the President of the ECB." (2011). *European Central Bank*, August 7. www.ecb.europa.eu/press/pr/date/2011/html/pr110807.en.html.

"Press Release: Technical features of Outright Monetary Transactions" (2012). *European Central Bank*, September 6. www.ecb.europa.eu/press/pr/date/2012/html/pr120906_1.en.html.

"Profile: Mario Monti" (2013). *BBC News*, February 18. www.bbc.com/news/world-europe-15695056.

"Protocol No (4) on the Statute of the European System of Central Banks and of the European Central Bank" (2012). *Official Journal of the European Union*, *European Central Bank*, October 26. www.ecb.europa.eu/ecb/legal/pdf/c_32620121026en_protocol_4.pdf.

Ramo, J. (1999). "The three musketeers." *Time*, February 15. http://content.time.com/time/world/article/0,8599,2054093,00.html.

Rankin, J. & Smith, H. (2015). "Eurozone chiefs strike deal to extend Greek bailout for four months." *The Guardian*, February 20. www.theguardian.com/business/2015/feb/20/eurozone-chiefs-meet-for-last-ditch-talks-to-avert-greece-cash-crunch.

"Reaching the debt limit: background and potential effects on government operations" (2013). *Congressional Research Service*, September 19.

"Recent developments in U.S. financial markets and regulatory responses to them" (2008). Washington, DC: US Congress.

Reiermann, C. et al. (2012). "German Central Bank opposes euro strategy." *Spiegel*, August 27. www.spiegel.de/international/europe/german-bundesbank-opposes-euro-crisis-strategy-a-852237.html.

"Report of the President's Working Group on Financial Markets" (1999). *US Department of Treasury*, November. www.treasury.gov/resource-center/fin-mkts/documents/otcact.pdf.

"Reserve requirements" (n.d.). *Federal Reserve Bank of New York*. www.federalreserve.gov/monetarypolicy/reservereq.htm.

"Resource center" (n.d.). *US Department of the Treasury*. www.treasury.gov/resource-center/data-chart-center/tic/Pages/external-debt.aspx.

Rodriguez, J. (2012). Interview with Jesus Rodriguez at Paraná 26 Piso 5 Oficina "I." Interviewer: G. Shambaugh.

Rogers, M. (2011). "2001–2011: the making of a crisis." *Argentina Independent*, December 27.

Rooney, B. (2012). "Draghi says euro is 'unsustainable' without action." *CNN Money*, May 31. https://money.cnn.com/2012/05/31/investing/ecb-draghi/index.htm.

"S. 2697 (106th): Commodity Futures Modernization Act of 2000" (n.d.). *GovTrack*. www.govtrack.us/congress/bills/106/s2697.

Scarpetta, V. (2013). "Where to publish an ECB letter setting your country's economic policy?" *Open Europe*, November 28. https://openeurope.org.uk/today/blog/ecb-letter-set-spain-economic-policy.

Schamis, H. E. (2002). *Re-forming the State: The Politics of Privatization in Latin America and Europe*. Ann Arbor: University of Michigan Press.

Schroeder, P. (2016). "GOP investigation: Treasury misled Congress, public about the debt limit." *The Hill*, February 1. http://thehill.com/policy/finance/267711-gop-probe-treasury-misled-congress-public-on-debt-limit.

Schulz, C. et al. (2016). "Germany economics focus." *Citi Research*, February 18. www.citivelocity.com/rendition/eppublic/uiservices/open_watermark_pdf?req_dt=cGRmTGluaz1odHRwcyUzQSUyRiUyRmlyLmNpdGkuY29tJTJGdU YwTkN4cTR6WWxBc1hoZldyeVpnS0tzZm1USXRZbGVGQkFXWGpL Vnd6UVNYYc3FhVUYzaFlmVDhlQkxxbm45NyZ1c2VyX2lkPTEtMUk0 UkFCQyZlc2VyX3R5cGU9Q1JN.

"SEC proposes rule to establish voluntary program for reporting financial information on EDGAR using XBRL" (2004). *US Securities and Exchange Commission*, September 27. www.sec.gov/news/press/2004-138.htm.

Secchi, C. & Villafranca, A., eds. (2009). *Liberalism in Crisis? European Economic Governance in the Age of Turbulence*. Cheltenham: Edward Elgar.

Shambaugh, G. (1999). *States, Firms and Power: Successful Sanctions in U.S. Foreign Policy*. Albany: SUNY Press.

   (2004). "The Power of Money: Private Capital and Policy Preferences in Newly Emerging Market Economies." *American Journal of Political Science* 48(2), 281–295.

   (2013). "States and Markets in the Age of Globalization: Is intervention by the Federal Reserve a substitute for Political Action?" Presented at the 2013 Annual Meeting of the International Studies Association, San Francisco.

Shambaugh, G. & Matthew, R. (2012). "Sword or Sheath: The Benefits of Imperfect Containment." *Japanese Journal of International Security* 39(4), 35–49.

Shambaugh, G. & Shen, E. (2018). "A Clear Advantage: The Benefits of Transparency to Crisis Recovery." *European Journal of Political Economy* 55, 391–416.

Shambaugh, G. & Weinstein, P. (2016). *The Art of Policymaking: Tools, Techniques and Processes in the Modern Executive Branch*. Washington, DC: CQ Press.

Sherman, M. (2009). *A Short History of Financial Deregulation in the United States*. Washington, DC: Center for Economic and Policy Research.

"Should President Clinton have reappointed Alan Greenspan as Fed chairman?" (2000). *CNN*, January 5. http://transcripts.cnn.com/TRANSCRIPTS/0001/05/cf.00.html.

Siebelt, F. & Koranyi, B. (2016). "Top German court clears ECB's OMT scheme with minor limits." *Reuters*, June 21. www.reuters.com/article/us-ecb-policy-germany/top-german-court-clears-ecbs-omt-scheme-with-minor-limits-idUSKCN0Z725M.

Siekmann, H. & Wieland, V. (2014). "Have markets misunderstood the German Court's decision on OMT?" *VOX CEPR Policy Portal*, October 3. https://voxeu.org/article/markets-and-german-court-s-decision-omt.

"Slaying the dragon of debt" (n.d.). *Regional Oral History Office, The Bancroft Library, University of California, Berkeley*. http://bancroft.berkeley.edu/ROHO/projects/debt/1993reconciliationact.html.

Smith, G. (2015). "Greece shutters its banks after the ECB turns off the taps." *Fortune*, June 28. http://fortune.com/2015/06/28/greece-capital-controls-bank-holiday-ecb.

Smith, H. (2009). "The new Iceland? Greece fights to rein in debt." *The Guardian*, November 30. www.theguardian.com/business/2009/nov/30/greece-iceland-debt.

(2010a). "Greece activates €45bn EU/IMF loans." *The Guardian*, April 23. www.theguardian.com/business/2010/apr/23/greece-activates-eu-imf-loans.

(2010b). "Greece struggles on after weak response to bond sale." *The Guardian*, March 29. www.theguardian.com/world/2010/mar/29/greece-bond-sale-weak-response.

Smith, H. & Gow, D. (2011). "Papandreou scraps Greek referendum as open warfare erupts in his party." *The Guardian*, November 3. www.theguardian.com/world/2011/nov/03/papandreou-scraps-greek-referendum-euro.

Smith, H. & Seager, A. (2009). "Financial markets tumble after Fitch downgrades Greece's credit rating." *The Guardian*, December 8. www.theguardian.com/world/2009/dec/08/greece-credit-rating-lowest-eurozone.

Sorkin, A. (2004). "What Timothy Geithner really thinks." *New York Times Magazine*, May 8. www.nytimes.com/2014/05/11/magazine/what-timothy-geithner-really-thinks.html?_r=2.

"Specific risk" (n.d.). *Investopedia*. www.investopedia.com/terms/s/specificrisk.asp?layout=infini&v=5B&orig=1&adtest=5B.

Sperling, G. (1992). "Economic Overview." Memorandum to the President of the United States, *Office of the Presidential Transition*, December 23.

Stacey, K. (2011). "Who originally broke the EU fiscal rules? France and Germany." *Financial Times*, December 6. www.ft.com/content/dfb8adf7-7ca4-384c-a737-f28c0dc46924.

Stahl, L. (2007). "Alan Greenspan: swimming with sharks." *60 Minutes*, Season 39, Episode 50, September 16.

Steen, M. (2012). "ECB bond buying likened to work of the devil." *CNBC*, September 19. www.cnbc.com/id/49082034.

Stewart, H. (2012). "European Central Bank hints it may forgo profits on its Greek bonds." *The Guardian*, February 9. www.theguardian.com/business/2012/feb/09/european-central-bank-may-forgo-profits-greek-bonds.

Suskind, R. (2004). *The Price of Loyalty: George W. Bush, the White House, and the Education of Paul O'Neill*. New York: Simon & Schuster.

Talley, I. (2015). "Emerging markets face rate-increase pressures." *Wall Street Journal*, December 16. www.wsj.com/articles/emerging-markets-gird-for-fed-rate-increase-1450261800.

"Targeted longer-term refinancing operations (TLTROs)" (2018). *European Central Bank*. www.ecb.europa.eu/mopo/implement/omo/tltro/html/index.en.html.

Taylor, R. (2001). "The dirty money war." *World Press Review*. www.worldpress.org/Americas/1175.cfm.

"Technical features of Outright Monetary Transaction" (2012). European Central Bank. www.ecb.int/press/pr/date/2012/html/pr120906_1.en.html.

"The budget battle" (n.d.). *CNN*, www.cnn.com/US/9512/budget/budget_battle/index.html.

"The committee to save the world" (1999). *Time Magazine*, cover, February 15.

"The Daily Shot" (2015). *The Daily Shot Brief*, July 17. https://us10.campaign-archive
.com/?u=451473e81730c5a3ae680c489&id=f69453a36e&e=3b53b92804.

"The definition of price stability" (n.d.). *European Central Bank*. www.ecb
.europa.eu/mopo/strategy/pricestab/html/index.en.html.

"The Dodd–Frank Act" (n.d.). *US Commodity Futures Trading Commission.*
www.cftc.gov/LawRegulation/DoddFrankAct/index.htm.

"The Dodd–Frank Wall Street Reform and Consumer Protection Act. Pub.
L. 111-203, H.R. 4173" (2010). January 5. www.sec.gov/about/laws/wall
streetreform-cpa.pdf.

"The economic effects of 9/11: a retrospective assessment" (2002). *Congressional
Research Service*, September 27. www.fas.org/irp/crs/RL31617.pdf.

"The ESCB's stability-oriented monetary policy strategy" (1998). *European Central
Bank*, December 7. www.ecb.europa.eu/press/key/date/1998/html/
sp981207.en.html.

"The Federal Reserve Act" (n.d.). *Federal Reserve Bank of New York*. www.federal
reserve.gov/aboutthefed/fract.htm.

"The Federal Reserve discount window" (n.d.). *Federal Reserve*. www.frbdis
countwindow.org/en/Pages/General-Information/The-Discount-Window.aspx.

"The first report of the Congressional Oversight Panel for Economic Stabilization"
(2008). *Congressional Oversight Panel for Economic Stabilization*, December 10.
http://money.cnn.com/news/specials/storysupplement/bailout_report.

"The last tango? Argentina's latest economic reforms have rattled markets in
South America" (2001). *The Economist*, June 21. www.economist.com/node/
666355.

"The potential macroeconomic effect of debt ceiling brinksmanship" (2013). *US
Department of the Treasury*, October. www.treasury.gov/press-center/press-
releases/Pages/jl2178.aspx.

"The targeted longer-term refinancing operations: an overview of the take-up and
their impact on bank intermediation" (2017). *The European Central Bank
Economic Bulletin* (3), 42–47. www.ecb.europa.eu/pub/pdf/other/ebbox
201703_05.en.pdf.

"The transition; excerpts from Clinton's conference on state of the economy"
(1992). *New York Times*, December 15. www.nytimes.com/1992/12/15/us/
the-transition-excerpts-from-clinton-s-conference-on-state-of-the-economy
.html?pagewanted=all.

Thomas Pringle v. Government of Ireland, CJEU, Case C-370/12, November
27, 2012. http://curia.europa.eu/juris/recherche.jsf?language=en.

"Time for bankers to intervene" (2012). *New York Times*, June 26.
www.nytimes.com/2012/06/27/opinion/time-for-bankers-to-intervene.html.

Time Magazine (1999). Cover: Rubin, Greenspan and Summers. http://content
.time.com/time/covers/0,16641,19990215,00.html.

"Transcript of President Jean-Claude Juncker's press conference on Greece"
(2015). *European Commission*, June 29. http://europa.eu/rapid/press-
release_SPEECH-15-5274_en.htm.

"Transcript of Senator Ted Cruz's filibuster against Obamacare" (2013). *Washington Post*, September 25. www.washingtonpost.com/sf/national/2013/09/
25/transcript-sen-ted-cruzs-filibuster-against-obamacare.

Traynor, I. (2010). "How the euro – and the EU – teetered on the brink of collapse." *The Guardian*, May 14. www.theguardian.com/business/2010/may/14/nicolas-sarkozy-angela-merkel-euro-crisis-summit.

Traynor, I. & Inman, P. (2015). "Greece faces banking crisis after Eurozone meeting breaks down." *The Guardian*, June 18. www.theguardian.com/world/2015/jun/18/greece-faces-banking-crisis-after-eurozone-meeting-breaks-down.

Traynor, I. & Wearden, G. (2010). "EU leaders reach Greek bailout deal." *The Guardian*, February 11. www.theguardian.com/business/2010/feb/11/eu-summit-greece-bailout-imf.

Treanor, J. (2015). "The 2010 'flash crash': how it unfolded." *The Guardian*, April 22. www.theguardian.com/business/2015/apr/22/2010-flash-crash-new-york-stock-exchange-unfolded.

"Treaty on European Union, as signed in Maastricht on 7 February 1992" (n.d.). https://europa.eu/european-union/sites/europaeu/files/docs/body/treaty_on_european_union_en.pdf.

"Trichet, former ECB President: the letter sent to Berlusconi's government succeeded in saving Italy" (2014). *eunews*, January 14. www.eunews.it/en/2014/01/14/trichet-former-ecb-president-the-letter-sent-to-berlusconis-government-succeeded-in-saving-italy/11812.

Trichet, J.-C. & Draghi, M. (2011a). "Letter of the European Central Bank to Silvio Berlusconi." *Voltaire Network*, August 5. www.voltairenet.org/article171574.html.

(2011b). "Lettera della Bce all'Italia, testo integrale." *Wall Street Italia*, September 29. www.wallstreetitalia.com/lettera-della-bce-all-italia-testo-integrale.

(2011c). "Trichet e Draghi: un'azione pressante per ristabilire la giducia degli investitori." *Corriere della Sara*, September 29. www.corriere.it/economia/11_settembre_29/trichet_draghi_inglese_304a5f1e-ea59-11e0-ae06-4da866778017.shtml.

Trichet, J.-C. & Papademos, L. (2008). "Introductory statement with Q&A." *European Central Bank*, July 3. www.ecb.europa.eu/press/pressconf/2008/html/is080703.en.html.

Tsebelis, G. (2002). *Veto Players: How Institutions Work*. Princeton: Princeton University Press.

"Two sides of the same coin? Independence and accountability of the European Central Bank" (2017). *Transparency International EU*. https://transparency.eu/wp-content/uploads/2017/03/TI-EU_ECB_Report_DIGITAL.pdf.

"UK financial regulation overhauled" (2013). *BBC News*, April 1. www.bbc.com/news/business-21987829.

"Understanding the federal debt limit" (2015). *Concord Coalition*, October 8. www.concordcoalition.org/issue-briefs/2015/1008/understanding-federal-debt-limit.

"United States of America long-term rating lowered to 'AA+' due to political risks, rising debt burden; outlook negative" (2011). *Standard and Poor's*, August 5. www.standardandpoors.com/en_US/web/guest/home.

"Urteil des Bundesverfassungsgerichts zum Vertrag von Lissabon" (2007). *Bundeszantrale für politische Bildung*, December 13. www.bpb.de/politik/hintergrund-aktuell/69361/urteil-zum-vertrag-von-lissabon-30-06-2009.

US Commodity Futures Trading Commission (n.d.). www.cftc.gov/index.htm.

US Congressional Budget Office (n.d.). Natural Rate of Unemployment (Long-Term) [NROU]. Retrieved from FRED, Federal Reserve Bank of St. Louis. https://research.stlouisfed.org/fred2/series/NROU.

US Department of the Treasury (n.d.). Fiscal Service, Federal Debt Held by Foreign and International Investors [FDHBFIN]. Retrieved from FRED, Federal Reserve Bank of St. Louis. https://fred.stlouisfed.org/series/FDHBFIN.

US Senate Committee on Foreign Relations (2018). "Corker, Coons introduce bill to modernize U.S. approach to development finance [press release]." www.foreign.senate.gov/press/chair/release/corker-coons-introduce-bill-to-modernize-us-approach-to-development-finance.

Van de Water, P. (2013). "'Debt prioritization' is simply default by another name." *Huffington Post*, November 19. www.huffingtonpost.com/paul-n-van-de-water/debt-prioritization-is-si_b_3957246.html.

Vann, B. (2002). "Argentina defaults on loan to World Bank." *World Socialist Web Site*, November 16. www.wsws.org/articles/2002/nov2002/arg-n16.shtml.

"Verbatim of the remarks made by Mario Draghi" (2012). *European Central Bank*, July 26. www.ecb.europa.eu/press/key/date/2012/html/sp120726.en.html.

Viegel, K. (2009). *Dictatorship, Democracy and Globalization: Argentina and the Cost of Paralysis, 1973–2001*. University Park: Penn State University Press.

Vogel, T. (2011a). "Papademos set to take over from Papandreou." *Politico*, November 8. www.politico.eu/article/papademos-set-to-take-over-from-papandreou.

(2011b). "Papandreou wins vote of confidence." *Politico*, November 4. www.politico.eu/article/papandreou-wins-vote-of-confidence.

Wallsten, P., Montgomery, L. & Wilson, S. (2012). "Obama's evolution: behind the failed 'grand bargain' on debt." *Washington Post*, March 17. www.washingtonpost.com/politics/obamas-evolution-behind-the-failed-grand-bargain-on-the-debt/2012/03/15/gIQAHyyfJS_story.html.

"Washington's budget fiasco: A timeline" (n.d.). *CNN Money*. http://money.cnn.com/interactive/economy/budget-follies-timeline/?iid=EL.

Wasson, E. (2011). "Boehner rebuts Obama's criticism, says the president moved the goal posts." *The Hill*, July 23. http://thehill.com/policy/finance/173099-boehner-rebuts-obama-criticism-says-president-moved-goal-post.

Watson, D. (2015). "There is only one solution to the debt limit." *Treasury Notes, Department of the Treasury*, October 16. www.treasury.gov/connect/blog/Pages/one-solution-debt-limit.aspx.

Wearden, G. (2013). "Eurozone crisis as it happened: German court holds crucial hearing into ECB's bond-buying programme." *The Guardian*, June 11. www.theguardian.com/business/2013/jun/11/eurozone-crisis-switzerland-german-court-uk.

Webel, B. & Labonte, M. (2010). "Government Interventions in Response to Financial Turmoil." *Congressional Research Service*, February 1.

Weber, A. (2010). "Monetary policy after the crisis – a European perspective." *BIS Review*. www.bis.org/review/r101018a.pdf.

Wehinger, G. (2013). "SMEs and the Credit Crunch: Current Financing Difficulties, Policy Measures and a Review of Literature." *OECD Journal: Financial Market Trends*, 2013(2).

Weisman, J. (2002). "Greenspan throws damper on permanent tax-cut plan."
Washington Post, November 14. www.washingtonpost.com/archive/politics/
2002/11/14/greenspan-throws-damper-on-permanent-tax-cut-plan/38a4468
5-056a-4af2-9d4d-33e5058dfc6a/?utm_term=.c0b681cefd15.

Whalen, K. (2013). "Ireland's economic crisis: The good, the bad and the ugly."
Presented at Bank of Greece Conference on the Europe Crisis, Athens, May
24. www.karlwhelan.com/Papers/Whelan-IrelandPaper-June2013.pdf.

"What is domestic liability dollarization?" (n.d.). *Forex News*. www.forex
news.com/questions/whats-is-domestic-liability-dollarization.

"What we do" (n.d.). *US Securities and Exchange Commission*. www.sec.gov/about/
whatwedo.shtml.

"Why are benchmark rates so important?" (2018). *European Central Bank*, September 21, 2017, updated October 31. www.ecb.europa.eu/explainers/tell-
me-more/html/benchmark_rates_qa.en.html.

Woodward, B. (1994). *The Agenda: Inside the Clinton White House*. New York:
Simon & Schuster.

——— (2002). "Behind the boom." *Washington Post*, November 12. www.washington
post.com/archive/lifestyle/magazine/2000/11/12/behind-the-boom/418c4dd0-
36fc-40fb-ab22-f5ae14090782/?utm_term=.0229a48a58e7.

——— (2018). *Fear: Trump in the White House*. New York: Simon & Schuster.

Wooley, J. (2008). "ECB offers longer-term finance via six month LTROs."
Euromoney, May 2. www.euromoney.com/article/b1322cm2dyyprq/ecb-
offers-longer-term-finance-via-six-month-ltros.

"World development indicators" (n.d.). *World Bank*. http://databank.worldbank
.org/ddp/home.do?Step=3&id=4.

"World economic outlook" (2018). *International Monetary Fund*, April. www
.imf.org/external/pubs/ft/weo/2008/01/pdf/c1.pdf.

Worrachate, A. & Walker, S. (2011). "Bunds lose to treasuries as swaps count costs
of rescue." *Bloomberg*, July 25. www.bloomberg.com/news/articles/2011-07-25/
bunds-losing-to-treasuries-as-default-swaps-count-costs-of-merkel-s-rescue.

Ygesias, M. (2012). "Jens Weidmann implies Mario Draghi and the ECB are
being manipulated by Satan." *Slate*, September 28. https://slate.com/busi
ness/2012/09/jens-weidmann-sites-goethe-to-imply-mario-draghi-and-the-euro
pean-central-bank-are-being-manipulated-by-the-devil.html.

Index